THE LAND
OF IONIA

ALAN M. GREAVES

THE LAND OF IONIA

Society and Economy in the Archaic Period

WILEY-BLACKWELL

A John Wiley & Sons, Ltd., Publication

This edition first published 2015
© 2015 Alan M. Greaves

Blackwell Publishing was acquired by John Wiley & Sons in February 2007. Blackwell's publishing program has been merged with Wiley's global Scientific, Technical, and Medical business to form Wiley-Blackwell.

Registered Office
John Wiley & Sons Ltd, The Atrium, Southern Gate, Chichester, West Sussex, PO19 8SQ, United Kingdom

Editorial Offices
350 Main Street, Malden, MA 02148-5020, USA
9600 Garsington Road, Oxford, OX4 2DQ, UK
The Atrium, Southern Gate, Chichester, West Sussex, PO19 8SQ, UK

For details of our global editorial offices, for customer services, and for information about how to apply for permission to reuse the copyright material in this book please see our website at www.wiley.com/wiley-blackwell.

The right of Alan M. Greaves to be identified as the author of this work has been asserted in accordance with the UK Copyright, Designs and Patents Act 1988.

Wiley also publishes its books in a variety of electronic formats. Some content that appears in print may not be available in electronic books.

Designations used by companies to distinguish their products are often claimed as trademarks. All brand names and product names used in this book are trade names, service marks, trademarks or registered trademarks of their respective owners. The publisher is not associated with any product or vendor mentioned in this book. This publication is designed to provide accurate and authoritative information in regard to the subject matter covered. It is sold on the understanding that the publisher is not engaged in rendering professional services. If professional advice or other expert assistance is required, the services of a competent professional should be sought.

Library of Congress Cataloging-in-Publication Data
Greaves, Alan M., 1969-
 The land of Ionia : society and economy in the Archaic period / Alan M. Greaves.
  p. cm.
 Includes bibliographical references and index.
 ISBN 978-1-119-02556-6   1. Ionia–Civilization.   2. Ionia–Antiquities.
3. Excavations (Archaeology)–Turkey–Ionia.   I. Title.
 DS156.I6G74 2010
 939′.23–dc22

                                                                2009032173

A catalogue record for this book is available from the British Library.

Set in 10.5 on 13pt Minion by Toppan Best-set Premedia Limited

I   2015

Contents

List of illustrations   *viii*

List of tables   *x*

Preface   *xi*

Acknowledgments   *xiv*

Prologue   *xvi*

1   FINDING IONIA   1

Introduction   1

The Source Materials   2

Excavation and Publication   22

Conclusions   26

2   CONSTRUCTING CLASSICAL ARCHAEOLOGIES OF IONIA   27

Introduction   27

Traditional Approaches to Classical Archaeology in Ionia   28

The German and Turkish "Schools" of Archaeology   32

Annaliste Perspectives on Archaeology   36

A New Approach to the Land of Ionia   39

Conclusions   43

3   A DYNAMIC LANDSCAPE   45

Introduction   45

Ionia's Geographical Zones   46

Landscape Dynamism   57

The Ionian Landscape and Ionian Identity   65

Conclusions   67

4 THE WEALTH OF IONIA 69

Introduction	69
Modes of Primary Production	71
Modes of Processing	79
Modes of Exchange	84
Ionia and World Systems	89
Conclusions	91

5 THE CITIES OF IONIA 95

Introduction	95
A Brief Survey of the Ionian Cities	96
Other Settlements in Ionia	107
The Size and Distribution of *Poleis* within Ionia	110
François de Polignac in Ionia	112
The City and Ionian Identity	115
Conclusions	118

6 THE IONIANS OVERSEAS 120

Introduction	120
Source Materials	121
Interpreting the Evidence	129
Colonial Interactions	131
Models of Ionian Colonization	137
Conclusions	143

7 THE IONIANS AT WAR 145

Introduction	145
Geographical Settings	147
Archaeological Contexts and Materials	148
Literary Sources	154
Discussion: Issues in Source Materials	156
The Fortification of Ionia	156
Naval Warfare	164
Mercenaries	166
Conclusions	168

8 CULTS OF IONIA 171

Introduction	171
Geographical Evidence	172
Archaeological Evidence	174

Literary and Epigraphic Evidence   179
Discussion of Source Materials   180
The Sacred Ways of Ionia   180
"Foreign" Influences on Ionian Cult   193
Burial Practices in Ionia   197
Conclusions   199

9 THE ORNAMENTS OF IONIA   201

Introduction   201
"Art" and Landscape   203
Ionia's Lost "Art" Treasures   203
"Art" and Literature   207
"Connoisseurship" of Ionian Pottery   207
"Reading" Ionian "Art"   214
Conclusions   218

10 WHO WERE THE IONIANS?   219

Introduction   219
Herodotos' Ionia   219
The Myth of the Ionian Migration   222
Ionian Identity and Archaeology   225
Conclusions   227

Epilogue   231
Glossary of ancient Greek [and modern Turkish] terms used in the text   233
Bibliography   235
Index   255

Illustrations

Figure 1.1	General view of Ephesos	3
Figure 1.2	Alluvium at Magnesia	4
Figure 1.3	The location of the cities of Ionia and major sites in Aegean Greece	8
Figure 1.4	The location of the cities of Ionia and major sites in Anatolia	9
Box 1.1	A view of Ayasoluk Hill at Ephesos (a) in 1907 and (b) today	25
Figure 3.1	Satellite image of the lower Büyük Menderes Valley	47
Figure 3.2	The *acropolis* of Priene	48
Figure 3.3	View of the modern Büyük Menderes Plain	51
Figure 3.4	The Büyük Menderes River near Miletos	53
Figure 3.5	GIS of the harbors at Miletos	67
Box 3.1	Progradation of the Büyük Menderes River into the Gulf of Latmos	59
Figure 4.1	Wild Goat style bowl with basket-like handles, made in Chios	82
Figure 4.2	Trade amphorae at Miletos	85
Figure 4.3	Electrum stater with image of a seal from Phokaia, c.600–550 BC	88
Box 4.1	The Susa *Astragalus*	78
Figure 5.1	Cult installation at the site of Myous	105
Figure 5.2	Excavations underway at Kato Phana in 2000	109
Figure 6.1	The harbor of Massalia	122
Figure 6.2	Site view showing the densely overlaid occupations levels at Kato Phana	125
Box 6.1	Sherds of East Greek pottery from the site of Al Mina	133
Figure 7.1	The Cappadocia Gate and adjacent defenses at Kerkenes Dağ	162
Figure 7.2	Ships attending the Battle of Lade	165
Figure 7.3	An inscription by Archon Son of Amoibichos, an Ionian mercenary, from Abu Simbel, Egypt	166
Box 7.1	The Maltepe section of the "Herodotean" Wall at Phokaia	158
Figure 8.1	Fragment of female sculpture from Ephesos	176
Figure 8.2	Marble head of a youth from Bronchidai-Didyma	179
Figure 8.3	The Ahmetbeyli Valley	182

Figure 8.4	A view of the sacred precinct at Klaros	182
Figure 8.5	Colossal *kouros* from Samos	189
Figure 8.6	Abu Simbel	190
Figure 8.7	Reconstruction of the Genelos group from the Sacred Way at Samos	191
Box 8.1	Marble statue of (a) Chares, ruler of Teichioussa, c.560 BC, and (b) woman seated in a chair from Didyma, c.530–510 BC	186
Figure 9.1	*My Bed* by Tracey Emin, 1998	202
Figure 9.2	Ivory furniture inlay from Kerkenes Dağ	206
Figure 9.3	Fikellura-style amphora with a running man, sixth century BC	208
Box 9.1	The Garstang East Greek bowl	213
Figure 10.1	The Karabel rock relief of "Sesostris"	225
Box 10.1	Artemis of Ephesos	228

Tables

Table 2.1 A summary of the tripartite *Annaliste* chronological framework
proposed by Fernand Braudel 38

Table 2.2 A model mapping different types of archaeological and historical
evidence onto areas of human activity in Maslow's hierarchy
of needs 41

Table 4.1 Different types of archaeological and historical evidence mapped
onto the four world-systems network types 90

Table 5.1 Known Archaic cult sites in Milesia 113

Table 6.1 A model of Ionian colonization based on world-systems analysis 138

Table 8.1 Sacred Ways of Ionia 181

Preface

J.M. Cook wrote: "The history of the eastern Greeks still remains to be written."[1] A complete history of the region would certainly be a large undertaking and this book does not claim be an encyclopedic account of the rise, fall, and eventual excavation of the great cities of Ionia. Rather, it is an exercise in archaeological interpretation that aims to highlight socio-economic themes and questions regarding the local practices and identity of those communities – the prolegomena to a new history of Ionia. It also aims to be an accessible introduction to these themes, and to the region itself, that is not overburdened with lengthy examples, theory, or footnotes. In this sense it has been inspired by Carl Roebuck's *Ionian Trade and Colonization*,[2] which remains one of the most accessible and useful introductions to Ionia. Through its bibliography and textboxes, it is hoped that this book can provide a point of entry into the rich archaeological material that exists for Ionia and thereby allow people to formulate their own interpretations of it.

Ionia, which consisted of the west coast of what is now Turkey and the Greek islands of Chios and Samos, was one of the most important regions of the ancient Mediterranean. It was simultaneously the meeting point and the battleground between East and West, a fertile birthplace of ideas, and an emblem of ancient civilization throughout time. In modern times, images of its monuments are iconic symbols of archaeology, and its leading cities, such as Ephesos, have become household names. Yet Ionia is a strangely unfamiliar friend. The critical reviews of the material available for the study of Ionia that are presented in this book often appear to highlight how little we actually know about the Archaic period in this most iconic region. Despite nearly a century-and-a-half of excavations and a wealth of discoveries, there have been relatively few works that have dealt directly with Ionia and none that have explicitly sought to examine and define the essential identity of the region and its society using archaeology as its primary source. However, this is changing and the exciting discoveries and modern approaches being applied in Ionia today provide a stimulating basis for any archaeological discussion.

[1] J.M. Cook 1962: 15.
[2] Roebuck 1959.

Geographically, Ionia cannot easily be defined. Its landscape is large and diverse and the limits of what was called "Ionia" in the ancient world do not appear to follow any clearly demarcated physical boundary. For the purposes of this book, discussion will largely be limited to the cities of the Ionian *dodekapolis* (league of 12 cities) that are named by Herodotos (1.142) and which he subdivided into four groups by their dialects. Chronologically, this study is limited to the Archaic period of 700 to 494 BC.[3] This was a formative period in the history of the Greek world and was also when Ionia was arguably at its peak. During this time a changing image of Ionia can be traced through Greek literature, from Homer's depiction of the "Carians" of Miletos as allies of Troy (*Il.* 2.867–75) to Herodotos' portrayal of it as a cultural extension of Greece. To attempt to map too closely onto the region's archaeology the apparent spatial and temporal changes in Ionian culture that can be gleaned from Greek literature would be an exercise in literary positivism (i.e. "cherry-picking" archaeological facts to hang off the existing narrative framework established by that literature; see Chapter 2). Although Archaic Ionia was birthplace to the works of great thinkers such as Thales and Anaximander, and although the importance of their work must be recognized, there is a danger of over-prioritizing these individuals when writing a general history of Ionia. Instead, the objective here is to conduct a systematic review of the evidence for different levels of economic and social activity in Ionia and to build on this an interpretation of the region's history and identity that is largely independent of literary sources. This book is essentially a postmodernist reinterpretation of the socio-economic history of Ionia, which may indeed provide a context in which to understand the production of cultural works such as philosophy, but which does not view them as the end point toward which all study of Ionia should be directed.

This book presents a critical review of the available archaeological information about Archaic Ionia, through an examination of key socio-economic themes that are constructed "from the ground up," i.e. beginning with landscape and the first principles of the agrarian economy and society, with the aim of identifying characteristics of the region and its people that distinguish it from the standard narratives of the Greek "mainland."[4] Several key topics emerge from this analysis: the role of landscape as a determinant of historical development in the region; the socio-economic contexts of Ionian culture; the Anatolian character of elements of the "Greek" communities of Ionia; and various unique elements of Ionian material culture and social practice.

Such a structured critical assessment of the availability and use of archaeological evidence reveals that, despite an apparent abundance of remains, there is often surprisingly

---

[3] This is the most commonly used starting date for the "Archaic." Some scholars may extend this definition to include the Geometric period, the so-called "Dark Age" of Greece, but restricting this study to these dates allows the author to examine the interplay of archaeological and written sources that are not available in the earlier "Dark Age" period. The end date of 494 BC marks the destruction of Miletos by the Persians following the Battle of Lade, an event that can truly be described as the end of an era in Ionia.

[4] The term "mainland" is used not to imply that Ionia was a region of secondary importance, but to recognize that the narratives constructed from the historically well-attested sites of Athens, Sparta, and Corinth will differ from those not only of Ionia, but also of other regions of the Greek world, such as the islands of the Aegean and Magna Graecia.

little hard archaeology for much of Archaic Ionia and many fundamental questions remain to be answered. In previous studies of Ionia the written sources of history and epigraphy have taken precedence over archaeological evidence, which has often been applied in a seemingly ad hoc way. However, this often belies an underlying set of assumptions about the inherent superiority of Greek culture over Anatolian, the primacy of the historical method over that of archaeology, and the acceptable standards of proof within different communities of practice. This book sets out to reverse such traditional approaches, by taking archaeology as its starting point and principal source material.

Following assessment of the source materials, this book follows a "pyramidal" structure, as laid out in Chapter 2, that builds up from an understanding of the landscape into a discussion of the essential elements of life in Ionia – agriculture and trade, settlement, and warfare – through to the less-urgent social imperatives of religion, art, and ethnic identity. In each of these thematic chapters, discussion of key themes is preceded by a critical review of the available evidence and textboxes provide more detailed explanations of key sites and ideas. Theoretically, the interpretations presented here are framed by the *Annaliste* and world-systems analysis perspectives. The *Annaliste* perspective integrates landscape, archaeology, and history and is therefore a useful method for any study of this kind, and world-systems analysis suggests a way to integrate local activity into inter-regional patterns of culture and exchange.

Casual readers might find that individual chapters are able to provide them with an insight into the evidence base and discussions that are of particular interest to them, whereas readers who follow the chapters from beginning to end will trace the development of the new "ground-up" approach propounded above. The overall aim of the book is to present new perspectives and to provoke discussion; if the reader is left with more questions than answers, then perhaps it has served its purpose.

Alan M. Greaves

Acknowledgments

Funding for the preparation of this book came from the AHRC Research Leave Scheme and the Holgate Visiting Fellowship at Grey College, University of Durham. Further financial support came from the University of Liverpool Research Development Fund and School of Archaeology, Classics and Egyptology and academic research facilities were provided by the British Institute at Ankara.

Many of the foundations for this book were laid whilst researching my PhD *A Socio-Economic History of Miletos* (Leeds, 1999) and I am grateful to my supervisor Roger Brock for his continuing support and Jeeves-like wisdom. That thesis was published as a series of articles (1999, 2000a, 2004, 2007b). My previous book, *Miletos: A history* (Routledge, 2002), was an attempt to produce a succinct archaeological account and diachronic history of that city. The inspiration for this current book came from the challenging and insightful questions of my students at the University of Liverpool during my course "Ionia: A Regional Study." They prompted me to think, and rethink, my ideas about Ionia and encouraged me to write an accessible scholarly book in English. I hope they will enjoy it.

The time and insight so freely given by my academic readers Lesley Beaumont, Alexandra Villing, and Wiley-Blackwell's anonymous reviewers have informed and greatly improved the final text, and are very much appreciated. I am enormously indebted to Susan Williams for proofreading the manuscript and preparing the index, for her diligent grammatical and academic comments, and for her unflagging encouragement and assistance – this book really would not have been possible without her. Throughout this project I have been guided by the fatherly and brotherly advices of Chris Mee and Tom Harrison, respectively. It is a pleasure to also acknowledge the generosity of so many friends and colleagues who have provided comments on specific chapters of the text, namely Zosia Archibald, Catherine Draycott, Warren Eastwood, Matthew Fitzjohn, Phil Freeman, Thomas D. Hall, Victoria Jefferson, Michael Kerschner, Gina Muskett, Joe Skinner, Michael Sommer, Geoff Summers, and Peter Thonemann. The views expressed here are entirely my own, not theirs, and so too are the errors and the oversights.

On a personal note, I would like to thank the many friends who have supported and encouraged me during the long gestation of this book. In particular I would like to thank Angela Burdick, Martyn Chamberlain, and the Grey College SCR, John Clifford, Rachel and Paul Newham, and Karen Wheatley. Finally, none of this would have been possible without the love and support of my brothers and my mother.

The ideas, opinions, and conclusions expressed in this book have grown out of my long association with western Anatolia, working with different research teams. I am grateful to all my collaborators and colleagues in Ionia and beyond for the opportunities they have afforded me and for the insights and perspectives that working with them has given me. I only hope that this book will direct readers toward their own excellent works and that the ideas presented here may prove to be a stimulus for discussion and further consideration of this important region by a new generation of interested readers.

Prologue

Even those who started from the Government House in Athens and believe themselves to be of the purest Ionian blood, took no women with them but married Carian girls, whose parents they had killed. The fact that these women were forced into marriage after the murder of their fathers, husbands, and sons was the origin of the law, established by oath and passed down to their female descendants, forbidding them to sit at table with their husbands or to address them by name. It was at Miletos that this took place.[5]

This passage of Herodotos clearly lays out the way in which the culture of Greece came to dominate the region of western Anatolia known as Ionia. A single influx of militarily and culturally superior Greeks swept aside the pre-existing "barbarian" (in this case Carian) population and took their land and their women for themselves. Herodotos demonstrates how residual Anatolian cultural traditions were allowed to persist and eventually become subsumed into the fabric of everyday life in Ionia, a life that was unremarkably Greek in other respects, like that of their founding city of Athens.

Anyone who began their study of Ionian culture with Herodotos' *Histories* and set about matching the archaeological evidence to it could easily construct a history of the region that would validate this interpretation.

Anyone who began their study from the starting point of landscape and archaeology, however, would weave an entirely different tale.

[5] Herodotos *Histories* 1.146 [trans. Sélincourt].

1

Finding Ionia

Introduction

Ionia in the Archaic period was at the core of the Greek world that centered on the Aegean Sea and it played a pivotal role in the events documented in the most important surviving historical work of that period: Herodotos' *Histories*. Consequently, in modern times Ionia attracted the attention of antiquarians and archaeologists from an early date and at the key sites of Ephesos and Miletos there have now been near-continuous archaeological excavations for over a century.

Considering this long history of exploration and research, when one begins to study the Archaic period of Ionia by conducting a critical review of the available archaeological source materials, the results are surprisingly, and remarkably, disappointing. Despite the size and crucial importance of this region in the ancient world, and despite its long history of research, the published archaeological information available is of mixed quantity and value and must often be handled with care. A similar review of the available literary and epigraphic evidence reveals that there is little hard evidence to be found here either.

Today there are important ongoing excavations using modern field methods of excavation and analysis at several sites in Ionia, yet the fact remains that the majority of our archaeological knowledge as yet still comes from those excavations that were conducted in an earlier era, often without systematic methods of recording. But as archaeological methods and the kind of questions we are seeking to ask of the material have developed, so the results of these old excavations are less able to answer them. For example, early archaeologists rarely logged and identified the animal bones from their excavations because they were interested in artworks, such as sculpture, and did not yet recognize that faunal evidence could tell us so much about past diets, environments, and human practices. Yet the systematic analysis of animal bones from a recently excavated sanctuary in Ionia, the Sanctuary of Aphrodite on Zeytintepe, Miletos, has been very illuminating and has told us a great deal about sacrificial practices at this site, for which there are no written records.[1]

---

[1] Peters and von den Driesch 1992.

It has long been recognized that the very act of excavation destroys that which we dig and therefore, once a site has been dug by archaeologists, it has been destroyed.[2] The need to create, and make public, systematic records of what is found during excavations is therefore paramount. However, a recent development in the theoretical understanding of the nature of archaeological evidence has been the recognition that the very act of excavating and recording is, in itself, based on interpretative decisions by the excavator.[3] That is to say that we, the archaeologists, create what we find by the choices we make about where and how to dig. Most archaeological evidence is therefore subjective, not objective, in nature.[4]

With this in mind, if we are ever to be able to make use of the large body of material from previous excavations, it is necessary to appreciate the motivations, interests, and methods of those previous generations of archaeologists who worked in Ionia in order to begin to compensate for biases that may be inherent in the archaeological record as a result. By understanding their objectives, we can begin to understand their methods and put them into a proper context for the age in which they operated. These objectives affected which sites they chose to excavate, the methods they chose to use, which artifacts they chose to keep (or publish) and which they chose to discard (or leave unpublished).

If the objectives of previous generations of archaeologists affected how the archaeological materials from Ionia were found, then they have also affected how they were interpreted. The aim of Classical archaeology has often been to establish, wherever possible, connections between the material remains of the Greek and Roman cultures and their literary and historical legacy. However, in our eagerness to make such connections, we can sometimes make associations between the archaeological evidence and passages of ancient history which might subsequently be interpreted differently, or indeed challenged.[5]

The Source Materials

There are three main categories of source material traditionally used by Classical archaeologists in their attempt to reconstruct ancient societies and their histories, namely archaeology, ancient literary sources, and epigraphy. The remainder of this chapter will review the quantity and nature of these sources as they exist from Ionia before discussing how these might be used and combined to deepen our understanding of society in ancient Ionia in subsequent chapters.

Archaeology

As a region, Ionia has exceptional potential for archaeological research. It is home to a number of exceptionally well-preserved archaeological sites, the most notable being New

---

[2] Wheeler 1956.
[3] Hodder 1998, 2000.
[4] This theme will be developed further in Chapter 2.
[5] e.g. Greaves 2002: 74–5 on Kleiner 1966.

Figure 1.1 General view of Ephesos.

Priene[6] and Ephesos. At both of these sites, there are ruins so perfectly preserved that visitors can imagine what it must have been like to inhabit the ancient city and walk down those same streets. The ruins of these places, and those of others in the region, are so exceptionally preserved because of certain physical characteristics within the landscape of Ionia itself.

The most famous archaeological sites in the world are often those that have captured a "snapshot in time," usually as the result of some natural disaster. Pompeii, Hercula-neum, and Akrotiri on Santorini were preserved because they were buried by volcanic ash in a sudden catastrophic event. In Ionia, Ephesos is one such site. Here, the central part of the excavated area seen by tourists, the Library of Celsus and the Street of the Curetes, was buried by a landslide that covered the ruins in a great depth of soil and resulted in remarkable preservation (Figure 1.1). The ancient city was located between two hills – Panayır Dağı, to the north, and Bülbül Dağı, to the south – from which the

---

[6] The excavated ruins at Priene are referred to here as "New Priene." These ruins date from the Hellenistic period and it has been argued that the city was refounded here from an as yet unknown location on the plain below. The site of the settlement referred to by Herodotos (referred to here as "Old Priene") has yet to be securely identified, if indeed it was different from its current location. For a summary of the debate see Demand 1990: 140–6. Archaeological research to find the location of "Old Priene" is ongoing.

Figure 1.2 Alluvium at Magnesia.

landslide apparently originated. Landslides are often triggered by seismic events like earth tremors, which are common across Ionia.[7] The hilly terrain and seismic nature of Ionia therefore combined to contribute to creating the superb preservation conditions seen at Ephesos. A catastrophic flood appears to have destroyed the eighth-century BC Temple of Artemis at Ephesos, and important finds, including a number of amber beads, were protected by the resulting layer of soft sand that covered its ruins.[8]

Close to Priene are another set of exceptional ruins – at Magnesia on the Maeander. Although Magnesia was not named as one of the Ionian *dodekapolis* in the Archaic period, its ruins are worth noting here because it is in a similar geographical zone to other sites in Ionia. Unlike New Priene and Ephesos, Magnesia does not sit immediately under a large hill. Instead, the site is in the low-lying valley bottom and consequently it has been covered in silt from the Büyük Menderes river system. The ruins of Magnesia are in such an excellent state of preservation because they became rapidly covered by a great depth of alluvium (Figure 1.2). Remarkable features of Magnesia that have been preserved in this way include the inscribed slabs of the *agora* (market place), the Temple of Artemis, and the famous Skylla capital. The alluviation of the Büyük Menderes may also have been responsible for covering over the ruins of Old Priene, so much so that despite exhaustive

---

[7] Ergin et al. 1967; Stiros and Jones 1996.
[8] Bammer 1990. See also Box 10.1.

research the location of the Archaic period settlement has yet to be securely identified.[9] If the current attempts at finding the ruins by means of geophysical survey are successful and the city is ever excavated, its ruins may prove to be in the same state of preservation as those of Magnesia.

The alluvial action of the Büyük Menderes River has also led to the preservation of the ruins of Ionia in other, less obvious, ways. The progradation (i.e. silting-up) of the bays on which the great cities of Ionia stood and the resulting swamps made these cities uninhabitable and isolated them from the sea. This meant that the cities were often abandoned, never to be reoccupied on a large scale. Without later settlement phases smothering the classical ruins it has been possible for archaeologists to uncover the complete plans of cities such as Ephesos, whereas excavating and exploring contemporary cities such as Athens are complicated by the presence of modern settlement. The alluviation also left the cities a long way from the coast. This meant that their abandoned ruins could not be easily robbed for stone and the blocks carried away by sea. In the case of Myous, the abandoned city was probably plundered for stone in antiquity and the archaeological remains at the site today are negligible.[10] The sea also played an important role in Charles Newton's work when he was collecting sculptures from the Turkish coast for the British Museum during the mid-nineteenth century. He deliberately began his excavations at Knidos in the theater because of its proximity to the sea and the ease with which its sculptures could therefore be removed.[11] Any visitor to the British Museum's Great Court will immediately be struck by the enormous size and weight of the Knidos lion that Newton retrieved. Such audacious acquisition of sculptures was only possible because of that site's proximity to the sea.

Researching the archaeology of Ionia is made difficult by the practical fact that, as a result of this early antiquarian interest, the artifacts from its most important sites are sometimes widely scattered between different museum collections. For example, statues from the so-called "Chares Group" of statues from Didyma are held in the Balat Miletos Museum, İzmir Museum, İstanbul Museum, the Louvre in Paris, the British Museum in London, and the Altes Museum in Berlin. In order to see the complete group, therefore, researchers need to visit six different museums in four different countries and on two continents. Seeing and appreciating these statues together as a coherent group is therefore impossible.

The landscape of Ionia is very dynamic, and the alluviation of the valleys is the most dramatic illustration of this. This dynamism meant that the cities of Ionia often shifted the focus of their settlements in response to changes in the landscape and this has sometimes had the effect of reducing the number of levels of settlement phases that are overlain or cut into by one another. At Miletos the focus of the city drifted about over time in response to various stimuli, within the general boundaries of the peninsula on which it was located, and as a result the Archaic settlement area on Kalabaktepe Hill, on the edge of the ancient city, was not covered over by subsequent Hellenistic, Roman, and Islamic period building works.[12]

[9] Raeck 2003.
[10] Bean 1966: 246.
[11] Jenkins 1992: 168–91, esp. 185.
[12] Greaves 1999.

Another geological factor that has contributed to the exceptional archaeological remains of Ionia is the fact that the region has good local supplies of marble. Consequently Ionia's architecture and sculptures are of the highest quality, as marble is more durable than many other types of stone. However, this has been a double-edged sword because such sculptural works also attracted the attention of the art market and illegal excavations as a result.

Today the Turkish government strictly forbids the export of antiquities and it has had considerable success in using legal and diplomatic means to force their return to Turkish museums.[13] Unfortunately, illegal excavations continue in Ionia but excavators of all nationalities now work closely with the Turkish and international authorities to identify looted artifacts and campaign for their return. For example, Hans Lohmann demonstrated that looting had taken place at the Çatallar Tepe temple site and was able to show that the building's decorative terracotta roof tiles were unique to that site. He was therefore able to prove that examples of the same tiles from a private collection must have been recently looted from this site and should be returned.[14]

It can be seen that Ionia has enormous potential for any archaeological study because of certain physical characteristics that are favorable to the formation and preservation of rich archaeological deposits. One might therefore reasonably expect that the archaeology of Ionia would be well understood, but this initial impression would be wrong. Iconic images of the ruins of Ephesos raise our expectations that there will be a wealth of archaeological data available for study but, in truth, much of the evidence dates from post-Archaic periods. In fact, the photogenic images that one has come to associate with Ionia often show monuments that obscure earlier phases that may lie beneath. This is particularly the case for the Bronze Age levels at some sites in Ionia.[15]

Exceptional preservation conditions are not uniform across Ionia or even across any one site and not everywhere is as well preserved as Ephesos and Priene. The ruins of Myous are virtually non-existent, for example. Others, such as Miletos, have a complex wealth of archaeology from many different periods, all intercutting and overlaying one another, and others still, such as Lebedos, are virtually unexplored in modern times. Trying to tease out the strands of evidence about Ionia in the Archaic period in order to test a complex set of archaeological questions about the character and identity of the region and its people is no easy task because of this piecemeal pattern of survival and excavation.

In some ways the character of the archaeology itself has been helpful to archaeologists. The fact that the Ionians built their largest and most important temples outside the city walls at Miletos (the Oracle of Apollo at Branchidai-Didyma and the Sanctuary of Aphrodite on Zeytintepe), Ephesos (the Temple of Artemis), Samos (the Temple of Hera), and Kolophon (the Oracle of Apollo at Klaros) meant that the excavation of these temples was unimpeded by an overburden of later settlement material from the city itself. However, the splendor of these temples and their early discovery and excavation has also worked to direct discussion of Ionia in general – and those cities in particular – toward

---

[13] e.g. Özgen and Öztürk 1996 on the so-called "Lydian Treasure."
[14] e.g. Lohmann 2007b.
[15] Greaves 2007a.

being focused on their large extra-urban temples at the expense of other questions. For example, there was scholarly interest in the temple at Branchidai-Didyma long before excavations of the city that built and effectively owned that temple, Miletos, began.

There have been advances in archaeological excavation techniques that now allow archaeologists to excavate strata that were previously unavailable to them. In the area of the Theater Harbor at Miletos, the raised water table prevented early archaeologists (and potential illicit excavators) from reaching some of the deepest levels. Today the use of modern vacuum-pump technology is allowing excavators to temporarily lower the water table in selected areas in order to expose the earliest levels of the city.[16]

While ongoing planned programs of excavation continue to reveal new information from Miletos, Ephesos, and the Temple of Hera at Samos, the situation is more complicated at sites where there are modern towns built over the archaeological deposits. At Chios town, Samos town (modern Pythagorio), and Phokaia (modern Eski Foça), excavation is limited to windows of opportunity of time and space between building works in the modern cities. These sites are located in relatively stable geological and environmental zones and therefore settlement has continued at the same place for centuries. This is in contrast to the landscape dynamism of the large alluvial valleys which led to the exceptional preservation of archaeological sites in those zones, as noted above. The historical character of these cities also makes them attractive to tourists and developers and at Eski Foça, in particular, archaeologists have had to struggle with developers to protect the city's heritage during a recent boom in building.[17] It is an irony that the growth of tourism, often built on images of Ionia's rich archaeological heritage, is thereby contributing to its destruction.

There are also some complex issues associated with the chronology of Archaic Ionia that complicate matters when attempting to research it. In the Aegean (Figure 1.3) there has existed for a long time a very detailed and precise pottery typology (i.e. a dated sequence of forms and decorative styles) by which archaeological sites can be dated. For the purposes of dating, the most important pottery styles are those of Corinth and Attica, where it has been possible to establish long sequences as a result of intensive studies of the styles from stratified archaeological contexts. Corinthian and Attic pottery was widely traded, and so it is used across the Mediterranean to establish the chronological framework of many sites. Only very recently, and as the result of years of meticulous research of the pottery from the stratified excavations at Miletos, has it been possible to establish such a typology for the pottery styles of Archaic Ionia.[18] This new system of classification, which builds on and incorporates into a new system the existing Ionian pottery classifications, such as Middle Wild Goat style and Fikellura, allows for the integration of Ionian pottery sequences with those of Corinth and Attica. As this new system of classification starts to be adopted, it will have important ramifications for the dating of sites and context in Ionia from which there is little or no imported pottery and for sites outside Ionia for which Ionian pottery is the predominant type, such as in the Black Sea.

[16] Niemeier and Niemeier 1997.
[17] Ö. Özyiğit 2006.
[18] Kerschner and Schlotzhauer 2007.

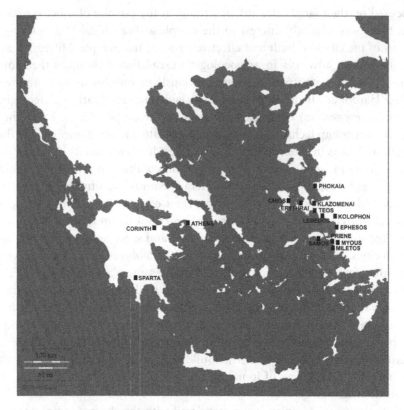

Figure 1.3   The location of the cities of Ionia and major sites in Aegean Greece.

There is, as yet, no comparable typological sequence for the pottery styles of Ionia's neighboring cultures in Anatolia (Figure 1.4). Although there are many good examples of pottery from these regions in museums and private collections, they have often derived from illicit excavations and so do not have a secure archaeological provenance or stratigraphic context. An example of this is Carian pottery, much of which is thought to come from the village of Damlıboğaz, the ancient city of Hydai, and includes many intact vessels, suggesting that it has been looted from graves.[19] Although many of the local pottery styles of western Anatolia, such as the Carian, appear to have been drawn from those of Ionia, the relationship between them is not always simply derivative. The pottery styles of Ionia and their relationship to those of its neighboring regions will be discussed more fully in Chapter 9.

Without the aid of a precise relative chronology based on local ceramic typologies, and often in the absence of quantities of dateable imported wares, archaeologists working in central Anatolia need to rely on scientific methods of absolute dating. At the Phrygian capital of Gordion, radiocarbon and dendrochronology (tree-ring) dating techniques have been applied in order to test the presumed date of the site, which had previously been based on assumptions about the date of the destruction levels found in the city as

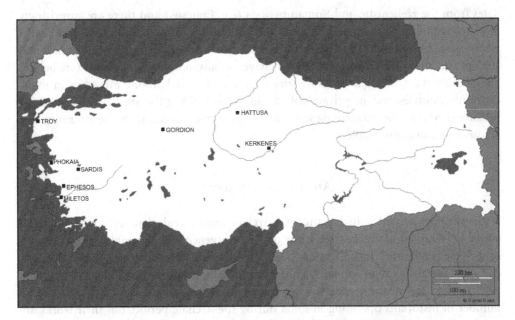

Figure 1.4 The location of the cities of Ionia and major sites in Anatolia.

referred to in historical sources. The application of these scientific dating methods has produced results that have challenged previous assumptions about the historical sequence of events at the site. In particular, the "Early Phrygian Destruction" level which had previously been assumed to have been caused by the Cimmerian invasions mentioned by Herodotos has now been redated to a much earlier period and has been reinterpreted by the excavators as being the result of an accidental fire of a considerably earlier date.[20]

Archaeologists working in the two regions that were Ionia's immediate neighbors and most important influences, the Greek world of the Aegean and Anatolia, are therefore using fundamentally different dating methods to achieve their chronologies – one relative and one absolute. The establishment of a system of pottery classification that corresponds to the existing pottery typologies of the Aegean will make it increasingly easy for us to make connections with the west, but the lack of such evidence to the east of Ionia, and the redating of Gordion in particular, has yet to be fully worked through and will make establishing precise correspondence to the east harder.

To sum up, Ionia has enormous potential for archaeological research and boasts some of the finest, and rightly most famous, archaeological sites in the world. Yet when we seek to explore the Archaic period the gloss of this apparent wealth of evidence begins to pale and we find that the state of the evidence is often patchy and unclear. Some of the Ionian cities are virtually unexplored to this day (e.g. Lebedos), some of them have been systematically destroyed (e.g. Myous), others are limited by the presence of modern settlements (e.g. Samos, Chios, Phokaia), and some have not yet been found (e.g. Old Priene). Even at those sites where there appears to be an abundance of evidence, much of this actually

---

[20] Voigt and Henrickson 2000.

dates from the Hellenistic and Roman periods (e.g. Ephesos) and there are surprisingly few sites with extensive Archaic deposits (i.e. Miletos, Klazomenai, Phokaia, and Erythrai). Accessing the results of these excavations is made difficult for many researchers and students because of the way in which they have, or have not, been published (see below) and because the artifacts from those sites are often scattered among museums in many different countries and in private collections. Even visiting the sites is made difficult because they span two modern nation-states, Turkey and Greece, with a relationship that is sometimes uncomfortable.

Ancient literary sources

A survey of the ancient written sources for Archaic Ionia reveals that here too the material available is limited in nature. In a study of the emergence and geographical distribution of the genres of early Greek literature, Joachim Latacz has demonstrated that the origins of Greek literature lay in Ionian Asia Minor in the eighth, seventh, and sixth centuries BC.[21] Yet very few of these early sources survive intact. There are known to have been a number of historians operating in Ionia during the Archaic period, but their works are either completely lost, as in the case of Kadmos of Miletos, or are preserved only in fragments, as with Hekateus of Miletos.[22]

There are two main bodies of historical material relating to Archaic Ionia. The first of these are the myths of the so-called "Ionian Migration." The second are references to Ionia in the Archaic period from later historians, such as Herodotos, that often deal in detail with events surrounding the Ionian Revolt, at the very end of the Archaic period.

According to mythic tradition, the cities of Ionia were established by migrants from mainland Greece. In this Ionian Migration, people from the Greek "mainland" were led to the shores of Ionia, often by men from Athens, and settled in Ionia, often only after enduring tribulations and hardships, such as war with the native population. We are told that these migrations took place soon after the date of the Trojan War. The pattern that many of these myths take is consistent with that of the foundation myths of the Archaic Greek overseas colonization movement.[23]

There are three schools of thought amongst historians about how to deal with the truth, or otherwise, of the historical tradition of the Ionian Migration. First, there are those who accept it at face value as being essentially factual and seek to apply archaeological evidence to prove the truth of these myths.[24] Secondly, there are those who reject the Ionian Migration and instead seek to develop an understanding of Ionian culture based principally on independent archaeological source material.[25] Finally, there are those who take a particularist approach and seek to nuance the understanding of the mythic tradition to find individual cases where it can be reasonably aligned with the archaeological

---

[21] Latacz 2007.
[22] Gorman 2001: 82.
[23] Dougherty 1993a. See also Chapters 6, 10, and the Epilogue .
[24] e.g. Vanschoonwinkel 2006.
[25] e.g. Cobet 2007.

evidence.[26] For the purposes of this book, the author will seek to adopt the second route, and reject the myths of the Ionian Migration in favor of trying to define an independent archaeology-based understanding of Ionian culture.

The other main body of literary evidence, including the works of Herodotos and Thucydides, was generated as part of the great flourishing of Greek literature in Athens in the fifth century. During this period, following the end of the catastrophic Ionian Revolt, the Greek cities of Ionia were often under Persian control and at times separated from the center of Greek political affairs and cultural development, but they nevertheless continued to appear in literature and to have had a role in Greek political and military affairs.

There is a danger that, in reading these sources, we may project onto Ionia that which we think to be true of fifth-century Athens simply because Athens is better attested and more widely researched and understood by academics. However, this easy approach would fail to appreciate Ionia's local identity as separate from that of Athens. Ionia is not unique in this respect because there are few regions of the ancient Greek world beyond Athens for which good, consistent independent sources exist, and any predominantly history-based approach to those regions will inevitably be inclined to be Atheno-centric. It is only relatively recently that scholars have sought to truly appreciate the diversity and regionalism that existed within the ancient Greek world.[27]

Neither are these two bodies of historical material, partial as they are, independent of one another. In passages such as his description of the foundation of Miletos (1.1.46), Herodotos is putting across a particular version of the foundation myth of that city that is consistent with the explanation of the origins of the Dorians and Ionians that had become widely accepted by most Greek writers in the fifth century BC.[28] According to some modern commentators, it was politically expedient for Athens to seek to "play up," or even invent, the myth of the Ionian Migration in the fifth century BC because at this time Ionia was being incorporated into the Athenian-controlled Delian League and Athenian Empire.[29] It had also been important for Miletos, the leading city of Ionia, to emphasize its putative Athenian origins when it had been seeking Athenian support for the Ionian Revolt of 499–494 BC. Whatever the Greeks' and Ionians' reasons for promulgating this myth of an Athenian origin for the Ionian Greeks of the Anatolian coast, it must be understood within the context of the fifth-century historians who are our primary sources, rather than as events with a firm foundation in fact. Convincing independent archaeological evidence that could corroborate such an origin is so far lacking.

When dealing with the archaeology of periods and cultures for which there are few, if any, historical accounts, there is a tendency to attach excessive importance to known "events." This is a phenomenon that Anthony Snodgrass has noted and written about with particular reference to the archaeology of the Aegean Bronze Age.[30] This fixation on "events" and the desire of archaeologists to identify them in the archaeological record

---

[26] e.g. Lemos 2007.
[27] J.M. Hall 1997.
[28] Alty 1982: 2.
[29] e.g. Nilsson 1986.
[30] Snodgrass 1985.

has the potential to cause misinterpretation of the archaeological record as we seek to "prove" the truth of these events. In the history of Archaic Ionia, significant historically documented "events" include the Ionian Migration;[31] the invasion of the Cimmerians that caused the destruction of sites across Anatolia (Hdt. 1.15); the Lydian incursion into Ionia and subsequent attacks (Hdt. 1.17); the Persian invasion of Ionia following the fall of Lydia, the Ionian Revolt and consequent attacks on various cities in Ionia (Hdt. 5.104ff.).

This brief list of the major attested events in Archaic Ionia illustrates two points: the primacy of Herodotos as the chief historical source, and the fact that most of the events described resulted in destructions. It is tempting to think that such destructions could be easily identified in the archaeological record, but one destruction deposit looks very much like another and it takes careful archaeological research to be able to determine the cause and the date of a destruction layer. At Miletos, the absence of finds from the ruined houses on Kalabaktepe was taken to mean that this late sixth-century BC destruction level had not been as the result of a sudden and unexpected natural disaster, such as an earthquake.[32] In this layer, there were no traces of Attic Red Figure or any more recent pottery styles, suggesting a date very close to that of the destruction of Miletos at the end of the Ionian Revolt. As in the case of the redating of the Gordion destruction deposits, the ability to provide precise dates for such levels, in this case based on imported Athenian Black and Red Figure pottery that could be related to sequences of locally produced pottery, is essential to making a secure identification with the sack of Miletos in 494 BC.[33]

The specific events of the Persian Wars have played an important role in influencing both ancient and modern interpretations of Ionia's position in Greek history. This was a defining point in Greek history because not only did it, even if only temporarily, unite a group of otherwise terminally factional Greeks in the face of an external threat and lead to the creation of a "Greek" identity in opposition to that,[34] but, through iconic battles such as Thermopylae, it has also gone on to define the image of Greece ever since.[35] The Persian War was an important moment that galvanized the formation of a common Greek identity in opposition to the Persians, but we know less about their individual identities prior to this event (i.e. in the Archaic period). The actions of the Ionians in the Persian War similarly shaped their portrayal in the works of Greek writers such as Herodotos and others.[36] The Persian War was crucial in influencing how ancient Greek authors and modern scholars alike have conceived of Ionia. Ionia's position in the war influences our thinking because the war itself, including the subsequent sack of Athens, had been precipitated by the Ionian Revolt. As a result of the Persian War, Ionia was excluded from Greek history for three reasons: the Ionian Revolt may have roused anti-Ionian feeling in Athens and in Herodotos;[37] Ionia remained under Persian control for

[31] e.g. Hdt. 1.146; for summary of sources see Sakellariou 1958.
[32] Senff 2007: 322.
[33] For further discussion of this topic, see Chapter 8.
[34] Hartog 1988; E. Hall 1993.
[35] Cartledge 2006.
[36] Tritle 2006; Harrison 2002.
[37] Although Herodotos is not straightforwardly pro-Athenian (Thomas 2006: 61).

considerable periods of time thereafter and was somewhat dislocated from the cultural and historical life of Greece as a result; and because the leading Ionian *poleis* of Miletos, Teos, and Phokaia had all been taken by the Persians (Hdt. 1.168, 6.18).

The Ionian Revolt, like the Persian Wars in general, has taken a great deal of significance in writings about Archaic Ionia. Yet the events leading up to the revolt took place only at the very end of the Archaic period in Ionia, and, some scholars believe, largely as the result of the machinations of a few individuals, namely Histiaios and Aristagoras of Miletos.[38] Although the states of Ionia united to fight the Persians in the Ionian Revolt, there is no evidence that they had ever previously formed any kind of military or political alliance. In fact quite the contrary – they appear to have had relatively little to do with one another prior to the revolt. It is therefore misleading to use any of the events associated with the revolt as a guide to what life in Ionia may have been like prior to this. For example, on the day of the Battle of Lade, the Samians broke rank, leaving Miletos to fall. This is often taken as evidence that there was a deep and long-standing Samian–Milesian rift. However, the archaeological evidence suggests that the material cultures of these two communities had more in common than they did with the other cities of Ionia. For example, a type of amphora found in the sea off Samos was thought to have been of Samian origin, but has been proved by scientific analysis to have been made in Miletos[39] and an example of Milesian sculpture was found at the Temple of Hera at Samos. Undoubtedly these cities might have been rivals, but we cannot read into the events of Lade that they had always been enemies. In truth we know very little about the region prior to the rising against Persia and we should be cautious about retrojecting assumptions about it based on the unique events of this short period of the region's history on to earlier periods of the Archaic.

Ionia was the birthplace of pre-Socratic philosophy, and its thinkers such as Thales of Miletos and Bias of Priene were held in high esteem by highly influential Athenian philosophers such as Socrates.[40] Ionian philosophy has been the starting point for many writers wishing to locate these important historical characters in their context, both popular[41] and scholarly.[42] But philosophical works are unlikely to tell us anything substantive about life in Archaic Ionia and the lives of these philosophers have been the subject of a great deal of mythologizing. Rather than being the starting point of any research into Archaic Ionia, the lives and works of the Ionian philosophers should more properly be its end point (see Chapter 2). We need to understand Ionia independently of its philosophy and the mythologies that have grown up around it and understand the whole society and wider social and economic processes that created and facilitated the production of that philosophy.[43] Such an approach may seem dully prosaic, but it is an approach that will contextualize the work of the intellectual minority within that of Ionian society as a whole.

---

[38] Gorman 2001: 129–45.

[39] Cook and Dupont 1998: 170–4.

[40] C. Osborne 2004.

[41] e.g. Stark 1954.

[42] e.g. Huxley 1966.

[43] See Greaves 2002: 148–50; Heitsch 2007.

In conclusion, there are very limited historical sources available for the study of Archaic Ionia. Of those that exist, Herodotos is the prime source. The events he describes that are most likely to be testable by archaeology are a series of destructions that affected a number of cities across Ionia during the Archaic period. Events such as the Ionian Revolt have taken on great significance for ancient historians and archaeologists alike, but it is harder to use such historical sources as evidence of social or political realities in Ionia prior to the Ionian Revolt. The fame and importance of the works of the Ionian philosophers have also thrown a long shadow over the interpretation of Ionian history and should be considered only within the socio-cultural context of Ionia as a whole.

Epigraphy

In addition to archaeological and literary sources of information, there exists another form of information relevant to the study of Archaic Ionia: inscriptions. These might be classed as a separate type of evidence because it is necessary to appreciate them not just as texts, but also as artifacts – the precise form and context of which was an essential element in their intended function and meaning. They are an invaluable source of information, but are perhaps the hardest of any for the non-specialist to access.

Archaic inscriptions are a rare find in Ionia and those that survive are generally either short or fragmentary. Responses from the oracle at Branchidai-Didyma are known to have been held in repositories located at the temple itself and in Miletos, where some were found in the Sanctuary of Apollo Delphinos. However, only three short oracular responses have survived from the Archaic period.[44] The study of Archaic Ionian epigraphy will therefore inevitably be fraught with difficulty.

As with the ancient literary sources, and perhaps because of their rarity, great emphasis has often been placed on the few inscriptions that do survive from Ionia, especially where these appear to give insight into the social or political organization of the region. Examples of inscriptions that have stirred up extensive academic debate are the *Molpoi* inscription (discussed below) and the inscription on the statue of Chares, which names him as *archon* ("ruler") of Teichioussa and which has prompted much debate about the nature of the settlement at Teichioussa and its relationship to Miletos.[45]

Inscriptions have been central to the discussions about the location of certain sites within Ionia. Historical writings about Ionia make mention of many different communities, not all of which have yet been securely identified. In the case of Assessos, this was named by Herodotos as being located within the *chora* of Miletos, but its precise location could not be confirmed for certain until the discovery of an in situ inscription during archaeological investigation at Mengerevtepe, several kilometers to the east of Miletos.[46] Inscriptions can also help give more detail about the nature of known archaeological sites, such as the inscriptions from the excavations on Zeytintepe Hill near

[44] Kawerau and Rehm 1914: 132a, 178; Rehm and Harder 1958: 11.
[45] Most recently by Herda 2006: 350, who suggests Chares was a Milesian official governing the settlement.
[46] Senff 1995; B.F. Weber 1995.

Miletos, which identified the cult site there as a sanctuary of Aphrodite, with the local epithet *Oikus*.[47]

As they did elsewhere in the Archaic Greek world, inscriptions in Ionia served a range of functions. They were used for votive inscriptions on dedications made to the gods, such as the Genelos group of statues from the Temple of Hera at Samos. They were used for monumental inscriptions dedicating temples, such as an inscription naming Kroesus on the Artemision at Ephesos.[48] Inscriptions were also used for keeping public records. An interesting example of this are the recorded responses from the oracle at Branchidai-Didyma, mentioned above, which were kept as a public record because the oracle was consulted on religious matters that were of significance to the whole community. For example, there is a fragmentary inscription of a response from the oracle that apparently declared that women should not be allowed to enter the Sanctuary of Herakles.[49] Although burial practices varied considerably across Ionia and *stelae* (stone slabs used as grave markers) were used in some places, including Miletos,[50] funerary inscriptions on *stelae* do not appear to have been common in Archaic Ionia.

The existence of inscriptions with such a variety of uses, and particularly in the public environment of temples and sanctuaries, appears to suggest that at least a section of Ionian society was literate and able to read them. In Athens, public inscriptions only began to be widely used in the fifth century BC, implying that a significant number of citizens could have read and understood them by that time. Less formal, but perhaps more telling, evidence for the level of literacy in Archaic Ionia comes from graffiti carved on the colossi at Abu Simbel in Egypt by Carian and Ionian mercenaries.[51]

One of the difficulties encountered in dealing with epigraphy from Archaic Ionia is the fact that some of the most important inscriptions date from later periods of history, but are thought by scholars to have been reinscribed from earlier, Archaic texts. The wording of the *Molpoi* inscription, for example, suggests that it is in fact a composite of several decrees dating from before 479/78 BC to 450/49 BC, which were re-engraved in c.100 BC.[52] Another crucial text that appears to be a reinscription from an earlier one is an inscription from Priene that apparently describes redistribution of land between various states of Ionia at an early stage in their history.[53] It is possible to show, with a reasonable degree of certainty based on close analysis of the language of such texts, which sections were originally composed in the Archaic period, and which are later insertions. Being products of a later era, the original location and archaeological context of the original document, which can have great significance for its interpretation, have inevitably been lost.

The precise details of how they came to be reinscribed, and of course why, cannot be so easily understood. A second-century BC inscription from Miletos records a delegation from the city of Apollonia-on-the-Rhyndacus in Mysia approaching the Milesians and asking

---

[47]   Herrmann 1995.
[48]   Jeffery 1990.
[49]   *Milet* 1.3.132.
[50]   von Graeve 1989.
[51]   Meiggs and Lewis 1969: 7; Dillon 1997; Boardman 1999: 115–17; see Chapter 7.
[52]   *Milet* 1.3.133; Gorman 2001: 176–86; Herda 2006.
[53]   Roebuck 1979: 59–61.

them if they had records in their archives, presumably from the oracle at Didyma, that would show them whether their city, like many in the region, had originally been founded as a colony of Miletos.[54] The Milesians happily confirmed this, even though Apollonia was most probably a foundation of the Attalid kings.[55] This tells us that the Milesians main-tained some form of archive of oracular responses that could be consulted at this time, but also that they were not above lying about what was in it and then carving those lies in stone. Great store appears to have been set upon the inscriptions of a previous era which evidently had the power to validate potentially contentious political decisions in the present era and for that reason the contemporary political and cultural context of events such as the delegation from Apollonia-on-the-Rhyndacus should always be borne in mind when seeking to use reinscribed or archaizing inscriptions as a source of historical evidence.

Naturally, in order to survive, inscriptions need to have been carved into durable materials. For the most part, in Archaic Ionia, this means stone – on *stelae*, architectural fragments, or statues. Inscriptions also survive on metals, such as bronze – for example a bronze votive *astragalus* (knucklebone) thought to have come from Branchidai-Didyma[56] – and lead, such as the Lydian ingot discussed below.[57] Inscriptions can also appear on other prestige materials that can be inscribed, such as tridacna shell and faience votives from Samos,[58] or more mundane artifacts such as terracotta loom-weights, which were also dedicated in temples. Texts could also be painted onto pots as *dipinti* (painted inscriptions), such as the numerous examples of pots dedicated at the Sanctuary of Aph-rodite at Miletos which have the goddess's name painted on them.[59]

The language of the inscriptions of Ionia in the Archaic period is predominantly, but not exclusively, Greek, and the particular letterforms used were a local variant of the Greek alphabet.[60] The recent discovery of so many potsherds with graffiti and *dipinti* from the Sanctuary of Aphrodite at Miletos will undoubtedly tell us more about epigraphic habits and paleography at that site, when they are published in full.[61] Inscriptions of more than one line were generally written *boustrophedon* (i.e. with lines alternating from left to right, and right to left) in Archaic Ionia (see Figure 7.3, pp. 166–7). Distinc-tive features such as these make it possible to allocate a date and, where the original provenance of the artifact is unknown, identify inscriptions as coming from Archaic Ionia. It was on this basis that it has been argued that the colossal bronze *astragalus* from Susa originally came from Ionia, probably as Persian booty following the sack of Branchidai-Didyma in 494 BC (see Box 4.1).[62] The Ionian script was also used in the

---

[54]   Kawerau and Rehm 1914, n. 155; Greaves 2002: 127–8; 2007b.
[55]   Magie 1950. See also Chapter 6.
[56]   *SEG* 30, 1290; Jeffery 1990: 334.
[57]   Adiego 1997. It is also interesting to note the Berezan Letter, which was inscribed on lead and is an indica-tion of how important letters may have been written in Ionia (Chadwick 1973).
[58]   Diehl 1965: 827–47.
[59]   Senff 2003.
[60]   Jeffery 1990.
[61]   Alexander Herda, speaking at the British Museum, March 14, 2007.
[62]   Although the provenance of this artifact has been questioned by some scholars, it is generally accepted by most, including the *SEG*, to have come from Branchidai-Didyma. See Greaves forthcoming (3) for a summary of the discussion.

colonies established by Ionian cities and it has been identified at sites across the Black Sea, such as Olbia-Borysthenes, Berezan, and Histria.[63]

Although most inscriptions from Ionia are in Greek, a number of items, including a lead ingot from Archaic Miletos,[64] a marble fragment found at the Artemision and some coins from pre-Achaemenid Ephesos were inscribed in Lydian.[65] The coins and the lead ingot bearing Lydian text are small portable items and do not imply that Lydian was read and understood in Miletos and Ephesos; however, the marble fragment from the Artemision may tell a different story, as inscriptions erected in temples were presumably designed to be read by someone. The total number of known Lydian inscriptions is very small, and so to find three examples outside of Lydia, and away from its capital of Sardis in particular, is noteworthy. Inscriptions in the languages of the other Anatolian contemporaries of the Ionians – such as Carian and Phrygian – are also rare. There are only 44 known Carian inscriptions in existence[66] and our understanding of Carian is often derived from placenames[67] and personal names[68] used in Greek literature. However, it appears that these peoples may have had a more lively epigraphic culture than may previously have been presumed as the discovery of a series of clay writing tablets at the Oracle of Labraunda in Caria is suggestive of mantic or votive practices that had built up around the use of writing.[69] An extremely rare find of a fourth-century BC bilingual Greek–Carian inscription at Kaunos not only gives us insight into the Carian language and its use in epigraphy, but also shows the co-existence of two literate groups of presumably equal status at that site.[70] The recent discovery of the use of the Phrygian language at Kerkenes Dağ, far to the east of what was previously presumed to be the extent of Phrygia, might show that, as in the case of the Greek graffiti at Abu Simbel, these Anatolian languages were capable of traveling beyond the presumed limits of the cultures that produced them.[71] Each language also has its own epigraphic culture. In the case of Lydian, the language may have been widely spoken, but it was evidently rarely committed to writing, despite having an established script. The fact that inscriptions in the Anatolian languages have not been a common find in Ionia does not mean that they were not spoken and understood here. The use of Anatolian words, names, and deities in the Greek inscriptions of Ionia suggests that there was a non-Greek speaking population here, even if they were not attested by the same quantity of epigraphic evidence as were their Greek contemporaries.

The fact that the majority of the inscriptions are in Greek and were apparently intended for public display on temples or on prestige items dedicated in, or on the approaches to,

---

[63] Knipovic 1971, Chadwick 1973, and Johnston 1995/96, respectively.

[64] Adiego 1997.

[65] Dusinberre 2003: 228, nn. 5, 6.

[66] Bryce 1986; Blümel 2007: 430.

[67] e.g. "Didyma," which is similar to Carian placenames such as Sidyma.

[68] e.g. names beginning with "Anax," such as Anaximander.

[69] Meier-Brügger 1983.

[70] The inscription is a *proxeny* (guest-friendship) decree, a Greek institution, but expressed in the Carian language. On the inscription see Frei and Marek 1997; Blümel 2007.

[71] G.D. Summers 2006.

those temples clearly presupposes the fact that there was a literate audience for these texts (see above). However, it is harder to demonstrate the use of Greek away from the social elite or temples. The best evidence for the widespread use of Greek (and literacy) in the population is not dedications on valuable statues or bronzes, but lower-order votive offerings bearing dedications in Greek, such as the pottery from the Sanctuary of Aphrodite on Zeytintepe, or the graffiti by soldiers at Abu Simbel, both mentioned above. There are very few, if any, inscriptions from Ionia that do not come from temples or other religious contexts connected with Greek deities. Interestingly, where there are thought to be Phrygian-style sanctuaries in Ionia, no inscriptions were found[72] and the inscribed Lydian ingot did not come from a temple context but from the domestic and artisans' quarter of Miletos, Kalabaktepe. This predominance of inscriptions from a religious context may be a product of Ionian Greek epigraphic habits at the time (i.e. the use of inscriptions may have been limited to cult purposes), or indicate that Greek was not widespread in the wider community, or that non-durable materials were used away from the temples, as they were in Athens, where laws were posted on wooden tablets in the *agora*.

It is, therefore, important to understand the precise archaeological context from which our epigraphic evidence comes because not only are inscriptions texts, they are also artifacts. Perhaps the bias toward religious contexts for inscriptions in Ionia, noted above, can be attributed to the objectives of the archaeologists who were responsible for finding them and their choice of sites (see Chapter 2). Another example of the importance of understanding the archaeological context of inscriptions and how the agenda of early archaeologists have affected our ability to understand them is the Chares inscription. This was inscribed onto a statue that was originally positioned somewhere on the Sacred Way from Miletos to Branchidai-Didyma. It is possible that this inscription is secondary, that is to say the statue was erected and then the inscription was added at a later date. The inscription is not in a prominent position on the statue, but runs down the leg of the chair on which the figure is seated (see Box 8.1). When the statue was found on the Sacred Way, it was not in its original setting, which may have been as part of a family grouping near the temple at Branchidai-Didyma.[73] In order to understand fully how this statue was originally intended to be seen and understood by its viewers it would be necessary to know where it was displayed, how it related to others in its original grouping or setting, whether its inscription was prominent and visible, and many other factors. It is interesting to note that a number of other statues from the Sacred Way at Branchidai-Didyma were inscribed on the rear side, presumably away from the viewer, and the reason for this practice cannot be fully understood now that the original orientation of the sculptures is lost.[74] Questions such as these cannot now be answered because the precise find locations of the statues were not always recorded when they were removed to the many museums in which they are now housed. In certain key respects, the questions that can be asked of the epigraphic evidence for Ionia will therefore always be limited and we should not

---

[72] See Chapter 8.
[73] Herda 2006: 327–50.
[74] e.g. Newton 1862, nn. 66, 73.

delude ourselves into thinking we can understand the epigraphic culture of the region when the precise archaeological context of the original findspots of inscriptions were not recorded, or have been lost. Another challenge when trying to understand the original context of inscriptions is that, with the exception of in situ architectural inscriptions on stone, most of them are on portable objects. It is also difficult to know the context of inscriptions in private collections, such as the inscribed Egyptian basalt statuette from near Priene.[75]

There are also lost epigraphic sources, which are known to have existed, but which we can never see. Herodotos describes how the Milesian Hecataeus had produced a map on a sheet of bronze, but this has never been found (Hdt. 5.49). As noted above, there is a later inscription that suggests there was an archive of responses from the oracle at Didyma, but this archive may have been another element of the invention of Apollonia-on-the-Rhyndacus as a Milesian colony. The original versions of the *Molpoi* and Priene inscriptions have never been located. There must once have existed a considerable body of Archaic inscriptions from Ionia, which are now lost to us, and of which only echoes survive.

The most significant epigraphic source for defining the region of Ionia comes not from Ionia itself but from Athens – the Athenian Tribute Lists (ATL). These lists literally carved a definition of Ionia in stone, and it is a definition that has often remained unchallenged by scholars. The purpose of the ATL was to record that proportion of the *phoros* (tribute) paid to Athens by its allies in the Delian League/Athenian Empire in the period from 478 BC onwards. The ATL inscriptions cannot be used as evidence for defining the extent of Archaic Ionia because they date from a later period of history and they were produced by outsiders for a particular administrative purpose. Whatever and wherever "Ionia" was in the Archaic period, it is perhaps best to try and appreciate it as an as yet ill-defined or mutable entity, as is clear even from the limited and tenuous epigraphic evidence that exists,[76] rather than the fixed administrative entity of the ATL.

Nevertheless, the Archaic epigraphy of Archaic Ionia has been very useful for determining the attribution of temples to certain gods,[77] or states,[78] where the archaeological evidence or location might otherwise have left these open to question. Inscribed dedications by individuals have also given us a body of data that can be used for prosopography, the study of personal names and kin relationships, in Ionia. Such studies show us that, in common with the epigraphic tradition in mainland Greece, names were accompanied by the individual's patronym (their father's name) and that names with the prefixes Hek- and Anax-, which are possibly of Anatolian origin, were common.[79]

---

[75] Boardman 1999: 280–1.

[76] It appears that at least two major cities disappeared from Archaic Ionia – Smyrna (which became part of Aeolis) and Melie (which was apparently destroyed). However, the source for this is the unreliable later inscription from Priene discussed above (Roebuck 1979).

[77] e.g. the attribution of the Zeytintepe sanctuary to Aphrodite was made by a single stone inscription and numerous graffiti and *dipinti* on pots (Herrmann 1995).

[78] e.g. Çatallar Tepe, where an inscription connects it with Priene, although its location between the territories of Priene, Samos, and Ephesos might have left this open to debate (Lohmann 2007b).

[79] See Herda 2006 for a recent discussion of this in relation to the Carian origins of Hekate.

There are, therefore, very few surviving inscriptions from Archaic Ionia, and of these, even fewer are from secure archaeological contexts. The language of the surviving inscriptions is predominantly Greek, but the use of inscriptions in Ionia appears to have been restricted largely to cult purposes and we know nothing about the use of Greek, or other languages current in Anatolia at the time, beyond this discrete cultic function.

Other sources

These three sources (archaeology, ancient literary texts, and epigraphy) are the traditional mainstays of Classical archaeology but there are other methods, developed for researching prehistoric cultures, which can provide potentially useful insights into Archaic Ionia. These are ethnoarchaeology and experimental archaeology. The conservation and restoration of monuments also may bring to light new and potentially useful evidence.

Ethnoarchaeology is the study of contemporary societies that are in some way comparable to the ancient society in question.[80] Observing these modern societies can provide new insights and understanding into how certain activities and practices may have been carried out in antiquity (pp. 79–80). These observations can provide a paradigm, or model, for understanding how certain aspects of ancient life may have worked. Although such observations do not generate "new" archaeological data as such, they can provide us with a framework within which to understand discard patterns that can be observed in the archaeology, or as models for behaviors that leave no archaeological trace at all.[81] Ethnographic observation of contemporary agricultural practices in a particular region can suggest ways in which ancient farming may have been practiced in that same region in antiquity. Where it is possible to predict how the inevitable changes in society, economy, or environment are likely to have changed these practices, these can be taken into consideration and accounted for. For example, in that part of Ionia that is now modern Turkey, some enduring elements of traditional agriculture can be identified, even though the modernization and mechanization of agriculture, mass tourism, and the introduction of Islam have all affected rural life in the region.[82] However, the value of such studies in Classical archaeology will be more limited than in other areas of archaeology, because there are now few analogous societies on which to base such study.[83] Ethnographic studies do still have the potential to provide us with new and original insights into ancient lifestyles in Ionia, but the application of such methods to the study of Classical Ionia is always likely to be limited.

Another potential source of information is experimental archaeology. In this method, hypotheses about the past are tested by rebuilding or re-enacting particular events, artifacts, or practices and comparing the results with archaeological evidence. An example of this from Ionia is the conjectured use of *astragali* (knucklebones) at the Oracle of

---

[80]   The major work on ethnoarchaeology in Turkey is Yakar 2000.
[81]   London 2000.
[82]   Greaves 2002: 16–24.
[83]   e.g. Sabloff 1986: 116 on the Maya.

Apollo at Didyma.[84] In order to examine how an ancient modified *astragalus* bone, which had been planed flat on both sides, behaved differently to an unmodified example, an experiment was conducted in which the bones were thrown and the results recorded. This showed that modifying the bone resulted in a more even distribution of falls between all four sides of the "dice." This suggests what the desired properties of a modified *astragalus* were and why this had been done. As with ethnoarchaeology, experimental archaeology does not generate new archaeological data, but it does provide a useful aid to interpretation and a point of discussion.

The large-scale conservation of architectural monuments at a number of sites in Ionia has also brought to light new information and insights into the histories of the buildings being conserved. The long-running program of restoration at the theater at Miletos has taught us a great deal about the construction, history, and use of this important Hellenistic structure, bringing to light new inscriptions, sculptures, and insights into the architecture of the building.[85] At Ephesos, the excavation of small trenches to accommodate the stanchions for a protective dome over the ruins of Roman houses revealed interesting new information. Mass tourism in Ionia has also led to new projects by archaeologists and museums that have required small-scale excavations, restorations, and other works that have resulted in research outcomes. For example, the planning and laying-out of a series of paths across the site at Miletos in an arrangement to match the original orthogonal plan of the city stimulated renewed research into the city's plan.[86] Conservation and reconstruction projects such as these can teach us a great deal, but their impact has been largely limited to the Hellenistic and Roman period, because these are the periods from which the largest monuments survive and restoration work has not yet provided any substantial new evidence about the Archaic period in Ionia.

Another important and rapidly developing field of archaeology is geoarchaeology. This is the study of ancient landscapes and environments using the methods of geologists, geomorphologists, and physical geographers. The understanding of landscape and environment and the impact it has had (and continues to have) on human settlement has such bearing on archaeology that these methods are now fundamental to the discipline. A great deal of this kind of research has focused on the lower Maeander Valley in the hope of explaining when and how the harbors of cities such as Ephesos, Miletos, and Myous silted up (see Chapter 3). Further work has also recently been conducted at Kato Phana on Chios in an attempt to understand the relationship of the Apollo sanctuary to the ancient coastline.

It can be seen, therefore, that there are a range of methods and approaches, beyond the traditional mainstays of Classical archaeology, that could provide useful new data, insights, and perspectives for the study of Ionia now and in the future, but the extent to which these are applied and used will depend on the kinds of questions being asked of the archaeology and the resulting forms of projects devised in order to answer those questions.

---

[84] Greaves forthcoming (3).
[85] e.g. Gresik and Olbrich 1992; B.F. Weber 1999a, 2001.
[86] B. Weber 2007.

Excavation and Publication

Sir Mortimer Wheeler summed up the greatest challenge and dichotomy of modern field archaeology in just three words when he wrote: "excavation is destruction."[87] This phrase encapsulates the understanding that although the very act of excavation recovers artifacts, it simultaneously destroys the most vital component of their interpretation: the archaeological context. Reaching this understanding is a critical "threshold concept" in any archaeologist's education.[88] Contexts are the essential clue to understanding the meaning of the artifact. For example, whether a figurine is found in a temple, in a tomb, or in a rubbish pit will have enormous significance for how it is to be interpreted and understood by archaeologists. Similarly, whether a coin is found in, under, or above a destruction layer will make a big difference to how that destruction is dated and interpreted.

What mitigates the destruction of archaeological contexts by excavation and ensures the secure interpretation of the artifacts and evidence found is the prompt and accurate publication of the primary excavation data: the excavation reports. These make knowledge available to a wider academic and public audience. Publication is therefore an essential part of the process of modern excavation. As will be discussed later, it would be entirely spurious to claim that any archaeological data is ever truly "objective," but as much as possible the overtly subjective interpretation of archaeological data should be separated from the reporting of the primary data. This may require excavators to differentiate between primary and secondary (i.e. interpretive) publications, or parts of publications, so that the conclusions they draw can be questioned against the data. It also requires them to make their interpretative frameworks and assumptions explicit. There are, however, many reasons why these things do not happen and why the available published evidence for the study of Ionia is limited.

In some respects there is such a superabundance of archaeological evidence about Ionia that it is almost too plentiful for any one archaeologist to absorb and process. A century of excavations at key sites such as Miletos, Samos, and Ephesos has resulted in a wealth of publications, but accessing, reading, and utilizing them is a challenging proposition. Relevant factors here include the fact that older publications may be rare, or inaccessible to many researchers and students.[89] The cost of some publications is prohibitive to many academic libraries. For example, the latest two-volume edition of inscriptions from Miletos cost US$400, and included reprints of a number of articles that had previously been published elsewhere. However, given the fundamental importance of the earliest excavations in Ionia and their enduring significance, it is important to note that many important publications that were previously out-of-print and unavailable are now being republished, making them accessible to a new generation of scholars.[90] Online publications are free, but are not yet a widely accepted feature of academic culture. It is also

---

[87] Wheeler 1956.

[88] Kirk and Greaves 2009.

[89] However, developments such as the systematic digitization of journal articles by services such as JSTOR are making some sources more widely available than was previously possible.

[90] e.g. www.Degruyter.de – made possible by digital printing.

important to point out that publications from Ionia appear in a multitude of languages, principally in German and Turkish, but there are also numerous important and relevant publications in English, modern Greek, French, and Italian. If one were to extend this to the Black Sea, where the Ionian cities had many colonies, then Russian, Romanian, Bulgarian, Georgian, and Ukrainian might also be added to that list.

Not only should all excavations be published in full if they are to compensate for the destruction of archaeological deposits that was necessary for their creation, but it is expected that such publications should appear promptly if they are to be of value to the academic community. Prompt publication is necessary because archaeological techniques, interpretative perspectives, and ethical agenda move on rapidly. There is therefore pressure on excavators to release the results of their latest excavation so that they can be incorporated into various contemporary debates. For example, in the time it has taken for the proceedings of the important Güzelçamlı conference to appear in print, many of the papers in it have been superseded by other publications.[91]

However, this desire for prompt publication that is brought to bear upon the archaeologist by wider archaeological communities may be at odds with the interests of his/her own smaller community of practice for high-quality publications.[92] This generates a tension between the need for speed and the need for the accuracy, quality, and completeness of the final publication. It can be seen that in Ionia there is a very powerful community of practice at work that values quality and completeness of final publications over the promptness of their appearance. The result is superbly presented, detailed, and comprehensive books which, although expensive to purchase, are considered to be definitive sources of information.

The interests of this community of practice also create another tension, namely with the requirement of the Turkish government for annual interim reports. It is a condition of receiving a permit to excavate in the Turkish Republic that excavators must make a presentation at the annual symposium, the papers from which are then published in *Kazı Sonuçları Toplantısı* (or KST). In this way the publication of KST has become a publicly available repository for archaeological evidence from across Turkey, especially as it is now available online.[93] Prior to this recent innovation, KST had very limited circulation because it was not for sale and was not very widely available outside of Turkey. However, articles in KST are not final publications and substantial revisions may be made in the final publications by the excavators. The other widely available sources of information on recent archaeological developments in Turkey are the annual "newsletter" published in the *American Journal of Archaeology*[94] and the *Current Archaeology in Turkey* website,[95] but both of these are inevitably subject to interpretation by their compilers and it is not considered good practice within certain communities of practice to cite them as definitive sources of evidence, for which only references to final publications will suffice. Yet when

---

[91]   Greaves 2008 on Cobet et al. 2007, e.g. compare Beaumont and Archontidou-Argyri 2004 and Beaumont 2007.
[92]   On the operating of such archaeological communities of practice in Turkey, see Greaves 2007a.
[93]   www.kultur.gov.tr
[94]   These newsletters are now available online at www.ajaonline.org, with back-issues available via JSTOR.
[95]   http://cat.une.edu.au

Box 1.1
British Excavations at the Artemision

From 1863 to 1874, John Turtle Wood (b.1821 d.1890) excavated at Ephesos, determined to find the Temple of Artemis, mentioned in the Bible and named as one of the Seven Wonders of the World.[a] In the 1860s, following the Crimean War, Anglo-Ottoman diplomatic relations were very favorable to a British excavator being granted the *firman* (royal mandate) needed to excavate. When he started his excavations in 1863 Wood was working as a railway engineer, as he continued to do during much of the long excavation that followed. His work attracted much attention and he was visited by the Ottoman Sultan, Prince Arthur (one of Queen Victoria's sons), and Heinrich Schliemann. Nevertheless, he received limited funding and logistical support from the British government and the British Museum.[b]

Wood was no scholar and he seems to have dismissed, or been unaware of, the previous researches of the British traveler Edward Falkener (b.1814 d.1896) who had proposed that the temple would be found beyond the city's Magnesian Gate. Wood wasted years in a fruitless search for the temple, before finally following Falkener's advice. The area in which the Artemision lay was swampy, which slowed down the excavations and the removal of sculptural fragments which were taken by train to İzmir, and from there to the British Museum. The swampy conditions were also extremely unhealthy and Wood suffered great ill-health and came to rely heavily on the support of his wife, Henrietta. Although archaeology was still in its infancy as an academic discipline, Wood was not following even the most rudimentary recording practices and this was noted by his contemporaries. Every year Wood had a struggle to renew his *firman*. The Anglo-Ottoman diplomatic climate was also changing, the Ottoman government was preparing stricter antiquities legislation, and finally Charles Newton (b.1816 d.1894) of the British Museum closed down the excavation.[c]

In 1895 excavations were begun by the Austrian Archaeological Institute, initially under the direction of Otto Benndorf (b.1838 d.1907), and have continued ever since, apart from breaks in excavation during the World Wars. There was a brief resumption of excavations at the Artemision by David Hogarth (b.1862 d.1927) for the British Museum in 1904 and 1905.[d] Wood had assumed that the altar must have been inside the temple building, but had not found it, but digging to the west of the temple building Hogarth had better luck and his spectacular finds, including coins and ivories, remain some of the most important discoveries from the site.[e] In 1907 the British traveler Gertrude Bell visited Ephesos. Her photographs remain an important historical document of the site and its surroundings during this important time.

Notes

[a] Wood 1877, 1890; Newton 1881.
[b] Challis 2008: 114–39.
[c] Challis 2008: 114–39.
[d] Hogarth 1908; Jenkins 1992.
[e] Hogarth 1908: 55ff.; Bammer 1968: 401–6.

(a)

(b)

(a) A view of Ayasoluk Hill at Ephesos, showing the line of the ancient aqueduct. Photograph by Gertrude Bell 1907. © Gertrude Bell Photographic Archive at the University of Newcastle upon Tyne.
(b) A view of Ayasoluk Hill today, surrounded by the modern town of Selçuk. Note that the piers of the aqueduct can still be seen in the midst of the modern buildings in the centre left of the image.

such publications are unavailable, or decades away from publication, tensions are created within those communities of practice that demand publications that use up-to-date information and are informed by the latest theoretical stances within contemporary archaeological thinking.[96]

Unfortunately, the delay between excavation and publication is too great – some final publications never appear and it is difficult to reconstruct the original excavation from the surviving records. Historical factors can also intervene, such as when excavations at Phokaia were halted by war in 1914,[97] or the 1922 excavations at Kolophon, when notebooks and finds were lost due to political unrest.[98] In some cases it is possible to return to unpublished material, where the artifacts, records, or preferably both, survive. For example, a recent reappraisal of the 1920s excavations of Archaic Ephesos by Josef Keil was able to access his sketchbook, photographs, notebook, and journal but still encountered difficulties in interpreting the precise meaning of some entries.[99]

Conclusions

Despite an apparent wealth of archaeological evidence from Ionia, on closer examination secure archaeological evidence from the Archaic period is in relatively short supply and comes from a few key sites. Although current ongoing excavations in the region are using modern techniques of recording and analysis and the potential new avenues of enquiry of ethnoarchaeology and experimental archaeology are starting to be explored, the bulk of our information about Ionia still comes from old excavations and we are reliant on the publication of detailed modern excavations and surveys from just a handful of sites across the region, especially when seeking to explore trans-regional trends and identities. There are also expectations and tensions within the communities of practice that generate and use this archaeological data that significantly affect its publication. These also affect the interpretation of data, as will be explored in Chapter 2.

Developments in the appreciation of identity have shown that in the Greek world this was constructed through the conscious use of language and literature and was often largely unconnected to material culture.[100] This is a useful perspective to adopt because it allows us to appreciate history and archaeology as two distinct disciplines and their materials as the distinct conscious and unconscious creations of the same people that we should not simply expect to be able to bring into a simple direct alignment. The written history of Archaic Ionia and the archaeological evidence for its material culture should therefore be studied in isolation from one another and we should seek to segue them together only cautiously and in an informed manner. This, also, will be developed in Chapter 2.

---

[96]   e.g. Rubinstein and Greaves 2004: 1077 note the lack of publications from Klazomenai and reference the AJA newsletters for key information.

[97]   Sartiaux 1921: 120.

[98]   Bridges 1974: 264.

[99]   Kerschner et al. 2008: 109–14.

[100]   J.M. Hall 1997.

2

Constructing Classical Archaeologies of Ionia

Introduction

As demonstrated in Chapter 1, despite an apparent wealth of archaeological evidence from this most important region in the ancient Greek world, the archaeological evidence for Archaic Ionia is limited to a few key sites. Also, to further complicate the application of modern methods of interpretation to that evidence, substantial early excavations took place at many sites before advances in excavation and recording techniques, historical events led to the loss of excavation archives and artifacts from some sites, and many excavations are only partially published. Although re-analysis is possible where detailed records and complete sets of artifacts have been kept, fully reappraising the results of earlier excavations is a time-consuming and often prohibitively costly process. As a result, the rigorous application of certain quantitative methods of analysis will be impossible at many sites in Ionia, and where it is possible, it will largely be restricted to those sites, and parts of sites, that are actively being researched at the moment. In effect the possibility to interrogate the evidence by the application of precise quantitative means has largely been lost and a methodology that seeks to balance limited hard data with more qualitative methods will need to be developed if an appreciation of Ionia as a region is to be achieved.

Ionia sits between two distinct cultural and geographical spheres: Aegean Greece and Anatolia. The aim, in part, of this book is to consider how the interplay between these two regions informed the cultural identities of the peoples of Ionia in the Archaic period. However, if we are to recognize that both of these extra-Ionian spheres influenced the development of the Ionians' own cultural identities it will be necessary to adopt methodological approaches that recognize and value both groups, rather than the traditional approaches of Classical archaeology, which are often implicitly Atheno-centric.

It is important to stress Ionian "identities" in the plural because it soon becomes evident when surveying the data that each community in Ionia had developed localized ways of expressing its identity that were unique to itself. It might reasonably be expected that these two cultural spheres of Greece and Anatolia would have played a part in the formation of these Ionian "identities," but it cannot simply be assumed that Greek and Anatolian culture melded in predictable ways at their Ionian interface because such simplistic geographical determinism would deny the fact that these identities were the results of conscious acts of creation by the Ionians, and were expressions of their own agency. However, even the constructs of individuals can be argued to be socially specific and are limited by the repeated everyday actions (the "habitus") of the societies around them.[1]

The other central theme of this book is the role that landscape played in the socio-economic life of Ionia. Landscape is not just a passive backdrop to the theater of historical events, but a dynamic and defining force in human culture. Nowhere is the dynamism and presence of landscape more apparent than in the changing rivers and deltas of Ionia and its striking valleys and mountains. Therefore, in order to appreciate the role of landscape in defining Ionian culture, a means must be found to accommodate geographical information in this general interpretative study.

Evaluating the relative contributions of the Greek and Anatolian cultural spheres to the formation of Ionian identities is, therefore, no simple task, as in order to provide assessments of their relative contributions to different aspects of Ionian society, some form of interpretative framework needs to be applied. Likewise, incorporating the results of an interdisciplinary overview that includes geographical, archaeological, and historical sources needs a balanced and reasoned approach if it is to be successful.

In this chapter, the traditional approaches to the interpretation of the archaeology of Archaic Ionia will be examined before exploring an alternative interpretative method: the *Annaliste* perspective. This is an approach to the study of the past that seeks to integrate geographical, archaeological, and historical information diachronically. This *Annaliste* approach will then be applied to a series of themes in the subsequent chapters as a means to provide new insights into Ionia that might not have been achieved by adherence to traditional methodologies.

Traditional Approaches to Classical Archaeology in Ionia

Archaeological evidence is not intrinsically self-explanatory and when dealing with it we are always applying an interpretative framework, whether we are consciously aware that that is what we are doing or not. Within Classical archaeology, which primarily concerns itself with the study of the literate cultures of Greece and Rome, the interpretative framework used by scholars has very rarely been made explicit.[2] Indeed, the popular view of Classical archaeology within the theoretically informed archaeological community at large is that it consciously avoids engagement with the theoretical debates going on within the broader archaeological community. It is argued that early on in its development archaeology bifurcated into "Prehistory" and "Historical archaeology" (including Classical and Medieval archaeology), the latter seeing archaeology only as an adjunct to the

---

[1]   For a useful recent discussion of the role of "agents" in archaeology see Knapp and van Dommelen 2008.

[2]   Precisely what "Classical archaeology" is, and whether or not it is a subdiscipline of classics, archaeology, or art history or is a discipline in its own right, is a matter of interpretation and personal preference (Snodgrass 2007: 11–19).

proper study of history.[3] Advances in the techniques and technology of Prehistoric archaeology, together with the challenges of understanding pre-literate societies, led to intensive debates between the different schools of archaeological thought. Popularizers of theoretical archaeology parodied Classical archaeologists for standing apart from such theoretical concerns.[4]

The theoretical evangelists par excellence of postwar Anglo-American archaeology were the New Archaeologists. Until the 1990s, this was the dominant theoretical movement, which sought to apply the methods and approaches of science to the interpretation of archaeological evidence. This resulted in "a dichotomy proclaimed by the New Archaeologists between history, viewed as particularizing and thus bad, and science, portrayed as generalizing and thus good."[5] It could be said that resistance to the intensity of theory-driven New Archaeology can be seen in the production of many works of Classical archaeology that were self-consciously "particularizing" and lacking in any outward appearance of the "emperor's new clothes" – theory. The publication of detailed excavation reports or encyclopedic catalogs of artifacts, meticulously footnoted and beautifully presented, but largely lacking substantial discussion or any theoretically informed interpretations, is one of the remarkable features of the data surveyed in Chapter 1 and can be cited as evidence of a conscious rejection of the New Archaeology movement.[6]

However, although some Classical archaeologists may pride themselves on not engaging with theoretical archaeology, they are nevertheless operating within an implicit interpretative framework that is well established and widely promulgated within their discipline. Ever since Heinrich Schliemann first excavated the site of Hissarlık, believing it to be the site of Homer's Troy, the interpretative framework of Classical archaeology has been set. In this framework Classical literature provides the overarching set of values, practices, and order of historical events (the "metanarrative" to use the language of postmodernism) into which archaeological evidence is either assimilated or accommodated.[7] Written sources are therefore always, however indirectly, the ultimate point of reference for all traditional Classical archaeology.

Classical archaeology can be seen as an extension of the "Great Tradition" of Classical scholarship. The study of Classical history is a central part of the European "Great Tradition" and it is a sophisticated field of research with its own lively culture of academic debate, of which Classical archaeologists are an important part – as the "materialist arm of Classical history."[8] It has been argued[9] that this places it at odds with the anthropological approach of much postwar New Archaeology, that is, "processualist" or "positivist"

[3] Bintliff 1986.
[4] e.g. Bahn 1996: 73; Johnson 1999: 183–4, figs 12.1 and 12.2 – both referencing the "Reality Gap" cartoons by Simon James. See Snodgrass's second definition of Classical archaeology (2007: 14).
[5] Smith 1992: 24.
[6] This is a "conscious rejection" and not just ignorance – as numerous conversations with colleagues working in Ionia have demonstrated to me.
[7] See Shanks 1996: 53–91, who notes that modern scholars cannot escape their own metanarratives, but instead recognize that the past and present are co-existent.
[8] Snodgrass 1991: 61.
[9] e.g. Renfrew 1980.

thought, which focused on the use of "hard" objective data that could be used "scientifi-cally" to prove the existence of patterns, processes, and laws of behavior in the past. However, it is now widely acknowledged that there are fundamental flaws in the proces-sualist approach and new, so-called "post-processualist" schools of archaeological thought have emerged.

One major drawback of the processualist New Archaeology was its claim to use "sci-entific" methods. The aim of such an approach is to take hypotheses, test them using scientifically proven evidence, and then generalize the results. This is the so-called hypo-thetico-deductive-nomological model. However, archaeological evidence is non-replica-ble in the way that scientific experimental data is, and, once excavated, archaeological sites can never be re-dug, or the past re-lived, in order to test emergent new hypotheses. This reliance on empirically tested data is called "logical positivism." Another drawback of such pseudo-scientific approaches to the past is that human beings have agency, or free will. The individual actions of humans cannot be predicted by reductionist scientific models.

There are two epistemological schools at work in archaeology: the natural sciences, which observe the world from a detached point of view, and the social sciences, which cannot be detached from human society.[10] Each of these has its own culture which informs its set of practices. Therefore, even in the "natural sciences" approach, especially as applied to archaeology, there is no such thing as objective scientific data. Ultimately, all archaeological data are produced by people (i.e. archaeologists) whose perceptions and behavior are determined by their social experiences and contexts. Any claim by archaeologists, whether in the name of processualism or *Wissenschaft* (see below), that their data is objective is therefore entirely spurious. For these reasons, post-processualist theories were developed that sought to address the limitations of processualist method-ologies by recognizing the inherent partiality of archaeological evidence, proposing new interpretative frameworks for dealing with that data, and recognizing the agency of past peoples.

Just as the positivist methods that underpinned processualism are being reappraised and challenged by post-processualist theory, so too can the "literary positivism" that underpins traditional Classical archaeology. "Logical positivism holds that through build-ing observation-based theories about the world, and testing those theories against the observed world, we are able to adequately describe the true nature of the world."[11] With this definition in mind, it could be argued that in the field of Classical archaeology, the traditional method of interpretation is one of "literary positivism" in which the theories are not tested against the "observed world," but against the "described world" of Classical literature. In this mode, the Classical "sources" provide the ultimate point of reference and the validity or veracity of any hypothesis is judged by its "best fit" to the metanarra-tive derived from Classical literature as it is currently understood.

An illustration of such "literary positivism" at work in Ionia is the interpretation of oval buildings found in the area of the Temple of Athena at Miletos. In this area, a number

[10]   A. Jones 2002: 1–22.
[11]   A. Jones 2002: 4.

of buildings of both rectilinear and oval plan had been found during excavation. In his interpretation of these structures, Gerhard Kleiner proposed that the oval structures must be Carian, and the rectilinear ones Greek, because Herodotos (1.146) told us that Miletos had a mixed Greek–Carian population.[12] However, more recent research has shown that such mixed building forms are typical of settlements across the region and should not be related to Herodotos' writings with such certainty.[13] Detailed reappraisal of the archaeological evidence from the period of the presumed Ionian Migration has shown that the evidence is not strong enough to show with absolute certainty that any such movement actually occurred. It is therefore a topic still very much open to debate and the Ionian migration myths must be handled with extreme caution when used as evidence.[14] Therefore, not only are alternative interpretations of the oval/rectilinear house evidence possible and sustained by comparison with other sites in the region, but the very basis of the historicity of this element of Herodotos' account is now being called into question. This highlights two issues for the literary positivist approach: that it is necessary to look beyond simple explanations based on readings of Classical literature; and that understandings of the meanings of those Classical works are not fixed and immutable.

For Ionia, there is also another issue that is of particular relevance to a study such as this, and this is that there will always be a tendency for literary positivist approaches to overvalue the culture that was the progenitor of the surviving literature (i.e. the Greeks) over the under-represented Anatolian communities, whose languages and literary inheritance are relatively little understood (see Chapter 1).

One of the criticisms of logical positivist approaches to archaeology, outlined above, is that the past cannot be re-run in order to test hypotheses in the same way that scientific experiments can be repeated in a laboratory. A similar problem applies to "literary positivism." Here there is an implicit assumption that the Classical historical metanarrative provides the ultimate form of irrefutable evidence about the past, against which hypotheses about the past can be tested. However, there is now an appreciation by scholars that, like archaeology itself, the historical and epigraphic sources of the ancient past are not self-explanatory sources of accurate information about the past. Works such as those of Herodotos are now seen as a series of consciously created "artifacts" (i.e. products of human manufacture) that developed within the cultural context of a past society, the precise values, practices, and nature of which are often lost to us. When we read the works of historian-logographers, such as Herodotos, we are not reading precise and accurate accounts of events in the past as they happened and which can be used as a test-bed for assessing, and rejecting, the acceptability of hypotheses. In works such as this we are reading only that version of events as perceived, interpreted, and imagined by Herodotos and then constructed by him into a work of literature, with a particular purpose in mind, and created by him within a particular cultural context (see Chapter 1). The full implications of this paradigm shift in the underpinnings of much Classical archaeological thought have yet to be fully worked through, but its result will undoubtedly be to put more

[12] Kleiner 1966: 14.
[13] Heilmeyer 1986: 107; Greaves 2002: 76.
[14] e.g. Lemos 2002, 2007.

pressure on Classical archaeologists to make their interpretative frameworks explicit and to reflect critically on the use of literary sources in their hypothesis-testing.

Another problem with the literary positivist approach is that we are in danger of denying the individuality of the majority of past peoples in favor of the minority who were the progenitors of the written evidence. That is to say, if we adopt the works of Classical literature as our template for behaviors in the past, then we are in danger of retrojecting onto the past the values of the society that surrounded writers such as Herodotos – namely male, elite, pro-Athenian, and non-Ionian. The main criticism of the processualist New Archaeology, and one which ultimately contributed to its rejection by many modern archaeological theorists in favor of heterogeneous post-processual approaches, is that it sought to predict patterns of human behavior based on spurious "scientific" data, and thereby denied past human societies their autonomy and individuality.[15]

Archaeological reports, however objective they appear to be, are just as much a product of the perception, interpretation, and imagination of the individual archaeologist as the works of Herodotos are of him. However, what the archaeologist is describing is not what happened in the distant past, but what happened in the near past, on the excavation, as he/she perceived it. Therefore, in effect the archaeological "data" recovered from excavations is entirely subjective to the person who excavated it. This is because the act of excavating itself, and whether material is kept and recorded or not, are all the result of a series of conscious decisions (where, when, how, etc.) made by the excavator in the field.[16] The mental schemata (i.e. the means or patterns by which people represent the world) of the excavator therefore influence the data itself, such as his/her methodological preferences, and problem-solving and prioritizing processes. There is, therefore, an interaction between the theoretical/interpretative framework of the excavator and their fieldwork practice.[17] Another complication for the application of specious scientific reasoning to archaeological data is the fact that the archaeological and historical artifacts that are our primary source, unlike the materials of "hard" scientific analysis, are all hermeneutic (i.e. the products of purposeful human activity about ideas, meaning, or symbols).

The German and Turkish "Schools" of Archaeology

It is not just the mental schemata of the individual archaeologist that will affect their fieldwork practice, interpretations, and any resultant "data," but also the social context within which they operate. Like any community of researchers, archaeologists are subject to social constructivism – that is to say, the questions they ask, the methods they apply to examine those questions, and the standards of proof that they accept in answer to them are determined by their community of practice. In the case of Ionia, there is a regional community of practice at work in archaeology, as there is in other regions of Turkey.[18]

---

[15] Goffman 1959; Bintliff 1991: 9–13; Dobres and Robb 1994.
[16] Hodder et al. 2000.
[17] Hodder 1998.
[18] Greaves 2007a.

German scholarship was central to the work of the Great Tradition of Classical scholarship[19] and German archaeologists have been responsible for the excavation of the largest archaeological sites in Ionia. The group of people responsible for publications here are graduates of a relatively small number of universities in Germany (and Austria). These excavation sites include Miletos, Samos, Priene, Didyma, Myous, and Ephesos (the last by the Austrian Archaeological Institute). Historically, the community of practice at work in Ionia created by the interaction (or lack thereof) between these different research teams has been the guiding force in the archaeology of the region. The diligent approach of so many archaeologists over a century has resulted in a rich dataset from certain sites in Ionia, and has also made valuable contributions to the development of archaeology as a discipline worldwide.[20] Although much of this data has been produced and published in an apparently untheorized context, it is nevertheless highly competent and has resulted in important reflections and advances in recent years.[21] It is wrong to dismiss the traditional approach to Classical archaeology, as practiced in Ionia and elsewhere, as being wholly detached from the more dynamic-seeming world of theoretical archaeology.

As shown above, Classical archaeology is engaged with the highly developed field of Classical historical research and has its own interpretative framework. Yet Classical archaeologists, and the German school of Classical scholarship in particular, are often caricatured as being theoretical Luddites, focused only on fieldwork and the establishment of academic dynasties. As the light-hearted, but by no means lightweight, British archaeologist Paul Bahn wrote:

> Other areas, such as Classical or historical archaeology, are still far more oriented towards fieldwork, analysis of texts, and the handling of real evidence. For example, some archaeologists in Germany, where very little attention has been devoted to theory, tend to consider the theoreticians as eunuchs at an orgy (especially as they are most uncertain to have any successors).[22]

Yet the largely untheorized approach of the German school of Classical archaeology is not just a product of the "Great Tradition," nor is it an unconscious choice by this particular group of archaeologists. In the early twentieth century, the "fanatical patriotism" of Gustaf Kossinna (b.1858 d.1931) had resulted in the interpretation of archaeological data becoming a vehicle for German nationalism based on the idea of a superior Indo-European race originating in Germany.[23] This style of archaeological interpretation found favor with the Nazi regime, which actively promoted it and dismissed or exiled many archaeologists who were politically or racially disfavored. The ideology of National Socialism, as with other causes that have hijacked the methods and materials of archaeology, was subsequently discredited and rejected,[24] but its influence has been pernicious and

---

[19] Renfrew 1980: 289.
[20] Shanks 1996.
[21] e.g. Kerschner and Schlotzhauer (2005, 2007) on the new classification of Ionian pottery.
[22] Bahn 1996: 66.
[23] Trigger 1989: 163–7.
[24] Trigger 1989: 381.

long-lasting.[25] One of the consequences of this period in German history when the past was consciously distorted may be the fact that in the postwar era there has been a reluctance by many contemporary archaeologists to actively engage with theoretical models that aim to reinterpret the past. The conscious rejection of highly theorized approaches to the interpretation of archaeological evidence by modern German Classical archaeologists can therefore be seen as a response to the historical experience of archaeology in that nation. Whereas Kossinna's work had marked the "final replacement of an evolutionary approach to prehistory by an historical one,"[26] postwar German archaeology has placed great emphasis on *Wissenschaft* – the scientific basis of knowledge. The "Wissenschaft" approach separates theory from method and the context of discovery of an idea from its context of evaluation; it seeks to find explanations that can be generalized and are testable; it rejects untestable statements as "unscientific"; and views scientific thought as independent of value judgments.[27] In this view of the past, historical records can, like archaeological evidence, be viewed as objective sources of evidence about that past that do not require interpretation or analysis.

The so-called "German school" of archaeology is, however, not the only one currently operating in Ionia – there are also Turkish and Greek scholars at work in Ionia, whose different national cultures influence how they perceive of the past. In Greece the link between archaeological monuments, both in Greece and in museums abroad, has historically been closely linked to ideas of nationalism and politics.[28] Many of the most important sites and the most influential archaeologists in the region are, of course, of Turkish nationality but the position of the "Greek" monuments in relation to Turkish politics and concepts of nationalism is a more ambiguous one. Archaeology played an important part in the political ideology of the early Turkish Republic.[29] In the early days of the Republic, a number of influential Turkish archaeologists were sent to be educated in Germany by the Republic's founder, Mustafa Kemal Atatürk, to whom archaeology was very important.[30] Of particular significance to the archaeology of Ionia, one of these individuals was the late Ekrem Akurgal (b.1911 d.2002), who proved to be an important influence on the archaeology of the region. Akurgal led excavations at a number of key Ionian sites, including Phokaia, Erythrai, and İzmir-Bayraklı (Old Smyrna).[31] He was also influential politically, as a teacher of future generations of Turkish archaeologists, and for the high esteem in which he was held by the whole archaeological community in Ionia.[32] Akurgal's work was firmly founded in the Great Tradition of Classical scholarship[33] and this can be seen to have influenced the early engagement of Turkish scholars

[25]   As an illustration of the influence of the Nazi regime on the archaeology of Ionia, the frontispiece of the publication of the Sixth International Archaeology Congress, which included the publication of the latest results from the excavations at Miletos (Weickert 1940), shows the Nazi flag flying over the conference venue.

[26]   Trigger 1989: 167.

[27]   Johnson 1999: 34–47.

[28]   Trigger 1989; Shanks 1996: 79–81.

[29]   Çiğ 1993; Özdoğan 2001: 28–47.

[30]   Ateşoğulları 2002: 75–92.

[31]   Ö. Özyiğit 2003.

[32]   The proceedings of the Panionion conference were dedicated to him – Cobet et al. 2007.

[33]   e.g. E. Akurgal 2007.

with the archaeology of the western coastal region of their country. The theoretical and methodological approaches of this "Turkish school" of archaeologists in Ionia may therefore be paralleled to that of the "German school," although the motivation behind the use of archaeology differed. During the early Turkish Republic, archaeology was used to prove that it was in Anatolia that Western culture found its origins – not in Mesopotamia which was the standard Orientalist view at the time.[34] This stance can perhaps still be detected in the work of some Turkish scholars.[35]

However, historical explanations for the theoretical approaches adopted in Ionia such as these, which are bounded by national identities, do not adequately explain the theoretical stance of the contemporary generation of scholars working in Ionia. Here, academics of many nationalities and disciplinary backgrounds work side-by-side on various excavation projects. For example, in regions where the community of practice has adopted theoretically informed approaches to the interpretation of archaeological evidence, German archaeologists have engaged with this as much as their peers of other nationalities. One region where this can be seen to have happened in Turkey is in the area of the Neolithic in the southeast.[36] The decision to present the results of archaeological excavations in Ionia without reference to theoretically informed interpretative frameworks has therefore been a conscious, and it could be argued a "creative," response by the community of practice operating in the region to the perceived deficiencies of such theoretical approaches. These perceptions may be informed by the awareness of the excavators of the long history of archaeological research in the region, their role as inheritors of that tradition, and the perception of final publications as "definitive" documents, which should be devoid of any faddish "trendy" archaeological theories which may pass out of fashion and thereby invalidate the overall work. Therefore, although the lack of engagement with archaeological theory by Classical archaeologists of the "German" and "Turkish" schools in Ionia may be decried by British theorists, Classical archaeology in Ionia is far from being intellectually moribund and its rejection of explicit theorizing is a deep-rooted, conscious, and principled stance which should be recognized and respected by those seeking to work in the region.

Once established, this emphasis on the "scientific" basis of archaeological interpretation is often driven and perpetuated by the demands of institutions such as funding bodies, or even social or educational institutions. This is what Matthew Johnson has referred to as "institutional intimidation"[37] and it can be a powerful force in perpetuating established theoretical and methodological practices within a community of practice such as that of archaeologists operating in Ionia.

It is the opinion of the author that scientific knowledge is not objective, but entirely subjective, relative to the social context within which the individual operates. The corollary of this argument is that there can be no division between theory and method.[38] This is contrary to the precepts of the positivist methodologies of *Wissenschaft* and therefore

[34] Atakuman 2008.
[35] See Chapter 9 on Fahri Işık.
[36] Greaves 2007a.
[37] Johnson 1999: 45.
[38] Shanks and Tilley 1992.

contrary also to received current practice within Classical archaeology, which sees itself as consciously rejecting theory. The importance of regionalized communities of practice within the archaeology of Ionia, as elsewhere in Turkey, has already been highlighted above. It is therefore within these communities of practice that social constructivism operates.

Strict adherence to positivist ideals along these lines is restrictive because, in order to be deemed valid, hypotheses must be "proven" and the means of doing this (i.e. weight of evidence and/or alignment with the established historical framework/metanarrative) mitigates against many hypotheses based on Anatolian evidence. Classical (i.e. Greek) history (which is a conscious construct of the Greeks) is therefore the ultimate and final point of reference for all "proven" hypotheses about the history of Ionia. Previous generations of archaeologists who generated much of the archaeological data in Ionia were also driven by a set of values (e.g. a high regard for the cultural aesthetics of Classical art and architecture) which were determined by their contemporary social context and which also mitigated against the recognition of non-Greek elements in the region.

The Classical archaeology community of practice within Ionia produced a wealth of archaeological data as the result of over a century of intensive and diligent research in the region. It is therefore important to recognize and address the implicit interpretative systems that have been at work in this community of practice if we are to achieve a more informed understanding of the region. The lampooning of Classical archaeologists for their lack of engagement with contemporary archaeological theory of the Anglo-American "anthropological" variety misrepresents the complexity of Classical archaeology as a subdiscipline and its enduring intellectual paradigm – that Classical writing provides us with the cultural scaffolding of, and the only secure framework for interpreting, the material culture of Classical societies. However, as this view has come increasingly under attack by Classical historians seeking to understand the Greek construct of ethnicity,[39] it is necessary to consider new frameworks that can accommodate both Classical literature and the independent study of archaeology if the discipline is to move forward successfully.

Annaliste Perspectives on Archaeology

The world is a big place in which little things happen – a fact that Prehistoric archaeology has always recognized by maintaining the understanding of the day-to-day activities of human subsistence as its central focus. However, the Classical Great Tradition and traditional approaches to the text-based study of literate societies and periods, such as Medieval and, by extension, Classical archaeology, were often concerned only with the architectural and literary works of "Great Men." These two approaches, respectively, present us with a "bottom-up" and "top-down" approach to understanding ancient society.

As an antidote to the traditional approach to writing Classical history which was derived from historical texts that were the conscious products of the male elite in society,

---

[39]   e.g. J.M. Hall 1997.

the *Annaliste* approach to the study of history advocates a broader understanding of diachronic processes at work within society at all levels. The *Annales* school has been very influential in the discipline of history and has also been important in the development of thinking about archaeology. The origins of this school can be traced back to 1929, and are exemplified by Fernand Braudel's monumental diachronic and interdisciplinary study *La Mediterranée et le monde mediterranéen.*[40] Since then, further generations of *Annaliste* scholars have developed and advanced its methodologies in multiple directions.[41]

The general philosophy of the *Annaliste* approach is that effective historical studies should be both interdisciplinary and diachronic: a "total" history. *Annaliste* history is "interdisciplinary" in the sense that not only does it go beyond traditional textual approaches to integrate the study of written sources with physical disciplines, geography in particular, but also it includes approaches derived from the social sciences, such as sociology. In *Annaliste* thinking, events can only be understood in a broad spatial context (i.e. the landscape and geographical setting). This emphasis on landscape and the nature of societies beyond the literary elite gives it an obvious affinity with the methods and objectives of archaeology. The *Annaliste* approach is also diachronic because it seeks to locate processes, societies, and events into a long-term chronological perspective. Again, in this respect it is a school of historical thought that has much in common with the traditional objectives of archaeology, which is often concerned with cultural processes and phenomena that can be traced over millennia.[42] For some scholars, the extensive gathering of detailed information that typified the massive works of *Annaliste* scholars such as Braudel was anathema to the generalizing approach of processualist archaeology, inspired by a perception of science that sought to define and then test pithy "laws" of human behavior.[43] For others, the *Annales* school approach built on New Archaeology (i.e. logical positivism) by building on quantitative, demographic, and social scientific works,[44] thereby making the connections between the individual and society clearer by bringing in the phenomenographic experience of the individual.

In his defining work, *La Mediterranée*, Braudel proposed a tripartite[45] chronological system for articulating the relationship between history and enduring processes and landscape. Table 2.1 provides a brief overview of terminology that might be applied to the three parts of Braudel's chronological scheme. An analogy can be made between these three registers and the sea, in which macrohistory is the underlying current, mediohistory is the tides, and microhistorical "events" are the curling crests of the waves of deeper historical processes.

---

[40] Originally published in 1949 and translated into English as *The Mediterranean and the Mediterranean World in the Age of Philip II* (1972).

[41] Knapp 1992 provides a concise overview of the development of the *Annaliste* approach, in which he identifies four generations of *Annaliste* scholarship. This article and Bintliff 1991 also examine its relationship with archaeology as a discipline.

[42] It has been a criticism of Braudel that his *longue durée* was conceived of as being only three centuries – which is relatively short in some archaeological timescales (Sherratt 1992: 138).

[43] Smith 1992: 24.

[44] Bintliff 1986: 26, quoting Hobsbawn 1980: 394.

[45] Although it is also possible to define it as a four-part system if one accepts differentiation of *intermediate-term conjonctures* and *long-term conjonctures* (Smith 1992: 25).

Table 2.1 A summary of the tripartite *Annaliste* chronological framework proposed by Fernand Braudel

"Macrohistory"	*"Mediohistory"*	*"Microhistory"*
La longue durée	*Conjonctures*	*Événements*
Centuries, (millennia)	Generations, decades	Years, days
Environment. Long-term processes and physical structures that place limitations on human action. Human ecology.	Land-use. Forms of human behavior that come to represent enduring "norms." Demographic, technological, and economic trends.	Behavior. The ephemeral "events" of narrative history and politics.

Braudel's chronological system is not only descriptive – it is also hierarchical, with the different levels being valued over one other. In this system the macrohistorical processes and structures of landscape and geography were emphasized as being the most important – they placed the ultimate limitations on human action, and historical events were insignificant in relation to these. Yet, it was noted by Anthony Snodgrass that there was a tendency for archaeologists dealing with historic or proto-historic cultures (such as the Bronze Age Aegean) to overemphasize the value of events.[46] In Braudel's scheme, this would be to focus on the "surface froth" of history without examining the deeper processes that can only be understood in the medium and long terms.

However, this particular aspect of Braudel's work attracted some criticism, as it was deemed to be too geographically deterministic – that is, that all human action was ultimately dictated by the limitations placed upon it by the physical environment. Post-Braudelian *Annaliste* scholars have addressed this issue in their work by recognizing and valuing the role of human agency.[47] The third generation within the movement sought to introduce more quantitative methods, although these are often difficult to produce given the limitations of the historical and archaeological data, and the contemporary fourth generation have focused on the understanding of *mentalités*, or the mental and emotional experiences of people in the past.[48]

Another potentially difficult concept in Braudel's chronological trinity is that it forces us to question the construct of time as a single, linear progression. In this framework there are three concurrent, sometimes coinciding, rhythms at work. It is precisely the indeterminate, "holistic" nature of this scheme that is its strength, but it presents a challenge to the traditional approaches of Classical archaeology which, being derived from history, demand precision and particularist measurability.

The *Annaliste* approach has been usefully applied to interpretations of the classical world.[49] It has also been used as a framework for landscape archaeologies of regions of

[46] Snodgrass 1985.
[47] Barker 1991: 3; Sherratt 1992: 137–9.
[48] Knapp 1992: 4–9.
[49] Austin and Vidal-Naquet 1977.

the Classical world including Boeotia,[50] the Biferno Valley,[51] and the Madra Çayı Delta.[52] In these cases it provides a useful interpretative framework by which to understand the diachronic processes at work within the chosen case-study region and counteracts the tendency of much ancient historical evidence to overemphasize the importance of events in the urban centers and of their elites.

It is only through intensive archaeological survey away from the urban centers that the *longue durée* and mediohistorical *conjonctures* will be identified and understood.[53] However, in choosing to apply the *Annaliste* framework to Ionia, this study differs from those of Biferno and Madra Çayı in that it does not take as its remit a defined geographical entity, such as a single river valley. Rather, as will be shown, Ionia is an invented and culturally defined construct that transcended any clearly definable geographical unit and included within it valleys, peninsulas, islands, and the sea between them (see Chapter 3). It is also more limited in its chronological scope than such long-term studies of historical landscapes as those of Barker (the Biferno Valley) and Lambrianides and Spencer (the Madra Çayı Delta). The aim of this study, and the reason why the *Annaliste* framework has been adopted, is to counterbalance the traditional text-based approach to the cities of Ionia, which is inevitably biased toward the urban elite who were the concern of such a historical evidence base. Instead it allows us to put those urban communities and the events that took place there into a broader spatial and temporal context.

A New Approach to the Land of Ionia

The written historical evidence for Ionia, outlined in Chapter 1, is limited in quantity, biased toward the Greek language sources, and written by non-Ionians. Therefore, the traditional Classical archaeology approach of using ethnohistorical sources to provide a framework for understanding Ionia's archaeological phenomena is a difficult methodology to sustain, particularly when dealing with regions or subjects that were peripheral to the prime concerns of Greek historian-logographers such as Herodotos. It is also a method that is liable to under-represent the non-Greek elements in Ionian society and to favor the study of the social elite. It is desirable therefore to find an interpretative framework for the study of Archaic Ionia that will accommodate the varying quality and quantity of archaeological evidence from so many sites, and to contextualize that evidence with regard to the geographical location of Ionia between the Aegean and Anatolia, as well as the specifics of its unique topography.

Therefore, for the purposes of this synthetic work, a new methodology will be attempted. The approach adopted for this will be to apply an understanding of the socio-economic structure of Ionia from the ground up. That is to say, in common with the *Annaliste* principle, landscape and geographical data will be freely incorporated into

[50] Bintliff 1991: 19–26.
[51] Barker 1991, 1995.
[52] Lambrianides and Spencer 2007. I am grateful to Nigel Spencer for discussing his research with me.
[53] Bintliff 1991; Snodgrass 1991: 67.

the consideration of the functioning of the Ionian economy and society. This will establish the physical structures that placed limits on human action within the region and within which mediohistorical "conjunctures" and microhistorical "events" took place at the instigation of human agency.

The chronological scope of this current work is primarily restricted to the Archaic period, but in order to understand macrohistorical physical and environmental changes it will sometimes be necessary to look outside that period (especially in Chapter 3). An example of where this has been done previously is in a study of the shifting settlement location at Miletos.[54] In this study macrohistorical processes such as the alluviation of the Gulf of Latmos, mediohistorical norms such as changes in the technology of warfare, and microhistorical events such as battles were incorporated. The outcome of that study was that processes that are identifiable in the *longue durée*, such as the silting up of Miletos' harbor, resulted in human actions such as changing the city's location or fortifications, and that such actions were often galvanized by immediate short-term events such as the imminent threat of attack. By way of contrast, a different study of the city walls of Miletos by Justus Cobet took a consciously historical approach, seeking to understand the significance of city walls in the mentality of the community that constructed them (or at least of its historians).[55] By following different methodological approaches to what was often the same subject matter, these two articles presented different sets of understandings of the meaning of Miletos' city walls. By developing the *Annaliste* approach to the much wider topic of Ionia as a whole, it is hoped that this study may also arrive at understandings that contrast with existing opinion and provide a point of interest or foil to discussion, and at the same time recognize the importance of a regional perspective on the development of the individual Ionian cities.

This new approach can be summarized as a pyramid. At the bottom, the foundation of the pyramid, is the landscape. A detailed appreciation of landscape will be the basis of this study, upon which other themes and ideas can be built. It is therefore applying the "bottom-up" approach typical of Prehistoric archaeology to Classical archaeology, a subject matter that is traditionally approached from the "top down" (see above).

The primacy of landscape within a study such as this is undeniable. In the *Annaliste* approach, landscape places the ultimate restrictions on what can be done and the greatest value is placed upon it. For this reason, Braudel's chronological system has been referred to as resembling a "wedding-cake."[56] This is justified by Braudel because although how a society chooses to practice agriculture in a landscape might be dictated by their social and religious conventions and their available technologies, ultimately the nature of the landscape in which they operate will place limits on what crops and animals can be grown and husbanded there.

For all we now understand about the sophistication of the ancient economy, it was always fundamentally driven by agricultural production, and the study of society cannot be divorced from the study of its means of existence and the accumulation of wealth. For

---

[54]   Greaves 1999.
[55]   Cobet 1997.
[56]   Sherratt 1992: 138, quoting Stone 1985.

Table 2.2 A model mapping different types of archaeological and historical evidence onto areas of human activity in Maslow's hierarchy of needs

	Area of human activity	Maslow's hierarchy of needs
5	Literature and philosophy	Cognitive and aesthetic pursuits of a small elite
4	Religion and art	Social, cognitive, and aesthetic needs
3	Warfare and defense	Safety
2	Agriculture and economy	Survival
1	Landscape and environment	[Ultimate limiting factor on all of the above]

the majority of people, even in a region supposedly famous for its role in trade, as Ionia was, achieving subsistence was the primary concern and trade and all other activities were secondary to that.

In this respect this pyramidal model can also be related to the hierarchy of needs proposed by Abraham Maslow (b.1908 d.1970) because only when the need of the individual (or the *oikos*) for survival and safety have been met can higher cognitive and aesthetic needs be considered (Table 2.2).[57]

There are interactions between all the levels of this pyramid, in both directions. For example, the landscape will determine the nature of any agriculture practiced there, but the practice of agriculture may bring about landscape change by means of erosion and deposition. Similarly, the agricultural cycle may determine when and how warfare is practiced and the methods of warfare will in turn determine certain choices of crops and how they are stored or otherwise protected against raiding and being laid waste. There may also be circumstances when social imperatives override the more primary drives toward safety and survival. Mapping Maslow's hierarchy of needs onto different aspects of ancient life, and then structuring these into a process of archaeological reasoning, is a similar tool to interpretation of the "ladder of inference" approach proposed by Christopher Hawkes.[58]

Traditionally, studies of regions such as Ionia have begun at the apex of this pyramid, with the products of the literary and epigraphic practices of the elite, by beginning with a survey of the available written sources and extrapolating out of these a chronological and cultural "scaffold" for whatever follows. Most archaeological evidence can then be fitted (or "assimilated") into this metanarrative, or "story," about what happened in the region in the past, whereas "difficult" archaeological evidence might require elements of the metanarrative to be finessed before it can be "accommodated." In effect, and by these means, the traditional strategy has been to approach the areas of life represented in the pyramid from a "top-down" approach, rarely presenting a serious challenge to the received understanding of the past as expressed in the metanarrative.

As mentioned above, in this synthetic study of Ionia it is hoped to approach these subjects from the "bottom up." Such an approach seeks, first of all, to achieve a general

[57] Maslow 1943, 1954.
[58] Hawkes 1954; Evans 1998.

understanding of the nature of the landscape, against which all subsequent discussions can be critically conducted and evaluated. Such a "bottom-up" approach owes much to Braudel, as it places strong emphasis on the primacy of landscape and environmental structures and processes as driving forces and limiting factors on the human activity within the chosen geographical arena of this study. However, in adopting such a methodology, one must be mindful to recognize and value the agency of humans to have acted within the environmental constraints in which they found themselves, thereby avoiding being prescriptively geographically determinist.[59] People are not machines whose behavior can simply be predicted by models of behavior derived from observing the landscape and seasons.

Such a new approach to the study of Ionia is timely because the results of modern systematic stratigraphic excavations at key sites are now starting to be published.[60] Excavations such as these and the results that they are likely to yield in terms of new understanding of paleobotanical and faunal evidence will be crucial for establishing the link between landscape archaeology and the archaeology of the urban centers, both of which are already well-established areas of knowledge. That is to say, the link between the physical environment (i.e. the macrohistory of the Ionian landscape) and the archaeology of the urban centers of the Ionian cities can only be securely established by understanding human land-use in the region – and the best evidence for this is environmental archaeology. Whereas traditional approaches, concentrating on texts, architecture, and archaeology of the urban center, often focused on the elite Greek-speaking elements within Ionian society, an approach that is more founded in landscape studies is likely to result in a broader understanding of cultural and societal issues in Ionia. This is similar to the *Annaliste* approach to history in which there is "a complex and oscillating interplay between environment, land use and society."[61] Compared with the very early start of archaeological excavations in the urban centers of Ionia, surveys of the landscape have been a relatively recent introduction, as has been the case elsewhere.[62]

If, as noted in Chapter 1, the nature of the historical evidence is such that it records primarily a series of destructions, then this new approach also has the possibility to balance our understanding of events such as these with broader and less chronologically discrete and narrowly defined social processes. In Braudel's terms, such events are just the historical "foam"[63] or "dust."[64] Although events such as the Ionian Revolt were undoubtedly important in the region and the lives of its people, their importance should not be overplayed to a point where our entire understanding of the region hinges on them. A landscape-derived understanding of Ionia is more likely to result in the identification of long- and medium-term processes that were at work concurrently with events such as these, and thereby give a more nuanced understanding of the context in which events took place than one derived from textual sources and traditional interpretations alone.

[59] Sherratt 1992.
[60] e.g. Senff 2007, on Miletos.
[61] Barker 1995: 4.
[62] Alcock 2007: 122–5; Greaves 2007a: 7.
[63] Braudel 1972: 21.
[64] Knapp 1992: 6.

In the case of the city walls of Miletos, noted above, a diachronic landscape-derived approach and a text-based approach can produce different perspectives on the same subject that are interesting and valid in different ways. However, this need not always be the case. For example, the Sanctuary of Aphrodite on Zeytintepe, just outside the city walls of Miletos, was discovered in the 1990s, then excavated and the results recently published.[65] It has been suggested that the character of Aphrodite as she was worshipped at this particular sanctuary was that of Aphrodite as goddess of the sea. This is a conclusion supported by both literary references to the character of the goddess[66] and epigraphic evidence from Miletos' many colonies.[67] Such an interpretation is consistent with the archaeological evidence from the site, which included evidence of sacrificial animals including a variety of sea creatures.[68] These studies are in effect "top down," because they seek to understand the character of cult at the site by reference to literary and epigraphic sources and by establishing connections between the extant written evidence and the archaeology of the site. However, were the site to be considered from a "bottom-up" approach, in isolation from any literary or epigraphic evidence, a similar conclusion might have been achieved because the precise geographical location of the sanctuary affords it excellent views of the sea and the city's harbors, but not of the land behind it.[69] In this case, the new methodology comes to the same conclusion as traditional methods, thereby validating and asserting the existing interpretation of the site.

To sum up, this synthetic overview of Archaic Ionia will start with a consideration of diachronic landscape processes and the medium- and short-term human activity that took place within the constraints of that physical environment. Such an approach has the capacity to both challenge and confirm existing interpretations of the archaeology of the region.

Conclusions

It has been argued here that the traditional mode of interpretation in Classical archaeology has been one of "literary positivism" in which Classical literature provides the ultimate point of reference against which hypotheses are tested. This, in part, has contributed to the perception that "Classical archaeology has too often seemed to be a treasure hunt where the clues are provided entirely by texts, in the tradition of Schliemann digging at Troy with Homer in hand."[70]

Classical archaeology has moved on, but our adherence to the Classical texts has not, even at a time when the value and meaning of our sources have been subject to considerable reappraisal by ancient historians. What is needed therefore is a framework for interpretation that seeks to balance textual and epigraphic sources with archaeological ones.

---

[65] Senff 2003.
[66] Senff 2003.
[67] Greaves 2004.
[68] Peters and von den Driesch 1992.
[69] Greaves and Wilson forthcoming.
[70] Alcock and Osborne 2007: 11–12.

The *Annaliste* "total" history method presents one such model. Not only can it incorporate textual and archaeological sources (and others such as geography and sociology), but its three chronological "wavelengths" of *événements, conjonctures,* and the *longue durée* can accommodate both the short-term history of texts and the longer-term histories of peoples and landscapes.

However, the "balance" that this model offers between texts and archaeology should not be misinterpreted as parity between them. The long-term structures of landscape and environment have primacy in this model; as Braudel himself wrote, "in historical analysis … the long run always wins in the end."[71] This primacy is also justified by the fact that the human hierarchy of needs will generally prioritize the means of existence, survival, and security, which are best attested by archaeological evidence, over social, cognitive, and aesthetic needs, which are often thought of as being the preserve of texts, but which can also be the subject matter of archaeology.

Therefore in this study, although not ignored, textual sources of evidence are properly contextualized into a secondary status to archaeological data. To further Alcock and Osborne's metaphor of Schliemann "digging at Troy with Homer in hand" the stance taken in writing this book is that, in contrast to previous generations of scholars who went to Ionia with Herodotos in the right hand and their trowel in the left, renewed emphasis should be placed on the archaeological data – putting Herodotos in the archaeologist's left hand and the trowel in their right.[72]

---

[71] Braudel 1972: 1244.
[72] In drawing this metaphor, I acknowledge and respect the rights of the left-handed community, who may wish to reverse this sentence in order to relate it to themselves.

3

A Dynamic Landscape

Introduction

The land of Ionia and the historical experiences and character of its people are inextricably linked. Having established in Chapter 2 that understanding the land is fundamental to understanding its people and their history, it is now necessary to describe that landscape and to draw observations from it which will have bearing on the interpretation of Ionia's Archaic period history and archaeology. The importance of understanding landscape in relation to Classical cities is now widely recognized,[1] even if the countryside itself is under-represented in ancient works of art and literature.[2] The geographical setting of the Ionian cities was more than just an attractive, but essentially passive, backdrop to the theater of history – rather it was the *raison d'être* for the existence of those cities, and it is the archaeology of that geographical setting that will provide the key to understanding the relationship between the two.

The immediate landscape vicinity of the cities affected their location and their rise, demise, and ultimate archaeological survival. The precise location of a city will be determined by its position in relation to the essentials of life (water, food supply – i.e. cultivable land, defense, communications); its ability to exploit those resources will determine its success; and various geomorphological and human factors will affect the survival of the archaeological remains of that community (as discussed in Chapter 1). Themes of economy and settlement will be developed in Chapters 4 and 5, whereas this chapter concerns itself with the Ionian landscape in general.

Visiting Ionia and observing its geological, geographical, and environmental character, and appreciating the archaeological monuments in their physical setting, is essential to

I am grateful to Warren Eastwood of Birmingham University for his assistance with this chapter. I was privileged to visit the Büyük Menderes in the company of Dr Eastwood and his colleagues and to have the chance to discuss this subject with him there.

[1]   van Andel and Runnels 1987; Foxhall et al. 2007; Alcock 2007.
[2]   R. Osborne 1987.

understanding the region and its history. However, when visiting Ionia today it is also necessary to imagine another landscape – that of antiquity. This landscape differed from the modern landscape in two ways. First, it was physically different. There have been considerable changes to the landscape of Ionia since the Archaic period that need to be taken into account before considering the history of that particular period. Secondly, the ancient landscape (like the modern) was overlain with social, religious, and political meanings for the contemporary population. These are harder for visitors and archaeologists to reconstruct and understand than is the nature of that ancient physical landscape, but are no less important.

In both senses, the physical and the social, the landscape of Ionia was a dynamic and changing environment. The modern visitor to Ionia is struck by this most forcefully when visiting Ephesos, Miletos, or Myous – harbor towns that are now disconnected from the sea by kilometers of accumulated alluvium. This rapid silting-up of the coastal inlets that must once have been such a feature of Ionia's coastline is a truly remarkable process, but it is not the only dynamic process at work in the landscape, of which we must be aware.

In this chapter, the physical environment of Ionia will be described, so as to provide a necessary basis for subsequent discussion of agriculture and settlement in Chapters 4 and 5. The different physical subregions of Ionia will be outlined and their geology, topography, and hydrology briefly examined. Next, the dynamic elements of this landscape will be examined before a more general discussion of the interaction of this dynamic landscape with Ionian settlement and culture. Archaeology and the earth sciences will be the main sources of data for this chapter and its chronological scope, in the *Annaliste* style, will aim to study the region over the longest period of time possible.[3] It is also a feature of the *Annaliste* methodology to consider regions not in isolation, but in their wider regional context. Just as Braudel considered the Mediterranean world of Philip II in relation to northern Europe and the Sahara,[4] so it is necessary to consider Ionia's regional situation, at the transitional point between the highlands of Anatolia and the Aegean Sea. Only by adopting a diachronic and regionally informed position such as this will it be possible to achieve a real understanding of the land of Ionia.

Ionia's Geographical Zones

Ionia can be divided into four geographical zones: the valleys, the peninsulas, the islands, and the sea between (Figure 3.1). These divisions are not based on any scientifically defined geological, geographical, or geopolitical criteria, but they are a useful means by which to begin thinking about the diverse character of the Ionian landscape. One could take any one of these physical elements and develop a discussion of its changing character and significance over time,[5] but for the purposes of this discussion it is the ways in which

---

[3]   Although the focus of this current work is the Archaic period, the author's experience of the region is based on writing a diachronic history of Miletos (Greaves 2002) and other studies of the region with a broad geographical and chronological remit (e.g. Greaves 1999, 2000a, 2007a).

[4]   Braudel 1972.

[5]   e.g. Greaves 2000a on the changing role of the sea in Miletos' historical development.

Figure 3.1 Satellite image of the lower Büyük Menderes Valley. Landsat 7 satellite image (SW Turkey), June 16, 2000.

they articulated with one another and affected human settlement and behavior in the Archaic period that is most important.

The ridges and peninsulas

Ionia is a land of mountains and valleys. The region's mountains are aligned east–west in formidable ridges that extend out into the sea, forming peninsulas and, beyond them, islands. Geologically speaking, these ridges are "horsts" – upstanding blocks of rock divided from one another by collapsed valley bottoms, or "grabens." These were created when the collapse of the Aegean Sea created block faults, which sank to create the grabens and left the mountainous horsts remaining.[6]

Two horst ridges cut across Ionia: the Çeşme (ancient Erythrai, or Mimas) Peninsula in the north and the Samsun Dağı or Dilek Dağları (ancient Mount Mykale) Peninsula in the south. These two bodies of mountains divide, and therefore define,

---

[6] Brinkmann 1971: 189.

Figure 3.2 The *acropolis* of Priene with the Hellenistic Temple of Athena in the foreground.

Ionia's three main valleys from each other (see below). They are composed of hard schist stone and rise from sea level to a height of nearly 1,300 m.

These mountainous ridges are the most important factor in Ionian geography. They are the most immediately striking feature of the landscape and were to play a crucial role in determining the historical development of the region. These giant ridges so totally dominate the landscape of Ionia that it is difficult to discuss the region's history without making reference to them. Visually, they dominate the landscape, creating huge unassailable divides between the different valleys and cities of Ionia.[7] One only has to look at the sheer wall of rock that rises up behind the columns of Priene's famous Temple of Athena, forming the natural fortress of that city's *acropolis*, to see how dramatic these mountains can be (Figure 3.2). Their influence on Ionian history was to be double-edged. On one hand, they were a divisive factor in Ionian history, separating one community from another, but on the other hand they formed the sheltered bays and trade routes that were to be the basis of the cities' commerce.

---

[7] It could be said that the alluvial plains are an equally striking feature of the modern landscape, but they would not yet have existed in antiquity.

These mountains slowed, or effectively stopped, north–south communications by land, making the sea, the valley bottoms, and the rivers appear much more attractive prospects for travel and transport. Originally, they would have been thickly forested and this would have further compounded their impression of impenetrability. The Samsun Dağı National Park[8] near Güzelçamlı gives an impression of how thickly forested this area may have been in its natural state, but how much of the forests had already been cleared in the Archaic period is not clear. Although an inscription from Priene does mention a pathway over Mykale to Ephesos, and there were probably other such local routes in use,[9] these would often be impassable in the winter months and may have been dangerous for lone travelers. This east–west orientation in the geology of western Anatolia strongly influenced its land communications. An illustration of this, dating from as early as the Bronze Age, is the failed attempt by Mursili II to sack the city of Millawanda, which is identified with Miletos, because the passage of his chariots was impeded by a mountain called Arinanda, which has been identified with the Samsun Dağı ridge.[10] The general pattern of communications across the Anatolian landmass has long been thought to be in an east–west direction, although in truth patterns of communication and exchange were more complex than this and often need to be understood at a local level.[11]

These mountain ridges and peninsulas might appear to have drastically divided and defined the territories of the different Ionian states, yet the interface between the territories of different states cannot always be precisely defined and between them there were often pockets of usable land. The geographically fragmented nature of the landscape is such that it created small island-like pockets of usable land, many of which can be assumed to have supported their own communities, separated from their neighbors by steep mountain ridges, seas, and forests. Consequently, the typical territory of an Ionian state can be conceived of as a mosaic of these small, discrete pockets that were held together by a central political and military authority for a period of time. Just as proximity to, and control of, these small parcels undoubtedly formed the territorial basis of the different Ionian *polis* communities, so too was the desire to control more of them the most likely cause of wars between *poleis* within Ionia.[12]

However, the influence that these ridges and peninsulas had could also be a unifying force in the history of Ionia. They created large sheltered bays, such as the Gulf of Latmos, across which the Ionian communities of Miletos, Old Priene, and Myous could easily interact, and even see one another. At one point during the Archaic period Miletos appears to have gained control over a number of smaller communities and territories around this gulf to create a "mini-thallasocracy" under its control.[13] This degree of micro-regional control might not have been possible had it not been for this physical feature of the Ionian landscape.

---

[8]   *Turk.* Dilek Yarimadası Milli Parkı.
[9]   Marchese 1986: 142.
[10]   Niemeier 2007b: 64.
[11]   See various papers in Fletcher and Greaves 2007.
[12]   e.g. the island of Ikaros appears to have changed hands from Miletos to Samos at some point in its history (Greaves 2002: 4).
[13]   Greaves 2000a: 51.

Ironically, these mountain ridges also allowed the smaller *poleis* of Ionia to survive alongside their bigger neighbors, by shielding and distancing them from these neighbors. For example, Lebedos and Old Priene are effectively enclosed by high mountains and even though they may have fallen under the sway of their larger neighbors, such as Miletos' control of Old Priene, they survived as independent communities for a long time. Even when Antigonos I ordered that Lebedos be *synoikised* (brought together into a single settlement) with Teos in 303 BC, the order does not appear to have been fully implemented and Lebedos persisted,[14] demonstrating how the physical nature of these "pockets" meant settlements could not easily be agglutinated into larger population centers.

These ridges and peninsulas are of fundamental importance to Ionia's history, but they have generally been given less consideration than the sea and the valleys when seeking to define the character of the region. Survey has revealed that where passes through the mountains exist, the very earliest human settlements are to be found.[15] Intensive archaeological survey of these mountain areas has been a relatively late innovation[16] and is hampered by the difficult terrain, thick forest, and modern military sensitivity on the border with Greece. Modern field surveys, aided by satellite imagery and GPS technology, are making important and impressive finds in these areas away from the ancient population centers, such as when a Hittite inscription was found on Mount Latmos.[17] A recently instigated survey of Samsun Dağı under the direction of Hans Lohmann has yielded a surprising amount of evidence from this crucial area.[18] As this survey work continues we will discover more about these areas and their relationship to the Ionian *poleis*. The discovery of rural sanctuaries, ancient military structures, and inscriptions will give us indications as to their significance to the centers of population as boundaries, borders, places of religious significance, and important resources for supplying timber and grazing.

The rivers and valleys

The east–west axes of the Erythrai and Mykale horsts, outlined above, divided Ionia up into three valleys. From north to south, these are:

- the Hermos Valley (modern Gediz)
- the Kayster Valley (modern Küçük Menderes)
- the Maeander Valley (modern Büyük Menderes).

The broad, abundantly flowing rivers that give these valleys their names (the Gediz, Küçük Menderes, and Büyük Menderes, respectively) dominate many aspects of life in these valleys, but it must be remembered that their drainages are not river valleys, but rift valleys created by tectonic faulting. Water draining into the grabens from the

---

[14]   Syll. 3.344; Demand 1990: 158.
[15]   Günel 2005.
[16]   Greaves 2007a: 7.
[17]   Peschlow-Bindokat 2001.
[18]   Lohmann 2007b.

Figure 3.3 View of the modern Büyük Menderes Plain, looking southwest from Priene toward Miletos.

surrounding mountains swells these rivers as they flow west across the flat bottoms of the grabens to empty into the sea. The drainage basins of these grabens are huge and this gives them a different character to many of the rivers and valleys in the Greek Aegean. The Büyük Menderes system alone drains an area of 23,889 square kilometers.[19]

One consequence of the sheer size of these river systems is that they carry down a huge amount of silt from their vast drainage areas, dumping it in the flat, shallow bottoms of the grabens and causing them to fill up with alluvium, thus causing the river mouths to extend further and further out into the sea, a process known as progradation. The net result of this process is the deposit of large, flat areas of newly created alluvial land on the coast that have completely transformed the landscape of Ionia. Today, these valleys are some of the most fertile agricultural areas in the world and are largely used for the intensive production of cotton (Figure 3.3). However, until the recent introduction of extensive drainage systems, these areas would have flooded annually and would have been unsuitable for permanent settlement.

In antiquity, this would have been a remarkable phenomenon as it would have made the inundated land very fertile as it laid down new silt and renewed the soil each year

[19] Aksu et al. 1987.

and allowed it to be cropped annually.[20] How much of these alluvial plains would have been available to the Ionians in the Archaic period is not clear and in such a rapidly changing environment it would be difficult to ascertain this. Our knowledge about the environment in this region prior to modern drainage commencing is therefore limited and large areas of it may have been too swampy to be cultivated. Also, the Ionian cities are somewhat distanced from where the valley bottoms were located at the time (although this too has changed as the river mouths advanced, in effect bringing the land closer to the cities). Miletos may have controlled part of the lower Maeander Valley,[21] but the precise details of this and other cities' relationships with the fertile areas in the nearby valleys are unclear. If one discounts the valleys, there would have been relatively little good cultivable land in the vicinity of most of the Ionian *poleis*, but whether the valleys were definitely inhabited and cultivated at this time, or if they were even habitable or cultivable at all, will need considerable geological and archaeological research to confirm.

The single most dominant feature in the landscape of the lower Maeander Valley between Miletos, Priene, and Myous would have been the vast expanse of the Gulf of Latmos – a major feature of the landscape which simply no longer exists. Today, one crosses the Maeander Plain easily by means of a modern elevated roadway, but in antiquity this expanse of flat swampy land, combined with a broad flowing river that needed to be crossed (a river which was constantly shifting and changing its course), would have been a formidable barrier to communications, exacerbating the north–south divisions created by the ridge-peninsulas.

The rivers of Ionia are supplied with meltwater from the mountainous interior of Anatolia and flow all year round. As they flowed across the flat bottoms of the grabens these famous rivers wandered in wide loops across the plain – entering into the English language as the verb "to meander" (Figure 3.4). They would have provided a potentially useful source of freshwater fish, as an addition to plentiful marine fish from the sea. Also, because of their size, the larger rivers would have been partly navigable along their lower courses.[22] If the rivers were navigable, even by small craft, this would have made travel and transport along the east–west axis of the valleys considerably easier than by slow and cumbersome land transport – further enhancing the east–west orientation of communications in this landscape. In the upper courses, braiding (where the river divides) may have made them impassable to river traffic, but at which point in the river's course this occurred in the Archaic period is not known and will, like so many other elements of such a dynamic river system, have changed over time.

The large islands

Two of the largest Ionian *poleis* were located on islands off the coast of the Anatolian mainland in the east Aegean. The islands of Chios and Samos were each large enough

[20] Hdt. 2.10; Greaves 2002: 102.
[21] Greaves 2002: 3.
[22] Marchese 1986: 141.

Figure 3.4 The Büyük Menderes River near Miletos. The Samsun Dağı (ancient Mykale) mountain range can be seen in the background.

to support a number of smaller communities in addition to the eponymous main *polis*.[23]

Chios is just a short distance from the western end of the Erythrai Peninsula. The island measures 842 km² and has a mountainous core with cliffs along the flank facing the Ionian mainland to the east. For this reason, the break in the cliffs at Chios town marks an important access point and an ideal location for the island's main harbor and settlement. The north and center of the island are hilly, but the southern side is gently sloping, with flatter and more fertile plains.

To the south of Chios, and just 1,300 m from the tip of the Mykale Peninsula, is the slightly smaller (477 km²), but no less significant, island of Samos. A ridge of hills running east–west cuts across the island. To the north of these, the land runs down steeply to the sea, but on the southern side of the island, as on Chios, is a broad, flat plain of cultivable land. Samos town stood at the eastern end of this plain, closest to the Ionian mainland and with a natural harbor, augmented by a built harbor mole.

---

[23] Boardman and Vaphopoulou-Richardson 1986; Shipley 1987; Rubinstein and Greaves 2004.

These islands are situated so close to the ends of the main Ionian ridge-peninsulas, and are separated from the mainland by such narrow sea passages, that they can be considered almost as extensions of the Anatolian mainland in their geological and geographical constitution. However, they are different in terms of their hydrology, because unlike their mainland counterparts they are not backed by such high mountains and vast river drainage systems. Shortage of water, especially in the summer months, is therefore likely to have been a more serious problem for these two Ionian states than it was for some on the mainland. This in turn will have affected the natural flora and fauna of the islands, as well as their agricultural capacity. Nevertheless, the islands are fertile and the two main *poleis* of Chios and Samos successfully sustained large urban centers. Each island also supported a number of subsidiary settlements, some of considerable importance, such as Emporio on Chios.[24] It would be wrong to assume that because the islands did not have large river systems their landscapes were not dynamic, as geomorphological research at Kato Phana has shown that the sanctuary here, that is now 300 m inland, was once on the sea.[25]

The sea passages that separate these islands from the peninsulas of the mainland are not only narrow – they are also bent. The dog-leg character of the passage between Samos and the Mykale Peninsula means that there are few vantage points from which one can see directly through – making the island appear to be a continuation of the mainland of Ionia. This indeed must be how it seemed in antiquity – that the islands were an integral part of this region – and their separation by sea posed little obstacle to transport and interaction with their Anatolian mainland peers. The small cluster of islands at Oinoussai, between Chios and the Erythrai Peninsula, would also have served as stepping-stones between that island and the Anatolian mainland. This closeness may have been uncomfortable for some of the islands' smaller mainland neighbors because, when they could, Chios and Samos asserted themselves over adjacent areas of the mainland to form *peraia* (areas of the mainland controlled by an island). This demonstrates how the aspirations of these island-states were not limited by their locations and that the geographical indivisibility of the islands from the Ionian mainland was perceptible to them in a way that the modern Turkish–Greek border and predominance of land transport make it difficult for us to appreciate today.

The two large islands of Chios and Samos can therefore be seen to be integral to Ionia because of their physical proximity and resultant intimate economic and military relationship to the Anatolian mainland areas of Ionia. In geological terms it is possible to view the islands as extensions of the ridge-peninsulas and, in common with their mainland neighbors, their *chorai* presented a mixture of physical terrain from flat and fertile (in the south on both islands) to mountainous (in their north and central areas). Their social and political histories were therefore also likely to parallel those of the mainland Ionian states, which in their own way were island communities divided by mountainous ridges (see above).

[24] Boardman 1967.
[25] Morgan et al. 2008: 87.

The space between: the sea

Far from being empty, the seas of Ionia are populated with numerous small islands, intersected by peninsulas, and probably crisscrossed by shipping routes.[26] As much as its peninsulas, valleys, and islands define Ionia, it is the sea that separates and defines those same peninsulas, valleys, and islands. "Separate" is perhaps a poor choice of word here, because the sea in fact served to bring the different constituent parts of the region together, rather than divide them. In Archaic Ionia the sea represented the quickest and easiest means of communication between the different parts of the region, not only because of the limited nature of land transport technology, but also because of the land's mountainous nature.

The open sea around Ionia is not especially deep and the waters of the bays at the mouths of the grabens must have been quite shallow. Nevertheless, these waters could be dangerous as storms rise up quickly in the Aegean and pose a genuine threat to shipping. However, sailors who knew the waters around Ionia would also know that they were never far from an island or headland that could provide leeward shelter. Yet the rocky character of the peninsulas and islands means that good natural harbors and safe places to make landfall were rare, and ancient shipwrecks have been found off Ionia's rocky coast. These include the Tektaş wreck near Teos,[27] a wreck off Chios,[28] and a presumed wreck off Taş Burun, near Branchidai-Didyma.[29] In addition to the threat of causing grounding during storms, these small rocky islands also provided cover from which pirates could attack and intercept traders or pilgrims visiting Ionia's cities, temples, and oracles. One such was Julius Caesar, who was himself captured by pirates and held for ransom on the island of Pharmakoussa south of Branchidai-Didyma (Plutarch *Caesar* 1–4). Strong currents, especially in the sea passages between Samos and Mount Mykale, and between Chios and the Erythrai Peninsula, must also have presented a hazard to sailors. When, in bad winter weather, the seas were closed and the mountain passes blocked, the island-like isolation of even the largest of the mainland Ionian cities must have been heightened and palpable to their populations.

Despite these risks, Ionia was still in many respects a perfect environment for ancient shipping. In the absence of navigation technology, ancient sailors navigated by island-hopping from one piece of visible land to the next. Around Ionia, the numerous small islands, peninsulas, and headlands would provide ideal landmarks for coastal navigation. Furthermore, on Cape Poseidon near Panormos in the territory of Miletos, a monumental altar had been constructed to act as a lighthouse to guide ships into the harbor as they carried pilgrims to the oracle at Branchidai-Didyma.[30] From Ionia it would be possible to navigate in this way, hopping between islands, across the Aegean as far as the Greek mainland, the Corinthian *diolkos* (dragway), and the western Mediterranean beyond.

---

[26] On military threats from the sea, see Chapter 7.
[27] Greene and Bass 2004.
[28] Hansson and Foley 2008.
[29] Greaves 2000a: 45.
[30] von Gerkan 1915; Greaves 2000a: 45–6; Herda 2006: 350.

Ionia is also well positioned on north–south sea routes. Following the coast of Anatolia to the north would bring ships to Aeolis, the north Aegean and the Hellespont – the gateway to the Propontis and the Black Sea. Heading south would bring them to Rhodes and from there to Crete. From here it would be possible to catch southerly trade winds to the coast of North Africa and the Greek cities of Kyrene and Barca, and to Egypt and the trading post at Naucratis, in which many Ionian states had interests.[31]

The waters around Ionia were rich with exploitable resources. Fishing was a useful and valuable addition to agriculture in the region, providing a nutritious and often highly prized addition to the ancient diet. The purple dye extracted from murex shells was another product for which the region was famous in antiquity.[32] The variety of marine and riverine environments would have resulted in a great variety of fish from the waters around Ionia. Some of the small islands were also a source of stone, and quarries have been found on the south side of Phourni, 10 km southwest of Samos.[33] Islands also offered another useful resource to the neighboring *poleis* – seasonal grazing land. For example, the Milesian Islands are likely to have been a potentially important additional element of Miletos' *chora*.[34] Small, but useful, islands such as these may have been a bone of contention between neighboring states who laid claim to them. If the medium-sized island of Ikaros could change hands between the authority of Miletos and Samos, then the same must certainly have been true of smaller islands.

The sea was evidently a central feature of economic, political, and religious life in Ionia and access to it would be a key concern for the cities of the region. However, the geology of the steep-sided horsts that dominate the region presented few ready-made natural harbors, and access to such harbors as there were was an important factor in the development of the cities that controlled them. It is difficult to know precisely what Ionia's ancient harbors were like, because many are now either buried by alluvium, as at Ephesos, Miletos, Priene, and Myous, or have been remodeled into modern harbor towns, as at Samos, Chios, and Phokaia. At Myous it is possible to see how the city, which was sited on a peninsula, would be presented, with two sheltered areas, one on either side. At Miletos, extensive geophysical and archaeological research has been directed into finding the shape, depth, and history of the Lion Harbor,[35] whereas at Priene similar methods are being used to try and locate the harbor, the precise location of which, together with the Archaic city itself, is as yet unknown. At Phokaia, excavations have been hampered by construction work in this small working harbor.[36]

Such was the importance of having access to a good harbor that at Samos a mole was built to create a harbor wall and to enhance the natural harbor. This was reportedly the work of the tyrant Polykrates (Hdt. 3.60) and the remains of this work can be seen at the site today (see Chapter 5). Lack of good natural harborage remains a problem, and

---

[31] Greaves 2000a: 48–9.
[32] Erim and Reynolds 1970.
[33] Kienast 1992: 206–13. On other sources of stone in Ionia, see also Chapter 4. Transporting stone was facilitated by sea transport.
[34] Greaves 2007b.
[35] Greaves 2000a: 40–3.
[36] Ö. Özyiğit 2006.

at Taş Burun a harbor mole has been constructed out of stone blocks in order to create a small, but viable, modern fishing harbor.[37]

When viewed from a satellite the distinction between land and sea – green and blue – is an easy one to make (Figure 3.1). Likewise, when viewed as a map it is easy to see where the mainland of Ionia stops and the islands start – it is, after all, now conveniently marked on any modern map by the dotted line of the Greek–Turkish border. However, for ancient sailors without such modern overviews on their land, the headlands and islands of Ionia merged into one another, separating out from each other or emerging from the hazy sea only as one drew close to them – creating mental schemata of the land of Ionia that transcended modern concepts of maps and national borders. Ionian cities could see one another across open water and crossing over by boat was easy – making them more closely connected than if they had been neighbors by land. For this reason, for example, it would seem reasonable that Phokaia was considered to be a part of the community of Ionian cities, even though it does not form a contiguous landmass with Ionia and is wholly surrounded by Aeolis.[38] Even today, standing on the hills above Miletos it is possible to see Samos – the island merging into the Mykale Peninsula and melding back into the Ionian mainland to which it was intimately linked in antiquity. This image perhaps sums up how the region felt before the imposition of a strictly controlled border between two nation-states was overlaid on the Ionian seascape.

Ionia is a liminal region with a long coastline relative to its area, but few good natural harbors. The seas were rich in fish and it was well positioned in relation to the trade routes. It was perhaps inevitable that the sea would play a key role in Ionia's historical development via colonization and overseas exchange (see Chapters 4 and 6). The choice of Poseidon and Aphrodite as patron gods by the Ionians also makes sense when we appreciate and accept the absolute centrality of the sea to Ionian life and culture.[39]

Landscape Dynamism

For Fernand Braudel, a historian, the landscape was a "structure" – a fixed framework that placed limitations on the human actions that took place within it (see Chapter 2). However, this is too fixed and simplistic a definition of landscape for archaeologists, who work with cultures and periods that can last millennia. In archaeological timescales environmental and landscape changes are often discernible and detectable and, using archaeological evidence, environmental and climate change can be traced against the development of past societies and be shown to have influenced them.[40] But environmental changes are not always so slow that they can only be detected by archaeologists with the benefit of modern scientific techniques and the miracle tool of hindsight. Such was the rapidity of the progradation processes at work in the gulfs of Ionia that they would have been

---

[37]   Greaves 2002: 23.
[38]   Rubinstein and Greaves 2004: 1054.
[39]   Hdt. 1.144; von Gerkan 1915; Greaves 2004; Schneider 2004.
[40]   Smith 1992: 25–6.

noticeable in human timescales and obvious to those living there and seeking to exploit those parts of their territory. There are also cataclysmic landscape events, such as the landslide that buried the center of Roman Ephesos, that can literally transform the landscape overnight (see Chapter 1). Processes of landscape change in Ionia are therefore happening at all three of Braudel's *Annaliste* tempos: the *longue durée*, the mediohistorical level, and at the level of individual events. Studying Ionia therefore requires us to challenge the notions that the landscape is "fixed" and that topographic and environmental changes happen at a tempo beyond everyday human cognition.

Neither is Braudel's concept of a structural landscape that affects human action, but is not in its own way affected by humans, applicable in archaeological contexts. Contemporary debates on global climate change illustrate, with characteristic egocentricism, that Western society of the third millennium AD believes that it invented human-made environmental disasters. Yet anthropogenic environmental change happened in the archaeological past just as it is doing in the post-industrial age, as archaeology has proven for Easter Island, which has been shown to have suffered great environmental degradation as a result of human action. In fact, since the first introduction of agriculture humankind has constantly modified its landscape, sometimes in ways that are permanent and detrimental. Human actions in the Ionian landscape, such as deforestation, irrigation, and agricultural intensification, might reasonably be expected to have affected the landscape in such ways and the effects of human action on the landscape must be precisely defined and clearly understood if we are to ascertain the true nature of the human–landscape relationship in Archaic Ionia.

The physical environment of Ionia's landscape should therefore not be viewed just as a passive structural element in the region's history, but rather as a dynamic context with which the people of Ionia were in an interactive relationship. But how are we to understand that relationship, and what methods, theories, and practices will we need to apply in order to best understand it?

Landscape dynamism in Ionia results from a complex set of interlinked processes which need to be taken into consideration when one begins to examine the environment of Archaic Ionia – or what might be described as "the Ionia of yesterday," to paraphrase Anthony Snodgrass.[41] Perhaps the most striking thing about the changes that have affected the landscape of Ionia since antiquity is their sheer scale – most obviously the progradation of the mouths of the grabens of the region's three big rivers. Other identifiable changes include shifts in the course of its meandering rivers, deforestation, earth movements caused by seismic events, and the formation of alluvial fans.[42] Not only have there been transformations of the land, but also of the sea – as the rise in sea level that is evident at Klazomenai and other places on the west coast of Anatolia demonstrate.[43] Of all these processes, it is the progradation of the grabens that has had the most dramatic impact on the landscape, and the following discussion will focus upon attempts to understand this process.

---

[41]   Snodgrass 1987.
[42]   Bay 1999a.
[43]   Erkanal 2008: 181–2.

Box 3.1
The Alluviation of the Gulf of Latmos

The Ionian cities of Miletos, Priene, and Myous, that once stood on the Gulf of Latmos, are all now separated from the sea by kilometers of alluvial plain. The scale and rapidity of this alluviation process is remarkable and is a product of the unique geography of the region.

The Gulf of Latmos was at the end of the large Maeander (modern Büyük Menderes) Valley. This steep-sided, flat-bottomed valley had been created by faulting and collapsing geology, not the usual processes of river erosion that shape many other valleys. As a result, the western end of the valley, which was inundated by the Aegean Sea to create the Gulf of Latmos, was broad but relatively shallow. It therefore silted up very rapidly as the large Büyük Menderes River discharged into it, depositing silt from across its 23,889 km² drainage area.

At first the rate of deposition was relatively slow, but it appears to have accelerated sharply in the first millennium BC. The reasons for this may be geological, or it may be a result of human actions, such as deforestation, that caused more soil to be washed into the Büyük Menderes system and deposited as silt at the river mouth. In terms of human settlement, the net result of this alluviation was that one by one the towns on the Gulf of Latmos became cut off from the sea and were subsequently abandoned.

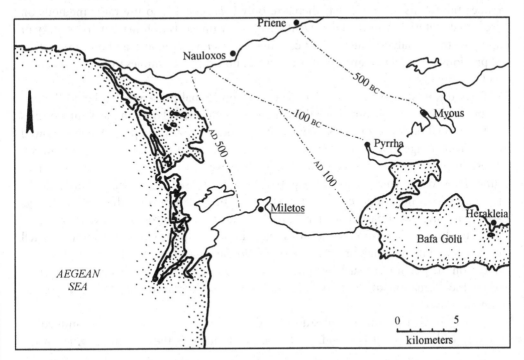

Progradation of the Büyük Menderes River into the Gulf of Latmos (after Aksu et al. 1987). Taken from Greaves 2002. © Routledge.

The geomorphology – that is, the changing elements in the landscape rather than the hard geology that underlies it – of Ionia's three major river valleys has been subject to a rapid and complex series of changes that have affected the character of the valleys and their relationship to the Ionian settlements around their river mouths. For example, changes in the course or character of a river that made it impassable to sailing craft, or the creation of lagoons[44] or malarial swamps,[45] would have had a considerable impact on the human–landscape relationship. However, there are serious difficulties in relating identifiable geomorphological changes to human processes and events. There are two main ways in which this can be approached: environmental archaeological analysis on excavated sites and by using chronometric means.

Relating the activities of humans to the landscape, either as farmers operating within that landscape or as active agents of change to the landscape itself, requires detailed environmental archaeology research. Environmental archaeology is a series of method-ologies, such as faunal analysis (the study of animal bones) and paleobotany (the study of carbonized plant remains), that can be used to ascertain what plants and animals were being brought into an archaeological site from the surrounding areas. However, there are a number of complications in using such methods.

First, in order to be accurate, correct sampling is essential. It is therefore really only possible to apply these methods to archaeological datasets that have been rigorously excavated by modern archaeological means, as any possibility of contamination would render the results invalid. It has therefore only been possible to use these methods on excavated material from the later twentieth century onwards in Ionia. The possibility of applying these analytical methods at certain sites has now been lost, and only excavation of previously unexplored areas of those sites can now retrieve samples from closed depos-its (see Chapter 1).

Secondly, it is necessary to understand the depositional processes that led to the for-mation of the contexts from which the samples or data derive. For example, faunal studies of the animal bones from the Sanctuary of Aphrodite on Zeytintepe in Miletos showed a very wide range of animals that were apparently brought to the temple as offerings.[46] These included wild and domesticated animals as well as a variety of fish and sea crea-tures. However, in contrast to the neighboring domestic settlement quarter of Kalabak-tepe, there was no evidence at all of pigs having been dedicated at the sanctuary. Pigs appear to have had a particular significance to the cult of Aphrodite and were therefore deliberately excluded from the sacrifices made in her temples. This observation may tell us much about the religious practices of the Ionians (see Chapter 8), but it also casts doubt on the potential of such evidence to tell us about the natural ecology of the region when the formation of deposits have been so self-evidently influenced by conscious human action.

Finally, evidence from faunal studies and paleobotany is specific to the immediate vicinity within which it is found. In the case of Ionia, it is the human activities in the

---

[44]   Such as the Alaman Gölü lagoon at the mouth of the Küçük Menderes, northwest of Ephesos (Karwiese et al. 1998: 31–3, esp. fig. 25).
[45]   Such as that at Myous (Demand 1990: 141–2).
[46]   Peters and von den Driesch 1992.

upper reaches of the region's big river valleys that will affect their progradation more than anything that happened within the immediate vicinity of the cities themselves. This is a theme that will be developed further below.

Another way in which geomorphological studies can be linked to the activities of archaeological cultures is by chronometric means. If accurate dates can be secured for geomorphological processes such as progradation, these can then be compared with the dates for archaeological processes and events, thereby allowing human–landscape inter-actions to be better understood. Increasingly precise and defined ceramic typologies have been established within Ionia in recent years[47] and these provide a scaffold of relative dates by which to understand the archaeology of the region. For example, fragments of pottery found in alluvial fans on the plain around Miletos, discovered during construc-tion of a well, allowed geomorphologists to date the sequence of alluviation that they were recording and also allowed archaeologists to accommodate those geomorphological processes within their own understanding of the development of settlement in and around Miletos.[48]

Unfortunately, though, for the much larger alluvial action of the big river valleys, coring is unlikely to recover pottery, and dating of the progradation process relies upon more scientific absolute dating methods, such as radiocarbon (^{14}C) and optical stimulated luminescence (OSL) dating. Issues of accuracy apart, these methods do not yet have the potential to give the same degree of precision as relative pottery chronologies do, espe-cially for the Archaic period. Whereas certain types of Archaic Ionian pottery can be placed within typological sequences that date them to within a decade or so, for absolute dating methods a standard deviation range of a century or more either side is not uncom-mon. These tensions between relative and absolute dating methods were previously explored in Chapter 1, in relation to the difficulty in contrasting dating systems in Ionia and central Anatolia.

Relating geomorphological processes that occur in the *longue durée* to shorter-term mediohistorical archaeological cultural processes is not an easy task. As an illustration of this, let us consider the movement to Athens of migrants from Miletos in the Hellenistic period. It has been suggested, based on literary sources, that the abandonment of cities on the Gulf of Latmos, such as Myous, was connected to the advancing mouth of the Maeander, which caused these settlements to be abandoned.[49] In the case of Miletos, Torben Vestergaard has proposed that the advancing river mouth resulted in the silting-up of Miletos' harbors, causing an outflow of people from Miletos to Athens, where their funerary inscriptions have been found in large numbers.[50] This interpretation would, *prima facie*, appear to accord with the available geomorphological evidence for the rate of progradation of the Büyük Menderes[51] and the silting-up of the Lion Harbor at Miletos.[52] However, Ottoman accounts show that the city had remained a busy trading port into the

[47]   e.g. Kerschner and Schlotzhauer 2005, 2007.
[48]   Bay 1999a, 1999b.
[49]   Demand 1990: 141–2.
[50]   Vestergaard 2000.
[51]   Aksu et al. 1987; Brückner et al. 2006.
[52]   Greaves 2002: 40–3.

fourteenth century AD.[53] How this was possible and where the city's harbor was located in this period is currently unclear,[54] but the historical and archaeological evidence for the presence of a lively trading community here in this period is unequivocal.

This example of Ottoman period Miletos illustrates two themes in the relationship between geomorphology and archaeology in Ionia. The first is that the geomorphological evidence, as yet, lacks the precision that archaeologists and historians require to relate changes in the landscape to mediohistorical social processes (such as the Milesians' migration to Athens) or even specific historical events. The second, and more important for the purposes of this book, is that it shows how, by taking a broad diachronic and multidisciplinary approach, a more accurate and informed understanding of mediohistorical social processes can be achieved. In effect this is a justification for adopting the holistic "total history" approach advocated by the *Annales* school (see Chapter 2).

The importance of such a multidisciplinary approach is widely recognized by archaeologists working in Ionia and they have been collaborating with geomorphologists for some time now.[55] However, when we attempt to combine geomorphology with history there is a danger that we might seek to accommodate the environmental data into the historical metanarrative, in order to reinforce our assumptions about the past based on a structure of ideas inherited from written sources (see Chapter 2). If this were to occur, then we would just be using the "scientific" evidence of geoarchaeology to perpetuate the literary positivist interpretations of the past by giving them a gloss of spurious scientific objectivity. To avoid such literary positivism, we should always seek to ensure that our geomorphological evidence is rigorously independent of any historical narrative derived from literary sources; only then can it be used to verify, or better still challenge, our existing interpretations of the past and thereby further our understanding of it.

This separation of geomorphology from history is not a straightforward task. For example, in the summary of his thesis on the progradation of the Büyük Menderes Delta, Bilal Bay suggested that the accelerated alluviation of the Gulf of Latmos in the Archaic period was a result of overfarming by Miletos as it attempted to feed its enlarged population.[56] He suggests that the resulting soil erosion would have made it impossible for Miletos to continue to support its own population, and that this would have contributed to the extensive Milesian colonial movement in the Archaic period. In this argument, Bay identifies the historical cause (i.e. overpopulation) and historical effect (i.e. colonization) for an observable geomorphological phenomenon (i.e. the progradation of the Büyük Menderes and pattern of deposition in alluvial fans on the hill slopes). It could be argued that in Bay's interpretation geomorphological evidence is merely being fitted into a preexisting historical metanarrative that is derived from the literary trope of colonization that abounded in fifth century BC Athens.[57] The geomorphological results that Bay

---

[53]   Greaves 2000b, citing Wulzinger et al. 1935.
[54]   At Ephesos there is evidence for extensive dredging of the harbor and its approaches, in the form of a levee of dredge material cast up alongside it (Kraft et al. 2007).
[55]   e.g. the many publications by Helmut Brückner. See Ehrhardt et al. 2007: 757–8 for a list of Brückner's publications based on his work at Miletos.
[56]   Bay 1999a.
[57]   See Chapter 6.

presents could not in themselves ever be capable of providing independent corroboration of the motivation of Milesian colonization, the very pursuit of which is in itself an inappropriate methodology to adopt as it seeks to explain the causes of colonization before considering the evidence base.[58] The basic historical assumptions about Miletos that are implicit in this argument are: that Miletos was indeed the founder of the many colonies attributed to its name; that Miletos was the sole progenitor of the entire population of those colonies; and that these colonies were all founded in the Archaic period. All these assumptions have now been challenged[59] and this should give us cause to re-examine the application of geomorphological evidence to questions of historical interpretation. Ultimately, despite presenting new scientific evidence, the questions that Bay is seeking to answer in his summary discussion are derived from historical interpretation and are ultimately answerable by historical interpretation. This discussion is a loop in the historical argument that geomorphological evidence neither breaks nor extends.

By seeking to relate the progradation of the Büyük Menderes river mouth to the history of Miletos and the other Ionian cities on the Gulf of Latmos, so as to support our simplistic historical narrative, we are in danger of misrepresenting the nature of estuarine geomorphology. The processes that affect the deposition of material at river mouths are the result of activities *upstream*, not those within the immediate vicinity of the river mouth. As noted above, the Büyük Menderes system is massive (23,889 km^2), of which Miletos' territory and that of other Ionian States forms only a small part,[60] and only a proportion of that territory lay in the Maeander Valley itself, the majority being made up of island and peninsular territories. Events and activities across the whole of the Büyük Menderes system would need to be taken into account in order to explain alluviation downstream. Deforestation was certainly an important contributory factor to soil erosion in antiquity,[61] but it does not adequately account for the staggering quantities of alluvium that would need to be carried downstream by the Maeander to effect such rapid and massive change at the mouth of the system. Likewise, a reference by Pausanias (8.24.11) about the agricultural practices of the Lydians can reasonably be read to suggest that agricultural overexploitation caused extensive soil erosion.[62] However, we should be cautious not to retroject this observation onto the Archaic period as Pausanias is a considerably later source and this is not an ethnohistorical account. If our starting point for discussion is always to be framed by questions that derive from literary sources such as these, then we will naturally seek to find anthropogenic causes that fit in with those sources, rather than seeking to construct a geomorphological history of Ionia that is independent of literary positivist thinking.

The capacity of humans to bring about landscape change on the scale witnessed in the Büyük Menderes Valley is limited and we flatter ourselves if we think humankind alone is capable of such things. For example, in the region of Yeşilova in the upper reaches of the Büyük Menderes River, natural erosion is occurring on a massive scale that may also

[58]   R. Osborne 1998b.
[59]   Greaves 2007b; see also Chapter 6.
[60]   Estimated at 1,380 km^2 by Greaves 2007b.
[61]   van Andel and Runnels 1987: 133–53.
[62]   Thonemann forthcoming, citing Horden and Purcell 2000: 315ff.

account for much of the deposition witnessed downstream at the mouth of the system. The geological, geomorphological, and possibly even seismic reasons why, how, and when this massive erosion process started will need much more detailed research in future. As Graham Barker wrote:

> In order to evaluate the respective roles of climate and people in shaping the Mediterranean landscape, we need to investigate Mediterranean valleys with integrated methodologies linking geomorphology, archaeology and history, so that we can compare like with like: reliable evidence for environmental change with reliable evidence for settlement process.[63]

Only when we have established an independent dataset detailing environmental change in the Büyük Menderes and the other valleys of Ionia can that information be applied to the discussion of historical or archaeological questions – thereby asserting the primacy of the essential natural structures and processes of the landscape over human encounters with that landscape, as suggested by Braudel (see Chapter 2).

A complicating factor in trying to achieve such a balanced geomorphological/archaeological understanding of Ionia and its hinterland is that there is only limited archaeological evidence from the hinterland regions from the early Iron Age (Archaic) period. In recent years there have been initial small-scale surveys of the territories of Chios,[64] Teos,[65] Klazomenai,[66] and Ephesos[67] and a large-scale ongoing survey of the *chora* of Miletos.[68] A survey of the Carian settlement of Latmos by Anneliese Peschlow-Bindokat has shown how slight the evidence for non-Greek settlements can be – in this case presenting only faint traces of negative rock-cut features.[69] But, as the discussion above on the effects of land-use and erosion processes in the upper Büyük Menderes Valley shows, it is not just within the immediate vicinity of the coastal sites that research is needed.[70] Extensive archaeological surveys of the region have now been done[71] but there is still a long way to go before the disparity in the quantity, precision, and understanding of the evidence from the Ionian hinterland begins to redress the inherent bias toward the coastal settlements that currently exists.

Where environmental archaeology has been carried out at excavated sites in the valleys, it has often been limited in nature.[72] Tantalizingly, in the current excavations at the site of Çine-Tepecik, where occupation levels from prehistory through to the Carian-Geometric have been found, there is apparently no evidence for a level that equates to the Archaic period on the coast.[73]

---

[63] Barker 1995: 11.
[64] Lambrinoudakis 1986.
[65] Baran and Petzl 1977/78; Ersoy and Koparal 2008.
[66] Aydın 2006.
[67] İçten and Krinzinger 2004; Bammer and Muss 2006; Bammer 2007; Aydın 2007.
[68] R.M. Cook 1961; Lohmann 1995, 1997, 1999, 2007a.
[69] Peschlow-Bindokat 1996: 22–8; Peschlow-Bindokat 2007.
[70] Greaves 2007a: 7.
[71] Günel 2003; Akdeniz 1996, 2002; Thompson 2007; Thonemann forthcoming.
[72] e.g. Lloyd and Mellaart 1965: 139–54; Joukowsky 1986; Greaves 2009.
[73] Günel 2007: 234–41.

Until such time as local chronologies, artifact typologies, and archaeo-environmental datasets exist it will be difficult to put the landscape archaeology of Ionia into its proper context. For example, the claim that deforestation was the cause of the accelerated progradation of the Ionian gulfs can only be postulated, but not proven, without evidence to link it to stratified evidence of human activity – namely, environmental archaeology of sites in the hinterland. Although an anthropogenic cause for such acceleration is possible, it is not the only possible cause, and we should not be tempted to short-cut the process of enquiry just to confirm the existing historical metanarrative.

Another way in which the advance of the river mouths may have affected the Ionian cities of the coast is by creating new areas of land which, once drained, became natural foci of settlement away from the coast. The largest towns in the lower Maeander Valley, which Miletos once dominated, are now the inland communities of Söke and Aydın. Aydın is the modern successor to the large and important Hellenistic and Roman city of Tralles, but Söke is a new town that has grown to importance through the cultivation of cotton on the newly formed and drained plains of the Büyük Menderes. At Ephesos there is a new settlement not far from the ruins of the ancient city at Selçuk, and Ephesos' function as a harbor has been usurped by Kuşadası. Viewed diachronically, population centers such as these benefited from the advance of the rivers as much as the towns lower down the valley suffered from it, resulting in a complex historical pattern of settlement development and demography in these dynamic environmental zones.

To sum up, considerable geological research has been done in those areas that are adjacent to major classical sites and in the lower river valleys. The approaches adopted so far have been largely those of coastal geomorphology and have been directed at answering specific archaeological questions about the nature and history of the Ionian cities and their harbors. This approach has been successful in answering the specific questions presented by the archaeological agenda – for example, by dating the silting-up of the harbors. However, in order to understand why this process happened and how it affected the cities concerned (e.g. Did malarial lagoons form in advance of the river mouth? Did usable river channels give them access to the sea after the river mouth had passed them by?) a more detailed and geographically wide-ranging program of research will be required. Such a program will also require iterative, interactive, and sustained collaboration between geomorphologists and archaeologists if it is to enable us to relate the results of geological research directly and securely to archaeological evidence.

The Ionian Landscape and Ionian Identity

One of the purposes of this book is to attempt to define identifiable regional characteristics of Ionia and the Ionians.[74] Landscape is fundamental to the formation of identity and culture in any society, but is it possible to identify ways in which it may have shaped the Ionian character in the Archaic period? The cities that constituted Ionia did not share a defined and contiguous body of land, such as an island, archipelago, plain, valley, or

[74] The political and ethnic aspects of Ionian identity will be discussed in Chapter 10.

peninsula. The physical space that "Ionia" occupied is a messy conglomeration of aspects of all of these more easily defined landforms that we might associate with a territorially defined state entity.

When viewed as a whole, one thing that is remarkable about the landscape of Ionia is that it is a land of extremes – from high mountains to fertile plains, from forest to scrub, and from expansive plains to rocky nameless micro-islands. Many different types of landform are found in the *chora* of each Ionian city, and this diversity of terrain is one of the main things that they shared. Within a few kilometers' radius of any settlement in Ionia one would have encountered a great diversity of different landscape forms (mountains, islands, etc.) and environments (maquis scrub, fertile plain, swamp). Far from being a problem for these *poleis*, this diversity was potentially beneficial to their agriculture and economy and must have played an important role in their historical development; even the maquis scrub had a productive role to play.[75]

As noted above, not only does Ionia encompass the islands of the Aegean, it also includes numerous island-like "pockets" of land backed by mountains and looking toward the sea. Today it is difficult to imagine how isolated the Ionian cities must have felt because of the expanse of newly formed and cultivated fields that surround them, but it is easier to imagine at those sites whose localities are little changed – such as Lebedos, Erythrai, or the island *poleis*. Access rights to, and ownership of, those areas that could be cultivated, grazed, or had other productive uses need to be considered on a case-by-case basis, as such pockets were difficult to unite successfully, even under a strong central authority. Although it is a glib analogy to say that Ionia was a "mosaic" of communities, each of which was in turn itself a mosaic of distinct territorial units, it is a hard one to deny.

The historian might argue that it was the political institution of the *polis* that made the Ionian states so fiercely independent and terminally factional, but viewed from a landscape archaeology perspective such disunity is entirely predictable. Although it was possible for larger *poleis* to assert themselves over larger territorial areas, such as Miletos' control of the Gulf of Latmos, or the *peraia* of the island-states, eventually such power-blocs would always dissolve down to their constituent parts once the central power began to wane.

If the landscape of Ionia can be characterized as being a diverse landscape of disconnected pockets, then it was the sea that bound it together. The importance of the sea's role as the mediator between these fragmented landscape components and the communities that they supported cannot be underestimated. If "Ionia" had, or has, any validity as an ethnic and political entity in antiquity, then the function that the sea played in its formation, operation, and identity must be recognized. But the sea not only connected the states and brought them into closer contact with one another – it could also be a divisive factor when the seas were closed by bad weather.

The loss of large parts of that sea to progradation has irreversibly changed how we perceive and understand that landscape. Yet it is only by "putting the blue back into the map of Ionia" that we can really begin to understand the region. One way it is possible

---

[75] Forbes 1996; Greaves 2002: 20–1.

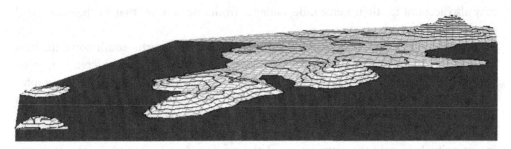

Figure 3.5 GIS of the harbors at Miletos.

to do this is by making visualizations of how these communities looked when they were still surrounded by the sea using virtual reality (VR) technology.[76] Such visualizations are attractive, but they are limited as the viewer cannot genuinely "feel" such virtual landscapes (the "haptic" experience), which is an important element of understanding the phenomenographic experiences of individuals in the past.[77] If our aim is to understand human–landscape relationships in antiquity, and not just see the landscape as some kind of geographical machine in which people played no part, then we must try to reconstruct that landscape as accurately as possible so that we can better understand their phenomenographic responses to it (see Chapter 8). Another disadvantage of static VR reconstructions is that they do not adequately describe the temporal changes in landscape discussed above (Figure 3.5).

Having emphasized the importance of the sea in informing Ionian identities, we must also recognize that if we view Ionia only from the sea, then we may overemphasize the role that the widely recognized maritime culture of the Greeks played in the region over the less easily defined and recognizable elements of the cultures of Anatolia. We therefore need to maintain a broad, Braudelian perspective that contextualizes the role of the sea with that of the highlands and other regions, and how these changed over time and were experienced by the people that lived there, if we are to achieve a true understanding of Ionia's character.

Conclusions

This chapter has outlined the interpretative possibilities and technical difficulties of studying the shifting and varied landscapes of Ionia and the necessity of such considerations in achieving a proper understanding of the region and its culture. It has been shown that Ionia was a "mosaic" of states, each made up of numerous small pockets of land, each of which had its own economic potential and character. As will be outlined in Chapter 4, this diversity was to be a source of economic strength for the Ionian *poleis*. It

[76] Greaves 2002: 139, fig. 4.4; Greaves and Wilson forthcoming.
[77] Tilley 1997.

may also account for their fierce independence from one another that has been adduced from literary sources.

Ionia occupies a stretch of coastline and islands that runs north–south down the west coast of the Anatolian landmass and this is how it has often been considered. Yet, when viewed objectively, the natural way to understand Ionia would be through the geographical units that dominate it – its east–west oriented valleys and ridge-peninsulas. In such an east–west scheme, the Ionian islands of Chios and Samos would be viewed almost as extensions of the peninsulas, which is how they appear and how they must have appeared in antiquity. It is only the retrojection of the modern Greek–Turkish border that sees them as being divided from the rest of Ionia. Likewise, the relationship between Ionian cities and their Anatolian hinterland would be deemed more significant than their relationships with one another, if the orientation of discussion was shifted from north–south to east–west.

Classical archaeologists have traditionally viewed the coastal cities of Archaic Ionia as being intimately connected to the "Greek" world of the Aegean by the sea, but separated from their "Anatolian" hinterland.[78] In part this is a consequence (and a cause!) of the disparity in the level of archaeological evidence between the coast and the interior that must be addressed if balanced understanding of Ionia is to be achieved. Such an approach would need to be an integrative one, combining cultural and paleo-ecology with geomorphology, if the role of these large and dynamic valleys and their peoples is to be understood correctly in relation to their coastal Ionian neighbors. Even though they were east–west communication routes par excellence, the valleys were not simply passive conduits through which cultural exchanges between the Greek Aegean and the Anatolian highlands occurred. Rather, the local cultures of the valleys would have been central to such exchanges and need to be understood in much more detail than has previously been possible.

Finally, it has been noted that the land of Ionia was a dynamic one. Understanding and recording those processes of change and mapping them onto the human experience of living in that landscape is no easy task, but it is underway. How humans related their settlements and economic lives to that changing environment will be the subject of the next two chapters.

---

[78] However, there has been a more integrated approach by prehistorians studying the region, such as Marchese 1986 and Thompson 2007.

4

The Wealth of Ionia

Introduction

Having established in the previous chapter the nature of the Ionian landscape, it is now possible to move on to consider how the physical nature of this landscape dictates the type of agriculture that can be practiced within it. It would be narrowly deterministic to assume that the landscape was the ultimate arbiter of what crops might be grown there and consequently how human societies and economies might flourish or fail in the region, but it did place the ultimate limit on what humans could achieve within its bounds.

Each *polis* of Ionia was in a position to exploit the neighboring territory that constituted its *chora*. As noted in Chapter 3, the nature of the Ionian landscape is such that these *chorai* were rarely contiguous blocks of land surrounding the community's chief town. The *chora* of an Ionian city typically consisted of an area of arable land nearest the city, plus additional pockets of cultivable land in the vicinity, mountainous grazing lands, and islands that could be used for grazing, farming, or fishing within reach of the city. Control of these islands, pockets of land, areas of plain, rural communities, and sometimes even other, smaller Ionian cities, was contested between competing neighboring states. The *chora* of a typical Ionian city therefore needs to be understood not as a single indivisible entity but as a series of land parcels, each with its own character and agricultural potential, which could be exchanged between states through warfare.[1] The size and character of each *polis'* *chora* would determine its success relative to its Ionian neighbors.

In *Annaliste* terms, the physical nature of landscape and the annual cycles of nature place limitations on human activity, but how humans choose to operate within these physical structures in mediohistorical and historical timescales is largely determined by them (see Chapter 2). For example, the soils and climate of Ionia are suitable for the cultivation of grapes and the production of wine. During the Archaic period, grapes were evidently grown and wine produced (see below). However, with the social changes that the introduction of Islam has brought to the region, production of wine has virtually

---

[1] Greaves 2007b; see also Chapter 7.

ceased and very few grapes are grown as a consequence.[2] Changes in the way the landscape is exploited can also be brought about by advances in technology. For example, changes in the technologies of drainage, crop intensification and management, and the creation of global markets and bulk transport have resulted in the lower Büyük Menderes Valley being drained and intensively cropped for cotton, which is then sold worldwide. Social and economic factors can sometimes also lead to the abandonment of previously viable agricultural land, or can lead to turning agricultural land over to other purposes. An example of this in Ionia is the explosion of building that has accompanied the growth of tourism in the region, for which previously farmed areas have been turned over for use for holiday homes and hotels.[3] Social and economic decisions such as these will therefore determine the nature of land-use and agriculture in mediohistorical timescales.

The fleeting glimpses of insight into the agricultural life of Ionia that we can glean from historical sources must be used with caution. For example, when Herodotos refers to the fields of wheat that grew around Miletos, he does so in an obviously allegorical way (Hdt. 5.92). However, what is interesting is that Herodotos refers to Miletos' fields four times, but never refers to the city as being an important center for the production and trade of pottery or other processed goods for which we now think of it as being famous. What is evident is that generations of scholars have constructed and recon-structed Ionian society according to the values, ideas, and economic models of their time (see below). The aim of this chapter, and this book in general, is to construct a new nar-rative that places the land at the heart of Ionian history in the hope that contemporary audiences may consider this to be closer to the reality of the Archaic Ionian experience than previously proposed models.

The rich ruins of Ionia's major monuments, widespread pottery, and frequent histori-cal references to the presence of Ionians abroad evidently combined to create the impres-sion of a region of successful overseas traders for previous generations of scholars.[4] Later written and epigraphic sources, such as the writings of Athenaios and the Diocletian Price Edict, in both of which Milesian woolens were a watchword for luxury, served to reinforce this impression. However, such impressions are formed by conflating sources for many different chronological periods and using works of art and short-term histori-cal episodes that are only partly representative of the Ionians in general. New interpreta-tions should also aim to encapsulate mediohistorical agricultural, economic, and demographic factors, and the environmental and geographical factors of the *longue durée*. Incorporating these into our reconsideration of the Ionian economy does not necessarily change the overall conclusion that this was a relatively prosperous and well-connected region, but it does provide us with a more nuanced understanding of how it came to achieve this status.

In contrast to previous studies which have tended to view trade and colonization as a continuum,[5] this work deals with these as two distinct elements of Ionian history.[6] Here

---

[2] Greaves 2002: 18.
[3] Greaves 2002: 19.
[4] e.g. Dunham 1915.
[5] e.g. Roebuck 1959; Gorman 2001.
[6] Other interesting studies of the economy of Miletos have been provided by Dunham 1915 and Röhlig 1933.

the phenomenal Ionian colonization movement is argued to have been largely demographic in origin, although commercial factors did play a role (see Chapter 6). This separation allows us to focus attention first and foremost on the processes of local production and exchange, and only then consider how these might articulate with long-distance networks. Rather than regarding Ionians only as global players, this recognizes that many Ionians remained modest farmers and that not all of the states of Ionia engaged in overseas colonization.

In the Archaic period, mainland Greece was sparsely populated and agricultural in nature, making it necessary to understand the rural economy first in order to understand Archaic Greece itself.[7] The landscape of Archaic Ionia was a diverse one, ranging from high mountains to coastal lowlands, and from fertile plains to marginal scrub. Braudel described the relationship between the uplands and lowlands, between farmers and shepherds, as the "slow-furling wave" of history that is a necessary part of understanding any region.[8] Unlocking this relationship in Ionia is the key to understanding how this diversity of landscape was also its strength, and it is only through adopting a holistic approach to landscape history that this can be achieved. As the results of new surveys of the *chorai* of Ionian cities such as Miletos, Ephesos, and Klazomenai start to be integrated into our understanding of those communities, we can begin to appreciate their development within the proper context of understanding the life of the territory in conjunction with that of the city.[9]

It is one of the central contentions of this book that the wealth of Ionia derived not from trade or the production of fine finished goods, but from the more fundamental activity of agriculture. In order to develop this theme, in this chapter the agricultural basis of Ionia will be examined first, so that the basis of the region's economy can be understood literally from the ground up. Next, the relationship between the agricultural fundamentals of the region and the processing and production of materials for trade will be surveyed. Finally, the modes of exchange of these traded goods will be examined and any new understandings of the nature of the ancient Ionian economy achieved will be discussed.

Modes of Primary Production

Agriculture

The land of Ionia had great agricultural potential. At the present time, the richest farmland is concentrated on the newly formed plains of the big rivers that provide an ideal environment for the intensive production of cash crops such as cotton. However, even

---

[7] van Andel and Runnels 1987; Alcock 2007.

[8] Braudel 1972: 88.

[9] On the importance and development of archaeological surveys of Classical chorai see Alcock 2007. For discussion and references for such surveys in Ionia, see Chapter 3. Archaeological research has generally been focused more on the lowland areas of Ionia than the uplands, although this is changing with the instigation of a survey project on Samsun Dağı (Lohmann 2007b).

before the formation, draining, and intensive cultivation of these alluvial plains, Ionia had great agricultural riches in comparison with many contemporary states in mainland Greece. Some Ionian states had access to considerable areas of plains that could be cultivated by dry agriculture. These include the southern plains of Chios and Samos, and the northern plain of Milesia, near Miletos. The region also had extensive areas of scrub for grazing, mountainous uplands for forestry, and seas full of fish. The exploitation of this diverse natural environment was the ultimate source of all Ionia's wealth.

However, Ionia's best agricultural lands were concentrated in the hands of just a few states. Samos, Chios, and Miletos had large areas of readily cultivable land that were clearly defined and easily controlled by virtue of being islands and, in the case of Miletos, a peninsula. As the plains of the big rivers grew, Ephesos and Miletos were able to assert themselves over the newly created land, as they did over the territories of their smaller neighbors. The differentiation between large and small states therefore became more pronounced over time, not less, leading to the phenomenon that we see at the Battle of Lade where the ships of a handful of large states comprised most of the Ionian fleet (see Chapter 7).

To try to understand how this landscape was used, it is possible to observe modern ways of life and make cautious parallels with past lifestyles and methods of exploiting the same landscape.[10] It is important to recognize the huge social and economic changes that have taken place in the region since antiquity, such as the introduction of Islam, the mechanization of farming, the introduction of cash crops, and mass tourism. The dominant type of agriculture in the Archaic period would have been dry agriculture based on Mediterranean polyculture. This is a mixed agricultural regime that combines three central crops: vines, olives, and cereals.[11] These were the mainstay of traditional Mediterranean farming because they are well suited to the region's climate and soils and can be combined well.

Vines

Grapes can tolerate the relatively dry climates and poor soils of the Mediterranean and viticulture was probably common in ancient times. However, storage of fresh grapes was impossible and they had to be dried or, more commonly, made into wine. When dried, they can be stored and consumed as sultanas, raisins, or as pressed *pekmez* (*Turk*. condensed grape juice, or must). As wine, they can be stored and transported in amphorae (see below). The ancient Greeks generally drank their wine mixed with water, not undiluted. Wine was consumed daily and it formed a significant component of their diet.[12] Paleobotanical analysis (the study of microscopic plant remains) of samples taken during excavations at the residential and artisan quarter of Miletos, on Kalabaktepe, provides evidence for the cultivation of grapes.[13]

The islands of Samos and Chios in particular had a good reputation for wines, a reputation that continues to the present day. Some traditional wines are still produced on the

---

[10]   Greaves 2002: 16–24.
[11]   Alcock 2007: 120.
[12]   Gallant 1991: 68.
[13]   Stika 1997.

Turkish mainland in the village of Sirince, near Ephesos.[14] DNA analysis of an amphora recovered from a fourth-century BC shipwreck just off Chios showed that it may have contained wine, to which mastic had been added.[15] Chian amphorae have been found further afield in the Black Sea and elsewhere, showing that these wines were widely distributed.[16] Finds such as these would seem to suggest that Chian wine was produced for regional and long-distance export markets. This does not, however, mean that any great quantity of wine was exported in this way, or that it had been produced solely for export. The vast majority of wine was probably consumed locally as part of the Ionian diet. Only excess production would have been available for trading, either locally within Chios, regionally within Ionia and the Aegean, or long distance to the Black Sea. If the majority of all wines can be assumed to have been made and consumed locally, often within the *oikos* or village, this would leave negligible archaeological evidence as the wine would be made and stored in wineskins, barrels, or possibly *pithoi* (large storage jars). Because the distinctive trade amphorae used for transporting wine over long distances survive so well, it is hard to gauge the relative importance of local markets (see below).

Olives

As with grapes, Ionia's climate and soils were well suited to the growth of olives. Pressed and stored as oil or preserved in brine, they evidently formed a significant proportion of the ancient diet.[17] Also like wine, olive oil can be readily transported in amphorae.

There is evidence to prove their abundant growth in the region in antiquity from paleobotanical analysis and palynology (the study of pollen) from samples taken at Miletos.[18] DNA analysis of another amphora from the Chios wreck showed not only that a form of amphora that was previously thought to be used for the transport of wine was in fact for olive oil, but also that the oil may have been flavored with oregano.[19] Today olive trees are a common feature of the landscape and can be found in fields, or on the foothills, where they can be grown on even quite steep slopes with or without the aid of small walls to retain the root bowl.[20] As with wine, most of the oil that was produced on farms in Archaic Ionia would probably have been consumed locally and leave little archaeological trace.

A remarkable feature of olive cultivation is the propensity of olive trees to periodically have glut years.[21] In such years, when communities find themselves with a superabundance of olives, there will be a surplus, while in a bad year they may need to import oil to satisfy local demand. It is impossible to quantify the level of production of olive oil in Archaic Ionia. The very fact that Ionian states were net exporters of oil in one year does

---

[14]   Although for cultural reasons there is a general lack of wine production in mainland Ionia; see Greaves 2002: 18–19.
[15]   Hansson and Foley 2008.
[16]   Lazarov 1982; Sarikakis 1986: 127; Dupont 1995/96; Foxhall 2007.
[17]   Gallant 1991: 68; Mattingly 1996: 222–3; Foxhall 2007.
[18]   Stika 1997; Wille 1995.
[19]   Hansson and Foley 2008.
[20]   Foxhall 1996.
[21]   Mattingly 1996: 219–20.

not mean that they were able to do so every year. Also, the presence of oregano in the DNA samples from the Chios wreck might suggest that these exported oils were special flavored oils, not an everyday household necessity. Therefore the wide distribution of Ionian oil amphorae should not be taken as evidence of regular bulk exports at this early date.

Cereals

The third and most important element of the so-called Mediterranean triad was cereal crops. They formed a crucial part of the diet, being the main provider of calorific energy. Parts of Ionia were well suited to the growth of wheat and barley. Although dry in the summer, the climate of Ionia does allow for the growth of cereal crops and in antiquity they were interplanted between olives and other trees to take advantage of the shade. This practice can still be seen in some areas of the region today although increasing mechanization and specialization of production is resulting in larger fields of cereals and separate olive orchards. Cereal cultivation cannot accommodate the same extremes of slope and dryness that vines and olives can, and so suitable arable land was always at a premium. Control of such land was the cause of wars and invading armies would deliberately set out to lay waste to crops in their enemies' fields (Hdt. 1.17; see Chapter 7). Storing and keeping the harvested grain safe has therefore always been a priority for households, ancient and modern.[22]

Preliminary paleobotanical research at Miletos showed that cereals were present, but that barley outnumbered wheat as the principal crop.[23] This is consistent with a domestic level of production as barley has a higher yield, but a lower commercial value, than wheat. Trade in cereals is very hard to prove and there has been much academic debate about the existence or otherwise of a large-scale trade in grain between Athens and the Black Sea in the Classical period.[24] Athens, as is often the case, is an exceptional state in this regard and the existence or otherwise of such a trade at Athens at that time does not provide a useful model for Archaic Ionia. The picture in Ionia appears to have been more complex. There were probably a few large Ionian states that were capable of producing large quantities of grain, but they may not have been in a position to export it and in times of crisis almost certainly imported grain.[25] The smaller Ionian states were probably in an even less secure position because their hinterlands lacked the extensive tracts of fertile arable land that their larger neighbors had (see Chapter 2). It has been argued that the distribution of Ionian coinage in Egypt shows that the larger Ionian states were procuring grain in Egypt and dealing in it back to other states in Ionia.[26] This observation is consistent with the vacillating pattern of import and export that unpredictable agriculture yields dictated, but it does not imply that Archaic Ionia relied on imported grain to the same extent that Athens came to do in the Classical period.

---

[22]   cf. Makal 1954: 19–20.
[23]   Stika 1997.
[24]   Recent discussions include Keen 2000 and de Angelis 2006.
[25]   Greaves 2007b, citing Hdt. 1.21.
[26]   Roebuck 1950.

The scale of production of grain in Ionia was probably considerable (see below), but at various times and for various reasons (drought, sieges, etc.) all Ionian states would have found themselves short of this most essential commodity. In such situations, the larger states with their harbors and trading ships would have been able to supply themselves with grain to tide them over the crisis. Smaller states would have been in a more vulnerable position and may have had to rely on trade from their large neighbors. This only reasserts the disparity between the larger and the smaller states of Ionia previously noted.

Other crops

In addition to the triad of cereals, olives, and vines, legumes and vegetables would be intensively cultivated in the sheltered courtyards of houses and in gardens on the edge of villages. These provided essential vitamins, variety, and flavor to a diet that derived its calorific intake mainly from bread, olive oil, and wine. Fruits such as apricots and figs can also be dried and stored until needed. Wild herbs and greens could also be gathered from the uncultivated uplands. Mastic was one of Chios' most famous products in antiquity, as it is today. Remains of pure Chian mastic resin have been found at Naucratis in Egypt,[27] and, as noted above, it was evidently used to flavor wine transported in amphorae.[28]

Animal husbandry

Mixed agriculture would have been the norm in Archaic Ionia, with households keeping animals such as sheep, goats, cattle, pigs, and bees. These animals were integrated into the agricultural life and cycles of Archaic Ionia and understanding this fact is an important element in unlocking their role in the economy. An effective way to get an impression of how human–animal interactions in the past may have operated is by observing contemporary behaviors in order to draw analogies or produce models by means of ethnoarchaeology (see Chapter 1).[29]

For example, one can observe that in modern small agricultural households each family generally keeps just one or two cattle. These are kept in byres in the farmyard adjacent to the house and are grazed and fed on melon skins and similar household waste; they provide the household with milk and meat. Given that keeping pigs is not permitted under Islamic tradition, the role that these cattle play by eating household waste in modern Turkish households might be assumed to have been fulfilled in Archaic Ionia by pigs. Faunal studies (the analysis of animal bones) have shown that pig bones were present in the domestic quarters of Miletos.[30]

Sheep and goats would have been grazed on the region's many hills, and let out to graze on the fields following harvest, as they are today. These sheep produce meat, milk, and wool, but conversation with shepherds reveals that their most valued function is to

---

[27] Mills and White 1989: 43.
[28] Hansson and Foley 2008.
[29] For a more detailed consideration of modern agricultural practices of Ionia and their relationship to ancient ones, see Greaves 2002: 16–24.
[30] Peters and von den Driesch 1992.

replenish the soil of the harvested fields with their manure. Taking this ethnographic observation into consideration, a new understanding of how sheep husbandry was integrated into the economy of Archaic Ionia can be achieved. Using this observation, it could be argued that sheep were kept *not* primarily for their wool, meat, or milk, but rather to replenish the fields. It was those crucial arable fields that were central to the life and economy of Archaic Ionia, and the keeping of sheep as part of mixed farming could almost be seen as secondary to that. Although Miletos, in particular, appears to have had a reputation for fine woolens in antiquity,[31] in this new interpretation of the Archaic Ionian economy wool was a by-product of a mixed agricultural regime in which the products of scarce arable land were at a premium, and wool was not a sought-after end-product in its own right.[32]

Another interesting observation about contemporary animal husbandry that has significance for our understanding of life in Archaic Ionia is the fact that herding of sheep and goats is the only activity that takes place across the whole region – its hills and mountains, its plains, and its coastlines.[33] Herding sheep therefore had an important role to play in integrating the Ionian landscape and forming the Ionians' understandings of their own surroundings.[34]

Extractive industries

Metals
Metals were an essential requirement for ancient societies. Gold and silver made coins and prestige goods for their temples and the elite; iron made weaponry and tools; and even in this Iron Age society tin and copper remained vitally important for making bronze armor. Judging by the few places where undisturbed deposits of metal artifacts have been found, metals were evidently not in short supply in Archaic Ionia.[35] Yet Ionia is almost totally lacking in the minerals that ancient societies most valued. Beyond some limited sources of lead and iron, it has no mineral reserves of any consequence and it could be argued that this forced the Ionians to look beyond their borders for the essential ingredients of their technology – a technology that through the production of arms and the practice of warfare was to earn them an international reputation (see Chapter 7). There may have been limited supplies of iron from Mount Latmos and lead from Myous,[36] but even though some local supplies were available, Ionia imported gold and lead from Lydia[37] and gold, copper, and iron from the Black Sea.[38] Tin may have had to come from further afield within central Anatolia, or be traded overland across the Near East from Afghanistan.[39]

[31] Ryder 1983: 148.
[32] Although on the probable existence of high-value cloth in Ionia, see Chapter 9.
[33] See Greaves 2002: 22, fig. 1.8.
[34] Greaves forthcoming (1).
[35] See Chapter 9.
[36] Greaves 2002: 32–7.
[37] Adiego 1997.
[38] Yalçin 1993; Lordkipanidse 2007.
[39] Greaves 2002: 32–7.

Processing of metals appears to have taken place in small workshops at a local level – examples of workshops for iron at Klazomenai[40] and bronze at Miletos have been found.[41] The mechanisms by which these metals came to be in Ionia will be examined below. As on indication of the volume of metal imported, see Box 4.1.

Stone

One natural resource that Ionia had in abundance was stone. The geology of the region is such that there are a variety of stones with different properties that were useful and exploitable in the Archaic period. The most obvious is the fine marble that occurred around the eastern Gulf of Latmos (modern Bafa Gölü). Evidence for its exploitation in antiquity comes from in situ stone blocks, column drums, and *sarcophagi* (coffins), partly finished and readied for transport by ship.[42] It is unlikely that Latmian marble traveled far due to its bulk, but also due to the fact that other good sources of marble existed at Paros and Proconnessos. For less conspicuous building works, gneiss from Myous was used. The trade in stone was evidently destined to be only intra-regional within Ionia and although stone was never going to be a great source of wealth for Ionia, it did facilitate the building of many fine monuments, and even small states like Myous had fine marble temples in the Archaic period. It is the remains of some of these monumental marble buildings that account for the region's very high profile in both the ancient and modern worlds (see Chapters 1, 8, and 11).

Timber

The mountainous terrain of Ionia's horsts was probably wooded with pine and other trees. These were an important resource and were useful for housebuilding and domestic fuel even if the timber produced was not of the high-quality, specialist type needed for shipbuilding.[43] Palynology and geomorphological studies suggest that there was deforestation of the region in historic times, and without proper management forests are not a permanent resource.[44] It is unlikely that this timber was traded beyond Ionia itself, due to high local demand, poor quality, and alternative sources.[45] The ability to supply timber from their mountainous hinterlands may have been an advantage for some of the smaller states in Ionia, such as Priene. Wood for use as domestic fuel was also an important necessity of ancient life,[46] and could be gathered in quantity from the region's extensive areas of maquis scrub.[47]

Fish

The coasts, islands, and river mouths of Ionia would have provided very favorable conditions for fish, as would the large bays of the Gulf of Latmos and the Gulf of Ephesos prior

[40] Ersoy 2007: 173–4.
[41] Greaves 2002: 92.
[42] Blackman 1973: 34–7; Peschlow-Bindokat 1981; Peschlow-Bindokat 1996: 52–7.
[43] Greaves 2000a.
[44] Thirgood 1981; Wille 1995; Bay 1999a.
[45] e.g. Rough Cilicia and the Black Sea.
[46] Forbes 1996: 84–8.
[47] It is estimated that 1 hectare of maquis can produce 1 tonne of timber per annum (Rackham 1996: 30).

Box 4.1
The Susa *Astragalus*

This solid bronze model of an *astragalus* (knucklebone) was found during excavations of the *acropolis* of Susa in Iran. It carries an inscription by two individuals, Aristolochus and Thrason, and was apparently dedicated in a temple of Apollo. The style on the inscription and the form of the letters indicates that this was made somewhere in Ionia in c.550–525 BC.[a] It is generally thought that it was probably dedicated at Branchidai-Didyma, although this can never be absolutely confirmed. How this Ionian artifact came to be in Susa is also unclear, but it seems likely that it was looted from the temple by Darius' troops during the sack that followed the defeat of the Ionian Revolt at Lade.[b]

Astragali are known to have had cult associations, being used in divination, and this would be an appropriate gift to give Apollo in one of his oracles. It measures 27.5 by 39 by 24.5 cm and weighs nearly 93 kg. The inscription implies that this was once one of a pair and it has loops that would have allowed it to be attached to its partner, which has since become lost. When complete this single dedication would have weighed almost 200 kg, giving an impression of the scale of dedications that were made in the great temples of Ionia and just how much is missing from the archaeological record as a result of the Persian sack of 494 BC.

Notes

[a]   *SEG* 30, 1290; Jeffery 1990: 334.
[b]   Parke 1985: 31.

The Susa *Astragalus*. Courtesy of Musée du Louvre.

to their silting-up. The islands would also have provided useful landfall for fishermen from the unpredictable storms that can rise up in the Aegean. Faunal evidence shows that a wide variety of different types of fish and other sea creatures were exploited, including murex that was used to make purple dye.[48] Although it can be dried, pickled, or smoked to preserve it, it is unlikely that fish was ever a major export commodity for Archaic Ionia.

Modes of Processing

The premise of this book is that understanding the land of Ionia is the key to understanding all other aspects of its ancient life. Nowhere is this clearer than when discussing the economy. The brief outline of primary production activities given above has shown that Ionia lacked the kinds of natural resources that were suitable for trading beyond the region itself and that although it was potentially capable of producing considerable amounts of agricultural produce, the amount available for trade as a surplus varied from one year to the next according to unpredictable natural cycles. The amount of surplus available would also depend on human factors such as the population of the region that relied on that produce for subsistence, the nature of land tenure, and besieging armies who periodically laid waste to the fields (see below and Chapter 7).

In order to understand the nature of the Archaic Ionian economy, it is necessary to consider the ways in which the available agricultural surplus was processed from its raw state into products suitable for trade and export. Understanding the scale of these processing activities will help us to understand the role of external trade within the overall structure of the Ionian economy. If processing can be shown to have taken place on a large scale, then it will prove that the economy of Ionia was geared toward the production of exportable materials that might account for the region's wealth and success. To elucidate this, the processing of three known export items will be examined: olive oil, decorated pottery, and woolen cloth.

Olive oil

Aristotle recounts a story that Thales of Miletos (b.642 d.547 BC) bought up the oil presses in Miletos and subsequently profited when the following harvest proved to be a glut year (*Politics* 1258b33). This story can be taken as evidence that in Archaic Ionia the processing of olives took place on a commercial scale and under the control of members of the elite.

However, this same story can also be interpreted differently. As noted above, olives are given to periodically having a "good" year and producing a glut of the type evidently being described in this story. Had the presses not been idle in the preceding "poor" year then it is unlikely that Thales would have been able to snap them up as he did. Whoever owned the presses before him was not necessarily a single individual. They may have been

---

[48]   Peters and von den Driesch 1992.

community installations shared between a group of households or a village, in the same way that *tandır* flatbread ovens are built and used by groups of neighbors in traditional Turkish villages today.[49] Viewed in this way, the story is a moral tale about how during a poor year a wily individual could procure the means of processing from the hands of individuals or communities and thereby gain a monopoly for himself.

Aristotle was writing about Thales in the fourth century BC and this is probably a morality tale for his own era rather than an accurate recording of historical events. It is also, first and foremost, an allegorical tale to demonstrate the cleverness of philosophers such as Thales, who was heralded as one of the Seven Sages of ancient Greece.[50] A papyrus records 25,000 liters of oil being shipped from Miletos and Samos to Alexandria in 259/58 BC[51] so the region was evidently capable of exporting oil on a large scale by the third century BC; however, the economy of the Hellenistic world was very different from that of the Archaic period and isolated references may only represent the exported proceeds of a single "good" year (i.e. a single microhistorical event, not the mediohistorical norm for the region).

More direct evidence for the scale of processing in Archaic Ionia comes from excavations at Klazomenai.[52] Here an oil installation consisting of oil presses and storage silos was found cut into bedrock. This installation is impressive, but before we start thinking of it as an oil "factory" we first need to consider how it was used and by whom. If, as has been suggested above, this was a community press in either collective or private ownership the scale of operations that it represents would have been sufficient for the needs of the households that were reliant on olives as a mainstay of their livelihood. Such a facility would have met the needs of the local community and any excess would have been available for trade. There is nothing inherent in its scale or structure to suggest that intensified mass production was taking place here. Oil-press stones can also be found in remote locations, where they were presumably used by rural farmsteads. However, dating these isolated finds is hard and many of these are likely to date from later periods of history. Therefore, proving where and on what scale production occurred is hard, although the Klazomenai press remains a remarkable early example.

Decorated pottery

The local pottery styles of Ionia have long been recognized by scholars for their distinctive style and there are many good sources of clay suitable for making pottery across the region (see Chapter 9). Ionian decorated pottery also provides archaeologists with essential dating evidence and it was evidently widely imitated, but it would be easy to overplay the importance of decorated pottery as a trade item and its commercial value was probably limited (see below).

---

[49] Parker and Üzel 2007.
[50] The first reference to the Seven Sages is in Plato's *Protagoras*, and dated to c.399–387 BC.
[51] Casson 1995: 162–3, n. 36.
[52] Ersoy 2007.

Recognized pottery centers in Ionia included Klazomenai,[53] Chios,[54] and Ephesos,[55] but the most comprehensively studied production site to have been published to date is in the Kalabaktepe area of Miletos. Here the two major Milesian pottery styles, Wild Goat and Fikellura, were made. Systematic stratigraphic excavations at Kalabaktepe allowed for the sequencing of pottery production to be established and uncovered a small pottery installation and kiln.[56] The size of this small kiln and its location in a mixed artisan area indicates that although Milesian pottery production may have been prolific, it was not specialist production on a mass scale.[57]

These two Milesian styles tell very different, yet informative, stories about the nature of pottery production and exchange in Archaic Ionia. The Wild Goat style was widely imitated and there were evidently production centers of imitation Wild Goat style pottery at locations in Caria[58] and in the Milesian colony of Histria.[59] It has only been through systematic typological and scientific analysis of this pottery style that the products of different Ionian and Carian workshops have been distinguished. As a result, it becomes clear that Miletos was not the only producer of this style and that other local centers existed to supply local demand. Wild Goat style pottery is found widely distributed, including at Al Mina (see Box 6.1), Naucratis (see Figure 4.1), and across the Black Sea.

By contrast, the Fikellura style was produced only in Miletos, where it is found in both the domestic settlement and in sanctuary deposits. In Samos it is found only in the sanctuary.[60] This pattern demonstrates that Fikellura pottery was produced and used locally and probably only a minority of that production was exported. Neutron activation analysis of pottery from Ephesos has shown that although it received, and was influenced by, pottery from North and South Ionia and from Lydia, it also produced its own pottery.[61] Similar scientific analysis of pottery from the Emecik sanctuary at Knidos, south of Ionia, has shown that the majority of the dedications here were locally produced, with a minority of imported wares.[62] Further studies of the local Archaic pottery styles of Ionia may continue to enhance and develop this general pattern of local production and consumption.

To sum up, although Wild Goat style was widely distributed and imitated, production was probably small scale and primarily concerned with satisfying local markets. The distribution of other styles was generally much more restricted and their appearance in non-local contexts is generally restricted to religious and funerary contexts. The commercial value of Ionian pottery was probably limited, but in religious contexts it would have taken on symbolic value, and it is useful to archaeologists as a dating tool and as an indicator of the trade in bulk commodities (see below).

---

[53]   Ersoy 2000, 2003.
[54]   Cook and Dupont 1998.
[55]   Kerschner et al. 2002.
[56]   Kerschner and Schlotzhauer 2007; see also Chapter 9.
[57]   Greaves 2002: 91–2.
[58]   R.M. Cook 1993; Cook and Dupont 1998.
[59]   Cook and Dupont 1998: 89–90.
[60]   Cook and Dupont 1998: 77; Schlotzhauer 1999.
[61]   Kerschner 1997; Kerschner et al. 2002, 2007.
[62]   Berges 2006: 199–204.

Figure 4.1 Wild Goat style bowl with basket-like handles, made in Chios. From the Sanctuary of Aphrodite at Naucratis, bearing a graffito by Sostratos, dedicating it to Aphrodite. © The Trustees of the British Museum.

Cloth

One processed material for which Ionia has developed a reputation is fine cloth. As is to be expected of a delicate biodegradable material, there are no preserved examples of cloth from Archaic Ionia.[63] There is therefore no direct evidence for this product, although there is indirect evidence in the form of weaving equipment such as loom weights and spindle-whorls. Made of terracotta and used on warp-weighted looms, loom weights were the commonest, but not the only, form of weaving technology at the time. The literary and epigraphic references that refer to Ionian cloth are generally of later date and limited usefulness. Although linen was probably produced in Ionia, there is little evidence for it and cotton had not yet been introduced, so woolens were the main product.

---

[63] Due to exceptional preservation conditions, some fragments of what are presumed to be Milesian wool were found at the Milesian colony of Nymphaeum (Wild 1977). Samples of this cloth are now the subject of research by the author. On cloth in Ionia see also Chapter 9.

Ionia was capable of producing considerable quantities of wool because the larger states in particular held sway over large expanses of territory suitable for rough grazing, including the many small islands that punctuate the seas around and between them.[64] Sheep could be reared in the hinterlands of even the smallest of the Ionian states. Faunal studies show that sheep husbandry in Ionia at this time included wethering, which is the castration of males to maximize their yield of wool and meat.[65] However, as noted above, an important purpose of these flocks, and possibly even their *raison d'être*, was to fertilize the lowlands by grazing on the stubble of harvested fields. The production of wool was, in effect, a by-product of the production of grain and here, once again, the larger Ionian states had an advantage over their smaller brethren.

As for scale of production, small pyramidal loom weights are a ubiquitous find in Archaic domestic areas and can even be taken as evidence of domestic settlement when found on archaeological surveys.[66] Inscribed examples were dedicated in the temples of Athena at Miletos and Erythrai.[67] Such a pattern of distribution and dedication is consistent with a domestic activity conducted in the home by women and overseen by the relevant goddess. There is nothing in their form or context of discovery to indicate the existence of "factories" or "sweat shops" for the mass production of textiles. Likewise, although there are later references to the dyeing of wool at Miletos, using murex, no significant archaeological evidence for this activity has yet been published.[68] Dyeing is a smelly process and is likely to have taken place away from the home and away from excavated areas, but nevertheless the large quantities of murex shells found at other sites have not yet been found at sites in Ionia.[69] There is no evidence of substantial dye works at Miletos, as previous generations of scholars may have hoped to find as proof of wool processing on a pseudo-industrial scale.[70]

The only near-contemporary reference to any trade in Ionian wool is in Aristophanes' *Lysistrata* (line 729). Interestingly, this passage refers to raw Milesian wool, not finished cloth. It was evidently the inherent quality of this wool and not its dyeing and weaving that gave it value. The Milesian breed of sheep, which may have been a precursor to the modern merino, evidently had a very fine fleece and probably originated in central Anatolia.[71] It was these sheep, raised on the extensive fields of Miletos, and presumably other Ionian states, that gave the region a reputation for quality woolens. Yet again, it was the land of Ionia and its connectedness to Anatolia that was the source of both its wealth and its distinctive character.

---

[64]   Greaves 2007b.

[65]   Peters and von den Driesch 1992; Zimmermann 1993: 13–29.

[66]   Pettegrew 2001.

[67]   Personal observations by the author.

[68]   Erim and Reynolds 1970.

[69]   e.g. Kinet Höyük on the coast of the Hatay region of Turkey, where many kilos of crushed murex shells were found in a single Iron Age context (M.H. Gates pers. comm.).

[70]   Dunham 1915: 8–10.

[71]   Ryder 1983: 149.

Modes of Exchange

Exchange and transport

One of the best forms of evidence for exchange of agricultural products is coarseware amphorae, also known as trade amphorae. These large, undecorated transport vessels could be used to hold a multiplicity of contents, not just oil and wine. In Ionia, the most common and important forms include those of Chios, Samos, and Miletos. Chian amphorae are distinctive because of their white slip and decoration.[72] Being from a known production center for wine, amphorae from Chios are assumed to have been used for transporting this commodity, although analysis has shown that they were also used for oil.[73] The high convex-lipped amphorae that were originally attributed to Samos[74] have been shown by clay analysis to have been manufactured in Miletos.[75] It has been suggested that the distinctive banded lip of these Milesian amphorae is a consequence of their having been used for transporting oil,[76] although residue analysis has not yet been applied to this group of vessels.

A quantitative study of the transport amphorae excavated in the Kalabaktepe area of Miletos, the city's residential and artisan quarter, by Alessandro Naso has revealed the proportion of vessels of local versus imported origin.[77] The results are perhaps surprising for a state with a trading reputation as great as that of Miletos and are summarized in Figure 4.2. Naso's research shows that 90% of the amphorae found at Kalabaktepe were of local origin. The second largest group were from elsewhere in Ionia, and only a very small minority were from in the Aegean or beyond. Elsewhere in Miletos, near the Theater Harbor, an amphora warehouse was found to contain a large number of intact Chian amphorae, again demonstrating the importance of intra-Ionian (i.e. regional) trade.[78]

The initial impression of Ionia that one might form, based on the exotica dedicated in its temples or from the wide distribution of Wild Goat style pottery, is that Ionia had very extensive trade networks. This may indeed have been so, but what this evidence from Kalabaktepe shows is that the majority of bulk trade was restricted to local exchanges within and between the Ionian states. For example, although Milesian amphorae are found in the Black Sea, they are only found in small quantities compared with the numbers in which they are found in Ionia and especially in Miletos itself.[79]

The means by which such exchanges took place was probably through cabotage – that is, small-scale maritime exchange in small- to medium-sized coastal vessels. These ships would pick up and offload goods in many different ports as they traveled by

[72] Cook and Dupont 1998: 146–51.
[73] Hansson and Foley 2008.
[74] Grace 1971.
[75] Grace 1971; Dupont 1982: 204–7; Dupont 2007.
[76] Cook and Dupont 1998: 177.
[77] Naso 2005.
[78] *Milet* 1.8: 79–81, figs 43 and 45.
[79] Dupont 2007.

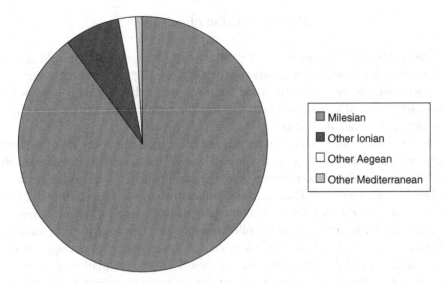

Figure 4.2 Trade amphorae at Miletos (after Naso 2005).

island-hopping and following coastlines. A wreck of one such ship from Ionia, dating from the third quarter of the fifth century BC, has been found off Teos, at Tektaş.[80] The amphorae in it, which were from Mende, Chios, and a "pseudo-Samian" type of local manufacture, contained wine, pitch, and butchered cattle bones, demonstrating the variety of commodities that could be transported in them – not just wine and oil. In total 60 amphorae were found, alongside a small quantity of fineware pottery. Another wreck, dating to the sixth century, off Pabuç Burnu near Bodrum, included Chian, Klazomenian, and Knidian amphorae in the same payload.[81] Wrecks such as these give valuable insights into the trade mechanisms in Archaic and Classical Ionia and confirm that ships' cargoes were made up of mixed commodities, not single-commodity bulk shipments. Decorated pottery formed only a small proportion of these cargoes and was probably of low commercial value relative to the bulk goods, but it is the distribution of the decorated pottery that accompanied these bulk cargoes that are so often invisible to archaeology that provides the most useful indicator of the cargoes' distribution. The exchange networks that emerge were not formed by the desire to acquire Ionian pots as *objets d'art*, but by the bulk goods they were traded with.[82] An example of an individual Ionian trader is the shipowner Kolaios of Samos (Hdt. 4.152) who we are told was blown off course from his planned trip to Egypt, only to land in Libya and then Tartessos. However, traders who dealt in Ionian goods and pottery were not necessarily Ionians themselves, as anyone could engage in cabotage and trade in Ionian products.

[80]   Gibbins 2000.
[81]   Greene and Bass 2004.
[82]   Morel 1983; Gill 1994; Greaves 2007b. This terminology should not be taken to imply that the Ionians themselves thought of these pots as "art," rather than as the practical products of craftsmen. See Chapter 9 for a full discussion of the perception of ancient Greek art by scholars.

The introduction of coinage

Ionia was one of the first regions to adopt the use of coinage and this would appear to be a significant development for facilitating the exchange of goods within the region. The reasons why coinage was first introduced are much debated.[83] Neither is it known who minted early issues of coinage – whether it was the central authorities of the different Ionian states, or private individuals.

As with pottery studies, which have tended to favor painted pottery over the study of coarsewares, our understanding of early Ionian coinage has been dominated by the study and cataloguing of high-denomination gold and silver coinage, with smaller denominations being largely ignored.[84] Their intrinsic and aesthetic value to collectors means that there is a ready market for illicitly procured coins, and some of the most important information about them comes from collections of coins that appear in the catalogs of auction houses or are seized from the black market.[85] New studies of coinage collections held in museums and the appearance of new hoards on the art market are continually changing our understanding of exchange in the region, and indeed of the history of coinage itself.

The Central Basis Deposit from the Artemision at Ephesos is a large deposit of votive offerings found under the Central Basis, a structure of unknown function that was evidently a focal part of the site's cult activity.[86] Stratigraphically, this deposit must be earlier than the mid-sixth century BC in date. In addition to 93 electrum coins, jewelry and ivories also of sixth-century date were found. All the coins found, with the exception of two, were made to the Lydian standard.[87] Electrum is an alloy of silver and gold and was used to make coins in the area controlled by Lydia (the probable source of the electrum, where it occurs naturally) for about half a century after their introduction in c.600 BC. As it is an alloy, the gold:silver ratio in electrum can vary and it was sometimes blended with copper to give it a uniform color. It may be this natural property of variability in electrum that led to it being stamped in order to standardize its value.[88] The Central Basis Deposit is important not only for its early date and use of electrum, but because it was found in situ during excavation. This is rare, as most coin hoards first come to light when they appear for sale on the art market. It is also important because the coins in it are of early date and relatively high value. However, it is important to note that this is not a "hoard" in the true sense of the word, but a votive deposit of coins sealed beneath a religious structure and never intended to be recovered. How, or even if, these coins were ever intended to be used for exchange cannot be known, but for a long time it was thought that the high denominations of early coins such as these meant that their intended use

---

[83]   Wallace 1987; Kurke 1999; Kim 2001; Le Rider 2001; Schaps 2004; Seaford 2004.
[84]   Kim 1994: 85–6.
[85]   e.g. Moucharte 1984 (15 Milesian silver coins that appeared in Brussels) and Becker 1988 (75 Milesian silver obols).
[86]   Hogarth 1908.
[87]   Kraay 1976: 20–40.
[88]   Wallace 1987; Koray 2005: 52.

was restricted to official transactions, such as paying off mercenaries. Unlike the coinage of Athens, for which lead isotope analysis has been used to show that it was sourced from Laurion, the use of electrum and silver bullion that had been "pooled" (i.e. melted down and mixed with metal from other sources) means that a similar analysis cannot easily be done for Ionia.

Coin Hoard I 3 is generally thought to have come from Kolophon, but its precise provenance cannot be proven as it was acquired from the art market.[89] This hoard consists of 77 silver coins and several large pieces of bullion. Detailed analysis of the coins shows that their weights were measured very precisely and that the products of a large number of different mints were present in the hoard.[90] These mints were evidently producing many small-denomination coins, alongside larger denominations. The sheer number of mints suggests that coins were being produced in early Ionia on a considerable scale, probably for official transactions, but the scale of production suggests that they were probably also intended for internal trade. The make-up of silver in Hoard I 3 shows that perhaps as many as three different monetary systems co-existed in sixth-century BC Ionia – namely, high-denomination coins for official transactions and services, such as mercenaries; small-denomination coins with limited circulation for day-to-day internal trade; and bullion, which had long been established for use in trade in the Near East.[91]

Another hoard was recently identified when a number of Samian electrum staters, which are generally rare, suddenly became available on the art market at once.[92] So far 44 coins from this putative hoard have been identified, which may have been recovered by metal detectorists working on the Turkish coast opposite Samos. The first Ionian states to strike electrum coins in c.600 BC were Samos, Miletos, Phokaia (see Figure 4.3), and Ephesos. In southern mainland Ionia the Milesian weight standard was used, in northern Ionia the Phokaiac standard was used, and Samos evidently used a different standard again, the Euboic-Samian.[93]

Various theories have been proposed to explain the reasons for the introduction of coinage, its economic and political contexts, and its early adoption in Ionia. The three coin hoards discussed here illustrate a number of interesting points in relation to these discussions, including the fact that coinage had a variety of uses (for official transactions, as votives, and for internal trade); that even in an inland Ionian state of modest size like Kolophon a large number of mints existed to produce considerable amounts of coinage of different denominations; and that a number of different monetary systems and weight standards co-existed within Ionia. It is also interesting to note that academic attention has traditionally focused on the high-denomination coins that appear most frequently on the art market, at the expense of studying the smaller, yet equally informative, denominations. In the opinion of the author, the most likely explanation for the introduction of

[89]   Kim 1994: 22–6.
[90]   Kim 1994: 23.
[91]   J. Kroll speaking in Oxford, November 27, 2008. On the use of bullion in the Near East, see Schaps 2004: 34–56.
[92]   Koray 2005.
[93]   Koray 2005: 43.

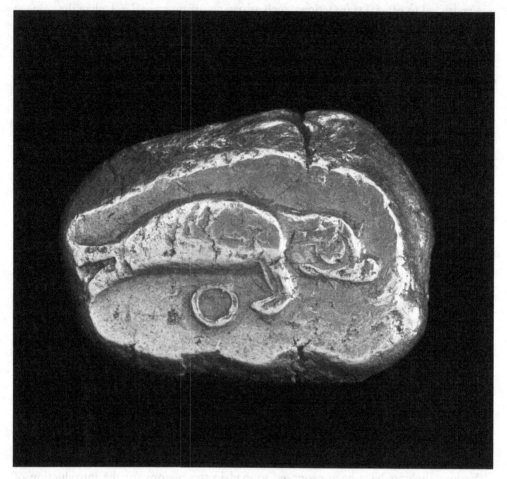

Figure 4.3 Electrum stater with image of a seal from Phokaia, c.600–550 BC. © The Trustees of the British Museum.

coinage is also the most prosaic: that the authorities that had accumulated quantities of bullion in their temples and repositories had to mint it in order to spend it.[94] Once minted, the rich dedications and mercenary spoils and other metal artifacts that had been deposited in Ionia's temples could then be spent on public works, such as city walls and fleets, or even new temples for the gods.[95] The grandeur of Ionia's temple buildings, its

[94] Wallace 1987: 396. C. Morgan 2003: 141–55 provides an excellent discussion of the role sanctuary authorities played in the processing and recycling of metals. If the redistribution of metal directly from temples, in coin or bullion form, is accepted, then this might account for the stamping of coins with religious or state insignia. These stamps would indicate that the metal had been legitimately given to the holder and was not the spoils of theft or simony.

[95] Greaves 2002: 98. See Chapter 7 on walls and fleets and Chapter 8 on dedications and the periodic renewal of major temple buildings during the Archaic.

early adoption of coinage, and the wide distribution of that coinage at an early date[96] might therefore be seen to be a product of the success of its priests and its mercenaries, rather than its merchants.[97]

Ionia and World Systems

Having considered how materials might be produced, processed, and exchanged, it is useful to consider theoretical models that can help us appreciate how these different activities operated within a coherent system.[98] One such paradigm is world-systems analysis.[99] This was first devised by Immanuel Wallerstein in relation to sixteenth-century AD Europe,[100] but has since been extended to cover many other periods and cultures, including archaeological ones.[101] A world system is a system of societies in which those societies interact with one another in ways that are "important ... two-way, necessary, structured, regularized and reproductive."[102] Only in modern times does "world" come to mean the whole globe; rather, the "world" of each historical period needs to be defined relative to itself.[103]

Christopher Chase-Dunn and Thomas D. Hall defined four different types of networks,[104] each one of which is generally progressively larger than the previous one, that constitute a world system:

- a bulk goods network (BGN), a system of exchange of low value-to-weight goods
- a political-military network (PMN) of regularized military or political interactions
- a prestige or luxury goods network (PGN) of more or less regular exchange of high value-to-weight goods
- an information or cultural network (IN) of regularized exchanges of information.[105]

Once established, world systems are not conceived of as static. As Hall wrote: "[world systems] all pulsate or expand and contract, with a net tendency to increase in size."[106] As they expand, so they "incorporate" new territories and peoples. This expansion can be related to Ionian colonization (see Chapter 6).

---

[96] e.g. the Assyut Hoard from Egypt shows that a number of Greek states, including some in Ionia, were producing and circulating coins at an early date (Holloway 1984).

[97] contra C. Morgan 1989: 18 who saw the temples of the sixth century BC as "an indication of the commercial wealth of the Ionian cities."

[98] For a recent discussion of the ancient economy, see Scheidel et al. 2007.

[99] Previously known as world-systems theory (Kardulias and Hall 2008: 573).

[100] Wallerstein 1974, 2004.

[101] See Kardulias and Hall 2008 for discussion of archaeology and world-systems analysis, which provides a useful overview and bibliography.

[102] Hall and Chase-Dunn 2006: 33.

[103] For discussion of the "world" within which Ionia existed, see Chapter 6.

[104] Chase-Dunn and Hall 1997.

[105] T.D. Hall 2006: 97–8.

[106] T.D. Hall 2006: 98.

Table 4.1   Different types of archaeological and historical evidence mapped onto the four world-systems network types

Network type	Evidence
Bulk goods network (BGN)	Wheat, oil, wine, timber, stone, etc. (see text)
Political-military network (PMN)	Diplomatic gifts (Hdt. 1.192, 2.159; Jeffery 1990)
	Political marriages (Hdt. 4.77)
	Mercenaries (see Chapter 7)
	Military engineering (see Chapter 7)
Prestige goods network (PGN)	Metals (see text)
	Luxuries, e.g. furniture, artworks, Egyptianalia (see Chapter 9)
Information network (IN)	Oracles as "clearing houses" of geographical information (Parke 1967: 45–6)
	Seasonal tunny runs (Greaves 2002: 106–7)
	Purple fishing (Hdt. 4.151)
	Coastal traders (Hind 1995/96)

The different types of networks that make up a world system can be related to different aspects of Ionian economic (and non-economic) activity. Examples of how this can be done are given in Table 4.1. Relating these different kinds of Ionian engagement with overseas societies from the world-system perspective presents a holistic model that not only accounts for the different patterns of bulk and prestige goods noted above, but also incorporates military, political, and religious activities.

To describe some of these activities as "trade" would be to misrepresent the means by which they came to be exchanged. Money was still a relatively new innovation and not yet universal (see above); in the case of diplomatic gifts and political marriages, what is being exchanged is political, and not monetary, capital; neither are such exchanges necessarily reciprocal, such as when the Ionians paid tribute to Persia. Due to the shifting nature of such networks, it is important to pay attention to the specifics of context and chronology before attributing artifacts or activities to one form of network or another. For example, a wine amphora might be considered to be part of a prestige goods network when found in a burial context at some distance from a nascent Ionian colony, whereas such an artifact found amongst others in the harbor area of a neighboring Ionian community might be considered as evidence of a bulk goods network.[107] The boundaries between the prestige goods network and the bulk goods network are therefore permeable because the value attached to artifacts is not fixed, but negotiated by the receiving society – and this may be especially true in pre-monetary societies.

The application of this aspect of world-systems analysis therefore suggests to us a model by which it is possible to understand the exchange of bulk commodities within

---

[107]   e.g. compare the context of Chian wine jars in Gute Maritzyn (Boardman 1999: 263) and the amphorae found at the harbor in Miletos (see above). For a detailed survey of the distribution, volumes, and context of amphorae in the Black Sea, see Tsetskhladze 1998.

and between Ionian states as being part of one network, and the appearance of those same goods in different quantities, locations, and contexts as part of another. The fact that Ionian traders and commodities appear in contexts across the Black Sea, the Near East, and Egypt does not imply that they were able to call upon those regions for the import of bulk commodities, such as wheat. Only in later historical periods had the bulk goods network developed to such an extent that such trade was possible for cities such as Athens.

Conclusions

Relative to some contemporary regions of Greece and the Aegean, Ionia was wealthy. Why it was wealthy will depend very much on how one approaches the question. Reading the works of previous generations of historians, such as Dunham, Röhlig, and Roebuck, one can see how they related their understandings of the economy of Archaic Ionia to the standards of their own time.

For example, Dunham was writing at a time when the British Empire was at its height, and perhaps influenced by the analogies being drawn at that time between the perceived cultural and economic superiority of the Greeks and that of the British Empire.[108] The influence of those analogies can perhaps be seen in Dunham's assertion that it was trade, via its colonies, that was the source of Miletos' wealth, a situation that paralleled Britain's own position at the time.[109] When approached from the point of view of an art historian, the remarkable wealth, quality, and evident Near Eastern influence of many Ionian works of art might lead one to assume that its wealth derived from overland trade via the Silk Road, or overseas to Egypt.[110] Even the study of numismatics, which can appear objective and scientific to the non-expert, is based on subjective interpretations. Literary positivism can influence numismatic interpretation as it can any aspect of archaeological evidence.[111]

This chapter has followed the line that appreciating the extent to which, and means by which, the economy of Archaic Ionia was fundamentally driven by the physical nature and cycles of the landscape can provide new points of entry to understanding it. This approach has provided new perspectives such as: seeing wool as a by-product of arable farming; seeing decorated pottery as an indicator of trade, not a prized commodity in its own right; and seeing that the availability of surplus agricultural produce will be largely dependent on the natural rhythms and vagaries of the local environment.

The key to developing deeper understandings of the Ionian economy along these lines will be dependent upon the continuing scientific analysis of samples from stratigraphic contexts by methods such as paleobotany, palynology, faunal studies, and DNA analysis of residues. That is to say, new analyses will be based not on the study of artifacts, but "ecofacts." These techniques have the ability to balance the detailed artifact studies of

---

[108] Snodgrass 2002; Hurst and Owen 2005.
[109] e.g. Dunham 1915: 15.
[110] See Chapter 9 for a discussion of these artworks and their context.
[111] e.g. it was once argued that during the brief period of unity during the Ionian Revolt the Ionian states minted common coinage, but this was subsequently disproved (Gardner 1911; Caspari 1916).

high-value materials such as sculpture and bronzes with the evidence of daily life in Ionia. By these means and by starting at the base of the pyramid, with the land and agriculture, we can then place the higher achievements of Ionian society into their proper context (see Chapter 2).

The Ionians needed metal for their technology and they got it, but the means by which they did that is not easily understood. Modern concepts of "trade" do not adequately describe the large-scale giving to temples by local elites and foreign powers that we witness in Archaic Ionia. Dedications such as that given by King Croesus of Lydia to the Milesian temple of Branchidai-Didyma (Hdt. 1.192) may have been in gratitude to Ionian merce-naries, purveyors of the second-oldest service industry (see also Chapter 7). In times of crisis the accumulated riches of the temples were evidently at the disposal of the state but metals were also imported in the form of ingots. The Ionians were not only recipients of metal, as in the Persepolis balustrade relief they are pictured giving up metal vessels (and cloth) as tribute to Persia.[112] However, when understood as being part of the political-military network of a world system, such exchanges can be integrated into our broader understanding of Ionia's economy.

It remains to be asked that if the control and effective exploitation of land was the ulti-mate source of Ionia's wealth, who owned that land? The nature of land tenure in Archaic Ionia is difficult to show, but essential for understanding how the economy worked.[113] It is evident from both archaeological and documentary sources that a wealthy aristocratic elite existed in Ionia.[114] The ownership and exchange of land, and other property such as slaves, was important to them.[115] The position of different elite groups undoubtedly shifted during the Archaic period and there may even have been moves to curtail the ostentatious display of wealth by members of this elite.[116] There were evidently periods of *stasis* (civil strife) such as the deadlock between the Milesian factions of the *aeinautai* and the *cheiromachei* (Hdt. 5.28). This dispute was resolved by an arbitration given by a delega-tion from Paros, who determined that those whose estates were well managed could rule the state. The precise meaning of this arbitration, like the constituency of the two groups themselves, is open to interpretation but the value placed upon effective land management is clear. The emergence of tyrants in the Archaic period may also have brought about changes in the way land was owned and managed. In Samos, Polykrates initiated large-scale public works that benefited many people economically, including the construction of a new harbor and a water tunnel to supply the city (see Chapter 5). In Archaic Athens meanwhile, Peisistratus (ruled variously between 561 and 528 BC) was reforming the Athe-nian economy to encourage specialization in the production of olive oil for export.

---

[112]   See Chapter 9.

[113]   e.g. David Tandy 1997 who has speculated about the nature of politico-economic changes in eighth-century BC Greece.

[114]   Archaeological evidence comes in the form of dedications such as the Genelos Group, a family group of statues on the Sacred Way to Samos, and a private sanctuary on the hills above Miletos, that it has been proposed belonged to an aristocratic family (see Chapter 8). Historical evidence comes from Hdt. 5.28.

[115]   e.g. Pedon of Priene mentions being awarded property in Egypt (see Chapter 7) and Matasys who gives his property and slaves to Anaxagoras in the Berezan lead letter (Chadwick 1973).

[116]   Morris 1987: 148, on the West Cemetery at Samos.

For the purposes of this chapter, it has been assumed that whoever owned the land, it was worked by smallholders or tenants based in family units comparable with the Greek *oikos*. The value of using ethnoarchaeological observations as a basis from which to propose models of ancient behaviors by such households has been shown above in relation to animal husbandry. Further ethnoarchaeological studies will be essential because to understand these historically invisible households, the smallest indivisible social and political units of ancient society, and their relationship to the land is to understand the very basis of Ionian society. This fact is something the Greeks themselves recognized and the English word "economics" derives from the Greek *oikonomikos*, meaning the management of a household. Physically, the buildings and lands operated by these family units in rural settings are not well understood, although they are known to have existed (Hdt. 5.28) and many possible sites have been identified by survey.[117] The majority of the population lived in the urban centers and commuted to their fields,[118] and here there have been detailed stratigraphic excavations of the domestic areas of the urban centers of Klazomenai,[119] Chios,[120] and Miletos.[121] It was in such rural and urban households that the majority of production and processing took place.

How the households as production centers articulated themselves with trade networks is again open to debate. Writing about eighth-century Euboea, Hesiod (*Works and Days*) implies that it is individual farmers or landowners who take their own produce by ship to markets abroad. However, it might be more reasonable to suggest that although local farmers may themselves have engaged in bulk goods networks, the prestige goods network probably operated by cabotage.

Just as the nature of land tenure is an essential component of the economy, so too is demography. The size of the population relative to the carrying capacity of the land and the make-up of that population are important factors in determining the possible level of surplus and the nature of the productive activities that could be engaged in. There is no accurate demographic data for Archaic Ionia although the number of ships attending the Battle of Lade in 494 BC has been used as a basis to calculate the population of the participant states.[122] Such calculations suggest that the populations of the major cities of Ionia were substantial, with Chios having an estimated population of 80,000, Samos 48,000, and Miletos 64,000. A certain proportion of these populations would have been slaves, who contributed to the economy as agricultural workers or in processing activities.[123] Whatever the population was, the factors that most limited its growth were the area of terrain available to support it and how that terrain was used. Changes in agricultural production could support population expansion and, conversely, loss of land caused

---

[117] e.g. during the Miletos survey (Lohmann 1995, 1997, 1999, 2007a – see Chapter 3). The best-known example of an excavated rural house is the Vari House in Attica, which yielded much useful information about the nature of agriculture and rural life around Athens (Jones et al. 1973).

[118] Alcock 2007: 126–8; see also Chapter 5.

[119] Ersoy 2007.

[120] Boardman 1967: 34–51.

[121] Senff 2007.

[122] Roebuck 1959: 21–3; Greaves 2002: 99–103; Greaves 2007b.

[123] Greaves 2002: 102–3.

out-migration.[124] In the opinion of the author, dependence on imported foodstuffs was not a viable option for Archaic Ionia, as it was to be in Classical Athens. The large cities of Ionia could only be supported by efficient use of the landscape in their possession, the physical nature of which placed limitations on how it could be used. In *Annaliste* terms, the physical structure of the landscape and changes in its character in the *longue durée* provide the means of subsistence that underpin demographic mediohistorical processes.

Overall, the Ionian economy defies analysis by reductionist economic models of goods exported and others imported – all mediated by new-fangled money. The reality was much more complex. Goods, be they oil, cereals, or even metals, were both imported and exported at different times and "money" was not yet universal. What is true though is that the Ionian economy was based on land and its peoples' relationship with it – a complex, organic relationship that is hard to prove archaeologically and hard to model economically.

It is not rocket science to say that Ionia, like all ancient societies, was dependent first and foremost on agriculture. Yet our attention is often easily distracted by Ionia's radical landscape transformations, the marble confections that are its ruins, and the great thoughts of its seminal philosophers. But most Ionians were not philosophers living a Panglossian existence in marble halls; they were farmers. Their land, much smaller than the one we see today, was nevertheless a fertile one. Its intimate connection to the sea made transporting produce out in times of surplus convenient, but its climate made importing produce necessary in times of crisis. By putting that land first and building up our understanding of the Ionian economy through the Ionians' relationship with it, we can achieve new perspectives on how life here worked. With these in hand we can now go on to explore the society and culture of these seafaring farmers.

---

[124] Greaves 2007b.

 5

The Cities of Ionia

Introduction

To think of Ionia is to think of cities. It is impossible to conjure up an image of Ephesos without picturing the Library of Celsus. In the popular imagination and in academic literature, Ionia *was* its cities. In this sense it is correct to use the term "city" (in the sense of the Greek word *asty*, rather than *polis*) because it is the image of the urban core and associated lifestyle that is being imagined. The *polis* was a composite of three parts: the urban center (the *asty*), the people (the *demos*), and the territory (the *chora*), including its constituent minor towns and hamlets. For Anthony Snodgrass the rise of the city-state was a "conjuncture … [that can] divert the forces of the *longue durée* into a different channel."[1] For him, the city-state became a natural state of being for Mediterranean settlements. It is the relationship that is at the core of the ancient *polis*, that between the *asty* and the *chora*, that is the subject of this chapter – the factors that determined the location of cities in Ionia, shaped their character, and ultimately limited, or facilitated, their growth.

What we see on the ground today and in guidebooks invariably dates from the post-Archaic periods. All the major visible Classical ruins in Ionia today are of Hellenistic or Roman date. Even buildings which originated in the Archaic period or earlier, such as the great temples of the Artemision, Heraion, and Branchidai-Didyma, have all been destroyed and rebuilt several times since. In the case of Old Priene, a whole city has been lost to the point that even its location is no longer known. The reasons for this state of the archaeological evidence were examined in Chapter 1, but the net result is that we know surprisingly little about the cities of this most urban region of Archaic Greece.

The landscape of Ionia, discussed in Chapter 3, played an essential role in determining where and how settlements formed. In this chapter the location and character of each of the 12 Ionian cities will be mapped onto the specific characteristics of its immediate landscape vicinity. It was these very specific localized factors, such as access to harbors,

---

[1] Snodgrass 1991: 69.

and good farmland and communications, that determined the relative wealth and importance of each city within Ionia and shaped the historical development of each. As Graham
Shipley observed, ancient cultures conceived of the countryside differently from contemporary Western society and "in studying the history of the Greeks and Romans we cannot
divorce the town from the country."[2] This chapter will attempt to map that town–country
relationship in Archaic Ionia and relate it to processes of *polis* formation, growth, and
identity.

There follows below a site-by-site survey of the 12 cities that made up the Classical
Ionian *dodekapolis*, with a brief assessment of the extent of their surviving archaeological
remains and landscape context. This is followed by a discussion on *polis* formation based
on the works of François de Polignac. Finally, there is a discussion of what these considerations of the nature of the cities of Ionia can contribute to the ongoing theme of Ionian
identity.

A Brief Survey of the Ionian Cities

The 12 cities that made up the Ionian *dodekapolis* were (from north to south): Phokaia,
Chios, Erythrai, Klazomenai, Teos, Lebedos, Kolophon, Ephesos, Samos, Priene, Myous,
and Miletos (Hdt. 1.142). Below is a very brief overview of each site, describing its
location and assessing the impact this had on the historical development of each city,
together with a critical review of the key archaeological remains and potential of each
site. These summaries are not meant to be exhaustive, but are designed to give the reader
an impression of the physical situation and state of preservation of each site. The biblio-
graphic references provided will direct readers to the most useful published literature on
each site.

Phokaia[3]

The city of Phokaia, once described by Ekrem Akurgal as "the most charming and magical
city of antiquity,"[4] is situated in an excellent natural location. From any vantage point
on the ring of hills that surround Phokaia, it is possible to see down into the old city's
harbors and across the dotted islands that hopscotch out across the bay and into the
Aegean. Any settlement here would be destined to look toward the sea for its livelihood
and cultural influences, and the Phokaians were renowned as great sailors (Hdt. 1.163,
6.11–12). In Herodotos' account, following its dramatic abandonment to the Persians,
the city played only a minor role in the Ionian Revolt and this may give the impression
that it was a place of relatively limited importance within Ionia.[5]

[2]   Shipley 1996: 8.
[3]   Sartiaux 1921; Roebuck 1959: 15–16; E. Akurgal 1976; Tuna-Nörling 2002; S. Özyiğit 1998; Ö. Özyiğit
2003, 2006; Rubinstein and Greaves 2004: 1090–1.
[4]   Ö. Özyiğit 2003: 109.
[5]   e.g. Roebuck 1959: 23.

However, in the current excavations under the direction of Ömer Özyiğit the archaeological remains he has been able to access beneath the modern town of Eski Foça have
provided evidence of an exceptionally large Archaic settlement. These excavations
have been greatly hindered by the existence of the modern city and the rapidity with
which it is being developed.[6] There have been three main phases of excavations here,
under the direction of Felix Sartiaux (1913–14, 1920), Ekrem Akurgal (1952–57, 1970),
and Ömer Özyiğit (1989–present).[7] Far from the small and insignificant place that one
might assume it to be from reading Herodotos, Özyiğit has been able to conclude that
"the length of the city's fortification walls [over 5 km] proves that at the beginning of the
6th century BC Phokaia was one of the largest and most important cities of the world."[8]

It was originally thought that the city was restricted to the peninsula by the harbor,
on top of which stood the famed Temple of Athena. This temple was built in tufa stone
in the Ionic style and stood on a walled podium 50 m long, which was built of such fine
ashlar masonry that it was once thought to be Hellenistic in date.[9] Beneath this temple,
a Sanctuary of Cybele was carved into the north side of the peninsula, overlooking the
entrance of the harbor.[10] Three other Cybele sanctuaries have been found, at Değirmentepe
Hill, the island of Orak Adası, and İncir Adası – which can be equated with the island of
Bakkheion mentioned by Livy (37.21). The current excavations have shown that the city's
real urban core was not on the peninsula but on the mainland, where it covered an
extensive area and was enclosed by impressive ashlar fortification walls.[11]

The city's Archaic *necropoleis* (burial grounds) have been only briefly explored, but
the use of terracotta *sarcophagi* is significant.[12] Archaic burials of this type were found at
the north of the peninsula and on the south side of the city, where large Archaic period
altars were also found.[13] Elsewhere in the hills south of the city is a Lydian-style tomb cut
into the rock-face,[14] and the mound of Maltepe, once thought to be a settlement, has now
been recognized as a *tumulus* (burial mound).[15] Seven kilometers east of the city stands
the monumental Taş Kule tomb, a Persian monument dated to 546 BC that may have
been the architectural inspiration for the Tomb of Cyrus at Pasargadae.[16]

Put together, its excellent location and the nature, diversity, and extent of its archaeological remains clearly point to Phokaia as having been an impressive and cosmopolitan
center in the Archaic period. Clearly able to rival its Ionian peers, such as Miletos,
Ephesos, Samos, and Chios, Phokaia is one of the most important, yet most overlooked,
sites in Ionia.

---

[6]   Ö. Özyiğit 2006.
[7]   These are the three phases of research-led excavations as defined by Ö. Özyiğit 2003. There have also been
rescue excavations conducted under the direction of İzmir Museum.
[8]   Ö. Özyiğit 2003: 116.
[9]   Ö. Özyiğit 2003: 117.
[10]   Ö. Özyiğit 2003: 118.
[11]   Ö. Özyiğit 2003: 115–16; see Chapter 7.
[12]   Ö. Özyiğit 2003: 118–19, fig. 8.
[13]   Ö. Özyiğit 2003: 118–19, fig. 10.
[14]   Known locally as Şeytan Hamamı; Ö. Özyiğit 2003: 114.
[15]   Ö. Özyiğit 2003: 116.
[16]   Cahill 1988; Ö. Özyiğit 2003: 119–20.

Chios[17]

Chios is a large island, with a mountainous northern half and fertile areas in the south. Its eponymous chief town sat on the fertile plain, known as the Kampos,[18] and was situated on a good natural harbor on the eastern flank of the island, looking toward the mainland of Ionia. The city's hinterland was the hilly interior of the island.[19] The island was agriculturally productive, especially in olives and wine. The island's most distinctive export was, and is, mastic.[20] The main city, with its position on a sea passage, natural harbor, and control of a large, discrete, and effectively unchallengeable territory, would appear predestined to be a major sea-power within Ionia, a role that it evidently fulfilled (Hdt. 6.8).

Most of the Archaic *asty* of Chios has been built over by the modern city of the same name which has effectively smothered the archaeological remains of its predecessor. The excellent city museum gives an indication of the wealth of material that we are missing, displaying finds from rescue excavations at various points within the modern town. On the south of the island is a substantial secondary settlement, from which much of our archaeological information about the site has come. This settlement, at Emporio, is known to have had a walled *acropolis* and at least two sanctuaries and a residential area, Prophitis Elias, which was densely settled.[21] Excavations and surveys of the coastal sanctuary site of Kato Phana have also yielded interesting further information about the island in the Archaic period (see below).

Erythrai[22]

Erythrai has perhaps the most perfect location of any town in Ionia. Situated on a peninsula jutting out into the bay, its high-sided and dominant *acropolis* can be seen from far away. The chief limiting factor in the city's growth was its hinterland, which although fertile in the area immediately around the city, soon tails off into the low hills and scrub of the Erythrai Peninsula. Its harbor was ideal for navigation, looking west toward Chios and with a string of small islets nearby.

The archaeological potential of Erythrai is considerable, because although there are numerous post-Archaic monuments covering the site, unlike Phokaia and Chios, it has been relatively undisturbed by modern building works. The site was briefly excavated by Ekrem Akurgal in the 1960s and remained largely unexplored until renewed investigations began in 2003. The majority of the remains date from the Hellenistic period and are located on the *acropolis* and in the *agora* area to the west of the *acropolis* summit. The

[17] Roebuck 1959: 16–17; Boardman 1967; Boardman and Vaphopoulou-Richardson 1986; Rubinstein and Greaves 2004: 1064–9.

[18] Roebuck 1959: 16.

[19] Lambrinoudakis 1986; Yalouris 1986.

[20] See Chapter 4.

[21] Boardman 1967.

[22] E. Akurgal 2002; Rubinstein and Greaves 2004: 1073–6.

most substantial Archaic ruins visible at the site today are the remains of the Temple of Athena, which dates from the eighth century BC, with rebuilding in the sixth century, and is built on a foundation of polygonal masonry, with an approach ramp constructed in the same style.[23] In 2006, a number of rock-cut niches were found with images of Cybele/ Athena. This strengthens the suggestion that the cult of Athena at the site developed out of the worship of Cybele (see Chapter 8).[24]

Klazomenai[25]

The physical setting of Klazomenai offered a number of attractive locations for human habitation, allowing the settlement here to shift its location over time.[26] The general location of Klazomenai was around a harbor, backed to the south by a coastal plain, with low hills behind it. Just north of this settlement area is the island of Karantina, which was also settled at certain points in the city's history. The ancient harbor has now silted up and the island is joined to the mainland by a causeway, giving the visitor a very different impression from what the Archaic site must have looked like. Liman Tepe, a low hill near the old harbor, has been the site of important Bronze Age excavations.[27] To the west, an Archaic settlement area and oil-processing area have been excavated (see Chapter 4).

The most remarkable feature of Klazomenai is the sheer number and variety of different Archaic burial sites and practices identified within its immediate vicinity.[28] This proliferation may be accounted for by these burial areas being used by different social groups within Klazomenian society.[29]

Teos[30]

Teos is situated on a low hilly isthmus between two bays and it had a good harbor area.[31] These bays provided the city with harbors and were an important feature of its physical location. The discovery nearby of a Classical period shipwreck, by the rocky islet of Tektaş, is also noteworthy in the context of Teos as a harbor town, which can be presumed to have been connected to the east Aegean network of ports (see Chapter 4). There have not yet been any substantial excavations at the site, although there have been three surveys of the site by Béquignon and Laumonier (1920s), Numan Tuna (1980s), and Yaşar Ersoy (present).

---

[23] Mitchell 1985: 83.
[24] http://cat.une.edu.au/page/erythrai, accessed May 14, 2009.
[25] Rubinstein and Greaves 2004: 1076–7; Ersoy 1993, 2007.
[26] See Greaves 1999 on the same process at work at Miletos.
[27] Erkanal 2008.
[28] Hürmüzlü 2004.
[29] Ersoy 2007: 175–7.
[30] Béquignon and Laumonier 1925; Tuna 1984; Rubinstein and Greaves 2004: 1101–2; Ersoy and Koparal 2008.
[31] Ps. Skylax 98.

The archaeological remains of Teos are scattered across a number of cultivated fields and areas of scrubby undergrowth, making it difficult to appreciate the original layout of the city. Remains of Archaic buildings were found on the *acropolis*.[32] The most remarkable features of the site are the theater and the Temple of Dionysus, both of which date from the post-Archaic period. However, a surface survey of the site has identified a long building of ashlar masonry.[33] The city's Archaic *acropolis* appears to have been on a low hill above the theater and was evidently fortified by the sixth century BC, when it is mentioned by Herodotos (1.168).[34] The extent of the Archaic city is hard to judge. A later city wall, dating from the Classical or early Hellenistic period, enclosed an area of c.80 ha.[35]

Lebedos[36]

The ruins of the small Ionian city of Lebedos are located near the modern town of Ürkmez. It sits in a clearly defined south-facing plain, surrounded by hills. The site itself is on a small, low-lying defensible peninsula in the middle of the plain that still juts out into the sea with beaches on either side. The plains surrounding it must have provided the basis for its agriculture. In Roebuck's opinion the south-facing aspect of this site must have been a disadvantage due to the summer heat. It is hard to tell what traditional land-use in the area may have been as the site itself is now almost completely surrounded by holiday developments. Nevertheless, it is quite conceivable that the area was capable of supporting a good agricultural base for the city and there are still cultivated fields away from the developments.

The archaeological potential of the site for Archaic period material is hard to judge. The peninsula itself is ringed by an impressive set of defensive walls that border the sea, which appear to be of Hellenistic date.[37] These can be traced for almost their full length around the site. There has been little archaeological investigation of the site, which is unfortunate as it is under very real threat (the central area has been built upon and the walls are covered in graffiti). The site itself would certainly warrant systematic architectural recording before further damage is done to it, and an archaeological survey of the hinterland, which has not been subject to such extremes of landscape dynamism as other Ionian *chorai*, would reveal a great deal about its diachronic exploitation and settlement history.

Kolophon[38]

The impressive steep-sided *acropolis* of Kolophon is c.15 km from the sea, making it the most inland of the Ionian cities. In the Archaic period the settlement appears to have

[32] Béquignon and Laumonier 1925: 283–98.
[33] Tuna 1984. This building measures 38.46 m by 7.30 m.
[34] Béquignon and Laumonier 1925: 284.
[35] McNicoll 1997: 159–60; Mitchell 1999: 148.
[36] G. Weber 1904: 228–31; Roebuck 1959: 11–12; Rubinstein and Greaves 2004: 1080.
[37] G. Weber 1904.
[38] Holland 1944; Roebuck 1959: 11; Rubinstein and Greaves 2004: 1077–80.

been on the slope of the *acropolis*, although over time its core shifted.[39] Herodotos (1.15) refers to the *asty* of Kolophon, and it was evidently already a developed urban center by the time of Gyges in the seventh century BC. The summit itself is small and flat with commanding views to the north and east, and high hills behind it to the west. The valley that connects Kolophon to the sea (and its harbor at Notion and chief sanctuary at Klaros) must have been of vital strategic and agricultural importance. However, trying to reconstruct precisely what the environment and communications in this valley were like in antiquity is hampered by the fact that it is now covered with deep alluvium. This is most evident when visiting the excavations at Klaros, which must cut through an overburden of meters of alluvium to reach archaeological deposits. This crucial part of Kolophon's territory must be radically different from its Archaic self, and these changes must be taken into account when considering the three sites of Kolophon, Notion, and Klaros and their relationship to their landscape and to one another. For example, a Sacred Way connecting the three is strongly indicated by epigraphic evidence, but archaeological and geophysical research has yet to locate its route through the valley (see Chapter 8).

Excavations at Kolophon in 1922 had to be abandoned, due to unrest in the region at that time. As a result some records from the excavations were lost, making publication difficult.[40] There have been more recent, limited excavations at the site, which apparently revealed material going back to the Geometric period, but there have been no major new publications. It is therefore difficult to say much about the site archaeologically in the Archaic period, although it was probably an important place.

Ephesos[41]

Ephesos, one of the most popular archaeological sites in the world, has yet to reveal one great secret: where is its Archaic period settlement located? The Artemision at Ephesos, which is 2 km north of the center of the Roman city, is known to have been an occupied site from the Bronze Age onwards, in a swampy area below Ayasoluk Hill.[42] However, as at Miletos and Klazomenai, the area around Ephesos presented several locations suitable for settlement and the city evidently moved between these over time, possibly even during the Archaic period.[43] It was also subject to the problems associated with the advancing of the Kayster (modern Küçük Menderes) River, which eventually clogged its harbors and led to the abandonment of the city.[44]

Bronze Age defenses, tombs, and a water sanctuary all existed on Ayasoluk Hill, largely obscured by the Byzantine church of St. John and adjacent citadel that dominates the area today. It has been convincingly argued that this is where the Bronze Age settlement

---

[39]   Rubinstein and Greaves 2004: 1079.
[40]   e.g. Bridges 1974 on a Mycenaean-style tomb found during the excavations.
[41]   Alzinger 1967; Hueber 1997; Rubinstein and Greaves 2004: 1070–3; Kerschner et al. 2008.
[42]   Bammer and Muss 1996.
[43]   Rubinstein and Greaves 2004: 1072, citing Hdt. 1.26.
[44]   Karwiese et al. 1998: 31–3.

of Apaša (Ephesos) was located.[45] By the Roman period, the city had moved to be near the natural harbor that can be seen from the top of the theater on Panayır Dağı Hill and which, like others in Ionia, is now silted up.[46] The Roman city was located between two hills – Panayır Dağı and Bülbül Dağı – the area between becoming filled by a landslide, resulting in the superb preservation of its monuments (see Chapter 1). On the history of excavations at the site see Box 1.1 and on the cult image of Artemis see Box 10.1.

However, where the main focus of settlement in this area was between the Bronze Age and the Roman period is not entirely clear. Arguments have been made for it being located on the north side of Panayır Dağı,[47] on Ayasoluk Hill,[48] on Bülbül Dağı,[49] and under the *agora* of the Roman city, where houses of the eighth and seventh centuries BC were found.[50] The location of the city in the Archaic period was evidently not static, as Herodotos refers to an "old town" (1.26); neither was it nucleated as there are references to at least two placenames, possibly suburbs or localities within the city – Smyrna and Koressos (Hdt. 5.100). Koressos was evidently on the coast and may have been the harbor area, but the old coastline of the area has been silted up and lost, like so many areas of the Ionian coast, and the remains of the Roman period city have hampered excavations. Geomorphological research to trace the old coastline, new excavations in soundings and slit trenches in and around the Vedius Gymnasium,[51] and a reassessment of old excavation records[52] have together shown that an Archaic settlement, which the excavators have equated with Koressos, existed on the north slope of Panayır Dağı and was adjacent to the sea. It has yet to be proven where else in the vicinity of Ephesos there was settlement in the Archaic period.

The city of Ephesos and its harbor were favorably located at the terminus of a trade route that came from central Anatolia down through the Maeander Valley and over a gap in the mountains to meet the sea at this point. This community was obviously capable of erecting a mighty temple to Artemis, but we cannot yet balance our understanding of that great monument with an understanding of the city that built it because the urban core of the city itself cannot be excavated. In truth, we know relatively little about the settlement archaeology of Archaic Ephesos and should be cautious not to retroject assumptions about it based on the later, better attested, periods in its history.

Samos[53]

The island's southern half is the most favorable for agriculture and it is here that the city and its chief temple were located. Samos city itself sits on the south-facing slopes that

[45] Büyükkolancı 2007; Bammer and Muss 2007.
[46] Kraft et al. 2007.
[47] Alzinger 1967: 20–3.
[48] Büyükkolancı 2007.
[49] Ö. Özyiğit 1988: 94.
[50] Karwiese et al. 1996: 12.
[51] Kerschner et al. 2008: 21–3.
[52] Kerschner et al. 2008: 109–14, citing the field notes of Josef Keil.
[53] Shipley 1987; Rubinstein and Greaves 2004: 1094–8.

run down to the harbor from Mount Kastro, and the principal agricultural plain extends to the west of the city. The great Temple of Hera stood in the center of this plain, on its southern shore, where a small river had created a swamp.[54] In the city, the natural harbor was enhanced by building works by Polykrates (Hdt. 3.60) and has been traced by under-water survey.[55] As noted in Chapter 3, water was in shorter supply for Samos than in some of its Ionian contemporaries and this may account for the enormous lengths that the Samians went to in order to supply their town with water, constructing the 1,036 m-long Eupalinos Tunnel and removing 7,000 m^3 of rock in the process.[56]

The first trial excavations at Samos were conducted by Joseph Pitton de Tournefort in 1702, and in 1879 Paul Girard discovered the statue of "Hera" of Cheramyes (a *kore* dedicated to Hera by Cheramyes). Excavations were conducted by the Archaeological Society of Athens in 1902 and 1903, before the first German excavations under Theodore Wiegand in 1910. Since 1925 there have been continuous excavations here by the German Institute at Athens, with a break from 1939 to 1951.

Despite its being covered by the modern town of Pythagorio, it has been possible for archaeologists to recover a considerable amount of information about the settlement of Archaic Samos, especially its city walls and burial areas.[57] The city's walls were mentioned several times by Herodotos[58] and the *acropolis* was probably first fortified in the sixth century BC. The foundations of a polygonal city wall have been traced.[59] The city's west *necropolis* was located on the sides of the road that led out from the city toward the *chora* and, more importantly, the Heraion.[60] A series of test-trenches across the city have been used to locate Archaic water channels and it is evident that a great deal of effort had been expended on water supply and management in this period of the city's history.[61] The city is also said to have had an *agora* (Hdt. 3.42).

(Old) Priene[62]

As noted in Chapter 1, the Archaic period site of Priene, wherever it is, should more properly be referred to as "Old Priene" to differentiate it from the widely known Hellenistic phase of the same city. The location of this "New Priene" is as stunning as its archaeological remains, situated at the foot of a sheer wall of rock that also served as its *acropolis*. Below, there is a strip of land between the east–west cliffs of the Samsun Dağı ridge-peninsula and the alluvial flats that were once the Gulf of Latmos. Assuming that Old Priene is eventually proven to have been located in the same approximate location as New Priene, it is possible to make certain observations on its location. Unlike Miletos

---

[54] See Chapter 8.
[55] Touchais 1989: 673.
[56] Hdt. 3.60; Jantzen et al. 1973a, 1973b, 1975; Kienast 1995.
[57] Tsakos 2007.
[58] Hdt. 3.39, 3.54, 3.143, 3.144, 3.16.
[59] Kienast 1978: 94–103.
[60] Tsakos 2001, 2007.
[61] Giannouli 1996.
[62] Rubinstein and Greaves 2004: 1091–3; Rumscheid 1998.

immediately opposite it on the Gulf of Latmos, Priene is backed by very steep mountains that come down almost to the sea, leaving limited space for agriculture on the coastal plain. Although there is likely to have been a small track over the mountains to the north, the main passage over the ridge was to the east of here, leaving it in a relatively isolated location. The possibilities for growth of such a position were few and Old Priene was likely to have been one of the smaller states in Archaic Ionia.

The location of the ruins of Old Priene is still unknown but there are two possibilities: either down on the smothered coastline of the Gulf of Latmos, or completely buried under the later town. In the case of the former, considerable effort is being focused on geophysical and geomorphological research to try and ascertain its location which, if successful, might result in good preservation of any remains (cf. Magnesia; see Chapter 1). In the latter case, continued excavations at the site have not yet found extensive Archaic levels in the few areas where it has been possible to dig down below the extant Hellenistic and Roman period ruins and, even if successful, could never result in the exposure of extensive Archaic levels. As with Ephesos, one must be careful not to extrapolate back assumptions about the well-documented later period of the site to its Archaic period predecessor.

Myous[63]

On visiting Myous one gets an immediate impression that this small, rocky peninsula jutting out into the sea (now land, of course) must have made an attractive defensible location (see figure in Box 3.1). However, looking away from what was once the sea toward its barren and inhospitable hinterland at the foot of Mount Latmos, the limitations of that site's agricultural potential become starkly apparent.

Even after Myous was abandoned to the mosquitoes and swamps of the advancing river Maeander and its population removed to Miletos, or beyond,[64] its ruins were not left in peace and its stones were carried away to Miletos to be reused.[65] Consequently, little is known about the architecture of the Archaic city, although enough fragments of an Archaic temple to Dionysus survived to allow for this structure to be understood.[66] There was also evidently a cult of Apollo here.[67] Some features do remain at the far end of the site near the later castle and also where the peninsula joins the mainland. Here, a number of rock-cut graves resemble those found in Caria.[68] However, one in particular, situated on a rocky outcrop and approached by a series of steps (Figure 5.1), bears similarities in its form and situation to rock-cut features that have been identified as Phrygian cult installations, possibly associated with Cybele.[69] The date and precise character and

---

[63]   Rubinstein and Greaves 2004: 1088–9.
[64]   Greaves 2000b.
[65]   Bean 1966: 246.
[66]   B.F. Weber 2002.
[67]   Bol 2005.
[68]   Peschlow-Bindokat 1996: 37–42.
[69]   Vassileva 2001.

Figure 5.1 Cult installation at the site of Myous. Note the steps bottom left, leading up toward the grave-like feature cut into the summit of the crag.

function of this structure are unclear. Although a reconsideration of the site and its architectural remains has advanced our understanding of it, its archaeological potential is always likely to be limited by the removal of much of its building stone in antiquity even though it remains uncluttered by modern settlement.

Miletos[70]

Finally, the most southerly and most important of the cities of Archaic Ionia is Miletos. The physical setting of Miletos has changed more radically than almost anywhere else in Ionia,[71] to the point that its great harbors, that were such a distinctive feature of the city's plan and character, are no longer visible. As we have already noted, Miletos was able to assert itself over the neighboring smaller communities of Priene and Myous and is presumed to have been in a constant power struggle with Samos. Standing on any high point of the city today, such as the Byzantine castle above the theater, it is obvious why this was. On all sides extend the flat alluvial plains that were once the Gulf of Latmos, over

---

[70] Useful recent works include: Gorman 2001; Greaves 2002; Rubinstein and Greaves 2004: 1082–8; Senff 2007. For a full bibliography see Ehrhardt et al. 2007. See also the Miletos excavations website: www.ruhr-uni-bochum.de/milet

[71] Brückner et al. 2006.

which Miletos had extended its power, with the aid of a powerful fleet and its excellent harbors.[72] Immediately to the north can be seen the *acropolis* of Priene, the hills where Myous is located are just to the east, and lurking on the horizon to the west can be made out the shadow of Miletos' arch-rival: Samos.

In terms of its immediate geographical situation, Miletos differs from other Ionian cities in that it sits on the northern side of a peninsula formed by a low-lying limestone escarpment, rather than a steep-sided gneiss horst. North of this peninsula is a relatively broad, fertile plain, watered by ephemeral streams that run down from the escarpment. For 16 km southwards from the city, the Sacred Way to Branchidai-Didyma ran across this escarpment. This road had a practical as well as a religious purpose and connected the city to its territory.[73] The city therefore had a large, integrated *chora* that combined fertile plains with useful grazing lands, and this was to be the main foundation of its wealth.

The site has the advantage of not currently being used as a town, although it was the site of the small town of Balat until an earthquake in 1955. Its Hellenistic, Roman, Byzantine, and Islamic ruins, which are impressive, do not entirely cover the Archaic remains because the city's urban focus shifted across the area around the harbors over time in response to changing settlement priorities and landscape dynamism.[74] The whole city was enclosed by an extensive defensive wall several kilometers long that enclosed an estimated area of perhaps as much as 110 ha.[75] In areas of the plain where this is now covered by alluvium, it has been traced by means of geophysics and deep sounding trenches.[76]

The areas where the most Archaic material has been found are around the Theater Harbor, Humei Tepe – the very northernmost tip of the settlement, and on the Kalabaktepe and Zeytintepe hills to the southwest of the city's main core. Around the Theater Harbor there were warehouses and the Temple of Athena.[77] The earlier Archaic phase of this temple building was replaced by a new structure in the late Archaic period, only to be destroyed in the Persian sack of 494 BC.[78] On Humei Tepe, remains of a sanctuary of Demeter have been found.[79] The hill of Kalabaktepe, the shape of which has been modified by terracing, is the site of another temple, to Artemis Kithone,[80] and the most important evidence for settlement and craft activities. At Kalabaktepe seven occupation levels were distinguished, including two destruction layers – one probably caused by an earthquake, and the other by the Persian sack.[81] This continuous stratigraphic sequence throughout the Archaic period has allowed the excavators to create a detailed typology for the development of Milesian pottery.[82] It has been estimated that the city once had

[72] Greaves 2000a.
[73] Lohmann 2007a.
[74] Greaves 1999.
[75] Müller-Wiener 1986; Greaves 2002: 99–103.
[76] Schröder et al. 1995; Stümpel et al. 1997; C. Schneider 1997.
[77] *Milet* 1.8.
[78] Niemeier et al. 1999; B.F. Weber 1999b; Held 2000; von Graeve 2005.
[79] Müller-Wiener 1979.
[80] Kerschner and Senff 1997; Kerschner 1999.
[81] Senff 2007.
[82] Kerschner and Schlotzhauer 2007.

as many as 4,000 houses,[83] but this is thought by some to be an overestimate. Although it is unlikely that the whole city was as densely occupied as the *acropolis* of Kalabaktepe, or the Theater Harbor area, Miletos was undoubtedly a very large city and must have housed a substantial population.

The city probably relied on wells for its water. Since antiquity, the water table has risen and the site is now frequently flooded during the winter months, causing damage to the exposed monuments.[84] Despite this high water table, there have been no true waterlogged deposits at the site that might preserve exceptional environmental evidence, even in the low-lying Temple of Athena area. The Persian sack of Miletos created a destruction horizon across the site that serves to link these disparate areas of Archaic material together, although the interpretation of this horizon needs to be approached with caution.[85] The Persian sack appears to have been total and systematic, even to the extent that the stones of the Temple of Aphrodite were systematically smashed down to tiny fragments, making architectural reconstruction virtually impossible.[86]

The tourist visiting Miletos may often find its sprawling multi-period ruins confusing. The excavators have gone to some lengths to make the site more understandable to visitors, but ultimately such a mass of overlapping historical ruins is inherently difficult to interpret to the casual observer. Even though the ruins of the Archaic period are not generally accessible to visitors, the Roman theater and baths, the mosque, and the new museum are all worth seeing and one can easily form an impression of what a great city this once was.

Other Settlements in Ionia

In order to understand these large Ionian city communities in context, and to reconnect them with their landscape and territorial settings, it is necessary to look at the smaller communities in the *chora* that also made up part of the *polis*. Anthony Snodgrass wrote that small towns such as this reflect the countryside, and we need to understand them if we are to put into proper perspective the transient effect of decisions made by the rulers in their capitals.[87] Such communities are also likely to reveal important information on mediohistorical processes at work within the *polis*, such as demographic change and rural–urban (or urban–rural) migration, as well as the connection of human activity to the annual cycles of the geographical "structure" that they operate in, such as transhumance.

In a summary of his exhaustive survey of the Milesian *chora*, Hans Lohmann defined four identifiable levels of settlement:

[83] Gates 1995: 238.
[84] Brüggerhorr et al. 1999.
[85] Senff 2007: 322; see also Chapter 7.
[86] Senff 2007: 320, 326.
[87] Snodgrass 1991: 66–8.

- the *metropolis* (Miletos)
- extra-urban temples (Didyma)
- nucleated settlements (Argasa, Assessos, Pyrrha, and Teichioussa)
- dispersed farmsteads and herding stations in the uplands.[88]

Other than in the *chora* of Miletos, there are several Ionian states where the pattern of rural settlement hierarchy is beginning to be understood as a result of intensive archaeological survey. These include Klazomenai, Ephesos, Samos, and Chios (see Chapter 3).

In some of these (e.g. Ephesos, Samos) we are in the position that the extra-urban temples are better understood than the *metropoleis* (mother-cities) themselves. This is partly a combination of archaeological preservation factors and the interests of previous generations of archaeologists (see Chapter 1). Although extra-urban sanctuaries are a distinctive feature of several of the Ionian *metropoleis* (Miletos, Ephesos, Samos, Kolophon) they are not universal. For example, there is as yet no indication that Phokaia had a large extra-urban sanctuary and it is unlikely that the smaller states, such as Myous and Lebedos, had them either. Neither were such sanctuaries exclusively religious entities. As noted above, the Sacred Way from Miletos to Didyma also served a practical function in the landscape[89] and a small secular community probably existed around the temple, although this is unlikely to have been independent of the Milesian polity, as some scholars have suggested it might.[90]

The Sacred Ways of Ionia also served to connect the cities not only to their temples and their territories but also to smaller nucleated settlements. For example, the Sacred Way from Kolophon to Klaros ran through to the harbor at Notion, connecting a string of three important, interrelated communities. Notion, which is located in a commanding position on a low hill beside a bay, was later to become a *polis* in its own right, even taking precedence over Kolophon.[91]

On Chios, where there have been intensive archaeological investigations of the settlement and sanctuary of Emporio,[92] the temple site of Kato Phana[93] (Figure 5.2), the fortifications at Delphinion,[94] and other sites in the island's interior,[95] we are in the position of knowing less about the *metropolis* than we do about its territory. In Milesia, two nucleated settlements have been excavated – at Assessos (identified with modern Mengerevtepe)[96] and Teichioussa (identified with modern Saplıadası),[97] which was probably ruled over by an official from Miletos.[98] In the case of the latter site, these investigations

[88]   Lohmann 2007a.
[89]   Lohmann 2007a.
[90]   Tuchelt 1988: 427; Ehrhardt 1998; Greaves 2002: 117–24.
[91]   Rubinstein and Greaves 2004: 1089–90.
[92]   Boardman 1967.
[93]   Beaumont and Archontidou-Argyri 1999, 2004; Beaumont 2007.
[94]   Boardman 1956.
[95]   See Rubinstein and Greaves 2004: 1064–9 for the known names of sites in the Chian *chora*.
[96]   Senff 1995; B.F. Weber 1995.
[97]   Voigtländer 2004.
[98]   Herda 2006: 350.

Figure 5.2 Excavations underway at Kato Phana in 2000. In antiquity the sea reached to the foot of the excavation area. © L.A. Beaumont.

have shown it to have been an established settlement from a very early date,[99] which evidently endured the upheavals that wracked its *metropolis* of Miletos. The excavation of sites such as these, especially when combined with the application of methods for sampling for environmental evidence (see Chapter 4), will have the potential to tell us much about human–landscape relationships, even more so than excavations in the cities themselves. However, very few of these sites have so far been investigated and they are under threat from the intensification of agriculture and the region's burgeoning tourist industry.

Finally, but perhaps most importantly, one must consider the individual farmsteads that must have peppered the landscape of Ionia. These are an elusive type of site to traditional archaeological survey methods, but intensive surface sampling of sherds, combined with soil analysis, can tell us a great deal about them without the need for excavation.[100] Ethnographic analogy to modern traditional farming methods and hamlets can also add a useful additional perspective to such studies.[101] The importance of these farmsteads in supporting their more glamorous urban counterparts is spelled out by two events. First, as mentioned in Chapter 4, when Miletos was in a state of political crisis caused by the *stasis* between the *aeinautai* and the *cheiromachei*, the two sides submitted

---

[99] Voigtländer 1986, 1988, 2004.
[100] Alcock 2007.
[101] Lambrinoudakis 1986; Greaves 2002: 16–24.

themselves to an arbitration given by the Parians that control of the state should go to those who had the best-managed farms (Hdt. 5.28). Secondly, when the Lydians failed to capture Miletos by force, they despoiled the farmland and removed the doors from every farmhouse – an act that put the Milesians under great pressure to submit.[102] Both these incidents show that the politics of the city and its very survival were never far removed from the land, even in a seemingly sophisticated urban community such as Miletos.

It can be seen, therefore, that the prominent first-order communities of the big cities of Ionia did not exist in a vacuum. Rather, they were part of a network of habitations that were the essential component in articulating the human–landscape relationship in Ionia, and thus the four levels of Lohmann's typology were interdependent. If the popular impression of life in Archaic Ionia is one of an essentially urban culture of thinkers and philosophers, it is one that has been formed because sites such as these were overlooked by earlier scholarship. Now that the results of intensive archaeological surveys and environmental archaeological analysis are starting to be available it is possible to rethink our understanding of Ionia. In particular, and in keeping with the general themes of this book, it is possible to view the settlement hierarchy outlined above in reverse. Instead of viewing the settlement history of Ionia from the top down – from the *metropolis* and the temple down to the farms – we can achieve a different understanding of the region if we approach it from the bottom up, starting with the farmsteads and small towns across the land of Ionia that fed and clothed its cities and left their wealthy citizens free to indulge their intellectual interests.

The Size and Distribution of *Poleis* within Ionia

Geography played a crucial role in the formation of settlements in Ionia and their historical development. As can easily be seen from the descriptions of each Ionian city above, those that had ready access to good harbors and relatively extensive areas of fertile plain were those that were destined to prosper. This distinction between larger and smaller Ionian states is evident in a graphical representation of the number of ships that each city was able to field at the Battle of Lade at the culmination of the Ionian Revolt (see Chapter 7).

The larger settlements in mainland Ionia were those that were able to command relatively larger, fertile tracts of plain which may, or may not, have included sections of the valleys. One such example was Miletos, which was in a position to control a large geographically defined peninsula, of varying agricultural value, but with extensive fertile plains on the north side.[103] For at least some of its history Miletos was also able to commandeer, by virtue of its size and military power, the lower portion of the Maeander river valley, giving it even greater access to fertile land.[104] Ephesos was in a similar geographical situation in relation to its own harbors and access to plains.

---

[102] Hdt. 1.19; Greaves 2007b.

[103] Greaves 2002: 1–4.

[104] Greaves 2007b.

The smaller states of Ionia were limited in their growth by having rocky hinterlands, and were often located on thin coastal strips that back onto the ridge-peninsulas, such as Priene and Lebedos, or clinging to small peninsulas, such as Myous and Erythrai. With such a poor agricultural base, and hampered by adverse topography, small settlements, such as Priene, could not control the large peninsulas on which they were located in the same way that Miletos controlled its smaller, flatter peninsula, or the island-states controlled their islands. As a result a number of states were often vying for control of the relatively large, topographically divided, but inhospitable ridge-peninsulas. Four Ionian states laid claim to sections of the Mykale ridge-peninsula: Samos, Miletos, Priene, and at one time perhaps Melie (see p. 19, n. 72 and below). A similar situation is evident on the Mimas Peninsula, parts of which were variously occupied by Erythrai, Chios, Lebedos, Klazomenai, and Kolophon. Far from being deserted, these mountainous ridges were fiercely contested and are evidently rich in archaeological material.[105]

Islands are naturally defined parcels of land of varying size. In Ionia these include large islands of a size suitable for control by a single state, such as Samos, or those so small as to be incapable of sustaining a *polis* community, and instead falling under the auspices of neighboring territories. The large rocky island of Ikaros, for example, is situated between Samos and Miletos, but apart from a short period in the fifth century BC when it may have been home to a *polis* that minted its own coins, it was under the control of one or other of its larger neighbors throughout its history.[106]

The topography of Ionia is such that it favored the development of *polis* communities, each with its own defined territory. The mountainous peninsulas divide off pockets of cultivable land of varying size, which individually or collectively could form the subsistence basis for a sizeable *polis* community. In the case of the larger pockets of land, that community might become a fully fledged city, whereas smaller pockets might only sustain a village, destined to become subsumed within the political structure of a neighboring *polis*. Where medium-sized parcels of land were sufficiently isolated as not to be easily combined with other territories, we see the phenomenon of small, enduringly independent *poleis* such as Lebedos. On the Gulf of Latmos, where Miletos apparently controlled the smaller Ionian states of Priene and Myous, at no point did these smaller *poleis* cease to exist because of the Milesian military or political dominance over them. This is because each filled an environmental niche, however small, and they made sense as local settlement responses to that environmental opportunity. It was only the advancing Büyük Menderes River that forced them to *synoikise* with Miletos.[107]

The only possible case of an Ionian city ceasing to exist entirely is that of Melie.[108] The origins, rise, and demise of Melie are very unclear. The site identified by archaeologists as Melie is located between Priene and Ephesos, near the site of the later Panionion (modern Güzelçamlı).[109] This appears to be a favorable location for settlement, but a later inscription suggests that the Ionians made war on their thirteenth member and divided

---

[105] Lohmann 2007b.
[106] Greaves 2002: 4.
[107] Greaves 2000b.
[108] Possibly to be equated with Karion (Rubinstein and Greaves 2004: 1060–1).
[109] Kleiner et al. 1967.

its territory between themselves.[110] The historical veracity of these events is highly dubious, as are the punitive reasons cited for the attack on Melie. Other than this unusual and dubious event, the settlement pattern of Archaic Ionia appears to have been pretty stable, except for changes in the political or military control of certain pockets of land, and the slow ongoing processes of landscape change noted in Chapter 2.

The topography of Ionia therefore favored the formation of *polis* communities of varying sizes, each independent from the next, but Ionia was not unique in this respect. As Anthony Snodgrass has noted, there is something favorable in the nature of the Mediterranean that predisposes it to the city-state as a form of settlement, which has flourished twice in the region: once in the Archaic period and once again in the later Medieval.[111] However, geographical determinism alone cannot explain the history of Ionia. *Polis* communities were not formed in social, political, or cultural isolation, and it is to the cultural factors associated with their formation that we now turn our attention.

François de Polignac in Ionia

An important contribution to thinking about the way in which landscape affected the formation of Greek *poleis* was proposed by François de Polignac in his book *Cults, Territory, and the Origins of the Greek City-state*.[112] In this he put forward the thesis that in the formative years of the Greek *poleis* states defined their territory by placing temples, shrines, and cult sites at important political boundaries or on natural boundaries at the point of transition from cultivated farmland to natural wilderness.[113] The best site in Ionia to be a test case of de Polignac's theory is Miletos, not only because it has the most plentiful archaeological evidence from both urban and rural contexts, but also because, although in some ways exceptional, it is in a good example of a large Ionian state. The known temples and sanctuaries in Milesia are listed in Table 5.1, sorted here into de Polignac's classifications of "urban," "peri-urban," and "rural."

At first glance de Polignac's theory would appear to fit with the distribution of three of these sanctuary sites in particular, as they ring the edges of the fertile plain on which Miletos is situated at the western end. These are the peri-urban Sanctuary of Aphrodite and the rural sanctuaries of Athena Assessia and an unnamed *temenos* (sacred enclosure) situated on a hilltop overlooking the city that may be identifiable with a location referred to as "*to akron*" ("The Heights") in the so-called *Molpoi* inscription (see Chapters 1 and 8). However, the location of these sites can also be explained in relation to the viewpoints that their locations afford them. The Sanctuary of Aphrodite was situated overlooking the sea and harbors, of which she was patron goddess,[114] and Mengerevtepe afforded Assessos good views over the plains and bay to its north, east, and west. The sanctuary at "*to akron*," like many of the other cults named here, was part of the Miletos–Didyma axis of cult activity associated with the Sacred Way that linked these two places. Its loca-

---

[110] Roebuck 1979.
[111] Snodgrass 1991: 69–70.
[112] de Polignac 1995.
[113] For discussion of these themes see also C. Morgan 2003.
[114] Greaves and Wilson forthcoming.

Table 5.1 Known Archaic cult sites in Milesia (names of cults in italics are known only from inscriptions)

Type	Cult	Location	Key references
Urban	Athena	Theater Harbor	von Gerkan 1925
			Held 2000
	Artemis Kithone	Kalabaktepe	Kerschner 1999
	Apollo Delphinos	Sacred Way	Kawerau and Rehm 1914
	Dionysus	Kaletepe	Real 1977/78
			Pfrommer 1989
	Demeter and Kore	Humei Tepe	Müller-Wiener 1979
	Zeus	[Unknown]	*Milet* 1.3: 153
			Koenigs 1996
	Herakles	[Unknown]	*Milet* 1.3: 132
	Hestia	[Unknown]	*Milet* 1.3: 133
	[?Phrygian cult]	Kalabaktepe	Brinkmann 1990*
Peri-urban	Aphrodite Oikus	Zeytintepe	Senff 2003
	Hekate	Sacred Way/City Gate	*Milet* 1.3: 133
	Dynamis	Sacred Way	*Milet* 1.3: 133
Rural	Athena Assessia	Mengerevetepe	B.F. Weber 1995
			Senff 1995
	Unnamed temenos	Sacred Way	Tuchelt et al. 1996
	[?"*The Heights*"]		[*Milet* 1.3: 133]
	The Nymphs	Sacred Way at	*Milet* 1.3: 133
		"the meadow"	[P. Schneider 1987]
	Hermes Enkelados	Sacred Way	*Milet* 1.3: 133
	Keraiites	Sacred Way	*Milet* 1.3: 133
	["*The Horned One*"]		
	Poseidon	Tekağaç Burun	von Gerkan 1915
	Apollo, Artemis, Zeus	Branchidai-Didyma	Fontenrose 1988
	Soter, Leto, and others		Tuchelt 1991
			Bumke 2006
			Herda 2006

* This rock-cut installation may be associated with Phrygian-style cult (Greaves 2002: 86). The date of the structure is unclear. It may originally have been sited outside the settlement core of Miletos, only to be incorporated at a later date when Kalabaktepe was first settled in the seventh century BC (Senff 2007).

tion here may have more to do with this being an epiphanic point on the journey from Miletos to Didyma from where one first saw the temple in the distance, than with the transition from "human" to "natural" landscapes. Even this "human"/"natural" distinction is somewhat spurious given the economic uses and management of maquis scrub,[115] and the Greek countryside was always well populated with sanctuaries.[116] In fact, there

[115] Forbes 1996; Greaves 2002: 20–1.
[116] Alcock 2007: 128–30.

are more attested cults at the single rural site of Branchidai-Didyma than there are in the urban center of Miletos itself and this major cult nexus and its associated Sacred Way appear to be the real focus of cult activity in this landscape.[117]

Major extra-urban temples like Didyma are a prominent feature of Ionian religious identity (see Chapter 8). The locations of these major temples appear to be related to particular landscape phenomena. The Artemision at Ephesos and the Heraion at Samos appear to have been positioned in swampy areas, whereas Klaros and Branchidai-Didyma (both oracles) were associated with natural springs. Any argument that attempts to find patterning in the distribution of cult sites across the landscape is inevitably open to criticism because cult is motivated by a belief in the irrational, which does not invalidate the truth of that belief, but does call into question any assumptions that we make as outside observers attempting to rationalize such behavior. The Ionians obviously did have their reasons for locating their temples and sanctuaries where they did, but it appears to have had more to do with the particular landscape features of each locality than to do with *poleis* using rural cults to appropriate the landscapes around them.

There is also a chronological problem when seeking to apply de Polignac's model to Miletos. The site itself had been established as a population center of some considerable size since long before the advent of the *polis*, in fact from as early as the Chalcolithic [Aegean Final Neolithic] period, c.5000–4000 BC.[118] During the Bronze Age, when Miletos was a substantial and established center, there were a number of smaller contemporary occupation sites in Milesia, suggesting that Miletos' ranking as primary settlement in the region was already well established. These smaller Bronze Age sites include Tavşan Adası, Kümüradası, Teichioussa-Saplıadası, and Didyma.[119] The cult at Branchidai-Didyma also appears to have started life as a Carian or "Phrygian"-style Anatolian cult site, which would suggest that it predates the reinvention of Miletos as a *polis* in the Greek mold.[120] The fact that it is possible that some rural cult sites may have predated the formation of *poleis* as political communities does not, however, invalidate de Polignac's hypothesis that such cult localities played an important role in the formation of those communities.

Although it would appear that de Polignac's theory of the placing of cult sites on the periphery of the *polis'* cultivable territory might be challenged when one begins to look in detail at the specifics of their location in the landscape, as an approach it does still have some value. The idea that rural cult centers integrate the landscape with the city is a useful perspective from which to deepen our understanding of human–landscape interactions beyond the geographical determinism of a purely topographic or economic model. It is a fact that rural cult sites are often identified on the margins of workable agricultural land. Such locations made them easily accessible to those working the fields (or shepherding in the case of the Sanctuary of the Nymphs), but it may also be an accident of archaeological preservation. One might also extend the marginal transition from the

---

[117] However, it is essential to note that most of the evidence for many of these cults, including the *Molpoi* inscription itself, comes from later epigraphic sources.

[118] Niemeier 2005.

[119] Greaves 2002: 39–73; see also survey results by Lohmann, discussed in Chapter 3.

[120] Gorman 2001: 187, n. 37; Greaves forthcoming (3).

"human" to the "natural" landscape to viewing the liminal positioning of sanctuaries such as the altar to Poseidon on Tekağaç Burun,[121] which is situated on a coastal promontory, or even the Sanctuary of Aphrodite on Zeytintepe.[122]

To sum up, de Polignac's model does not appear to be directly applicable to Ionia because the chief settlements here seem to have been early foundations in their own right, predating the earliest evidence for cult activity at their rural sanctuaries. It is hard to demonstrate that the location of cult sites across the *chora* bears any relation to the formation and location of the *polis*; rather their location can be explained in terms of the local phenomena of the landscape, either physical (e.g. on crests or summits that offer epiphanic views of the land or sea) or religious (e.g. on the Sacred Ways connecting the Ionian *poleis* to their major extra-urban temples). In keeping with the general theme of this book, this discussion illustrates that it is only through a detailed appreciation of the specific phenomena of the landscape of Ionia that the region's history, and that of its cults, can be properly understood. That is not to say that the appropriation of those landscape phenomena and the cults associated with them into the physical territory and political operation of a single *polis* entity was not important to the development of such entities, but that the cult nature of these localities often predated, and was not dependent upon, the *polis* as a political construct.

The City and Ionian Identity

The modern visitor to Ionia is often introduced to its cities as being the apex of Mediterranean Greek urban culture, but how the Ionians themselves conceived of their land and their cities as part of that land may have been a very different matter. To try and understand the Ionians' relationship with their cities it is necessary to understand how they experienced their cities, that is to say their phenomenological relationship with them. In so doing we can begin to understand what the *Annaliste* school would call the *mentalité* of the era (see Chapter 2).

Despite the very solidity of their construction, cities are mutable entities. This applies not only to their dynamic landscape setting and the buildings that compose their urban environment, but also to the way in which their meanings are negotiated by societies. One only need cite the example of the reinvention of inner-city living in contemporary Britain and the clash between this and equally reinvented "traditional" country lifestyles to see how this can happen, and how fundamental it is to individuals' concepts of personhood and those of broader British society. The example of Sparta which was undefended and evidently lacked any lavish public buildings, although an extreme one, is perhaps an illustration of how considerably the physical structure of a Greek *polis* can differ from that of the Athenian "norm." Prior to the start of their association with Athens via the

---

[121] von Gerkan 1915; Greaves 2000a. This sanctuary is not located in farmland, but on a scrubby headland. The transition here is not from one of farmed "human" landscape to "natural" sea, but from one "natural" landscape to another.

[122] Greaves and Wilson forthcoming.

Delian League in the fifth century BC, the Ionian *poleis* may have had a very different relationship to the built environment of their cities from that which one might predict by drawing parallels to Athens or elsewhere in Greece.

To illustrate how the *mentalité* of the Ionian people could influence, and be influenced by, their built environment let us consider their cities' defenses. Walls often form an important part of our mental schemata regarding ancient cities. The image of Medieval European cities, for example, is synonymous with oppressive encircling stone walls with heavily defended gates. In Archaic Ionia likewise, walls were an integral part of the *polis'* self-identity.[123] In fact, the existence of walls has been used as a defining criterion for the *polis* itself as a political institution.[124] But the presence of walls also affects the social and sensual experiences of living in a city and it is this phenomenological aspect of Ionia's city walls that will be focused upon here, rather than their connection to the *polis* as a literary and political construct.

Excavations and surveys in recent decades have brought to light the sheer size and extent of the defensive walls at a number of Ionian cities.[125] These include Ephesos, Samos, Miletos, and most especially the so-called "Herodotean" walls at Phokaia. Surprising features of these defenses include their early date, their extent, and their design. At Miletos the gneiss foundations of the defensive wall on Kalabaktepe date from early in the life of the settlement here, its second occupation phase – the third quarter of the seventh century BC.[126] At Miletos, Samos, and Phokaia, tracing the circuit of the Archaic defenses has shown that each enclosed a very large area – in the case of Miletos perhaps as much as 110 ha.[127] But it is at Phokaia where the unusual structure of some of these Ionian defenses is most apparent. Here, in front of the forward face of the wall itself, a glacis (a sloping forewall) was constructed – a feature associated with the massive Iron Age defenses of sites in the interior of Anatolia.[128]

The existence of walls also imposes a hard delimitation on the spread of the urban core, increasing settlement density within their bounds and dislocating the urban population from the land. Although enclosed defended areas of large cities cannot have been entirely covered with housing or public buildings, areas such as the Milesian *acropolis* of Kalabaktepe or the Prophitis Elias hill of Emporio on Chios might reasonably be expected to have a higher density of habitation than an undefended low-lying rural community.[129] Ethnographic observation in rural Turkish villages shows that there are often multiple points of egress from the villages to the land, to give daily access to the intensively tended in-fields and vegetable patches. The relationship between villages and the land is therefore almost an osmotic one, with no clearly defined boundaries. In cities, the defensive necessity of strictly limiting and controlling entry points served to break this connection

---

[123]   Cobet 1997.
[124]   Hansen and Nielsen 2004: 9.
[125]   On the fortification of Archaic Ionia, see Chapter 7.
[126]   Senff 2007: 323.
[127]   Müller-Wiener 1986; Greaves 1999.
[128]   i.e. Sardis and Kerkenes Dağ – see Chapter 7.
[129]   Here Boardman 1967 estimated more than 50 houses in an area of 0.04 km^2 (quoted by Rubinstein and Greaves 2004: 1065).

to the land and must have had a considerable effect on the mind-set of the urban population of Ionia and their cultural and aesthetic interests.[130]

Another, and perhaps more interesting, way in which the city walls display and affect the identity of the city is in their actual architecture and external appearance. In the case of Phokaia, the city walls and the associated sloping glacis that fronted them were constructed of finely carved, close-fitting stone blocks. This sloping glacis structure finds parallels in central Anatolia at Kerkenes Dağ, in stone, and at Sardis, in mudbrick. Could it be that the Ionian cities were modeling their defenses on those of their Anatolian contemporaries as a form of competitive emulation, in the same way that Anthony Snodgrass has suggested they did with temples[131] and Yaşar Ersoy with burial *tumuli*?[132] This might account not only for their design, but also for their size which, although impressive, is dwarfed by those of Sardis and Kerkenes Dağ. If then, as Cobet has suggested, the walls are an integral part of Ionian cities' identity and self-representation,[133] then that identity was one that looked toward Anatolia.[134] Of course, it would be possible to dismiss these Anatolian parallels as being a predictable response to the forces that historically assailed Ionia from the Anatolian interior – the Cimmerians, Lydians, and then the Persians. However, in imitating Anatolian fortification systems the Ionians' regard toward Anatolia was not necessarily a hostile one and there are other reasons why they may have adopted such systems.[135] Whatever their reasons, the decision to adopt one particular form of architecture over any other is an expression of the Ionians' agency and their choices of identities, not those of their assailants.

A subject that has concerned many scholars of Ionia is whether or not Miletos, and the other cities of Ionia, were executed on some kind of orthogonal grid plan, or not.[136] The motivation for this interest has been the historical figure of Hippodamos of Miletos (b.498 BC d.408 BC), who is credited with having introduced city planning to the Greek world (Aristotle *Politics* 2.8). In a brilliant piece of research, combining geophysics with excavation and meticulous architectural analysis, the late Berthold Weber (b.1954 d.2005) was able to demonstrate that the southern part of the Archaic city was executed in long, thin blocks measuring 36 m by 90 m, with the Temple of Athena being oriented to fit within this scheme.[137] Such a system of elongated *insulae* has much in common with the plans of Archaic Greek colonies such as Metaponto in southern Italy.[138] This might seem very neat, that the Greek cities of Ionia adopted city planning from the Greek colonies overseas (including their own) and that this is then attributed to Hippodamos. However,

---

[130]   Humphreys 1972: 765–6.
[131]   Snodgrass 1986.
[132]   Ersoy 2007: 175.
[133]   Cobet 1997.
[134]   The theme of the form of these Ionian defenses is developed further in Chapter 7.
[135]   One is reminded of the Heuneberg, which was equipped with Mediterranean-style fortifications, perhaps by Greek military advisors (Kimmig 1975). Being on the Upper Danube, its enemies were unlikely to be Greeks.
[136]   e.g. Gorman 2001: 155–63.
[137]   B. Weber 2007: 355–9.
[138]   Owens 1991: 42–3.

when one looks away from the Greek world, and away from later textual sources, an alternative inspiration for Ionian city planning can be found in Anatolia. At the site of Kerkenes Dağ, which has already been mentioned as a possible inspiration for Ionian city defenses, extensive topographic and geophysical survey by Geoff and Françoise Summers and their team has shown that the city was laid out in blocks, some time during the late seventh century BC, and that the architecture of its large halls was inspired by western Anatolian (Phrygian) examples, not the Near East.[139] Although it cannot be proven that the Ionians (and their colonists) adopted the idea for city planning from Anatolia, or from their own experience of having to lay out and build cities virtually from scratch in the colonial world, the fact remains that if we only look for paradigms for Ionian action within the Greek world, we will only ever conceive of the Ionians as Greeks, and this may be misrepresenting them. Although Greek, they operated in the Anatolian world as much as they did in the world of the Aegean and they were not immune to its cultural influences.

Controversially, it is possible that the inspiration for the Ionian *polis* as a political entity also came from within Anatolia. This was the suggestion of the late Ekrem Akurgal (1997: 318), an influential figure in the history of scholarship in Ionia (see Chapter 2). Akurgal likened the Ionian *poleis* to the neo-Hittite kingdoms of Anatolia, describing them with the Turkish word "*beyli*" ("emirate" or "principality"), that is, small independent state entities with a defended core settlement and a single leader. Following a long history as a great power in central Anatolia and the Near East, the Hittite empire had collapsed in the early 12th century BC. Out of its collapse arose a number of small neo-Hittite successor kingdoms, one of which appears to have evolved into the Phrygian kingdom.[140] In the 8th century BC this kingdom can be seen to have influenced Greek pottery, metalwork, music, cult and mythology during Greece's so-called "orientalizing" period. In this context, it is possible to admit that the nascent city-states of Ionia were as likely to be influenced by developments in their Anatolian neighbours as they were the Aegean Greeks, whose formulation and promulgation of the *polis* as a political concept is well attested in their own literature of a later era. In the mediohistorical timeframe these neo-Hittite "*beyliks*" are as likely to be progenitors of the Ionian *poleis*, which were not only their peers but were also politically monarchies, as the Greek concept of the *polis*, which would only be articulated in literature centuries later. It therefore behoves us to keep an open mind about the Anatolian-Aegean context into which the Ionian *poleis* were born.

Conclusions

The physical structure of the city itself (the *asty*) would have been the largest construction project undertaken by any community in Archaic Ionia and its location and physicality would both reflect and determine the character of that community.[141] The physical

---

[139]   Summers and Summers 2006, 2008; G.D. Summers 2007.
[140]   Collins 2007: 80–90.
[141]   Although it should be noted that the construction of the city walls was probably the largest single construction event – see Chapter 7.

form of the cities, their size, planning, and defenses, can be seen to have reflected not just Greek cultural and political aesthetics, but perhaps also those of Anatolia, their nearest neighbor.

By mapping human settlement in Ionia onto the physical landscape we have seen in this chapter that the nature of the land was predisposed to the formation of small, independent communities that included a settlement, usually in a defensible position with access to harbors, and an adjacent pocket of cultivable land. Such "pockets" could be agglutinated into a larger territory by those states naturally advantaged by having good fertile land in their immediate vicinity. The land of Ionia therefore also predisposed itself toward the creation of larger and smaller *poleis* and the almost inevitable build-up of power-blocs under the larger states.

The cities of Ionia may dominate popular and philosophical writings about Ionia, but they were only one component of settlement patterns in the region, the others being cult centers, nucleated towns, and farmsteads. Although the natural state of the smallest agricultural communities is to be intimately connected to the land, this was not possible in defended communities, which created a disjuncture between the urban community (and the urban elite) and the land. However, they were not so inured to the agrarian basis of their state that when the Parians arbitrated in the Milesian *stasis*, governance of the state was rendered to those who had continued to manage their farms most effectively with, apparently, the consent of both parties (Hdt. 5.28; see Chapter 4). The true history of Ionia is more than just the sum of the experiences of a dozen leading states; instead it is built on an understanding of these rural settlements and being able to reconnect the cities, their politics and economy to the land that supported them.

6

The Ionians Overseas

Introduction

Having established in Chapter 4 that the economy of the Ionian cities, for all its apparent wealth and sophistication, was essentially based on agriculture, let us now consider another phenomenon for which the region has become famous, namely colonization.[1]

The colonization movement is one of the most remarkable achievements of Archaic Greece. In just a few centuries, hundreds, if not thousands, of overseas settlements sprang up around the coast of the Mediterranean and the Black Sea. Later historical traditions connect their foundation to various *metropoleis*, some of which are apparently confirmed by epigraphic sources from the overseas settlements themselves. Among these colonizing states were a number of Ionian cities, most especially Phokaia and Miletos. Phokaia is notable for the geographical spread of its colonies, from the Hellespont to the western Mediterranean; Miletos for the sheer volume of its foundations, said to be as many as 90 in number (Pliny *NH* 5.122). In this chapter, we will examine the complex economic and social motors that drove the Ionians to such extensive and prodigious overseas settlement.

The Greek language distinguished between two types of colonies: *apoikia* (an away-settlement) and *emporion* (a trading post).[2] It is not always possible to differentiate the two archaeologically. How can one distinguish between a settlement where a farming community also engages in trade and a trading post where the traders also farm? For the purposes of this discussion, the intentionally non-specific English word "colony" will be used, even though it must be recognized that this term carries some unhelpful meaning in the English language.[3]

There are many factors that might prompt people to leave home and set up new settlements overseas. These include shortages of food or land, to procure much-needed

[1]   Major publications on this topic include Ehrhardt 1988, Tsetskhladze 1998, and Möller 2000.
[2]   For discussion of the Greek term *emporion* see Hansen 2006.
[3]   Snodgrass 2002; Hurst and Owen 2005; Tsetskhladze 2006; Greaves 2007b.

commodities, to engage in trade, to flee from political persecution, or for religious reasons. There is no single explanation for the large-scale outward migration that was evidently taking place in Archaic Ionia, and elements of all these reasons can be read into the available historical and archaeological sources.

Understanding the nature of production of these historical sources is, once again, going to be essential to understanding the process in context. If we consider stories associated with the early founders of America, we see tales of religious persecution, famine, refugees, commercial opportunism, military cunning, success in adversity, chances for personal advancement in a new land, and a proud empire brought low. Some, but not all, of these narrative threads are also woven into the histories of the Greek colonies. Although no meaningful analogy can be drawn between these two settlement movements, what they do have in common is the creation of sets of stories that are varied and complex in nature and cannot easily be constructed into a single and unequivocal explanatory narrative.

Understanding Ionian colonization will therefore require not just an understanding of the archaeological facts and contexts in which the movement took place, but also a certain degree of the mythologizing and storytelling that necessarily accompanies it. This chapter will begin by analyzing the source materials available and the historical and archaeological problems inherent in their use. It will then go on to consider different models that have been used to account for Ionian colonization, and to propose a new one.

Source Materials

Studying the Greek colonization movement, including that of the Ionian states, presents us with a particular set of methodological issues. Crudely defined, there are two main bodies of evidence that one can use to reconstruct the Greek colonial movement: the foundation myths and other historical references, and the archaeological evidence from the colonial sites themselves. To this may be added the geographical character of the chosen sites. As will be demonstrated below, these datasets are often flawed and difficult to use. There are also limitations in the ways in which these datasets have traditionally been combined and interpreted by scholars (see below). In keeping with the general *Annaliste* methodology of this book, this overview of the nature of the available evidence is presented with the geographical information first, then the archaeological and finally the historical.

Location of the colonies

As with the *metropoleis*, understanding the geographical position and landscape context of the Ionian colonies can provide useful insights into the reasoning behind why they were established.[4] Although it is impossible to characterize Ionian colonies as being

---

[4]   Given the sheer number of Ionian colonies, this is necessarily a broad-brush survey based on readings and personal observations of the locations of some sites by the author.

Figure 6.1 The harbor of Massalia.

different from other Greek colonies in terms of their choices of physical location, they do share a number of common features in the way they relate to geographical phenomena in the landscape. Phenomena that appear to have been of importance are:

- good harbors: Massalia (see Figure 6.1), Apollonia Pontica, and virtually every other known Greek colony
- defensible location on a promontory or headland (e.g. Olbia-Borysthenes, Priapus), an isthmus or large peninsula (e.g. Sinope, Cyzicus), or small offshore island, perhaps made accessible by a man-made causeway (e.g. Apollonia Pontica)
- rivers giving access to riverine communications networks and the interior, e.g. Massalia (the Rhône), Istria (the Danube), and Olbia-Borysthenes (the Bug/Dneiper)
- proximity of mineral resources, e.g. Apollonia Pontica (copper),[5] Sinope (iron),[6] and Massalia (tin)[7]
- proximity to other natural resources, e.g. Olbia-Borysthenes (the timber of the Hylaea forest)[8] and Ankhilos (the Pomorie salt-pans).[9]

[5] Greaves 2002: 35.
[6] Yalçin 1993; Greaves 2002: 36–7.
[7] See Treister 1996: 152 for discussion of how it is thought tin came to Massalia.
[8] Hdt. 4.9, 18, 54, 76.
[9] Khristchev et al. 1982.

In themselves, there is nothing exceptional about any of these phenomena. They are all assets that any Archaic Greek community would find desirable and most Ionian colonies combine several of the desiderata of any viable settlement. What is interesting though is that their positioning relative to cultivable land is not so clear. This is a theme that will be developed further below. Neither were these chosen locations static. As was noted in the discussion of the physical locations of the Ionian cities of Klazomenai, Ephesos, and Miletos, their environment presented a range of possibilities for settlement and the way in which they occupied that space changed over time. For example, the early colony of Berezan was located on a peninsula but the settlement appears to have moved on-shore to the site of Olbia-Borysthenes after a period of time.[10]

The regions that the Ionians are credited with colonizing appear to have been quite specific. Miletos, or those who colonized under its auspices (including citizens of Erythrai and Klazomenai), appears to have settled its colonies in the north Aegean, Hellespont/Dardanelles, Propontis and, most importantly, the Black Sea. Phokaia chose the far western Mediterranean for its colonies, including Sardinia, southern France, and the coast of Spain. This regional division between the two major Ionian colonizers is easy to discern, but the reasons for it are less easy to see. This distribution and the apparent lack of rivalry between these two colonizing states may be accounted for by the way in which their colonial activities were mediated by an oracle, presumably Branchidai-Didyma.[11] Even so, it was evidently still possible for these two colonizers, and other Ionians, to consider founding a new joint community together on the eve of their defeat by Persia (Hdt. 1.170).

The geographical distribution of the Ionian colonies also demonstrates that they had no intention of making a contiguous bloc of colonies of the type that we might consider an "empire" on the Roman model. Each colony appears to have been an opportunistic foundation to take advantage of the physical attributes of its immediate environs. Evidence for the "strategic" placing of colonies only comes from later, non-Ionian, examples such as foundation of Byzantium by Megara and the Athenian *klerouchies* (colonies of Athenian citizens).

Archaeological sources and issues

The most intensively studied area of Greek colonial settlement is the region known in antiquity as *Magna Graecia* ("Great Greece"). This area of southern Italy and Sicily was so densely occupied by Greek cities that it was considered (and called) an extension of Greece itself. There developed here a Greek *koine* (common culture), essentially independent of its founding *metropoleis*, that has come to be extensively studied as a region in its own right. This region was an important theater in the Peloponnesian War and was consequently mentioned by Thucydides as a part of his narrative on that war. In later

---

[10]   The timescale and reasons for this shift are disputed. It is interesting to note a similar shift occurring at another famous early colony site – Pithekoussai on the island of Ischia, which apparently moved to the Italian mainland to form the colony of Cumae (Ridgeway 1992).

[11]   Greaves 2007b, and forthcoming (2). See also Bol et al. 2008.

history, this region was close to the core of the Roman Empire and was documented by Roman authors, and has since been the subject of much continued archaeological investigation.

Although there are some Ionian colonies in Magna Graecia, such as the Phokaian colony at Elea, for the most part the Ionians' main colonies are outside of this area, in which the most intensive scholarly research into Greek colonization (both ancient and modern) has been focused. It is therefore necessary to be cautious when extending ideas from Magna Graecia into the world of Ionian colonization, which presents its own set of challenges.[12] Ionian colonies are located either further west in the Mediterranean or north of the Aegean, in the Black Sea. These regions were less well documented by ancient Greek authors and so fewer contemporary literary references to the foundation of Greek colonies remain.

There are a number of particular challenges that face the archaeologist wishing to make a study of Ionian colonization. The factors that limit this kind of archaeological investigation include:

- *Sea-level change.* There has been eustatic sea-level change in the Black Sea since antiquity, causing the water level to rise, and inundating and destroying large sections of many known Greek colonies, which were invariably located on the coast.[13] For example, the lower town at Olbia-Borysthenes is flooded, restricting archaeological investigations to the area of the upper town. There is also the possibility that smaller or more low-lying settlements have been completely destroyed leaving an incomplete settlement pattern on which to base discussion.[14]
- *Modern cities.* Many of the localities chosen by the Ionians for their colonies were situated in order to take advantage of useful geographical phenomena. Consequently, these locations have remained important foci for settlement ever since. Sites such as the Phokaian colony of Massalia (Marseilles), which was located at the point where the Rhône-Saône corridor meets the coast and was equipped with a good natural harbor, are now the seat of major modern settlements. This makes the investigation of the earliest levels of the Greek colonies difficult and archaeological work in the heart of modern towns such as Marseilles is often restricted to temporal and spatial "keyholes" that present limited opportunities for excavation. Archaeology is therefore the victim of the Ionians' success in choosing good locations for their colonies.
- *Archaeological overburden.* As a result of this long settlement history, there is an overburden of material from later historic periods of occupation covering, and cutting into, the earlier settlement levels (Figure 6.2). Archaeologists have a responsibility to record and conserve all of these levels and cannot simply ignore or remove them in their pursuit of the earliest settlement at that site. Therefore, our ability to open up

---

[12]   Greaves forthcoming (2).

[13]   e.g. Khristchev et al. 1982: 201 on the salt-pans of Anhialo. This situation is not unique to the Black Sea. The same is true of the Aegean coast of Ionia itself, where the Bronze Age settlement of Liman Tepe can be seen to have a submerged harbor area, visible in satellite imagery (Erkanal 2008).

[14]   e.g. underwater exploration of the Taganrog Straits has recovered seventh-century BC East Greek pottery that has been interpreted as evidence of a possible pre-colonial trading post (Boardman 1999: 254).

Figure 6.2   Site view showing the densely overlaid occupations levels at Kato Phana: foreground – foundations of the Temple of Apollo; middle-ground – apse of the Early Christian basilica; top right – present-day chapel of Agia Markella. © L.A. Beaumont.

the Archaic levels of such settlements is even further restricted. There are some examples of colonies that have not been extensively built over since antiquity, most notably Olbia-Borysthenes and Histria, but we should be mindful not to overemphasize their importance just because they are better documented.

- *State of evidence in the metropolis.* Until relatively recently, there was a lack of modern stratified excavations and recording at the Ionian mother-cities themselves. Without such excavations it was not possible to compare the archaeologies of colony and *metropolis*. For example, in order for pottery studies to be made, there needed to be published typologies and results of analyses from the production site (see Chapter 9). This has only recently been resolved by publications based on the stratified excavations of the Archaic settlement area at Kalabaktepe at Miletos.[15] Even more recent has been the start of renewed systematic investigations of the archaeology of Phokaia which is buried beneath the modern town of Eski Foça, and like its most famous colony of Massalia, discussed above, archaeological work here is often restricted to keyhole operations.[16]

- *Publication.* Once systematic excavations have been completed it is essential that they are published, in order for the information from the excavations to be disseminated

[15] Kerschner and Schlotzhauer 2005, 2007.
[16] Ö. Özyiğit 2006.

and become accessible to other scholars. However, the excavations of both colony and *metropolis* sites take a long time to bring to publication and some key sites are as yet not adequately published.

- *Volume of data.* Despite the lack of publications at some sites, the sheer quantity of material that has been published from the many different colonies and *metropoleis* is considerable and it would be hard for any one individual to read and adequately synthesize them all.

- *Languages.* Once published, scholarship based on these excavation reports is further hampered by the fact that they are written in different languages. In order to access the primary archaeological material for the regions in which the Ionians founded their colonies, one would have to be proficient in a number of major languages including Russian, French, and Turkish, not to mention German for the Miletos excavation reports, and a number of less commonly used languages such as Bulgarian and Georgian, which are also used for academic purposes. There is, as yet, no single recognized *lingua franca* for archaeological publications in the Mediterranean and Black Sea regions.[17]

- *Cold War politics.* Scholars have been separated from one another by not only linguistic but also political divides. The politics of the Cold War made it difficult for scholars to cross the divides between East and West to visit excavation sites and museum collections, or to participate in academic conferences. Such things are a necessary part of archaeological research, in order to understand contexts, trace comparable material from different sites, and to exchange information, ideas, and perspectives. In the latter part of the twentieth century, trans-national studies of the Greek colonies in the Black Sea finally became possible.[18]

- *Methodologies.* As well as there being no single language, it has not been possible to agree on and adopt a single systematized approach to archaeological research.[19] For example, there has not yet been a single archaeological survey of the Black Sea coast, using an agreed methodology, that has proven to be effective in finding traces of Greek colonies, and there is continued over-reliance on historical sources. The post-Cold War availability of satellite images and new technologies, such as geographical information systems (GIS), means that systematic research into the location of Greek colonies in the Black Sea can now be conducted in ways not previously possible.[20]

- *Literary positivism.* A factor that has done much to limit the imaginative use of archaeological methods has been the fact that archaeology has so often been seen only

---

[17]   A very important publication that did much to begin to open up the great body of Black Sea publications to Western scholars was Balin de Bellu 1965 which presented French language abstracts of articles originally published in Russian. English language reviews of recent developments in Black Sea archaeology, such as those published in *Archaeological Reports* by John Hind (1984, 1993), have also been very useful for maintaining Western scholars' interest in the region.

[18]   In British scholarship, Gocha Tsetskhladze and David Braund were particularly important individuals.

[19]   It should be noted that the British Academy Black Sea Initiative (BABSI), coordinated by the British Institute in Ankara, is currently creating a number of useful databases of archaeological information from around the Black Sea. See www.biaa.ac.uk/home.

[20]   Greaves 2007b.

as an adjunct to history and sought only to confirm history, and not to follow its own agenda in the exploration of these colonial communities as entities in their own right. Archaeology has sought to provide a confirmation of the historicity of these sources, but very often cannot. For example, discussion surrounding the existence or otherwise of the Athenian grain trade has dominated studies of the economy of the northern Black Sea colonies, and yet there is much more to communities, such as Olbia-Borysthenes, that facilitated that trade than this one presumed activity. There is a danger that these important communities might appear to be one-dimensional if the full value and significance of their archaeological remains is not appreciated in its own right.

These are the factors that hamper attempts to achieve an *archaeological* appreciation of the Ionian colonial movement. Nevertheless, we are now in the position of knowing more about the Ionian colonies than we do about their *metropoleis*.[21] As an example of this, Norbert Ehrhardt's epigraphic, historical, and numismatic study of the colonies of Miletos was able to predict that there may have been a significant cult of Aphrodite in the mother-city, which was in fact subsequently found by the excavators there.[22] The political and intellectual landscape has changed in the latter part of the twentieth and early twenty-first centuries and there is now a renewed impetus behind collaborative archaeology projects in the Black Sea and a desire to understand the archaeologies of colonial lands and their *metropoleis* in conjunction.[23]

Literary sources and issues

The most important literary source for Archaic Ionian colonization is undoubtedly Herodotos because he is closest in date to the foundation of the colonies. Herodotos makes mention of a great many places in his work, but it was never designed to be a systematic gazetteer of Greek settlement and gives only passing references to Ionian colonies. Even so, it is possible to cautiously glean some useful impressions of the nature of the Ionian colonies from such sources.[24]

Writing in the first century AD, Pliny the Elder appears to be quite specific when he wrote that Miletos had established over 90 colonies in the Black Sea (*NH* 5.122) but it is not clear on what evidence he based this figure. Not only had much time passed between the putative foundation of the earliest Ionian colonies and the later writers who provided their foundation stories,[25] there had also been conscious historical reinvention of those stories by writers and the communities themselves to meet the needs of their immediate

---

[21]   Greaves forthcoming (2).

[22]   Ehrhardt 1988; Senff 2003; Greaves 2004.

[23]   e.g. the Panionion conference in 1999 (Cobet et al. 2007) was significant for the inclusion of scholars from both Ionia and the Black Sea regions.

[24]   e.g. a survey of historical sources by John Hind demonstrated the ubiquity of trade and traders in such early accounts of colonies in the Black Sea (Hind 1995/96).

[25]   e.g. Pindar in the fifth century BC.

political and social context.[26] There are a number of factors that need to be taken into account when using historical sources about the foundation of Ionian colonies:

- *The passage of time.* Many of the sources were written long after the initial supposed foundation date of the colonies themselves. For example, important sources include the first-century BC geographer Pseudo-Skymnos and Strabo, who was writing in the early first century AD. Even Herodotos is writing in a period when Ionian colonization was already long since finished.
- *Indirectness.* The foundation stories of colonies are often mentioned *en passant* as a part of the background to a description of historical events or localities. They rarely form the focus of historical narratives themselves.[27]
- *Mythologizing.* Foundation stories often incorporate obviously mythic elements, such as gods, heroes, or nymphs. Although it is often clear which elements of the story are mythic tradition or obvious invention (e.g. for reasons of etiology), this undermines their general sense of historicity.
- *Literary genres.* An entire genre of writing foundation stories developed as a poetic form. For example, the works of Pindar were written in honor of Olympic victors and included an elaborate back-story on the origins of the victor's home city. Such tales were designed to entertain and were not historically accurate accounts of the foundation of the city, and they need to be understood as actively constructed works of poetic invention, and not viewed as passive repositories of historical evidence.[28]
- *Invented tradition.* The foundation stories of cities can be invented, or reinvented, at a later date. There is at least one known incidence of this, when Apollonia-on-the-Rhyndacus invented a claim to have been an early Milesian colony, even though archaeological evidence suggests it was a later foundation.[29] As Irad Malkin has written, such traditions were "malleable" within the limits imposed by the collective memory of the community.[30]
- *Oikist cults.* The popularity in later history of *oikist* (founder) cults might also be seen as part of this trend toward inventing a foundation tradition for a city in later periods of history that may or may not have any bearing on the historical truth of the city's origins.[31]
- *Multiple foundations.* In a number of cases there is more than one foundation story for a single colony. This is often rationalized as the colony having been "refounded" at a later date, but other reasons may also account for such apparently contradictory foundation traditions.[32] Conversely, some colonies have no foundation traditions and

---

[26] Malkin 2003.

[27] Herodotos does, however, provide a detailed story about the foundation of Cyrene by settlers from Thera (Hdt. 4.150).

[28] Carol Dougherty's *The Poetics of Greek Colonization* (Dougherty 1993a) did much to bring about an important and much-needed reappraisal of the literary context within which such stories were created.

[29] Apollonia-on-the-Rhyndacus in Mysia (Aybek and Öz 2004; Greaves 2007b).

[30] Malkin 2003: 169–70.

[31] On *oikists* see Graham 1964: 29–39.

[32] e.g. Gorman 2001: 248 on the presumed destruction of Sinope by the Cimmerians and its refoundation.

important sites have been identified by archaeology for which no known name survives, let alone the identity of their *metropoleis*.

To sum up, the available historical sources are generally late in date and subject to conscious invention within literary and historical contexts that it is not always easy to identify or account for. As a result, even such fundamental historical "facts" as the date of foundation or the identity of a colony's *metropolis* may be skewed or invented to an extent that makes many literary sources unusable as reliable historical evidence.

Interpreting the Evidence

Narratives constructed from the tales and foundation myths preserved in literature are likely to be influenced by the literary, social, and political contexts within which these literary works were composed.[33] These foundation myths can be seen to generally conform to a standard template, as follows:

- *Oikist* consults Delphi (usually about something unrelated)
- Oracle issues typically cryptic pronouncement
- *Oikist* ignores whole or part of the oracle's pronouncement
- His community (home or away) suffers
- *Oikist* realizes meaning of oracle and fulfills it
- New community flourishes.

The moral of such stories is that the oracular pronouncements are (in the long run) always accurate, the gods are real and all-knowing, and mortals suffer if they ignore their religious obligations. It is also a necessary process for the *oikist* to go through because, by consulting Delphi and fulfilling an oracle, he is absolved of some other religious guilt or imperfection, which makes him purified and therefore a suitable person to found a new Greek community with all the religious responsibilities that this entails.[34]

In reading Greek literary sources about foundations and recognizing that they adhere to this template, we must also recognize that the template was a conscious product of a literary genre of a later era and that the details of historical events are likely to have been changed considerably in order to be accommodated within the template.[35] For example, Herodotos provides a detailed story about the foundation of Cyrene by colonists from Thera, led by their *oikist* Battos (Hdt. 4.150). Thera had been suffering a seven-year drought because Battos had ignored an oracle telling him to found a colony. This drought has been taken as literal evidence of climate change in the Aegean.[36] However, when understood within the context of the foundation myth template it can be seen to fulfill

---

[33] Dougherty 1993a; Malkin 2003.
[34] Dougherty 1993b.
[35] See R. Osborne 1998b on the influence of fifth-century BC Athenian practices on the writing of histories of earlier colonizations.
[36] Cawkwell 1992.

the role of the community "suffering" that ignoring an oracle brings. The fact that the drought lasted seven years and there are seven villages on the island should also make us suspect that the drought motif is a literary invention, or at the very least an embellishment of the core tale, because seven was a magical number that was associated with oracles.[37]

If we unquestioningly buy into these foundation myths, then we are also buying into the social and cultural contexts and attitudes that produced them. One such attitude is that the Greeks were inherently superior to the peoples they encountered both militarily and culturally. The reality of this position will be challenged below, but it was a position that was utilized by British scholars when they drew an analogy between their own empire in the late nineteenth and early twentieth centuries AD and the colonies of the supposedly culturally superior Greeks and their "barbarian" neighbors.[38] This erroneous analogy went on to inform the way in which Greek colonization was conceived of for nearly a century afterwards. For example, writing about Milesian colonization in 1915, Adelaide G. Dunham wrote: "The city served as the centre of a kind of colonising agency, and to it flocked those Greeks who were in search of fresh homes, much as the unemployed of modern times tend to drift into the harbour towns."[39] It is therefore not just the culture and attitudes of the ancient Greeks that can influence our interpretations, but also those of the contemporary culture within which we produce our interpretations (see below).

Starting with the location of the Ionian colonies, we can see that their position in relation to geographical phenomena of the landscape indicates that they were well placed to take advantage of opportunities for the exploitation of natural resources and trade. They evidently also chose positions that gave them security.[40] They were not, however, always well positioned in relation to accessible cultivable land. Only later did they develop a *chora* of the type seen in their homeland. For example, the early site of Berezan was abandoned and Olbia-Borysthenes flourished and developed a *chora* at a later date, when the Ionian presence in the region became more firmly established.[41]

The archaeological evidence shows that, initially, Ionian pottery at Berezan was found in contexts alongside local material, but that over time the Greek material became predominant.[42] Away from the colonies themselves, Ionian materials such as pottery and transport amphorae appear in prestige burial contexts – their apparent value being negotiated to give them new meanings by the local community that was using them.[43]

From historical evidence, we have an example of a Greek woman from the Milesian colony of Histria marrying a local chieftain (Hdt. 4.77). Their son married a woman from Olbia-Borysthenes and held an important place in his tribe, but was killed when they turned on him for following the Greek cult of Dionysus.

---

[37]   A text that purports to be from the Ionian oracle of Branchidai-Didyma makes repeated use of the number seven (Burkert 1994).

[38]   Snodgrass 2002; Hurst and Owen 2005.

[39]   Dunham 1915: 47.

[40]   See also Chapter 7.

[41]   Wasowicz 1975.

[42]   Solovyov 2007: 536–7. The earliest pottery is an Ionian piece dating to the seventh century BC (Kopeïkina 1972).

[43]   e.g. the Chian pottery in the tomb at Gute Maritzyn, discussed in Chapter 4.

Starting with the geographical evidence and then using the archaeological and historical evidence in this way allows us to construct a very different narrative about the process
of Ionian colonization than that which has previously been constructed based on earlier
readings of the literature. In this new narrative, the Ionians can be seen to choose sites
that are defensible and give them access to materials and trade, but not land. Over time,
their presence becomes more dominant and engagement with the landscape develops
into a recognizable *chora*. Finally, an isolated historical incident gives insight into how
they engaged with the local elite as equals in order to cement their position in a region
through marriage alliances, but that such "cement" was weak and the local population
could still assert themselves by means of violence. Such a narrative would no doubt have
been a revelation to those British historians who saw Greek colonization as a paradigm
for their own empire and justified their policy of racial superiority over colonized populations by invoking that analogy.

Colonial Interactions

Metropoleis and one another

The two Ionian cities that were attributed with having founded the most colonies were
Miletos and Phokaia, and the archaeological investigation of these two sites will continue
to inform, and question, our thinking about Ionian colonization. Other states that were
mentioned as having been involved in colonization were Chios, Erythrai, and Klazomenai. Historical and epigraphic evidence is the most important for identifying a *metropolis*,
because exchange of archaeological identifiers such as pottery was not exclusive to the
city that made them, as they could be carried overseas by cabotage, and not just as a
consequence of colonization (see Chapter 4). For example, Chian pottery is a common
find in many Black Sea colonial sites, even though their foundation is attributed largely
to Miletos.[44]

There are historical instances of Ionian cities collaborating to found a colony. However,
it is not really possible to describe these foundations as being "pan-Ionian" because only
two or three states were involved, some of which were not Ionian. Examples of joint colonies include Kardia in the north Aegean, founded jointly by Miletos and Klazomenai;[45]
Parion in the Propontis, founded jointly by the Ionian cities of Miletos and Erythrai and
the Kykladic island of Paros;[46] and the site of Amisos (modern Samsun), which may have
been a joint foundation of Miletos and Phokaia.[47]

The Ionians were also involved in settlements that drew their population from across
Greece, including the famous sites of Naucratis and Al Mina. Before the official foundation of Naucratis, which Herodotos describes as both an *emporion* and a *polis*, there may
already have been a Milesian base on the Nile Delta (Strabo 17.801–2) but under the

---

[44]   Bujskikh 2007.
[45]   Gorman 2001: 244.
[46]   Gorman 2001: 245–6.
[47]   Gorman 2001: 249.

Pharaoh Amasis (Ahmose, b.570 d.526 BC) Greek involvement in the region was formal-
ized into (and presumably limited by) the concession of a settlement at Naucratis.[48] The
site of Naucratis (modern Kôm Gi'eif in Egypt) was located on the Canopic (west) branch
of the Nile Delta, and excavations between 1884 and 1903 uncovered a scarab workshop,
a large fort or storehouse building, and several temples. Herodotos (2.178–9) lists nine
Greek cities that appointed port officers and were involved in the construction of the
largest of these temples – the Hellenion – including Ionians from Chios, Teos, Phokaia,
and Klazomenai.[49] Samos and Miletos were also present and had their own temples – the
Samians to their patron goddess Hera and the Milesians to Apollo and possibly also to
Aphrodite.[50] The most common pottery that survives from the site is that of Chios,[51] and
pseudo-Egyptian artworks made in Naucratis appear in sanctuaries in Ionia.[52]

Another site of interest to Greeks was Al Mina, an *emporion* on the mouth of the
Orontes River, a position that gave it ready access to the interior of the Near East.[53] There
are no historical references to the site and its ancient name remains unknown. However,
significant quantities of Ionian pottery have been found, especially from levels VI–V, and
Ionian merchants or mercenaries may have operated here.[54] Unlike Naucratis, the level
of Greek involvement in this site is unclear, but it is thought that they may have been in
a relative minority at the site, working alongside other groups.

Another interesting phenomenon of Ionian *metropoleis'* relationships with their colonies is when a colony supposedly went on to establish colonies of its own – in effect
the "grand-daughter" colonies of the original mother-city. Examples of this include the
Phokaian colony of Allalia on Corsica, which went on to establish the community of Elea
on the Italian mainland, and the Milesian colony of Sinope, which is attributed with
founding a number of colonies of its own, including Phasis, Dioskurias, and Gyenos in
Colchis.[55]

Even bearing in mind the multi-participant ventures such as Kardia, Parion, Naucratis,
and Al Mina, it is possible that we read too much exclusivity into the *metropolis–colony*
relationship. It has been suggested by this author that "Milesian" colonies were in fact
colonies sanctioned by Miletos' oracle at Branchidai-Didyma but that their populations

---

[48] Hdt. 2.178–9. Naucratis had evidently already been established by the start of Amasis' reign. The most
recent full treatment of the site is Möller 2000. See also Villing and Schlotzhauer 2006. For further bibliography
see www.sace.liv.ac.uk/apoikia.

[49] The non-Ionian states named as being involved in the Hellenion were Rhodes, Knidos, Halikarnassos,
Phaselis, and Mytilene.

[50] Aphrodite was evidently an important deity to the Milesians, and her cult was transported to a number
of its colonies (Ehrhardt 1988; Senff 2003; Greaves 2004; Nazarov 2007). Greek involvement in Naucratis
predates its official foundation by Amasis, and Miletos had evidently been heavily involved in the region and
the early development of the site (Strabo 17.801–2; Bowden 1996). It therefore seems reasonable to the author
to hypothesize that the as yet unattributed Temple of Aphrodite was built by the Milesians. It is from here
and the temple to the other main god of Miletos, Apollo, that the site's earliest pottery comes.

[51] Boardman 1986, 2006.

[52] e.g. a Falcon figurine from the Sanctuary of Aphrodite at Miletos (Hölbl 1999: 357–61).

[53] Robertson 1940; Woolley 1953; Boardman 1999, 2006. For further bibliography see www.liv.ac.uk/apoikia.

[54] Kearsley 1995.

[55] Lordkipanidse 2007.

🐎🐎🐎 Box 6.1 🐎🐎🐎
The *Emporion* of Al Mina

Al Mina is a mound located on the mouth of the ancient river Orontes, a position that gave it access to the interior of the Near East. Some of the earliest Greek Iron Age pottery to be found in the Near East comes from this site. Al Mina is unlikely to have been a Greek foundation as there is no evidence for settled Greek life, such as cult or burials, only pottery. More likely the site was an *emporion* (trading post) in which many different Greeks, and non-Greeks, were involved.

The archaeological evidence from the site shows that there was Greek pottery even from the very earliest levels, and throughout its history. The Greek pottery in the earliest levels was Euboean (from levels X–VIII, c.800–

700 BC) after which time the site was abandoned. When it was reoccupied Greek pottery included less Euboean and more Corinthian, Athenian, and East Greek (Wild Goat) styles (levels VI–V, c.700–600 BC). In the sixth century BC there was a gap in occupation. There are no literary references to the site ("Al Mina" is the modern Arabic placename).

At Al Mina, pottery from Ionia can be seen to be appearing alongside the pottery from mainland Greece. This does not mean that Ionians settled, or even traded, at Al Mina. However, the Ionians were evidently well known in the Near East and in the Old Testament all Greeks were referred to as "Yavan" (from "Ionian") (Genesis 10.1–32).

Sherds of East Greek pottery from the site of Al Mina. © Garstang Museum of Archaeology at the University of Liverpool.

may have been mixed.[56] The fact that these colonies appear to share the religious calendars and other religious institutions of Miletos would be entirely fitting with such an interpretation.[57] In effect colonists were traveling under a "flag of convenience" supplied by the oracle of Branchidai-Didyma and its own *metropolis* of Miletos.

Metropoleis and their colonies[58]

The most often cited evidence of enduring cultural associations between the colonies and *metropoleis* is cult and religion. In some ways this is a very good indicator of colony–*metropolis* relations because religion is often an obvious and self-consciously constructed expression of a society's identity. By contrast, burial traditions in both the *metropoleis* and the colonies were very varied and it is hard to relate them to one another.[59]

As we saw above, the Samians took the cult of their patron goddess with them to Naucratis and the Milesians' preference for worshipping Aphrodite as a goddess of the sea, rather than of sex and marriage, is also expressed in the cults of their colonies.[60] Epigraphic evidence shows that the colonies of Miletos also adopted the religious calendars and other religious institutions of their Ionian *metropolis*, such as its *phyle* (tribe) system.[61] However, there is no firm evidence that the Anatolian cults that are present in the Ionian *metropoleis* were transferred to the colonies alongside those of their local variants of "Greek" deities. Cult images that are similar in form to images of Cybele from Anatolia have been found in the Ionian colonies of Apollonia Pontica and Massalia.[62] It has been suggested that there is evidence for the cult of Cybele at the Phokaian colony of Massalia,[63] but the epigraphic[64] and iconographic evidence used to support this argument is generally late in date and of questionable value.[65] Whether this distinction between the presence of "Greek" cults and absence of "Anatolian" ones in the Ionian colonial is significant, or just an artifact of our inability to recognize the "Anatolianized" elements of their art, remains to be seen (see Chapter 9).

The Ionians were evidently distinguishable from other Greeks by their dialect (Hdt. 1.142) and the physical manifestation of their language is the epigraphic scripts of Archaic

---

[56] Greaves 2007b, and forthcoming (2).

[57] cf. Ehrhardt 1988 on the cults and calendars of Miletos' colonies.

[58] The most important studies of this subject are Ehrhardt 1988 (on Miletos); Ersoy et al. 2004 (on Klazomenai); and Morel 2006 (on Phokaia).

[59] Greaves forthcoming (2). See also Chapter 9.

[60] Senff 2003; Greaves 2004; Nazarov 2007. The cult identity of Aphrodite was complex – see Pironti 2007.

[61] Ehrhardt 1988. On the Ionian *phylae* see Roebuck 1961 (reprinted in Roebuck 1979) and Nilsson 1986: 143–9.

[62] These are on display in the museums of Bourgas and Marseilles, respectively.

[63] Naumann 1983: n. 90; Salviat 1992: 147–9; Roller 1999: 130. See Roller 1999: 131, n. 49 who disputes the identification of a presumed image of Attis, Cybele's associate, from Massalia, arguing that it is a Roman product. For a summary of cult sites of Cybele found at Phokaia see Ö. Özyiğit 2003.

[64] C.I.L. XII 405: a Latin (and therefore post first century AD) inscription to the Great Mother of the Palatine from Pennes, c.15 km north of Marseilles.

[65] I am grateful to Victoria Jefferson for sharing sections of her forthcoming thesis with me and discussing this question.

Ionia.[66] The letter forms and other features of the inscriptions of Olbia-Borysthenes show that it derived its epigraphic traditions from those of Miletos,[67] and the subject matter of these inscriptions is often religious.[68] Therefore, as might be expected, the epigraphic culture of the Milesian colonies also seems to mirror that of the state that is attributed with their foundation and which provided the model for their political and religious institutions.

Religion remained an important and abiding tie between the colonies and their *metropoleis*, and is reflected in the choice of deities, the character and epithets of those deities, the calendar of festivals and sacrifices, and the sacred texts inscribed in their honor.[69] Moving the cult of any deity so that it might be established in a new home was a significant religious act. One can understand therefore why it would seem necessary to the later writers of foundation myths that an oracle would need to be consulted prior to the establishment of a colony, so that divine sanction for the removal of cult objects, paraphernalia, and personnel could be secured.[70] Whether the imperative to consult an oracle before setting out on such ventures would have been so strong for the Archaic settlers themselves is unknown.

Pottery and other goods produced in the *metropolis* could be traded to the colonies by intermediaries via cabotage and do not necessarily reflect the identity of the trader or his customers (see Chapter 4). However, terracotta roof tiles of the type used on prestigious buildings, such as temples, were exported directly from Miletos to Olbia-Borysthenes and Istria, where they were imitated and developed into local forms of their own.[71]

Other than public monuments that used such tiles and adopted the forms of architecture familiar from temples in the *metropolis*, metropolitan influence on the domestic architecture of Ionian colonies is harder to show. For example, the earliest houses at Berezan were semi-subterranean pit dwellings and debate has raged about what the source of inspiration for this form of domestic architecture was. It has been argued that this form of building had its origins in the local population,[72] in Anatolia,[73] or even in Ionia itself.[74] The origin of these houses and their precise function needs further exploration through detailed excavation and recording, although debate on their origins and ethnic associations is likely to rumble on for some time to come. However, the fact that traceable Ionian influence can be seen in the public architecture of some colonies, but apparently not in their earliest domestic architecture, may have important implications for how we interpret the social, cultural, and ethnic composition of these communities

---

[66] Jeffery 1990.

[67] Knipovic 1971.

[68] Ehrhardt 1988.

[69] It must be remembered that the use of inscriptions was largely limited to religious contexts in Archaic Ionia.

[70] These writers are, of course, often reflecting the experiences and values of the foundations of fifth-century BC Athens (R. Osborne 1998b).

[71] Greaves 2004; Zimmermann 2007.

[72] Solovyov 2007.

[73] Greaves forthcoming (2), citing Voigt and Henrickson 2000.

[74] See Tsetskhladze 1998: 19–22.

and may lead us to question the depth of their so-called "Hellenization" (or "Ionianiza-tion") in their earliest phases.

Another way in which Ionian colonial settlements may have resembled their *metropo-leis* is in regard to their town planning. Hippodamos of Miletos is named by Aristotle as having been the first city planner.[75] New research at Miletos has shown that the Archaic city was planned in long, thin blocks that are reminiscent of Greek colonies such as Poseidonia (Paestum).[76] However, it may have been that city planning as a way of organ-izing Greek communities was first developed in the colonies, where they had a "blank canvas" to work with, and was only taken up by the *metropoleis* at a later date.[77]

The forms of relationships that can be established between the colonies and their *metropoleis* are therefore complex and, in the case of city planning, arguably two way. In their earliest phases in particular, these colonies were in no way carbon copies of their founding communities and great attention needs to be paid to the chronology of the interplay of Ionian and pre-existing traditions.[78] The most apparent similarity was in their cults and associated activities such as public architecture and epigraphic culture, but when, and how deeply, such Ionian institutions came to be adopted, both temporally and spatially, within these overseas communities needs careful consideration.

Colonies and local populations

Historical and literary sources connected with the foundation of Greek colonies fre-quently portray the native populations they encountered as outwardly hostile (e.g. during the foundation of Taras – Pausanias 10.10.6–8) or untrustworthy (e.g. during the founda-tion of Cyrene – Hdt. 4.157). However, the archaeological evidence, as outlined above, can be interpreted to tell a very different story.

Matthew Fitzjohn has argued that when "hybrid" forms of architecture are present in the earliest phases of certain colonies of Sicily, this is evidence that a state of equality may have existed between the in-coming Greek population and those they encountered (in this case the Sikels).[79] "Hybrid" behaviors are hard to identify securely in the archaeologi-cal record, and even harder to find in the one-sided historical record. Identifying exam-ples of "hybridity" from the Ionian colonial world is difficult because we do not always fully understand the precise nature of both the local and the Ionian cultures prior to the colonial encounter. Possible areas of "hybrid" behavior in the Ionian colonies might include their diverse burial practices, for example, but this needs careful site-specific consideration (see Chapter 8). If evidence of hybrid behaviors can be identified in the archaeological record of the Ionian colonies then, following Fitzjohn's reasoning, it might be seen to be evidence of parity in power relations between the two parties in the initial

---

[75]   *Politics* 2.8; Gorman 2001: 155–63.
[76]   B. Weber 2007: 355–9.
[77]   Owens 1991; Greaves 2002: 82.
[78]   The new typology of Ionian pottery proposed by Kerschner and Schlotzhauer (2005, 2007) will be of real benefit to those dealing with questions of relative chronology of colonies and *metropoleis*.
[79]   Fitzjohn 2007.

phases of the colonial encounter. From literary sources, evidence of equal power relations may come from incidents of intermarriage.[80] As will be argued below (in Chapters 8 and 9) finding evidence of hybrid artifacts and traditions is difficult when we know only little about the material culture of the populations with whom the Greeks were mixing. An example of hybridity from an Ionian colonial site is an Archaic bronze casting mold from Berezan that would have been used to produce artifacts that combined both Greek and Scythian features.[81] This suggests that, at the very least, elements of Scythian cultural aesthetics may have been adopted at the site.

It is necessary to judge each site on a case-by-case basis as the reactions of the local and the Greek populations to the colonial encounter are likely to have varied considerably. In some cases the nature of the relationships between Greek colonists and the peoples they encountered were likely to have been balanced and relatively harmonious, yet non-Greek "natives" were generally depicted as aggressive or deceitful in many foundation myths. The reasons for this may be twofold. First, in myths such as the foundation of Taras by Phalanthus, the "natives" represent a motif for the "suffering" that the *oikist* must go through in order to fulfill his oracle (see above p. 129). Secondly, in the period between the foundation of the colonies and the writing of the foundation myths, the Greeks had successfully repelled the Persian Empire (but only after much of Ionia had been destroyed). After this date, Greek literature established the "barbarian" as a model of non-Greek behavior.[82] It was therefore part of the literary culture of their time to depict non-Greeks as unreasonable and aggressive, but ultimately inferior, when faced with Greek culture. Once again, the reality of Archaic Ionian colonization may have been very different from the ideal image that we may construct from reading textual sources only.

Models of Ionian Colonization

It is becoming clear from new evidence from Ionian colonial settlements such as Berezan,[83] Olbia-Borysthenes, and Histria[84] that there were distinct phases or "waves" of Ionian colonization.[85] For example, in a study of sites in the territory of the Milesian colony of Istria, Alexandru Avram has concluded that Milesian *epoikoi* (settlers) arrived in waves around 600 BC and the mid-sixth century BC and were accommodated by the native population.[86]

There has been much discussion of the causes of Greek colonization, with varying emphasis being placed on the role of trade, politics, climatic change,[87] and demographic

[80] e.g. Hdt. 4.77 from the Milesian colonies of Histria and Olbia-Borysthenes; and from the Phokaian colony of Massalia Justin. 43.3.4–12; Aristotle frag. 549 Rose; and Plutarch *Sol.* 2.
[81] Treister 1998.
[82] E. Hall 1993.
[83] Solovyov 2007.
[84] Avram 2007.
[85] Identified by Tsetskhladze 1994.
[86] Avram 2007.
[87] Cawkwell 1992.

Table 6.1 A model of Ionian colonization based on world-systems analysis

Phase	Network type*	Evidence
Pre-colonization	Information network (IN)	Greek goods appear, or references to traders and travelers, but no evidence of permanent settlement.
"Emporion"	Prestige goods network (PGN)	Trade in prestige goods, evidence of permanent settlement (sometimes mixed in character).
"Apoikia"	Political-military network (PMN)	Greek culture predominates in religious and civic establishments. Creation of a *chora*.
Full assimilation	Bulk goods network (BGN)	Territory assimilated into *chora* of the *metropolis*. Exchange of large volumes of low-value goods.

* After T.D. Hall 2006: 97–8. See Chapter 4 for further discussion. On networks see also Malkin et al. 2009.

explosion.[88] However, the author has proposed a two-stage model for Ionian coloniza-tion, in which in the first stage a colony can be seen as a commercial outpost, which later becomes consolidated into a full settlement colony with the arrival of mass population from the *metropolis*.[89] In this model two phases of activity in the life cycle of an Ionian colony can be identified. In the first, the so-called "*emporion*" phase, the settlement exists as a trading post.[90] Archaeologically, in this phase of the settlement there is likely to be evidence of a mixed population with Greek and non-Greek pottery and cultural traditions being present. In the countryside around the colony, there are likely to be small numbers of Greek finds in prestige locations, such as burials. In the second phase, the so-called "*apoikia*" phase, increased numbers of migrants arrive from the *metropolis*, either in waves or en masse as the result of catastrophic events in the homeland. In the case of Miletos, Phokaia, and Teos, this can be clearly related to the taking of these cities by the Persians. In this phase of the settlement the culture and organization of the colonies comes under much more intensive Ionian influence. In the landscape, there is likely to be evidence that territory has been appropriated and now forms the *chora* of the fully fledged colonial community.

This model can also be related to the different elements of a world-systems analysis perspective, as shown in Table 6.1. In the context of Ionian colonization, the information network that typifies the pre-colonization phase of a colony might be conceived of as a network of independent traders operating by cabotage, the infrequent appearance of prestige Greek goods in native contexts, and the informational networks created by

[88]   Snodgrass 1980: 10.
[89]   Greaves 2002: 99–109; Greaves 2007b.
[90]   Greaves forthcoming (2).

oracles and cabotage. Tangible archaeological or epigraphic evidence for this phase of Ionian colonization will inevitably be hard to find, and it also existed on the edge of recorded history. Nevertheless, historical evidence for the pre-colonization stage of the model comes in the form of a Samian purple fisher in Herodotos' story about the foundation of Cyrene by Thera (Hdt. 4.151). Archaeological evidence that might be cited includes the isolated finds of seventh-century BC East Greek finewares at Nemirov, 200 miles up the river Bug from Olbia-Borysthenes in Ukraine.[91] Although we do not know precisely how oracles in the Archaic period operated, it has been conjectured that because they were visited by travelers seeking to make dedications and get advice and divine approval (but also to deposit information) before and after their journeys, they began to operate as "clearing houses" of geographical information for the age of Greek colonization.[92] Such geographical information could have come from traders, who appear to have been a ubiquitous feature in writings about Greek colonies in the Black Sea,[93] and from fishermen.[94]

At the start of the "*emporion*" phase one might expect to see the beginnings of a settled Ionian population in the archaeological record. Berezan was settled in the last decade of the seventh century BC and for much of the sixth century BC its architecture consisted of semi-sunken "dugout" houses, with plentiful imported amphorae, and Greek and locally produced pottery.[95] Away from the settlements, in the countryside around the colonies, Ionian materials might be expected to turn up in contexts that are suggestive of trade and there may be some adoption of Greek behaviors, but the population probably remained predominantly non-Greek. For example, a Milesian silver obol coin found in the hinterland of Phasis has been cited as evidence of metals being exported via Milesian sub-colonies on the coast of Colchis.[96] In the modern global world system, bulk goods such as metal ores and the fuels needed to process them are transported long distances to processing centers and factories overseas. However, in an age before bulk transport on this scale was possible, mineral ores were likely to have stayed at the periphery and workers to have moved to them.[97] In such a construction of Ionian colonization, the foundation of these sub-colonies by the Milesian colony of Sinope on the coast of Colchis would have facilitated the processing in the colonies of metal ores extracted from the hinterland.[98] As discussed in Chapter 4, metals were a key commodity in the prestige goods network.

The shift from "*emporion*" to "*apoikia*" phase marks a gear-change in the lifetime of a colony in terms of the volume of settlers. That shift might be slow and incremental, or equally it might be rapid. At Berezan in the third quarter of the sixth century BC there is

---

[91]   Boardman 1999: 243–4.

[92]   Parke 1967: 45–6.

[93]   Hind 1995/96.

[94]   Greaves 2002: 106–7. For a discussion of pre-colonization see Greaves 2002: 104–9.

[95]   Trade amphorae make up 80% of the pottery assemblage and include imports from Klazomenai, Chios, Lesbos, and Miletos. Of the fineware pottery the ratio of Greek to local is in the order of 80:20. See Solovyov 2007: 532–4.

[96]   Lordkipanidse 2007.

[97]   Kohl 1987; Kardulias and Hall 2008: 576; *contra* Snodgrass 2006: 229–31.

[98]   Metals were cast in the Greek colonies of the Black Sea – into shapes that include local Scythian motifs and are suggestive of the development of "hybrid" Ionian–Scythian forms (Treister 1998); see also Chapter 9.

a noticeable shift in the settlement, and semi-subterranean houses were replaced by "Greek"-style houses built on the ground surface, although some dugout houses continued.[99] As happened elsewhere in the Black Sea and across the Mediterranean, there was also a change in the pottery assemblage toward Athenian pottery styles[100] and a shift away from cremation burial rites with the presumed arrival of more Greek settlers.[101] Within the framework proposed above, this stage can be equated with the establishment of a political-military network of the world-systems analysis perspective. The types of evidence that might be cited to support such a shift toward a military presence in the colony are discussed further below.

Given the technological limitations of the age, and the geographical distance to the areas being settled, the phase of full assimilation of the colony into the territory of the *metropolis* was not possible. Examples of where this might have occurred in Archaic Ionia are when the islands of Patmos, Leros, and Ikaros effectively became part of the Milesian *chora*,[102] but it was never a feature of Archaic Greek colonization for *metropoleis* to create contiguous blocks of territory out of their colonies.

Development along the scale proposed above is not a foregone conclusion; pre-colonial contacts do not always result in "*emporion*"-phase settlements and such settlements do not necessarily develop into full "*apoikia*"-phase colonies. It would be wrong to think of the pre-colonial information network only as a form of commercial reconnaissance that was the prelude to full colonization, as settlement did not always follow. Examples of arrested development between the "*emporion*" and "*apoikia*" phases can be seen in Ionian overseas settlements at Naucratis[103] and the Phokaian colonies of Massalia[104] and Gravisca.[105] In these cases, established pre-existent and powerful first nations or local populations limited the development of the Greek presence within their territory and prevented them developing a *chora*. There are also examples of colonies that acquired a *chora* very soon after foundation, such as Chersonessos in the Crimea, which appears to have resembled a conscious "*apoikia*"-style foundation from the outset.[106] It has also been suggested that colonies that may have originally been established by Ionians later took on a Dorian identity as they grew, demonstrating that the ethnic identity of a colony (or rather that of its institutions) was mutable as it developed.[107]

The role of military activity within this framework needs careful consideration. As with the discussion of amphorae in Chapter 4, it is important to understand the precise context

[99]   Solovyov 2007: 534–7. That is not to say that the form of house, or indeed pottery, relates to the origins of the individuals who lived in or used it, but it may be taken to be indicative of a cultural, if not ethnic, shift within the character of the community.

[100]   Solovyov 2007: 537.

[101]   Damyanov 2005.

[102]   Greaves 2002: 3–4; Greaves 2007b.

[103]   Hdt. 2.178–9.

[104]   Bats and Tréziny 1985.

[105]   Morel 2006: 372.

[106]   Carter 2006.

[107]   Vinogradov 2007 on Herakleia Pontika and Kallatis, which were named as Dorian foundations in the literary tradition, but where new archaeological research has shown that they were originally purely Milesian and Megarian–Dorian colonists were received into them at a later date.

in which Greek/Ionian military presence was negotiated by the populations which encountered it. For example, it is possible that Greek mercenaries, military engineers, or specialists were valued by local non-Greek societies for the benefits and status that they afforded, without any element of feeling threatened by them.[108] In contexts such as these, limited military activity can be seen as part of the prestige goods network, rather than the more developed political-military network in which their presence, it might be argued, should be capable of effecting political change, or upholding or removing ruling regimes.[109] More subtle evidence of the existence of a political-military network is the ability of colonies to create a *chora* in the territory around them, which necessarily presupposes the ability to extend their settlement beyond the limits of the colony settlement itself without fear of attack or retribution.[110] However, references to battle with autochthonous groups can be viewed as part of the literary motif of "suffering" that the colonists must go through before their oracle is fulfilled and cannot be taken as firm evidence of conflict.[111]

The application of the world-systems analysis perspective to archaeological datasets has been criticized.[112] In particular, criticisms have been leveled that world-systems analysis is a product of the contemporary globalized world, and not applicable to less technologically advanced and integrated pre-modern societies. Such criticisms have been accommodated within the second generation of world-systems analysis, but the fact remains that the concept of world systems is born of our contemporary globalized society, just as the false analogy between the British Empire and Greek colonization was a product of its era. We must be cautious when making any kind of analogy between the present world and the past, but we must also recognize that by making such analogies we have a powerful tool for deepening our ability to relate to and understand past societies. As P. Nick Kardulias and Thomas D. Hall noted, world-systems analysis "facilitates comparisons," and concluded that "whatever detail is lost by taking this big picture approach is more than compensated for by the ability to link geographically dispersed cultures and perhaps to derive some of the lessons from the past that remain salient for the present."[113]

Another criticism of world-systems analysis is that it can appear to deny individual peoples their agency. In the case of Ionian colonization, as has been discussed above, the progression from pre-colonization to "*emporion*" or "*apoikia*" status was not inevitable, and first nations and local populations were important players in limiting and informing the nature of colonies' development. Although it may appear that within this model the

---

[108]   e.g. Kimmig 1975; Goudineau 1983. See also Chapter 7 for discussion of the significance of military engineering at Heuneberg. As an analogy, consider how the Scythian archers of Athens were perceived and deployed by that state.

[109]   As may have been the case for large groups of Greek/Ionian mercenaries deployed in Egypt, for example.

[110]   The existence of defenses around the colony itself is not evidence of a political-military network, as their chosen locations reflect an interest in defensibility even from their earliest days (see above).

[111]   A clear example of this is Pausanias 10.10.6–8 on the foundation of Taras, cited above, but Justinius (43.3) and Strabo (4.1.5) provide an example from an Ionian colony – Massalia.

[112]   For a summary of these criticisms see Hall et al. forthcoming, who note that many of these are leveled against Wallerstein's original 1974 formulation of a world-systems theory, not the updated world-systems analysis (Wallerstein 2004).

[113]   Kardulias and Hall 2008: 578.

Ionians were just part of a process of Persian expansion that pushed them in front of it, it is possible to see individual agency at work within that process. When the Lydians attacked Ionia and the Persians took land from Miletos after the failure of the Ionian Revolt, it reduced their capacity to feed their own populations and individuals must have faced choices about how to deal with this situation – one choice being to move overseas.[114] Where they settled would be determined by where they as individuals had opportunities to settle, namely where they had existing social contacts, such as family members, or a *proxenos* (guest-friend) – i.e. the colonies. In this way the redirection of displaced populations from the *metropoleis* to the colonies can be understood not as the *metropolis* exerting its rights over its colonies, but as a web of individual social obligations.

Like world-systems analysis, early *Annaliste* approaches to interpreting history were accused of denying individuals their agency and subsuming their personal choices within the faceless workings of a geographical machine.[115] It was demonstrated earlier in this chapter how forms of evidence for the three different tempos of the *Annaliste* structure could be identified in relation to Ionian colonization. Working within the geographical structure of landscape, it was the mediohistorical processes of demographic change and loss of territory to advancing powers from within Anatolia that prompted mass Ionian colonization.[116] Historical references, such as the Ionian defeat at the Battle of Lade, are only short-lived temporal episodes that crystallize those mediohistorical shifts and illustrate new geopolitical realities.

Such a drastic re-evaluation of the significance of key events in the history of Greece is not the nub of the challenge that the interpretation proposed here makes to traditional historical understandings of Ionian colonization. The real challenge is that it forces us to look beyond the narrative offered by the Hellenocentric literary texts and the narratives that they contain and to see the Greeks not as the key players in their own history, but as reacting to the expansion of the economic and military "core" created by the Persian Empire.

Konstantinos Vlassopoulos has argued that the nature of Greek history and the nature of the *polis* as a political institution mean that the Greeks stood outside of ancient world systems and cannot easily be reconciled with them.[117] Instead, he argues, the Greek world can be understood as a series of networks that connected it to larger world systems. Gocha Tsetskhladze has written that the motivation for the Ionians to leave their homeland and settle in the colonies was that they would rather live as politically "free" Greeks than remain under the Persian yoke.[118] However, interpretations such as these only perpetuate the literary constructs of Greek history – that the Greeks were different from other people and had higher moral values that rose above the demands of basic subsistence. When viewed demographically and economically, their engagement with the Persian world system and their need to move as it expanded is evident, because within

---

[114]   Greaves 2002: 104–9; Greaves 2007b.
[115]   See discussion in Chapter 2.
[116]   Greaves 2002: 99–109; Greaves 2007b.
[117]   Vlassopoulos 2007.
[118]   Tsetskhladze 1994.

the hierarchy of needs, subsistence and security are more important than the social imperative to live as "free Greeks" (see Chapter 2).

The nature of Greek historical writing is such that it always places the Greeks at the center of historical events, and there are no ethnohistorical sources to support the role of non-Greek groups, either Anatolians or the local populations of colonized areas, in the process of colonization. It therefore behoves us to try to extract a history for those non-Greek peoples from the archaeological evidence alone, and in doing so to see that they interacted with the Greeks sometime as equals[119] and even sometimes as superiors, not just as lesser "barbarians." Only after the Greek victory over Persia can this process be seen to have been stemmed, but that victory came after the end of the period under consideration in this book. Following that victory, Greek literature increasingly became influenced by the construct of "Greek" and "barbarian" as diametrically opposed ideals. Nowhere is that construct more clearly illustrated than in the *proem* (introduction) to Herodotos' *Histories* – our main historical source.[120] The attitude of the Ionians to the non-Greek peoples they encountered, both Persians and the local populations and first nations of colonized areas, is likely to have been more complex and more positive than this black-and-white literary fiction of the Greek/barbarian divide would suggest. The challenge then is not just to accept that the Greeks were not the only actors, or perhaps not even the main actors, in the story of their own colonization, but to try to understand them as players in a much more complex and subtle pattern of interactions that we must view through careful archaeological interpretations, and not just through the prism of later historical writings.

Conclusions

The archaeological and literary source materials for Ionian colonization present a particularly difficult set of challenges. In this case the archaeological evidence can tell a very different story to the foundation stories recorded by historians, which are subject to more obvious conscious mythologizing in their re-telling than perhaps any other type of historical evidence.

It has been proposed here that Ionian colonization occurred in stages. Following a period of pre-colonial contact, the commercial "*emporion*" stage was followed by a stage of mass colonization that was a response to the demographic pressure caused by the expansion into Ionian territory of powers from within Anatolia, at first Lydia and then Persia.

These were not the only reasons for colonization. Other reasons cited in historical records for sending out colonies from Ionia include the expulsion of tyrants.[121] One must also question whether the scale of colonization suggested by the historical records is genuine, as the case of Apollonia-on-the-Rhyndacus suggests there were later invented

---

[119] Fitzjohn 2007.
[120] See Chapter 1 for further discussion of the importance of Herodotos.
[121] The foundation of Sinope by the expelled Milesians Koos and Kretines (Parke and Wormell 1956: 81, n. 85). See Greaves 2002: 128.

traditions about colonization. The attribution of colonies to certain *metropoleis* must also be questioned, as archaeological evidence has shown that the ethnic identity of a community might shift during its lifetime (see above on Megarian colonies) and colonies that were described as "Milesian" may in fact have been foundations sanctioned by Branchidai-Didyma and composed of a mixed Ionian, or even non-Ionian, population.[122]

Colonization was not the only remedy for political, economic, and demographic pressures within the *polis*, and we see evidence of other solutions in historical texts. Alternatives included arbitration,[123] territorial expansion,[124] and the overthrow of existing political regimes.[125] In effect all these alternatives, like colonization itself, can be seen as alternatives to war either within the *polis* or with other states. What happened when these failed and war did break out will be the subject of the next chapter.

---

[122] Greaves 2007b, and forthcoming (2).
[123] e.g. the Parian arbitration – discussed further in Chapter 7.
[124] This was a common feature of inter-polis struggles within Ionia. See Chapters 3 and 7.
[125] e.g. the assassination of Leodamas, the last king of Miletos (Greaves 2002: 95).

 7

The Ionians at War

Introduction

Wherever there were borders in ancient Greece there was war.[1] In a land divided into fiercely independent *polis* communities, some of which had sizeable resources and ambitious leaders, warfare would have been a fact of life in Archaic Ionia and it was the medium through which the Ionians sometimes related to one another. The aim of this chapter is to examine the evidence for warfare in Ionia and to consider the ways in which the military practices here differed from those elsewhere in Greece and to consider if these represent evidence of a uniquely "Ionian" approach to war.

Again, landscape appears to have played an important role in the practice of warfare in Ionia, as it did in every aspect of its culture and identity. As we saw in Chapter 3, this was a region in which cultivable parcels of land were few and far between and *poleis* vied over control of these parcels, seeking to agglutinate them into a viable *chora*. It can be assumed that such exchanges of land might often have been concluded as the result of conflict. As always, the sea must be included in any discussion of the Ionian landscape and so we must include in any review of warfare in Ionia discussion of naval warfare and bear in mind the role that small islands played as parcels of land to which Ionian *poleis* laid claim and counter-claim.

Language, social customs, and dress are all important indicators of a shared cultural identity, yet when seeking to define the culture of ancient societies these particular traits prove to be intangible, elusive, and controversial. More tangible "hard" evidence comes from the artifacts that made up the material culture of past societies. The most commonly cited of these when discussing evidence of cultural identity are religious paraphernalia and art, including the pottery so beloved of archaeologists for its ubiquity and indestructibility (see Chapters 8 and 9).

Another category of material evidence that is useful when discussing matters of cultural identity is the materials of war. This is an extensive and varied class of artifacts, and

[1] van Wees 2004: 28–30.

includes weapons, armor, and artworks that depict warriors and battle scenes. The archaeological assemblages they are found in are also many and varied, including groups of votive deposits in temples and sanctuaries, burials, battlefields, and destruction horizons. To this list may be added fortifications and other defensive structures, which are not only artifacts but also contexts in their own right. War was the inspiration for the greatest works of Greek literature, including those of Homer, Herodotos, and Thucydides, and the importance of these to understanding the political context in which wars occurred in Ionia cannot be ignored. This rich assortment of material can be combined to tell us not only about how these artifacts came to be deposited, but also about the culturally informed behaviors behind their usage.

Warfare is an important expression of cultural identity because the making of war by one ethnic, social, or political group with a shared cultural identity against another group, with its own identity, throws their differences into high relief. Indeed those differences may have precipitated the very conflict itself. However, the way in which wars are conducted often demonstrates that there were also values that were common to both groups. For example, there may be common ethical attitudes toward when and how it is acceptable to make war, the treatment of the dead or of prisoners, and other key moral choices made during war. It is in these "choices" that we see the expression of societies' unique identities and their agency, their innate autonomy, to make decisions that reflect who they are and how they think. Warfare is therefore a useful indicator of common values, identities, and behaviors that are made manifest in the material culture of those societies and in the bricks and mortar of their city walls.

Yet, having stated that the materials of warfare can be used as an important indicator of cultural identity, it is necessary to qualify that with one important observation. There is an essential dichotomy at the heart of the study of warfare of which we must be aware: if one makes choices about the design of a piece of armor or the architectural form of a defensive wall, that decision is informed not just by the aesthetic values or cultural imperatives of one's society, but also by the prevailing technology available to one and, more importantly, one's enemy. The decision to shape a piece of armor or a wall in one way or another is literally a life-or-death decision and must be made in the light of an awareness of the very latest developments in military technology.

Furthermore, warfare was of such paramount importance that entire societies were structured around its practice. In contemporary Athens and Sparta it can be seen that Solon's creation of citizen classes and the construction of Sparta as the "ultimate *hoplite* (infantry) state" were responses to the introduction of the *hoplite* style of warfare. In Ionia, where there is limited historical evidence about the structure of society and the role of the lower orders in particular, it is virtually impossible to postulate how warfare may have been embedded in the socio-political structures of the Ionian *poleis* and even the existence of a *hoplite* class comparable to that seen in mainland Greek states is hard to prove.

This chapter will begin with the geographical features of the land of Ionia and how they may have affected the conduct of war. There then follows a critical survey of the archaeological evidence for warfare in Ionia and an assessment of the literary evidence. These will be combined to examine a number of key issues in Ionian warfare, including fortifications, Ionian mercenaries, the development of navies in Ionia, and finally an evaluation of what insights the practice of warfare in the region might give us into Ionian culture and identity.

Geographical Settings

As we saw in Chapters 5 and 6, the locations chosen for the Ionian cities, and those of their colonies, all offered good defensible positions. These included hills (e.g. Kolophon), peninsulas (e.g. Myous), and small offshore islands (e.g. Klazomenai).[2] As the majority of these sites were coastal, an adjacent hill would be used as an *acropolis* (e.g. Erythrai). Although the locations of some Archaic Ionian settlements have yet to be securely located (i.e. Old Priene), it is likely that wherever these settlements were they were probably defensible.

A diachronic study of the city of Miletos, whose environment offered several suitable niches for settlement, shows that the focus of the settlement shifted between the islands,[3] hills,[4] and peninsula[5] of the city's environs over the millennia of its occupation. Defensibility was the paramount concern in all phases of the settlement and major shifts were prompted by military threats posed by new enemies or technologies.[6] In *Annaliste* terms, the long-term geographical structure of the city's environment offered it certain possibilities for defensible settlement. How it positioned itself within that environment was determined not only by processes in the mediohistorical timeframe, such as changing demography, but also by specific historical events which served to highlight emergent new threats to the city.[7]

With secure control of the adjacent seas, having adjacent small islands and a good harbor close to the heart of the city was a distinct advantage for many Ionian communities. However, when that security was lost, they became a defensive liability. For example, the city of Miletos was taken twice by sea – in both cases loss of control of the island of Lade gave the enemy easy access to the harbors that penetrated deep into the core of the city.[8] Therefore, certain geographical features of the Ionian cities could be either an asset or a liability depending on the specific circumstances of each military engagement, and their defensive value needs to be judged accordingly.

---

[2] These positions, although defensible, are all relatively low-lying. It was only with later changes in military technology and tactics that elevated positions were sought (Shipley 1996: 10). On the importance of defense in general see Rowlands 1972.

[3] In prehistoric times the area the city now occupies was apparently an archipelago of small islands (Niemeier 2005; Brückner et al. 2006). The island of Lade, which can clearly be seen nearby, was too far away to be reached by a causeway and was apparently never occupied, although it had an important defensive function (Greaves 2000a; see below).

[4] Kalabaktepe was occupied from the Geometric period until the end of the Classical period (Senff 2007). Kale Tepe was occupied from the Archaic period onwards and became the focus of the Byzantine settlement (Greaves 1999).

[5] Once formed (see n. 4, above), the city peninsula of Miletos was to be the main focus of the settlement from the Archaic period until the abandonment of the Turkish village of Balat in AD 1955.

[6] Greaves 1999.

[7] Greaves 1999.

[8] Greaves 2000a – the Persian attack of 494 BC and that of Philip V in 200 BC.

Archaeological Contexts and Materials

As with any archaeological artifacts, in order to interpret their use correctly it is essential to understand the materials of war in their proper context of discovery. For example, when considering highly decorated arms and armor dedicated in temples we must question whether they were ever designed to be used in combat or whether they are merely ornamented display items.[9] An example of such materials from Ionia is a series of metal discs, which may have been the decorated bosses of shields, found in the Sanctuary of Aphrodite on Zeytintepe at Miletos.[10]

There is an important difference between ways in which arms and armor enter the archaeological record and those of other artifacts. Pottery and similar domestic materials are usually deposited by accidental breaking and dropping, or as rubbish. However, arms and armor are generally deliberately deposited in specific contexts and accidental loss is rare. They can also be hoarded for recycling or for personal curation. Destruction deposits and battlefields are an exception but even these yield surprisingly few artifacts as the scene would have been scoured for any arms that might be reused or retrieved to erect a trophy or use as dedications in temples. Therefore most arms and armor are found as the result of deliberate acts of deposition and this should affect how we interpret them.

Another complicating factor in the survival of military artifacts is the fact that they were made of metal and are subject to the three Rs: rust, reuse, and robbery.[11] Under normal soil conditions, metal artifacts might be expected to survive reasonably well but the value of metal means that it will almost always be recovered and smelted down for reuse. Temples, where many weapons would have been deposited, have long been the target for those seeking booty, either ancient invaders, or modern illegal excavations seeking goods for the art market.

Votive deposits

In common with many ancient cultures, weapons were probably left as votive offerings in temples in Ionia and so the region's major temples are once again a key source about Ionian cultural life. The recent discovery of a temple 800 m up in the Samsun Dağı mountains at Çatallar Tepe, purportedly the "Panionion" itself, included a room in which were deposited seven spearheads, a *sauroter* (a point on the opposite end of a spear to the head), and a bronze cuirass.[12] Although not on the same scale as the major *panhellenic* (sacred to all Greeks) sanctuary at Olympia, where 350 helmets, 280 shields, 225 greaves, and 33

---

[9]   e.g. some of the armor recovered from Olympia is finely decorated and it is unlikely that it was intended for use in combat.

[10]   e.g. von Graeve 2007, esp. figs 6 and 7.

[11]   Greaves 2007b: 12.

[12]   Lohmann 2007b.

breastplates that had been dedicated over centuries have been found during excavations,[13] it does show that Ionians followed the practice of dedicating arms in temples. Perhaps the elevation and sheer remoteness of the Çatallar Tepe temple protected it from robbery in antiquity, although sadly not in recent times when it was attacked with a bulldozer.[14] Examples of dedicated arms and armor from Ionia are few because most temples were systematically robbed in antiquity.[15] It might be assumed that dedications of the materials of war would be deemed inappropriate in the repositories of the best-preserved temples in Ionia, such as the temples to Artemis at Samos and Ephesos, as she is a deity not generally associated with warcraft.[16] For example, the *acropolis* sanctuary of Athena at Emporio on Chios included military paraphernalia, whereas the votives in the harbor sanctuary featured mainly fish-hooks.[17] Written accounts similarly record great wealth in the temples of the near-contemporary eastern Anatolian culture of Urartu, such as Mussair.[18] Such reports might appear exaggerated, but when the temple repositories of the Urartian site of Ayanis[19] were found intact, they held a phenomenal number of bronze shields and weapons because the site had remained unrobbed since its destruction in a single cataclysmic event.[20] It is interesting to note that shields of Urartian type have been found at sanctuaries across the Greek world, including Miletos,[21] and elements of Urartian temple architecture may have influenced the design of the temple at Branchidai-Didyma.[22] Whether dedications of arms and armor were made in the early Ionian temples on the same scale as those of their contemporaries in Urartu is unclear, but the two cultures do appear to have been in some form of contact. Perhaps it is only at sites like Olympia and Ayanis that we get a real glimpse of just what is missing from the temples of many ancient cultures, including Ionia, in terms of the volume of arms and armor dedicated there.

Burials

Warrior burials are an important source of archaeological finds of arms and armor in many cultures, but they are generally not a feature of Archaic Greek culture.[23] In Ionia, where Archaic cemeteries have been found and graves are intact, they generally do not contain arms.[24] Even where a high-prestige Archaic grave, the Lion Tomb in Miletos, was

---

[13]   J.M. Hall 2007: 165.

[14]   Lohmann 2007b: 576.

[15]   At Branchidai-Didyma, for example, Herodotos (1.92) writes that the sanctuary was endowed with great riches, but these were taken when the site was sacked by the Persians in 494 BC.

[16]   Although Simon 1986 notes that the character of the god is a secondary factor in determining votive objects over that of the dedicator.

[17]   R. Osborne 2007: 253. On the martial character of the East Greek Athena, see Villing 1998: 159–63.

[18]   Thureau-Dangin 1912; Luckenbill 1927.

[19]   Urartian Rusahinili[KUR]Eidurukai.

[20]   Çilingiroğlu and Derin 2001; Çilingiroğlu 2007.

[21]   Boardman 1999: 58–60.

[22]   Greaves 2002: 111–14.

[23]   A famous, and significant, exception is the three warrior burials from Argos (Snodgrass 2006: 309).

[24]   This was evidently not the case in Ionia in the Bronze Age as a number of swords were found from the Değirmentepe tombs of Miletos (Niemeier 2005).

found unrobbed no arms were found despite there being other metal goods including two silver bowls.[25] Burial practices appear to have varied substantially from one Ionian city to the next, but burial with weapons does not appear to have been a feature of any of these local burial traditions in the Archaic period (see Chapter 8). In this regard, the Ionians shared a common practice with their fellow Greeks across the Aegean.

Battlefields

No battlefields on land have been securely identified in Ionia. This is to be expected for a number of reasons: the historically attested conflicts that we know about involved besieging and destroying cities (e.g. Hdt. 6.18); some attacks involved only laying waste to the enemy's *chora* (e.g. Hdt. 1.19); and because battlefields are notoriously hard to identify in the absence of explicit literary evidence. The most important recorded battle in the history of Archaic Ionia was the sea battle off the island of Lade immediately adjacent to Miletos. Control of this small, yet strategically vital, island was the secret to control of the city of Miletos itself.[26] It is hard to understand just how the battle around this island may have unfolded because it has since been engulfed by the advancing alluvium of the Maeander River and today it is just a low hill in the flat alluvial plains that surround the now land-locked ruins of Miletos (see Chapter 3).[27]

Destruction deposits

Herodotos recorded the destruction by the Persians of Miletos (6.18), Branchidai-Didyma (6.18),[28] and Sardis (1.85). Excavations at all these sites have uncovered evidence of destruction levels that have been equated by the excavators with the events described by Herodotos. Together, the excavation of these destruction levels creates a "destruction horizon" of near-contemporary destructions across the region and has given us valuable insight into the Persians' methods of war at that time.

An example of how careful excavation has given us one such insight comes from the Temple of Aphrodite on Zeytintepe at Miletos.[29] This was evidently an important and sizeable sanctuary that had recently been rebuilt toward the very end of the Archaic period,[30] but when the Persians sacked the building in 494 BC it was so totally destroyed that it appears to have been systematically broken down into small pieces, making it impossible to reconstruct its original architecture. This strategy of total destruction

---

[25]   Forbeck and Heres 1997.

[26]   Greaves 2000a.

[27]   Myres 1954 provides a detailed description of the area and speculates on the conduct of the battle.

[28]   It is now generally agreed that the temple was taken as part of the sack of Miletos in 494 BC (Tuchelt 1988: 427–30).

[29]   Senff 2003.

[30]   von Graeve 2005.

appears to have been a deliberate policy of the Persians targeted at this important sanctuary, a practice that is seen elsewhere in the Near East.[31]

At Miletos, Herodotos' description of the Persian sack of the city has dominated the interpretation of many of the city's remains. For example, a great deal of debate has surrounded the dating of the "new" Temple of Athena near the Theater Harbor. Stylistically the temple is so close in date to the destruction of 494 BC that its construction could be argued either way. New excavations recovered a fragment of architrave from a nearby well filled with rubble from the destruction of 494 BC.[32] This proves that the temple must have been in existence before the destruction. Also, excavations at the Temple of Aphrodite showed that it had two construction phases in the Archaic period, as is now being proposed for the Temple of Athena, further strengthening this interpretation.[33] This debate has only served to highlight the absolute necessity of rigorous excavation methods of all archaeological deposits, even those that apparently result from a major cataclysmic event.

During excavations elsewhere in Miletos, a layer of black soil containing fragments of what appeared to be degraded and burnt pottery was found in a deep sounding under a Hellenistic *heroon* (shrine to a hero) in the heart of the Hellenistic/Roman city. This initially had the appearance of another destruction deposit from the Persian sack of 494 BC, but was actually found to be mixed redeposited material including prehistoric Minoan pottery.[34] Rather than being a destruction deposit from 494 BC, this layer appears to have been a leveling-off of material from that destruction, presumably as part of a later building program.[35] Even at a site that is historically famous for its total destruction at the hands of the Persians, it is only through careful attention to detail that genuine destruction deposits can be identified. For example, in the domestic and artisan quarter of Miletos, at Kalabaktepe, a destruction layer was found which contained very few finds of any description in any of the houses. Of the pottery, there was no Attic Red Figure, and this absence dated it to the late sixth century BC. This date, together with the absence of finds, led the excavator to conclude that the later destruction level must represent the Persian sack and de-population of the city.[36] An earlier destruction deposit in the stratigraphic sequence of layers contained a more plentiful assemblage of pottery and other materials and this was attributed to an earthquake, which would not have resulted in the emptying-out of the houses, as the Persian sack did.

This shows that it is only through the very careful excavation and examination of artifacts from destruction deposits that the nature of the events that led to their formation can be understood. In some cases it was the absence, rather than the presence, of archaeological materials that led to the excavators being able to identify a level as being the result

[31]   Senff 2007: 326, citing Flavius Josephus.
[32]   Niemeier et al. 1999; von Graeve 2005.
[33]   von Graeve 2005.
[34]   Gödecken 1988: 313, n. 7.
[35]   B.F. Weber 1985: 33.
[36]   Senff 2007: 322. Deposited over this destruction deposit was a thick layer of rubble that included Fikellura sherds of a later date that represents a post-destruction leveling-off similar to that seen during the soundings at Heroon III.

of war-like destruction. Together with deposits from the temples of Athena and Aphrodite, this evidence is consistent with a "destruction horizon" across the whole site of Miletos at the date that is consistent with the narrative given by Herodotos. However, the discovery of this "horizon" has required careful excavation and finds analysis across the whole site. This serves as an example of how important the application of careful excavation methods and open-minded interpretation and reinterpretation of the evidence is to identify even the largest of historical "events" in the archaeological record; it also serves as a warning of the need to question the presumption of an easy congruence between literary traditions and archaeology.

The artifacts

Weapons

Excavations at Phokaia and Miletos recovered many dozens of arrowheads that are associated with deposits from the Persian attacks on these cities. Finds like these are perhaps a better source of evidence for the kinds of weapons used in combat than votives as they are found in situ, where they fell. In addition to the weapons from Çatallar Tepe (see above), a number of bronze arrowheads were also found in a ritual context at the Sanctuary of Apollo at Kato Phana on Chios, as were also an iron axe and a knife, the latter of which is more likely to have had a ritual function than to have been dedicated as a weapon.[37] This example demonstrates that, even in votive deposits, arms are a rare find, with arrowheads being the most common.

Armor

Finds of armor from Ionia are even rarer than those of weapons. The Çatallar Tepe cuirass had holes in the bronze so that it could originally be attached to a leather jacket.[38] Another example is a large bronze disc, probably a shield, with a tree-of-life motif and dating from the seventh century BC, which was found at the Temple of Athena at Miletos.[39]

Artworks

Although there are examples of Ionian figured vase-painting with apparently narrative themes, the common "Wild Goat" style was generally restricted to scenes of animals (see Chapter 9). Whereas in Corinth and Attica, vase-painting is an important source of information about the technology and tactics of war (or at least images of them), for Ionia this important source of information is mostly lacking. However, there is an important group of artifacts that do provide us with images of warriors in the later Archaic period and these are the famous painted *sarcophagi* of Klazomenai. A number of these are painted with images of warriors in *hoplite* armor on the rim of the coffin, including at least one battle scene.[40] The two-dimensional nature of the vase-painting technique

---

[37] Beaumont and Archontidou-Argyri 2004: 227–31; R. Osborne 2007: 249.
[38] Lohmann 2007b: 579.
[39] Kleiner 1966: 18, fig. 16.
[40] R.M. Cook 1981: 44ff.; Hackbeil et al. 1998.

and the restricted space on the side panels of these *sarcophagi* mean that painters were limited to showing straightforward agonistic battle scenes, in which one warrior is directly opposed by another. The larger battle scene across the top panels of a *sarcophagos* in Berlin features multiple figures,[41] but in a chaotic mêlée, and it would be hard to conclude from these alone that *hoplite* tactics, of the type that have been commonly assumed were already in place in mainland Greece, were used in Ionia.

A rare example of sculptural art is the Samos Warrior *Kouros*.[42] *Kouroi*, sculptures of standing male figures, of the period in Attica and other regions of Greece are generally depicted nude, but in Ionia there are examples of clad and seated male statues.[43] Unusually, the Samos Warrior *Kouros*, which is dated to c.520 BC, is dressed in armor with a cuirass and Corinthian-style helmet. A sculptural frieze of chariots from Myous, and the battle scene on the Klazomenian *sarcophagos* in Berlin, appear to suggest that these may also have played some role in Ionian warfare. However, it is not clear if the Myous chariot is a sporting scene or not and the Berlin *sarcophagos* includes an image of a winged deity, probably Athena,[44] and is therefore in a mythical setting, not during a real-life battle.

A seventh-century BC terracotta model of two helmeted warriors has been recently found at Çatallar Tepe.[45] This terracotta is interesting because it shows two warriors pressed close together, one behind the other, with their heads turned away to the left. Although it has been interpreted as a scene of the mythological many-headed giant Geryon,[46] perhaps a more likely explanation of this unusual pose it that it represents a battle formation, a *phalanx* (rank), in which the soldiers are lined up to face an enemy but have turned their bodies sideways to minimize their frontage to the enemy and maximize the protection they receive from their shields. The seventh-century BC date of the context of discovery is consistent with the introduction of *hoplite* weapons, and presumably tactics, to mainland Greece. The discovery of spearheads, a *sauroter*, and cuirass – the tools of the *hoplite* – in the same temple might also be cited in support of this interpretation. Given that many of the dedications in Ionian temples were procured by means of mercenary service, and that Ionian warriors were famed for their armor (see below) the commissioning and deposition of such an image in a temple would have been entirely appropriate. If the identification of this image with mythology is rejected in favor of the interpretation proposed here, then this artifact represents the best evidence yet for the adoption of *hoplite*, or pseudo-*hoplite*, tactics (but not necessarily culture – see below) in seventh-century BC Ionia.

[41]   Berlin inv. No. 3145 – Cook and Dupont 1998: 124–5, fig. 17.2–3.
[42]   Boardman 1978: fig. 176.
[43]   A robed male figure in Samos Museum and the Chares Group (see Box 8.1), respectively.
[44]   Villing 1998.
[45]   Lohmann 2007b: 581, fig. 10.
[46]   Lohmann 2007b: 581, citing a parallel to a bronze plate from Samos. Depictions of Geryon and the mythical conjoined twin the Molionides vary (Dasen 1997). In some cases, they are shown with multiple bodies, like the Çatallar Tepe terracotta, but in others they have a single body, but multiple heads (e.g. National Museum Athens 11765 – an engraved bronze fibula).

Literary Sources

As noted above, war is used as the central theme or motif in many great works of ancient literature, including Herodotos,[47] but such sources need to be used judiciously, especially when seeking to use them in conjunction with archaeology. It goes without saying that there are biases and weaknesses inherent in any historical account of war. It is a glib adage to say "the victors wrote the histories," but we are forced to continue to use histories of victors regardless because they are our only source of written evidence. The truth behind historic "victories" is often much more complex. In Archaic Ionia, a region where there were multiple non-Greek powers who had expanded into the region in waves, it would be fairer to change the adage to say "the Greeks wrote the histories (and they usually lost)." This is because the Greeks were the only society in the region for whom we have a surviving body of literature and we do not have the other side of the story from which to begin to reconstruct a more even-handed account of the Ionians' interaction with their Anatolian neighbors (see Chapter 1).

It is remarkable that in Greek literary sources, there are virtually no references to the standard set piece land battles on open ground that typify their writing about mainland Greece. Rather the battles that take place in Ionia are sieges, with the exception of the sea battle at Lade. The reasons for this will be examined below, but the contrast with the tradition of writing about *hoplite* warfare between peer *poleis* in mainland Greece is probably significant and indicates a key difference in warfare practices between the Ionian cities and their mainland contemporaries.

With regard to the Ionians' relations with one another, Herodotos' accounts of warfare in Archaic Ionia paint a complex picture of the social and political context in which war took place. There were evidently friendships, treaties, alliances, and wars between the Greek *poleis* of Ionia. There were various ways in which these states could mediate their differences, including consulting oracles, arbitration, the Panionion, and going to war. Of these, we should not assume that going to war was necessarily the last resort for ancient diplomacy. It might be better to view it as just another diplomatic tool that one might use with an enemy or neighbor. War is the only one of these forms of diplomatic intercourse that leaves tangible physical evidence, so it needs to be balanced with an appreciation that others existed and may have been used without leaving any historical or archaeological trace. Examples include:

- *Consulting oracles.* There were a number of active oracles in Archaic Ionia, but one appears to have been of particular importance – the oracle of Apollo at Branchidai-Didyma. In a dispute between Miletos and Kyme, Aristodikus of Kyme approached the oracle seeking a resolution (Hdt. 1.158–9). Aristodikus did not appear bothered by the oracle's close connection to the *polis* of Miletos, in whose territory it lay. This status did not appear to affect its role as an impartial arbiter and holy place and it was widely consulted across Ionia and beyond.[48] An oracle also de-fused the long-running military

---

[47]   Harrison 2002; Tritle 2006.
[48]   Greaves 2002: 124–7, fig. 3.19.

stand-off between Miletos and the Lydians (Hdt. 1.17). In this episode, the Temple of Athena at Assessos was accidentally burned by the besieging Lydian forces and their king Allyates fell gravely ill as a consequence. Having consulted an unspecified oracle, he was told to rebuild the temple in order to appease the goddess, which required that he negotiate a peace with Miletos. In this story the Milesians and Lydians were able to negotiate their peace without a climb-down because of their expressed mutual belief in the gods of the other. In effect the oracle facilitated a peace between the two – something that oracles, as the only institution above the *polis* in the Archaic Greek system, could do.

- *Arbitration.* During a civil dispute between two groups within Miletos, the city found itself in a state of *stasis* and invited representatives from Paros to adjudicate and resolve this (Hdt. 5.28–9). Seeking arbitration by a friendly state that was outside the dispute could de-fuse a situation that might otherwise lead to civil unrest.

- *The Panionion.* This was a focal religious center for the Ionians, where they met to discuss issues of common concern.[49] It might reasonably be assumed that the annual meetings that took place here resolved minor issues between the Ionians about which we now know virtually nothing. The only recorded instance of it being used as such is during the Ionian Revolt (Hdt. 1.170). Being on the eve of war, this meeting took place under a very exceptional set of circumstances and must be used cautiously when trying to consider how the Panionion may have facilitated discussion between the Ionians under normal circumstances (if indeed it did at all), but there are sources to suggest that this is how it may have been used after the revolt.[50]

Historical sources also give us an insight into another very important aspect of ancient warfare, and that is the role of religion. States could enter into binding treaty agreements that were sealed with a vow. For example, when the people of Phokaia abandoned their city to the Persians, they made an oath never to return. As part of this oath, they dropped a piece of iron into the sea with the vow that they would not return until it floated (Hdt. 1.165). This oath is similar to that later entered into by the founder members of the Delian League, many of whom were Ionians. In another example, during the siege of Ephesos by Croesus, the Ephesians strung a rope between the city and the Temple of Artemis, in order to bring it under the protection of the goddess (Hdt. 1.26). Although apparently to no avail, this does indicate the expectation (or at least the hope) that Croesus would respect the Ephesians' goddess.

Oaths, treaties, truces, and similar agreements between states were made binding by a shared recognition of one another's deities and cult places. This was especially important in a region such as Ionia, where non-Greek powers sought to interact with the Greek *poleis* of the coast. Mutual recognition of one another's cults gave the Ionians and those with whom they had dealings a shared diplomatic language and a medium through which to interact. Important dedications were made to Ionian sanctuaries by the Egyptian pharaoh Necho (Hdt. 2.159) and the Lydian king Croesus[51] whose dedications can be interpreted as diplomatic overtures toward the Ionians.

---

[49] Roebuck 1979; C. Schneider 2004. See also Chapter 10.
[50] Debord 1999: 176–7; Rubinstein and Greaves 2004: 1056, citing Hdt. 6.42.
[51] Jeffery 1990.

Discussion: Issues in Source Materials

The interface between historical sources, the events that they purport to recount, and the archaeological record is complex and how such questions are approached and the evidence deployed are the fundamental issues underlying all Classical archaeology.

On the face of it, our sources appear to present us with unambiguous historical events, such as the Persian sack of Miletos in 494 BC. There is also a danger that our archaeological researches will become teleological. That is, by setting out to prove that the historical sources are "true," we are already predetermining the outcome. In other words, we think we already know how the story ends and we are simply working toward that end instead of keeping our interpretation of the data open-ended. Even with such a major event as this it has sometimes proved a challenging task for the excavators to piece together secure evidence for the different elements of the destruction horizon across the whole city, as the example of Miletos shows. The task of securely identifying the archaeological evidence for these historical events is therefore not as easy as it might at first appear.

In some cases, the archaeological evidence is less equivocal. For example, Herodotos (1.17–22) describes how the Temple of Athena at Assessos, a site within the *chora* of Miletos, was destroyed by fire during an assault on the city and its lands by the Lydians. Excavations on a hilltop settlement near Miletos, at Mengerevtepe, found the remains of a temple, with an inscription to Athena, on top of a destruction horizon.[52] Although never absolutely secure, evidence such as this can be more clearly related to the account of this event given by Herodotos and might confirm, at least in part, its historicity.

In other cases, however, the archaeological evidence appears to contrast with the historical accounts of events. For example, Herodotos (1.164–5) describes how the Persian army under Harpagos began to lay siege to the city of Phokaia, but did not take it by force; yet recent excavations by Ömer Özyiğit in the area of the city gate show signs of intense fighting.[53] There are numerous reasons that may account for this apparent mismatch in the historical and archaeological evidence, but whatever the outcome of the debate, we must always keep an open mind about the reliability of *both* the archaeological *and* the historical sources, rather than just seeking ways of interpreting the archaeology differently so that it quietly elides to leave our comfortable historical narrative intact. It is for this reason that Classical archaeologists must be especially rigorous with their excavation methods, so as to ensure that the stratigraphic position, interpretive context, and relative date of the material found is not open to question.

The Fortification of Ionia

A brief look at either the archaeological or the historical evidence for fortifications in Ionia will reveal that they were not permanent features. Box 7.1 gives a brief overview of the available evidence for such fortifications in the Archaic period, but for some key sites,

---

[52] Lohmann 1995; Senff 1995; B.F. Weber 1995.
[53] See Chapter 5 and below.

such as the city of Chios,[54] little or no data is available. Despite their size, large defensive walls can prove to be surprisingly hard to trace, and academic attention has traditionally been focused on the sanctuaries and public buildings of the urban core, rather than how it was defended (see Chapter 1).

Although the fortifications of the third quarter of the seventh century BC at Old Smyrna have been known about since the 1950s,[55] the walls of its Ionian neighbors have proved harder to find, despite their size and the serious efforts of archaeologists.[56] Tracing fortifications can be difficult because they are repeatedly rebuilt and reused (e.g. Samos), because they are robbed of their stone (e.g. Phokaia), or because they have become covered in alluvium (e.g. Miletos).

They are also less likely than other archaeological contexts to lay down continuous and meaningful stratigraphic sequences and their excavation often yields little material relative to that from domestic, cult, or burial contexts. For these reasons fortification systems have rarely been the focus of extensive systematic archaeological excavation and are notoriously difficult to date. Yet such walls represent the single biggest capital building project of any Archaic *polis*. They are also an important cultural signifier and were fundamental to the character and continued existence of the city (see Chapter 5). For these reasons (the difficulty in dating them and their importance), Classical archaeologists have often sought to make connections between the construction of fortifications and attested historical threats to the state.

At Klazomenai, Ephesos, and Miletos the remains of earlier Bronze Age fortifications have been found, and these may still have been visible to the Archaic builders.[57] Although the first phase of settlement on the *acropolis* of Kalabaktepe was unfortified, Miletos was the first of the Archaic cities in Ionia that we know to have constructed fortifications, in the third quarter of the seventh century BC.[58] This wall was built in mudbrick on a socle (foundation layer) of gneiss stone. The remaining cities of Ionia for which we have information appear to have been fortified sometime during the sixth century BC, as their walls are mentioned by Herodotos (see Box 7.1). The most closely dated are the walls of Phokaia, for which Ömer Özyiğit has proposed a date of 590–580 BC,[59] placing them in the early sixth century, several decades after Miletos had been fortified.

Not only were the walls of Miletos the earliest in Archaic Ionia, they were also the longest lived. From their construction in the seventh century BC they were to stand intact until the Persian sack of 494 BC. The Phokaians' walls were apparently attacked in the Persian assault of 546 BC, during which the gate was burned.[60] Thucydides reports how

---

[54] There is, however, good evidence from the defenses of the *acropolis* of the settlement at Emporio (Boardman 1967).

[55] Nicholls 1958/59; M. Akurgal 2007.

[56] e.g. it was E. Akurgal who recognized it would be hard to find the city walls at Phokaia because they had been based on bedrock. See Ö. Özyiğit 2003: 113.

[57] Klazomenai (Liman Tepe): Erkanal 2008. Ephesos: Büyükkolancı 2007. Miletos: Niemeier 1998, 2005, 2007a; Greaves 2002: 59–62, figs 2.3 and 2.4.

[58] Senff 2007.

[59] Ö. Özyiğit 2003: 116.

[60] Ö. Özyiğit 2003: 116.

Box 7.1
City Walls of Archaic Ionia

Klazomenai[a]
Fortified: Second half of sixth century BC.
Technique: n/a.
Sieges: n/a.
Size: n/a.
Description: The mainland urban center on the acropolis was walled, but the island part was evidently unfortified in 411 BC (Thuc. 8.31.3).

Phokaia[b]

Fortified: 590–580 BC.[c]
Technique: Ashlar, with glacis, and step-like beddings cut into bedrock.
Sieges: Harpagos for King Cyrus of Persia 546 BC (Hdt. 1.161–4).
Size: Walls over 5 km in length.
Description: According to Herodotos, the walls of Phokaia (see photograph) were supposedly built with the financial support of the king of Tartessos. The section of these so-called Herodotean Walls that was covered by the Maltepe tumulus is exceptionally well preserved and shows that they were of high quality and constructed of finely cut stone blocks, as Herodotos had described. Elsewhere, the walls were removed down to their rock-carved beddings, which were mistaken for stairs by Felix Sartiaux.[d]

Miletos[e]

Fortified: Third quarter of seventh century BC.[f]
Technique: Gneiss socle with mudbrick superstructure.

Sieges: 14 annual sieges by Lydians in seventh century BC (Hdt. 1.17). Persians 494 BC (Hdt. 6.18).
Size: Enclosed area of c.110 ha.
Description: The walls of Miletos, which supposedly held out during 14 annual sieges by the Lydians (Hdt. 1.17), have proved remarkably difficult to trace. This is due to the great depth of alluvial deposits that have accumulated over the lower plain and the fact that they were obscured in part by later fortifications.[g] It has been possible to trace them across the plain between Kalabaktepe and the harbors by means of geophysics and deep sounding trenches.[h]

Samos[i]

Fortified: Sixth century BC.
Technique: Polygonal.
Sieges: Sparta 524 BC (Hdt. 3.54).
Size: Enclosed area of c.103 ha.
Description: The tyrant Polykrates is credited with having built the walls of Samos, and the city's acropolis was certainly first fortified sometime during the sixth century BC. Athens forced the Samians to dismantle their walls in 439/38 BC (Thuc. 1.117.3) which remained unfortified until 411 BC when the Athenians were forced to hurriedly re-fortify the city in advance of an imminent attack by Spartan forces (Thuc. 8.51.2). Three building phases can be distinguished with the lowest, polygonal-style, masonry being the remains of the Archaic wall. Built on top of this is a second phase of ashlar masonry, which is presumed to date to the fourth century BC.

Teos[j]

Fortified: Sixth century BC.
Technique: Polygonal.
Sieges: n/a.
Estimated size: (Classical walls enclosed c.80 ha).
Description: Polygonal blocks of hard limestone.

Ephesos[k]

Fortified: Early sixth century BC, or before?
Technique: Massive squared stone blocks.
Sieges: King Croesus of Lydia, c.560 BC (Hdt. 1.26).
Size: Unknown.
Description: The early defensive walls of Ephesos were found, but never fully published, during Josef Keil's excavations of 1926. Photographs from these excavations show that the wall was composed of giant (c.1 m+) stone blocks, roughly squared off

and incorporating sections of bedrock. The full extent of the fortifications is unknown, although a stretch of walls c.250 m+ long was traced on the north side of Panayır Dağı.

NOTES

[a] Hdt. 1.163; Mellink 1983: 440.
[b] Hdt. 1.161–4; O. Özyiğit 1994.
[c] O. Özyiğit 2003: 116.
[d] O. Özyiğit 2003: 116.
[e] Hdt. 1.17, 6.18; von Gerkan 1935; Blüm 1999; Senff 2007.
[f] Senff 2007: 323.
[g] Blüm 1999.
[h] Schröder et al. 1995; Stümpel et al. 1997; C. Schneider 1997.
[i] Hdt. 3.39, 3.54, 3.143, 3.144, 3.16; Kienast 1978.
[j] Hdt. 1.168; Béquignon and Laumonier 1925: 283–98; Tuna 1984; Ersoy and Koparal 2008.
[k] Hdt. 1.26; Kerschner et al. 2008.

The Maltepe section of the "Herodotean" Wall at Phokaia. Note sloping glacis.

the Samians were forced to demolish their walls by the Athenians in 439/38 BC,[61] only to have the Athenians rebuild them in 411 BC in the face of an imminent threat.[62] It appears that the Athenians may have required many of their other Ionian subjects to dismantle their defenses in the fifth century BC.[63]

Episodes such as that of Samos, above, and the decision by Themistocles of Athens to redefend the city hurriedly against a perceived imminent Spartan threat give us the impression that defensive walls can be built at relatively short notice in response to impending danger. This may be so, but walls built in a hurry can be differentiated by their rushed construction methods from those that have been constructed more system-atically. For example, walls built in the face of imminent attack are likely to incorporate a great deal of *spolia* (reused architectural and sculptural fragments) rather than specially cut stone. The so-called Themistoclean wall of Athens and the post-Archaic wall of Miletos[64] are examples of walls built when these cities had been destroyed and then rebuilt, with walls constructed in a relatively short timeframe.[65]

Herodotos describes the Cimmerians sweeping through Anatolia to raid and destroy sites, including Ionia (Hdt. 1.6). It has been suggested that the first walls of Miletos may have been built in response to the threat posed to the city by these raiders.[66] However, during the excavation of the settlement mound at Gordion, two destruction levels were found, the lower one of which dated to c.800 BC and was initially equated with the coming of the Cimmerians. However, the recent redating of the Gordion destruction by means of new radiocarbon and dendrochronological samples has completely changed the way in which the site's history is understood, and the reality of the Cimmerian destruc-tion of Gordion (and presumably their threat to Miletos) is now called into question.[67]

The redating of Gordion, once again, demonstrates how literary positivism can lead us to interpret archaeological materials in a way that fits in with metanarratives con-structed from textual sources (see Chapter 2). In this case, it may lead us to assume that the walls of the Ionian cities were built in response to historically attested threats, such as the Cimmerians, even if these threats subsequently turn out to have been non-existent. Looked at objectively, it seems inconceivable that the walls of Phokaia, Miletos, or any of the other cities for which we have evidence were a historical "knee-jerk" response to immediate military threats. City walls, such as those of Athens, Miletos, or Samos, may be *rebuilt* in a short timeframe, but engineering projects of this size are not planned, prepared, and erected from scratch overnight.

At Phokaia, the construction of a 5 km-long wall made of cut stone blocks and embed-ded in the carved bedrock would have been a colossal undertaking. Its construction would require the organized bringing together of resources of materials, skills, labor, and finance

[61]   Thuc. 1.117.3.
[62]   From the Spartans: Thuc. 8.51.2.
[63]   Thuc. 3.33.2.
[64]   Blüm 1999.
[65]   A reappraisal of the plan of early Classical Miletos by B. Weber 2007 showed that it closely matched that of the Archaic town and it may have been rebuilt relatively quickly after the destruction of 494 BC.
[66]   e.g. Senff 2007: 323.
[67]   Voigt and Henrickson 2000.

that could only arise out of a convergence of social, economic, political, or military needs in the mediohistorical timeframe. Although an imminent external threat may have necessitated the need for new defenses, all that such threats do is crystallize in the minds of the defenders an already outstanding need, which may have emerged due to changes in the environment or the technology and practice of war.[68] The construction of defenses on the scale seen at Phokaia is therefore a response to mediohistorical processes (e.g. the rise of expansionist kingdoms and empires within Anatolia) which historical sources (e.g. Hdt. 1.163) may illuminate, but do not fully explain.

Another reason that might account for the scale of Phokaia's walls and those of other Ionian states is that they were entering into competitive emulation – either with one another, or with their Anatolian neighbors. It has long been suggested that the *poleis* communities of Archaic Greece engaged in a form of competition with one another via the construction of increasingly lavish temples.[69] As they are also highly visible public works, might not the construction of impressive city walls be interpreted as another way by which the Ionian *poleis* could compete with one another? There was apparently no love lost between Samos and Miletos, and although they may have raided one another's territory periodically,[70] all-out assault seemed unlikely. However, one can well imagine that when Polykrates ordered the building of Samos' walls it would have been a significant act of political one-upmanship over Miletos. The very fine standard of workmanship on the stone of Phokaia's walls is also unnecessary in purely functional terms and suggests their construction was as much a political statement as a military one.

The Ionians' walls may also have been built not in emulation of one another, but of the defenses of the power centers of Anatolia. The Ionian cities were under the control of Lydia from at least as early as the mid-sixth century BC and the Lydian capital of Sardis was surrounded by defenses of a breathtaking scale that dominated the surrounding landscape and influenced visitors' phenomenological responses to approaching the city.[71] These walls were built of mudbrick on a wattle foundation and were equipped with a glacis. Another site in Anatolia with impressive defenses and a glacis is Kerkenes Dağ (see Figure 7.1). Here there were 7 km of defenses, 8 m high and built in polygonal stone and perhaps topped by a wooden parapet.[72] Although the form of these walls is comparable to those of Phokaia, they are executed in different materials and on a much larger scale. Nevertheless, as noted in Chapter 5, the visual impact of approaching Phokaia would have been significant and the visual reference to the form of Anatolian defensive systems would not have been lost on those who viewed them.

This discussion has highlighted the fact that the construction of walls such as these may have been motivated by more than just military necessity. Another non-military function that they may have performed was as a form of diplomatic interaction.

[68]   Greaves 1999.
[69]   Snodgrass 1986.
[70]   Jackson 1995.
[71]   Dusinberre 2003: 19–20.
[72]   G.D. Summers 2006: 173–4.

Figure 7.1   The Cappadocia Gate and adjacent defenses at Kerkenes Dağ. Note the sloping glacis (bottom, left). Courtesy of Geoff and Françoise Summers.

Herodotos tells us that the walls of Phokaia were paid for by the king of Tartessos to protect them from the Persian threat (Hdt. 1.163). The truth of the king's motivations may be open to debate but the giving, and more importantly in this context, the *receiving* of diplomatic gifts of this magnitude was evidently an important part of inter-state diplomacy in Archaic Ionia. King Croesus of Lydia paid for the construction of the Artemision of Ephesos, and the construction of such conspicuous public works as the fine city walls of Phokaia might reasonably be considered a project of comparable, or even greater, scale. To have such fine walls was clearly a feather in Phokaia's cap, but to have had them paid for by a powerful foreign sponsor was a stroke of diplomatic genius!

To return to military matters, the very fact that the Ionian cities felt the need to construct extensive defenses at a time when many states in mainland Greece, most notably Sparta, did not is worthy of consideration. The population of Archaic Sparta did not coalesce into a single large settlement and remained *kata kōmas* (in villages).[73] Perhaps inspired by the Spartan model, Plato took the stance that fortifications made citizens cowardly (*Laws* 78d–79a). The Ionians, however, had no such luxury and faced with enemies using non-*hoplite* forces they needed their defenses to repel them. Agonistic

[73]   Thuc. 1.5.1, 1.10; Humphreys 1972.

hoplite engagements took place in the open on level ground and siege warfare was evidently not an important part of military practice in mainland Greece.[74] Ionia's potential enemies included the Lydians and the Persians, who made extensive use of siege tactics (Hdt. 1.17, 1.162).

The glacis of the so-called Herodotean Wall at Phokaia (see Box 7.1) may have been intended as a counter-siege measure to prevent sappers hiding close to the foot of the wall. Without a glacis defenders on the ramparts could not aim at the foot of the wall from above without leaning out and endangering themselves. As the final siege of Miletos was to be broken by sappers, the fear of this tactic appears to have been well founded.

There were various tactics that might be employed to break a siege. The commonest appears to have been to try and starve the city out by destroying its fields. This was a widely used tactic in Greece[75] and was evidently used in Ionia during the Lydian sieges of Miletos (Hdt. 1.17).[76] The effect of this may have been more psychological than real, as the besieged population watched their livelihoods being destroyed. The fact that most Ionian cities were on the sea and may have had additional opportunities to supply themselves with food this way may have helped them withstand sieges to a limited extent.[77] Sappers were used to break the Persian siege of Miletos by undermining its walls (Hdt. 6.18). The Persians might also have used the technique of piling earth up against an enemy's walls to create a ramp, as the Lydians had done during the sack of Old Smyrna.[78] Another effective strategy was simply to watch and wait. During the Persian siege of Sardis, which lasted only 14 days, one of the defenders dropped his helmet and when he climbed down to retrieve it the enemy saw their way in and took the city (Hdt. 1.84–5). Archaeological evidence from Phokaia shows that in the Persian siege of 546 BC, the gates were burnt and arrows and catapults were fired. One stone catapult recovered from the scene, which weighs 22 kg and is 29 cm in diameter, is the earliest example known to date and shows that the Persians had other tactics and technologies at their disposal that are not mentioned in texts.[79]

The archaeological and historical evidence for the sack of Miletos shows that the Persian assault on the city was brutal and its devastation total. Unlike the *hoplite* warfare of mainland Greece, which some commentators have construed as being a form of symbolic military engagement between peer *poleis*, the stakes were high in this form of siege warfare. In the Ionian context, being on the edge of Anatolia, the importance placed upon the scale, design, and location of fortifications and even cities themselves is entirely understandable.

---

[74] Hartog 1988: 46.

[75] van Wees 2004: 121.

[76] Archaeological evidence apparently confirming this incident comes from excavations at Mengerevtepe; see above.

[77] Although it appears that they could not adequately supply themselves in this way – Greaves 2002: 101, citing Hdt. 1.21.

[78] Remains of a siege ramp built of earth, stones, and timber were found during excavations at Old Smyrna. Nicholls 1958/59; Boardman 1999: 96–7, esp. fig. 110.

[79] Briant 1994.

Naval Warfare

It was demonstrated in Chapter 3 that the sea was an integral part of life in Ionia. Access to the sea, possession of harbors, the physical nature of the coastline and the resources that it offered were all central to the Ionians' economy and way of life. This is as true of warfare as it is of any other part of that life and so the consideration of naval warfare in Ionia would seem to be an important point from which to view Ionian history and identity.

In geographical terms, possession of a defensible harbor would seem to be the natural prerequisite of any aspiring Ionian sea-power. Evidence for a *liman kleistos* ("closable harbor"), the entrance to which might be closed by a chain or boom, is hard to identify but in Ionia Samos, Miletos, and possibly Phokaia might have had such harbors.[80] Geo-morphological research at Ephesos and Miletos has revealed the probable locations, shapes, and alluviation histories of their harbors[81] and the practice of warfare itself might have had an impact on those processes as the burning of fields and deforestation of hill-sides for shipbuilding accelerated soil erosion.[82]

The archaeological evidence for Archaic navies is virtually non-existent, and we are forced to rely instead on the historical writings of Classical period Greek historians for the majority of our evidence.[83] This immediately presents us with a number of problems. The main source of our historical evidence is Herodotos' account of a single event – the Battle of Lade – which, being a momentous turning point in his narrative about the Persian Wars, can be assumed to be overlain with multiple layers of meaning for him and his readers, some of which are hard to disassociate from any core "facts" that it may contain. An example of this is the numbers of ships that he tells us attended the battle; for the smaller states these numbers seem quite specific, but when we get to the larger states, such as Samos, Chios, and Miletos, the figures come in suspiciously convenient multiples of 10 (see Figure 7.2).

Going back before the Battle of Lade, the Archaic period appears to have been an important one in the development of navies in the eastern Mediterranean because it marks the shift from the "Homeric" tradition of private ownership of warships, to the state-owned navies of the Classical period.[84] It is also the period in which there was a technological shift from the smaller 50-oared *pentekonter*,[85] to the technically advanced triple-banked 200-oared *trireme*.[86] It is also important to note that, prior to the Ionian

---

[80] de Souza 1998: 275. These are the "built" harbor of Polykrates at Samos and the Lion Harbor at Miletos. The publication of new excavations at Phokaia since the writing of de Souza's article point to this being a much larger settlement than previously thought, extending beyond the peninsula on which the Temple of Athena stood. It is therefore conceivable that its harbor, the entrance to which was overlooked by a sanctuary of Cybele, might also have been "closable." See Chapter 5.

[81] Brückner et al. 2006.

[82] Hdt. 1.17; Greaves 2002: 13–14.

[83] de Souza 1998: 271.

[84] de Souza 1998.

[85] e.g. the Phokaians sailed to Tartessos to trade using *pentekonters* (Hdt. 1.163).

[86] e.g. the Ionians fielded 353 *triremes* against the Persians' 600 at the Battle of Lade (Hdt. 6.8).

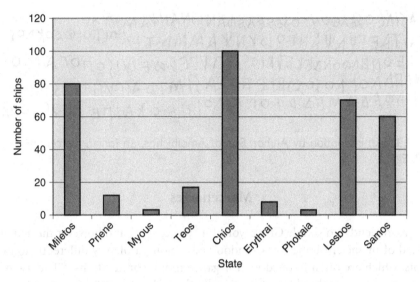

Figure 7.2 Ships attending the Battle of Lade (after Hdt. 6.8).

Revolt, Miletos' ability to conduct large-scale naval operations overseas without Persian support was limited (Hdt. 5.31), and that the ships fielded by the Ionians at Lade were Persian ships that they had commandeered.[87] It was noted above that the construction of city walls on the scale of those built by the Ionian cities required the convergence of numerous socio-economic factors across a mediohistorical timescale. The same must surely be true of the construction of large fleets, which required not just resources of labor, timber, and other specialist materials, but also craftsmanship and an ongoing financial commitment to their maintenance. Perhaps, as with the walls of Phokaia, the construction of fleets on the scale of those fielded at Lade was beyond the financial means of the Ionians without external finances, in this case from Persia. In the Classical period the financial and technical demands of building and maintaining large fleets can be seen to have been a major stimulus to the creation of large *hegemonies*, such as the Delian League, and the lack of such cooperative (or rather, coercive) institutions in pre-revolt Ionia is a reflection not just of their independence from one another, but also the ultimate inability of their short-lived *symmachy* (military alliance) to withstand the Persian Empire's response to their revolt. Militarily, to control the sea was to control Ionia and vice versa.[88] The sea gave the Ionians a lifeline when besieged by their Anatolian neighbors and a means of escape from such sieges (e.g. Phokaians: Hdt. 1.165). However, ultimately, the Ionians' command of the seas around them in the latter part of the Archaic period was made possible only by utilizing the immense financial resources of the Persian Empire.

---

[87] Wallinga 1987.
[88] Greaves 2000a: 56.

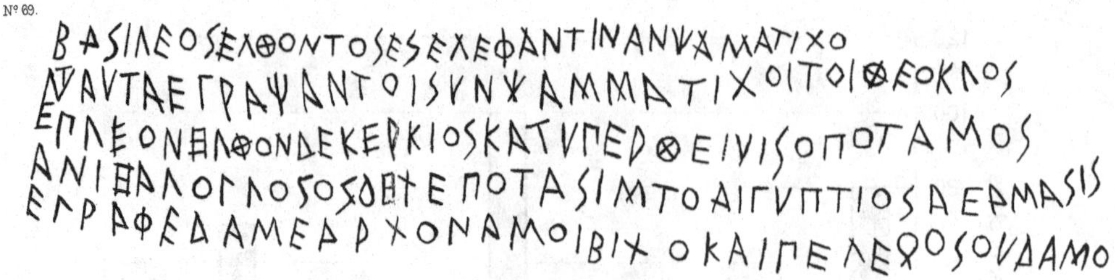

Nº 69.

BASIΛEOSEΛΘONTOSESEΛEΦANTINANYΧMATIXO
NAYTAEΓPAΨANTOISYNΨAMMATIXOITOIΘEOKΛOS
EΠΛEONAHΛΘONΔEKEPKIOSKATYΠEPΘEIVISOΠOTAMOS
ANIHAΛOΓΛOSOSΔEYEΠOTASIMTOAIΓYΠTIOSAEAMASIS
EΓPAΦEΔAMEAPΧONAMOIBIΧOKAIΠEΛEQOSOYΔAMO

Figure 7.3 An inscription by Archon Son of Amoibichos, an Ionian mercenary, from Abu Simbel, Egypt.

Mercenaries

There was evidently no simple Greek word for "mercenary" and however the activity was conceived of in ancient Ionia it was undoubtedly thought of very differently to modern concepts, which are often imbued with negative moral connotations.[89] The use of mercenaries varied geographically and temporally throughout Greek history and one must therefore be careful to avoid making generalizing statements about their presence in Archaic Ionia. Matthew Trundle has mapped out a history of ancient Greek mercenaries[90] in which their appearance marks a departure from the traditional citizen-army in the late Archaic period, through an era in which the Persian threat called upon the citizen-armies as never before in the late Archaic/early Classical, to an age in which mercenaries were decisive in establishing control of the Aegean by those who could employ them in the Classical period, and finally to the Hellenistic period in which all armies were professionalized and the concept of a "mercenary" becomes hard to clarify.

Greek mercenaries may have been operating in Egypt as early as the late Bronze Age,[91] but it is in the Archaic period that firm evidence for Ionia mercenaries in the service of the Egyptian pharaohs appears. Evidence for the use of Ionians as mercenaries by foreign powers includes a graffito by Ionian and Carian mercenaries in the service of the Pharaoh Psammetichos[92] on the colossi at Abu Simbel (see Figures 7.3 and 8.3),[93] translated as follows:[94]

When King Psammetichos came to Elephantine
This was written by those who, with Psammetichos son of Theokles,
Sailed and came above Kirkis, as far as the river permitted;
Potasimto commanded the non-native speakers, and Amasis the Egyptians;
Archon son of Amoibichos wrote us and *Pelekos son of Oudamos.*[95]

---

[89] Trundle 2004: 1–4.

[90] Trundle 2004.

[91] Schofield and Parkinson 1994.

[92] Egyptian Psamtik (reigned c.664–610 BC, after Clayton 1994).

[93] Meiggs and Lewis 1969; Boardman 1999: 115–17.

[94] Meiggs and Lewis 1969: 7a. Transl. Dillon 1997: 129.

[95] "Pelekos son of Oudamos" can literally be translated as "Axe son of Nobody" and in this translation can therefore be read as a pun on Homeric poetry, when Odysseus escapes Polyphemos (Dillon 1997).

Further evidence includes a dedication at Branchidai-Didyma by the Pharaoh Necho[96] after the Battle of Megiddo in c.609 BC presumably in recognition of the role of Milesian mercenaries in his victory (Hdt. 2.159),[97] and the possible inclusion of Ionians and Carians in the army of the Lydian king Gyges sent to help Psammetichos I, recorded on the Assyrian Rassam cylinder.[98]

The people who employed Ionian mercenaries were not only foreign potentates, but also members of the Ionian aristocracy, who wished to use their force for personal gain. An illustration of this is Aristagoras of Miletos' Naxos campaign in 498 BC (Hdt. 5.34).[99]

If Ionian mercenaries were working for such foreign potentates, what did they do? It is too simplistic to assume that they were shipped in just to fight in decisive battles, such as Megiddo, and then paid off and sent home. Christopher Tuplin's meticulous study of the garrisons of the Achaemenid Empire[100] shows that the Persian deployment of paid soldiery in the Classical period was a complex matter. Greek mercenaries were highly valued, most probably for the devastating effectiveness of the *hoplite phalanx*, both its armor and its tactics, against less tightly trained or heavily armed troops.[101] In an Archaic period context, it is assumed that the superior bronze armor of the Greeks, and their training, gave them a unique advantage over the non-Greek forces that they were deployed against – they were *khalkeoi andres*, "brazen men."[102] There is also evidence from the site of Heunenburg on the Upper Danube to suggest that Greeks may have advised the builders about the construction of timber-and-mudbrick defensive walls of Mediterranean style.[103] For their foreign paymasters, the Greeks evidently supplied services and technical expertise that went beyond simple fighting for booty and that provided their employers not just with military victories that secured them power, but also prestige.

If the benefits of Ionian mercenary service can be identified for the regions in which they were employed, what effects did their service have back home in Ionia? It has been suggested that the extensive use of mercenaries may have been a factor in the early adoption of coinage in Ionia, as they were paid off with pieces of bullion at the end of their service.[104] Mercenaries may also have played a role in the foundation of Naucratis/Milesian Teichos, the formal constitution of which by Ahmose can be interpreted as an attempt to limit Greek military power in the Nile Delta, whilst giving Greek mercenaries a base from which to operate in the service of the Pharaoh.[105] Greek mercenaries may also have been involved in another settlement on the edge of the Near East, at Al Mina

---

[96] Egyptian Nekau (reigned c.610–595 BC, after Clayton 1994).

[97] Parke 1985: 14.

[98] Boardman argues that, given the extent of Lydian control at the time, it is possible that the Lydian forces included Ionians and Carians (Boardman 2006: 525, citing Braun 1982).

[99] Trundle 2004: 6, n. 13.

[100] Tuplin 1987.

[101] This is in contrast to the Persians who are described by Herodotos (9.62–3) as being *anoploi* (without arms) – Hartog 1988: 44–50.

[102] Boardman 2006: 525. See above.

[103] Kimmig 1975.

[104] R.M. Cook 1958.

[105] See Chapter 6.

(see Box 6.1).[106] Although the materials that came out of Egypt and the Near East into Ionia have been much discussed,[107] what the Ionians had to offer in return is less clear and mercenary service appears to suggest one factor that might have helped "balance the books."

The place where the effect of Ionian mercenary service overseas can be most clearly seen is in the region's temples. Although their architectural form and scale may have been influenced by individuals' exposure to Egyptian prototypes (see Chapter 8), it is particularly in the temples' votive deposits that real influence can be seen. The best illustration of the connection between the temples and presumed military service in Egypt is an inscribed Egyptian basalt statue dedicated by Pedon and found near Priene.[108] This includes a testimony to his services to King Psammetichos, for which he was rewarded with a gold armlet and property. High-value Egyptianalia brought back by mercenaries, and other Ionian visitors to Egypt, found their way into temples as early as the eighth century BC.[109] These prestige votive offerings inspired Egyptianizing imitations, which were produced in the Greek settlements of the Aegean and at Naucratis. The Heraion at Samos has the most important collection of Egyptian artifacts in Ionia,[110] but they have also been found at Erythrai,[111] Ephesos,[112] Priene (see above), Miletos,[113] and Branchidai-Didyma.[114]

The volume of real Egyptian material found in Samos, and also at Rhodes, far outweighs that in comparable sites in mainland Greece,[115] much of which one might reasonably imagine to have been brought back by those who had performed military service there. Yet, although the Ionian temples were beneficiaries of such rich dedications, they were not just passive recipients of mercenary spoils, but actively encouraged this form of activity. Hugh Bowden has suggested that by dedicating his cloak at Branchidai-Didyma, the Pharaoh Necho was soliciting new mercenaries to come and work for him.[116] This same oracle probably sanctioned privateering raids from which it directly benefited in the form of a tithe on the recovered booty.[117]

Conclusions

Perhaps it is ultimately only in the denouement of the Ionian Revolt that we can really understand the reasons for the Ionians' adoption of apparently Near Eastern forms of defensive walls. Throughout his account of the Persian Wars, Herodotos clearly differ-

---

[106] Kearsley 1995. See also Chapter 6.
[107] e.g. Roebuck 1950 on the grain trade.
[108] Boardman 1999: 280–1.
[109] Hölbl 2007.
[110] Bumke 2007; Hölbl 2007.
[111] Hölbl 2007.
[112] Bammer and Muss 1996.
[113] Hölbl 1999.
[114] Bumke 2002.
[115] Boardman 2006: 524.
[116] Bowden 1996: 36.
[117] Greaves forthcoming (3), citing Jackson 1995.

entiates the way in which Greeks and Persians fought.[118] In the sack of Miletos, the Persian army systematically stripped its defeated enemy bare – a very different practice to the symbolic "agonistic," almost gentlemanly, forms of engagement between peer *poleis* that it has been argued were the norm in contemporary mainland Greece. The city was razed, its temples smashed and robbed, its men killed, and its women enslaved. Perhaps most interestingly, the Branchidai priests of the oracles of Apollo were carried away like booty – valued for their "craftsman"-like abilities of prophesy,[119] silencing the city's most important temple. By the standards of contemporary Greek warfare the sack of Miletos was brutal indeed, but in all these actions the Persian forces were behaving in accordance with norms of Near Eastern warfare, not those of the "*hoplite* code" of Greece, and in accordance with Herodotos' portrayal of their "barbarian" way of fighting.[120] This chapter set out to find evidence of common, and contrasting, cultural practices associated with war and what we see is that there was commonality between Ionia and its Anatolian and Near Eastern contemporaries, but a contrast with some of the practices of mainland Greece.

As noted above, there are historical references to fighting between the Ionians themselves, and there is even the possibility of civil strife within states, as happened at Miletos between the *aeinautai* and the *cheiromachai*. The fact that, despite these tensions, there are so few incidences of open hostilities is perhaps testimony to the existence of various forms of mediation. Central to these was the premise of mutual respect of one another's gods – the central tenet of treaties, going back to the aftermath of the Battle of Qadesh and the oldest known peace treaty (agreed in c.1258 BC). During the Ionian Revolt, the Ionians themselves appear to have broken with this tradition when they burned the Temple of Cybele at Sardis, and the Persians cited this wanton destruction as their reason for burning the temples of the Greeks (Hdt. 5.102). Elsewhere in Herodotos, the Lydians had paid due respect to the Ionians' temples, such as when Alyattes made peace with Miletos in order to rebuild a temple of Athena that his forces had inadvertently burned (Hdt. 1.17). In the broader context then, the Persians' actions in attacking the temples of the Greeks can be seen as a departure from their normal practices of war. The taboo against the destruction of temples that was in place until the Ionian Revolt can therefore be viewed as a common bond between the Ionians and their Anatolian neighbors, even in times of war.

One of the most important and tantalizing questions in the history of Ionia is why did Miletos instigate the Ionian Revolt? According to Vanessa Gorman, Herodotos' narrative places the blame at the feet of Histaeaus, and his personal ambitions,[121] whereas Thomas Harrison has emphasized "reversal of fortune" as a key motif in Herodotos' construction of his Persian War narrative[122] and this might also account for the great fall of Miletos (Hdt. 6.19). Whatever the truth behind the historical accounts, when viewed from a longer timescale, the Ionian Revolt can be seen to be doomed to failure because it goes against the tide of Ionian history in the *longue durée*. In this timeframe it was the

[118]   e.g. the Persians are shown goading their soldiers on to fight, using whips (7.223).
[119]   Burkert 1994: 60.
[120]   Hartog 1988: 44–8; Tritle 2006: 220.
[121]   Gorman 2001.
[122]   Harrison 2002.

emerging regional powers within Anatolia that ultimately prevailed in Ionia; something that was only to change when Alexander conquered Anatolia and brought control of it into the Greek world. Not only was it a fool's errand to try and stand against a power that had control of their Anatolian hinterland, but the Ionians had the audacity to do so with a fleet of ships that the Persians had built and which was beyond their means to have built for themselves. With Miletos, arguably the most natural candidate for *hegemon* (leader) of Ionia, utterly destroyed the region was weakened and it fell under the control of external powers, thereafter vacillating between control by Athens, Sparta, and Persia.

As noted at the start of this chapter, in matters of war, the adoption of one form of technology over another was not an aesthetic decision informed by culture, but a life-or-death choice informed by the need for survival. In choosing Anatolian forms of defenses, the Ionians showed that the enemies they anticipated engaging with from behind those walls practiced a different kind of warfare to that of their mainland contemporaries. Once again, the ability of Anatolia to determine the progress of events in Ionia is clear.

8

Cults of Ionia

Introduction

The religious practices of the Ionians, the penultimate theme of this book, provide us with perhaps the richest of all fields of source materials for study of their identity. As Elspeth Dusinberre observed in relation to her study of Achaemenid Sardis, religious sites are important because "emotional investment in cult is great; sacred practices are particularly sensitive indicators of human relationships in their demonstration of authority and status, or their overseeing of social transitions."[1]

It is, in part, the very nature of religious materials to be prominent in the archaeological record, as Robin Osborne has written: "Just as potential divine intervention pervades the superstitious man's life, so the material contents of and context for acts of religious cult pervade the archaeological record."[2] The construction of elaborate temples, the sacrifice of animals, and the deliberate laying down of votive deposits and burials are behaviors that are tailor-made to create abundant archaeological deposits.

However, there is another factor at work in the history of the exploration of Ionia that has skewed the archaeological dataset toward creating this abundance of evidence for religious practices, and that is the motivations of the excavators. The late nineteenth and early twentieth centuries were the era of the "great sanctuary excavation" in which the European "Great Powers" competed with one another to uncover yet more and more spectacular archaeological treasures.[3] This era not only continues to color the popular perception of Classical archaeology, but the results of these excavations remain some of the most important contexts that we have in Ionia, as discussed in Chapter 1. Recent excavations of temple sites in Ionia, such as those at Kato Phana and the Sanctuary of Aphrodite at Miletos, have benefited from the application of modern techniques of

---

[1] Dusinberre 2003: 199, citing Geertz 1973; Alcock 1993: 172, 175–8.
[2] R. Osborne 2007: 246.
[3] Shanks 1996; Whitley 2001: 32–6; Snodgrass 2007: 17–18.

recording and analysis, but they can only do so much to redress the inevitable loss of irreplaceable archaeological data caused by the mass excavation of so many temple sites at an early date in the development of archaeological methodologies.[4] However, the fact that those early excavators were so focused on identifying temples that were recognizably Greek meant that a number of non-Greek cult sites escaped their notice and have only recently been identified (see below).

It is not the purpose of this chapter to summarize the many excellent and detailed publications of the many different cult sites in Ionia. Rather, the aim here is to balance those discussions, which have often sought to align or contrast Ionian cult practices with those of the mainland Greeks, with perspectives drawn from trans-Ionian and non-Greek comparisons. The overall aim of this discussion is to illustrate the broader context within which we should seek to understand Ionian cult practice, even where this poses serious methodological challenges that comparisons to mainstream Greek materials alone do not.

An overview of the available source materials will be presented and discussed in accordance with the general approach of this book, namely geographical, archaeological, and then written source materials. Following this, a number of illustrative themes will be developed to demonstrate the potential value of these new methodologies and perspectives.

Geographical Evidence

As noted in Chapter 2, the physical location of temples in relation to the landscape can be an important clue to their interpretation, in the absence or otherwise of epigraphic or literary sources. The location of cult activities is very important to their function. Their location may be associated with a particular mythological event,[5] it may have certain physical attributes that are desirable for cult practice, such as a water source,[6] or there may be some phenomenological characteristic of its location that might be considered pleasing to its resident deity, such as a commanding view. In the colonial world, it has been argued that the act of locating temples in the countryside was a means of appropriating the landscape as a *chora* for the newly established community,[7] and in de Polignac's formulation of the emergence of the *polis* in mainland Greece, they represent a connection between the *polis* and the land.[8]

The variety of localities chosen by the Ionians for their temples and sanctuaries corresponds to that of sites in mainland Greece but also to the location of Anatolian cults.

Acropoleis are appropriate locations for cult sites for reasons of "both natural and political geography."[9] In Ionia, examples of temples on *acropolis* locations include the

---

[4] Even in the 1870s when J.T. Wood was excavating the Temple of Artemis at Ephesos, it was already recognized that his recording techniques left much to be desired (Challis 2008: 134).

[5] R. Osborne 2007: 254.

[6] Whitley 2001: 134–6.

[7] Carter 1994.

[8] de Polignac 1995. See Chapter 5.

[9] R. Osborne 2007: 254–5.

Temple of Athena at Emporio on Chios,[10] the Temple of Athena Polias/Poliouchos at Erythrai, and the Temple of Artemis Kithone on the East Terrace of the Kalabaktepe *acropolis* at Miletos.[11]

Harbors were another favored location for sanctuaries. At Phokaia, there are two sanctuaries on the harbor – the Temple of Athena and, immediately below it, one of the city's four known sanctuaries of Cybele. At Miletos, the Temple of Athena stood by the Theater Harbor and the Temple of Apollo Delphinos[12] was next to the Lion Harbor. On Chios, a sanctuary was located next to the harbor at Emporio,[13] and the temple at Kato Phana was once located on the sea.[14] Promontories were also popular, as attested by the temples of Dionysus at Myous, Demeter and Kore at Miletos, and Poseidon at Tekağaç Burun (Cape Monodendri near Branchidai-Didyma).

One of the most striking features of the location of that most famous of *panhellenic* sanctuaries at Delphi is its spectacular commanding views, but at its comparator in Ionia, Branchidai-Didyma, the temple was located in a hollow and would have afforded the visitor very poor views indeed.[15] Perhaps the purpose of this temple, and others like it in Ionia and elsewhere, was to be seen from a distance and not to be a place from which to look out (see below). With the application of GIS, it is possible to model the viewpoints from ancient temples, even where the landscape itself has now changed beyond recognition. Viewshed analysis of the Sanctuary of Aphrodite on Zeytintepe near Miletos shows that it would have had commanding views of what was once the Gulf of Latmos.[16] This analysis should remind us to question our modern, and very subjective, aesthetic reactions to the views offered by ancient temples.[17]

Two important oracular shrines were located on springs: at Klaros and at Branchidai-Didyma. These may originally have had an important role to play in their function as oracles, but then, proximity to a water source is a common feature of Greek and non-Greek cult places.[18] However, it is possible at Branchidai-Didyma that the sheer weight of the temple building itself may have closed off any spring, and a presumed water channel that supposedly drained out from the spring inside the *sekos* of the temple has now been redated to the Classical or Hellenistic period.[19]

Despite being generally unhealthy environments for humans, swamps also appear to have been a favored location, with two of the largest temples in Ionia being located in them – the Temple of Hera at Samos and the Temple of Artemis at Ephesos. Their cultic

[10] Boardman 1967: 4–23.
[11] Kerschner 1999.
[12] Once thought to be god of dolphins and associated with travelers, he is more commonly associated with state governance. Gorman 2001: 168–71.
[13] Boardman 1967: 54–97.
[14] See Chapter 2. Deep soil coring at the site has revealed that it was originally on the sea.
[15] Greaves 2002: 109, *contra* Fontenrose 1988: 1.
[16] Greaves and Wilson forthcoming.
[17] Another example of this is the altar of Poseidon at Tekağaç Burun which, although relatively low-lying and offering no great views out across the sea, would have been visible to ships, so as to render it a lighthouse for sailors (Greaves 2000a: 45–6; see also Chapter 3). In ancient times, access to temples was restricted and the majority of the population could not enter them and look out. Rather, they would observe temples only from the outside.
[18] Whitley 2001: 134–6; Berndt-Ersöz 1998: 97; Berndt-Ersöz 2003: 11–13.
[19] Furtwängler 2007: 409.

associations may stem from the proliferation of native fauna and flora that is found in Mediterranean marshlands. In both cases, the local environmental conditions have changed considerably since antiquity, but it is thought that they were originally marshy. In the case of the Temple of Hera at Samos, the small Imvrasos River that entered the sea nearby created a marshy environment in which the temple was located. At Ephesos, the situation is less clear, but it is also thought to have been a marsh and a sacred spring appears to have flowed down the north side of Ayasoluk Hill, from which the temple is located toward the southwest. This spring appears to have been associated with a Bronze Age sanctuary and so there may be a precursor to the ritual association between water and this location (see below). Although this location was evidently prone to flooding, leading to the destruction of the first temple building, it was felt to be sufficiently sacred to rebuild the temple on the same spot, which necessitated the ground level being raised by several meters, despite its obvious disadvantages.[20]

In fact there is evidence of Bronze Age activity at a number of key sanctuaries in Ionia – the Temple of Athena at Miletos, the Temple of Artemis at Ephesos, the Temple of Apollo at Branchidai-Didyma, the Temple of Hera at Samos, and the Temple of Apollo at Kato Phana.[21] Although there is not always direct evidence of cult activity in the Bronze Age at these sites, the fact there was some Bronze Age activity does raise the question of whether the patterns of cult activity that we are seeing in the landscape of Archaic Ionia are in fact the products of the Ionians' own Archaic cult traditions, or an inheritance from an earlier age. At the Temple of Artemis at Ephesos, Ulrike Muss has argued that the use of amber demonstrates cult continuity from the Bronze Age,[22] and at the Temple of Athena in Miletos in particular, Wolf-Dietrich Niemeier has argued that there may yet be evidence for continuity of some form of cultic practice from the Bronze Age through to the Archaic period.[23]

These examples of locations cover a wide range of natural landscape phenomena, all of which appear to have attracted cult attention in different ways and for different reasons, but there were also human features of the landscape that began to take on a cult significance of their own. Rural sanctuaries were linked to the centers of population by religious processions.[24] The routes of these festivals in turn became processional ways that might be paved and become lined with dedicated statues and minor sanctuaries of their own. Sacred Ways, of which Ionia has a number (see below), can therefore be seen to become mediohistorical features of the landscape that attract cult activity to themselves, and to determine its patterning and practice in the landscape (see Chapter 5).

Archaeological Evidence

Ionia's temples are one of its most outstanding features, although the remains of few Archaic period temples are visible to casual visitors today, perhaps with the exception of the

---

[20]   Bammer 1990: 144.
[21]   Beaumont and Archontidou-Argyri 2004; Beaumont forthcoming.
[22]   Muss 2008.
[23]   Niemeier 2007a.
[24]   R. Osborne 2007: 255.

foundations of the temples of Athena at Erythrai and Phokaia. In many cases, the remains of the Archaic period buildings are buried under the later phases of the same temples, obscuring them and making them hard to determine the precise plan, or even size.[25] Nevertheless, the largest Archaic temples of Ionia were of an impressive size and the development of the characteristic "Ionic" style has been one of the Ionians' lasting legacies.

With regards to their size, each temple building can be considered as a stage in a process of development and growth that began much earlier. A number of important temple sites in Ionia appear to have been in some form of use as early as the Bronze Age, but only a few of these have identifiable cultic associations (see below). A number of Ionia's key temples were also rebuilt during the Archaic period, with each phase of building being larger than the last. For example, there were four Archaic temples to Artemis at Samos,[26] three temples to Artemis at Ephesos,[27] two at the so-called "Panionion" at Çatallar Tepe,[28] two to Apollo at Branchidai-Didyma,[29] and two to Athena and Aphrodite at Miletos.[30]

The ever-increasing size of these temple buildings is significant for two reasons. First, it is illustrative of the process of peer–polity interaction. Secondly, it allows us to trace a relative chronology for the invention and adoption of the "Ionic" architectural style.

Peer–polity interaction was discussed in Chapter 7 in relation to the Ionian states' construction of defensive walls. This theory suggests that states of similar size, and operating within the same cultural milieu, engaged in a form of competitive emulation with one another. Anthony Snodgrass related this theory to the construction of monumental temples by the competitor *poleis* of Archaic Greece[31] and this argument certainly seems to have some mileage in relation to the scale on which the Ionian cities built their temples. As Robin Osborne wryly observes: "It is hard to believe that it is mere coincidence that the fourth Temple of Hera at Samos just surpasses the first Temple of Artemis at Ephesos in ground area (6,038 square metres compared to 6,017)."[32]

However, although it is tempting to think that the Ionians not only competed with one another through the construction of their temples, but also found a group identity through the development of a common "Ionic" architectural style, the evidence does not appear to support this latter suggestion. Although the familiar elements of the "Doric" style were in place by the sixth century BC, this did not happen for the "Ionic" style until the fifth century BC and there appears to have been a great deal of variety in Archaic

---

[25]   e.g. the plan of the Archaic Temple of Apollo at Branchidai-Didyma is largely obscured by the later Hellenistic temple building, and the precise form and dimensions of the Archaic temple are still under discussion. See Tuchelt 1991 and Greaves 2002: 109–29 for summaries of the site and its reconstructions. However, new excavations have provided new evidence that call into question these previous reconstructions (Furtwängler 2006a, 2006b, 2007).

[26]   Shipley 1987.

[27]   Hogarth 1908; Bammer 1990.

[28]   Lohmann 2007b.

[29]   See Tuchelt 1991.

[30]   Recent discoveries at Miletos have shown that the temples to both Athena and Aphrodite were rebuilt on a newer, larger scale just prior to the city's fall in 494 BC; von Graeve 2005.

[31]   Snodgrass 1986.

[32]   R. Osborne 2007: 256.

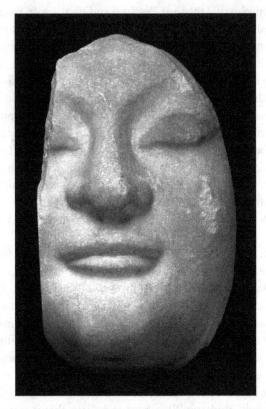

Figure 8.1 Fragment of female sculpture from Ephesos, perhaps part of a sculpted column base or other architectural element. © The Trustees of the British Museum.

Ionian architecture.[33] The distinctive "fluted" columns that are the most easily recognizable feature of the "Ionic" style were not used on many Archaic temples in Ionia. Instead the columns of the Temple of Artemis at Ephesos and the Temple of Apollo at Branchidai-Didyma were decorated with human figures (see Figure 8.1). Archaic temples in Ionia had elaborate roof tiles, decorated with gorgons' heads and other ornamentation, that were produced using molds specific to each temple-building project.[34] Another distinctive feature of the fully fledged "Ionic" style is the *peripteral* temple (i.e. with columns on all sides). Although the earliest known *peripteral* temple in Ionia, the first Temple of Artemis at Ephesos, dates to the eighth century BC,[35] this architectural innovation was not universally adopted by the other Ionian cities. In fact, if Hans Lohmann's assertion that his recent discovery of a temple on Çatallar Tepe can indeed be identified with the Temple of Poseidion Hellenikos – the "Panionion" – then it is interesting to note that this central sanctuary for all Ionians had columns that were neither fluted nor *peripteral*.[36]

---

[33] Koenigs 2007.
[34] Lohmann 2007b; Zimmermann 2007.
[35] Bammer 1990.
[36] Lohmann 2007b.

Within the precincts of these temples sacrifices were conducted and votive offerings dedicated that provide us with some of the most telling information about the socio-economic character of Ionia. Although once disregarded by archaeologists in favor of more attractive treasures, the detailed analysis of the remains of sacrificial animals gives modern archaeology valuable insights. A particularly interesting faunal study from Archaic Ionia comes from the Sanctuary of Aphrodite in Miletos. Here, Joris Peters and Angela von den Dreisch compared the bone assemblages from the sanctuary on Zeytin-tepe with those from the domestic quarter on Kalabaktepe.[37] The results of this compara-tive analysis highlighted a number of differences between the two that were in keeping with what we understand of Greek sacrificial practices from other sites and from written sources. The standard Greek custom that the animals for sacrifice should be young, fit specimens was evidently observed, as revealed by the comparative age profiles of the two assemblages. It was evidently also the practice that no pigs were sacrificed to Aphrodite as this was thought to be an offense to the goddess because her lover had been killed by a boar (Pausanias 2.10.4). Both wild and domesticated animals were sacrificed to Aph-rodite at Miletos[38] as they were to Artemis at Ephesos, as is appropriate to her character of huntress.[39]

As important as these insights from faunal analysis are, this method is limited in its application to identifiable pieces of bone, and as it was the practice to burn the bones on the altar within sight of the temple building during sacrifices, these are not always avail-able.[40] One such burnt altar was found in front of the Temple of Apollo at Branchidai-Didyma and found to contain lead models of votive *astragali* amongst the ashes, but no faunal evidence was recorded.[41]

Patterns of votive dedications are also in keeping with standard Greek practices else-where.[42] Votives were left intact[43] and they were appropriate to the character of the deity as worshipped in that particular locale[44] and were occasionally inscribed with the deity's name. In common with sacrificial practice, votive offerings were often of high value rela-tive to the status of the dedicatory event in the life of the individual, and their personal means,[45] although the value of some dedications may have been more symbolic than economic. The materials dedicated range from statues and elaborate bronzes, gold, and ivories to modest pottery and probably even more humble materials, now lost, and reflect the wide range of social participation in such cult activity. Votives were probably

---

[37] Peters and von den Driesch 1992.

[38] Peters and von den Driesch 1992: 119–23.

[39] Bammer and Muss 1996.

[40] Voyatzis 1990: 42, 269–73; Whitley 2001: 134–6.

[41] Wiegand 1911: 41–3; Greaves forthcoming (3).

[42] Simon 1986.

[43] i.e. they were not ritually "killed" as votives in some other cultures, including some cults in Greece, were.

[44] e.g. at the Temple of Aphrodite at Miletos, a wide variety of fish bones and sea shells were found among the faunal remains, reflecting the maritime nature of the goddess as worshipped at this site – Peters and von den Driesch 1992; Senff 2003; Greaves 2004; Greaves and Wilson forthcoming.

[45] Simon 1986.

displayed in the temple, although the richest archaeological deposits have been from *bothroi* (pits) into which votives appear to have been cleared periodically.[46]

The so-called Central Basis Deposit found during excavations at the Temple of Artemis at Ephesos included coins of high value from many different states and may show that this large temple was attracting dedications from across the region.[47] Literary sources tell us that the largest temples in Ionia apparently attracted vast quantities of high-value dedications, including those from foreign leaders.[48] However, little remains of these large dedications for archaeologists to discover, and the more mundane dedications made in smaller sanctuaries and systematically excavated in recent years provide more important evidence for the reconstruction of life in Ionia.

Votives should be pleasing to the gods, and as the gods are created in the imaginations of the dedicators, the artifacts dedicated in temples reflect the cultural values and aesthetics of the dedicator.[49] A great number of Egyptian, and Egyptianizing, artifacts were dedicated in temples in Ionia, particularly at the Temple of Hera on Samos (see below). Despite their foreign origin, these artifacts were laid down in a manner that was consistent with Greek practices, reflecting the value attached to such orientalia for their rarity and exotic value. Once again, the importance of understanding artifacts in context is paramount.

Extant images of deities are uncommon in Ionia. The majority of sculptures from Ionia probably represent human dedicants (see Figure 8.2; see also Chapter 9). Although not a universal feature, the central part of many Greek temples was occupied by the image of the god. Often made of wood, none of these survive from the temples of Ionia, but there are tantalizing references to them in much later literature that may indicate their original attributes and appearance, which in turn gives us insight into the identity and image of the god being venerated at that particular temple.[50] The preference of southern Ionian vase-painters for animal scenes means that we do not have the same wealth of imagery that Attic Black and Red Figure vase-painting provides for contemporary Athens. In North Ionia, the local painting traditions do provide us with some figurative images, including an early image of Athena with spear and shield on a Chian plate from Emporio,[51] and winged female figures on Klazomenian *sarcophagi*.[52] These latter, once thought by R.M. Cook to be non-specific supernatural beings, have since been reinterpreted as representing Ionian images of a war-like winged Athena.[53]

Much of this evidence relates to the images and practices associated with Greek deities. Finding secure evidence for non-Greek cults in Ionia has proven to be more difficult, but there have been a number of advances in this field in recent years, discussed below.

---

[46] See Senff 2007: Beilage 1, for a location of the numerous pits excavated in the vicinity of the Sanctuary of Aphrodite at Miletos.

[47] Hogarth 1908; Kraay 1976: 20. This is in contrast to the Kolophon hoard, which is composed of "pure" Kolophonian issues and probably represents a local, economic deposit. See Chapter 4.

[48] See Chapter 7.

[49] Or their antithesis – see R. Osborne 2007: 260–2 on dedications of "voodoo dolls" and curse tablets.

[50] e.g. Pausanias (7.5.9) on the statue of Athena in her temple at Erythrai, discussed in Chapter 9.

[51] Boardman 1967: 23–4, 163–4, n. 785, pl. 60; Villing 1998: 160, fig. 12.

[52] R.M. Cook 1981: 121–2.

[53] Villing 1998: 159–63.

Figure 8.2   Marble head of a youth from Bronchidai-Didyma. © The Trustees of the British Museum.

Literary and Epigraphic Evidence

As noted in Chapter 1, the surviving epigraphic language of Ionia was Greek and our evidence for its use is largely restricted to temples. Other languages are generally not represented in the epigraphic corpus of Archaic Ionia, and where non-Greek style sanctuaries have been identified, none of them contain any inscriptions, Greek or otherwise. This lack of a non-Greek epigraphic tradition, combined with a general lack of finds, makes such sanctuaries harder to date and interpret than those that adhered to more typically Greek modes of cult practice, but they should not be discounted from our consideration just because of this. The surviving Archaic inscriptions that we have tend to be very short and the longest pseudo-Archaic inscription that we have, the *Molpoi* inscription (see below), appears to be a reinscription of an earlier text that has been considerably altered and added-to in the process, a fact which presents many problems to its interpretation.[54]

Compared with some of the other themes discussed in this book, there is a relative abundance of historical references to religion in Ionia. However, many of these are

---

[54]   *Milet* 1.3.133; Gorman 2001: 176–86; Herda 2006.

oblique references (e.g. to the location of a temple, such as the burning and rebuilding of a temple to Athena at Assessos – Hdt. 1.17) or recounting exceptional events (e.g. Apollo speaking directly from his oracle at Branchidai-Didyma – Hdt. 1.158–9). In searching for the essence of the "Ionian" identity, scholars have placed much emphasis on the role of the festival of the Apatouria[55] and the Panionion.[56] The only temple in Ionia to which Herodotos could be said to have devoted particular attention was the Oracle of Apollo at Branchidai-Didyma and his purpose in doing this might only have been to build up its importance in order to make its sack at the hands of the Persians seem more brutal.[57] As in previous chapters, understanding these passing references within the context of the macro- and mediohistorical processes by the application of geographical and archaeological evidence will serve to deepen our understanding of their proper context.

Discussion of Source Materials

The consideration of Ionian cult buildings and practice within a Braudelian framework will present us with a new appreciation of their role in Ionian culture in general. For example, the selection of different ages and species of animals for sacrifice, and the treatment of their bones, can tell us a great deal about the preferences and practices of the Ionians, but ultimately the animals at their disposal were determined by the nature of the geographical structure (Braudel's *longue durée*) within which they were reared. As Alcock and Osborne write: "As the prominence of animal sacrifice indicates, civic ritual continued to centre upon the products of agriculture and to keep in the foreground the precarious provision of subsistence."[58] Another advantage that the Braudelian "holistic" methodology has over traditional text-based Classical archaeological approaches is that it will balance the under-representation of Anatolian cults in the region, by incorporating and valuing landscape and archaeological data, and not just historical arguments.

The Sacred Ways of Ionia

One of the most remarkable features of cult in Ionia is the existence of a number of Sacred Ways. At least four of these are known to have existed in Ionia, each linking a city to its major sanctuary (see Table 8.1). Sacred Ways are by no means unique to Ionia – the processional way that linked Athens and Eleusis[59] is more famous than any in Ionia – but

---

[55]   Hdt. 1.147.

[56]   See Chapter 7.

[57]   Harrison 2002 – reversal of fortune is a key theme in his historical writing about the Persian Wars. For example, he likens the wealth of dedications in the temple to those of Delphi (Hdt. 1.92), which would be familiar to his readership, and then reminds his readers of this fact when the Persians come to sack the temple (Hdt. 6.18).

[58]   Alcock and Osborne 2007: 245.

[59]   Another Sacred Way on the Anatolian coast is that between Pergamon and the Asclepion.

Table 8.1 Sacred Ways of Ionia

From	To	Distance
Kolophon	Oracle of Apollo at Klaros*	13 km
Ephesos	Temple of Artemis	2 km
Samos	Temple of Hera	7 km
Miletos	Oracle of Apollo at Branchidai-Didyma	16 km

* The Sacred Way probably ran a further 2 km south to Notion, making its total length 15 km.

they provide a useful entrée into understanding the application of the Braudelian methodology proposed in this book because of their physical relationship to the landscape. Sacred Ways were not purely ritual phenomena because they also had, or had developed, practical functions (see Chapter 5). They represent multifaceted archaeological phenomena that are worthy of serious consideration and serve to highlight many of the issues of geomorphology and phenomenology that were highlighted earlier in this book.[60]

Let us begin by considering each one of these Sacred Ways in detail, starting with the most northerly, to assess their archaeological remains, routes, and relationship to the location of the main temples.

Kolophon

The c.13 km-long Sacred Way from Kolophon to Klaros ran north–south through the bottom of the steep and narrow Ahmetbeyli Valley (Figure 8.3), the bottom of which has become covered by alluvium from the Ales River that flows there.

This alluvium has hampered attempts to trace the Sacred Way beyond the limits of the temple precinct, the entrance to which was marked by a propylon in the Roman period. The Sacred Way presumably connected Kolophon to Klaros and ran on toward the sea at or near the harbor town of Notion, 2 km further south. The earliest pottery is Geometric, but the spectacular ruins seen at Klaros today mostly date from the Hellenistic and Roman periods.[61] From the Archaic period there are remains of a temple to Apollo, altars to Apollo and Artemis, two Archaic *kouroi*, and an apparently robed image of Apollo Klarios.[62] As at many other sites in Ionia, excavations here are hampered by the great depth of alluvium and the raised water table (Figure 8.4) and there is therefore no evidence for the nature of the road surface or any roadside shrines. Between Kolophon and Klaros, there were *tumuli*[63] and rock-cut tombs[64] which the road presumably passed. Assuming the route of the Sacred Way followed the general course of the Ahmetbeyli Valley it would have been relatively straight and presented a generally gentle descent from Değirmendere, where Kolophon is located.

---

[60] This will be the subject of a larger forthcoming project by the author.

[61] Şahin 1998.

[62] Şahin et al. 2007: 600, esp. 607. This figure, which also wears a *polos*, may be female.

[63] Şahin 1998: 95, based on Schuhhardt's 1886 map.

[64] Şahin et al. 2007: 600–2.

Figure 8.3 The Ahmetbeyli Valley, looking north from Notion towards Klaros.

Figure 8.4 A view of the sacred precinct at Klaros showing the high water table. © Nikater 2008 (GNU Creative Commons Licence).

Ephesos

The Sacred Way from Ephesos to the Temple of Artemis was c.2 km long. Relatively little is known about the city of Ephesos in the Archaic period, although there is at least one known area of settlement on the north side of Panayır Dağı (see Chapter 5) and the route of the Sacred Way in the Archaic period is likely to have been similar to that of the better preserved Hellenistic and Roman route. That later route, through the city and out across the plain to the Temple of Artemis, was to become a major focus of religious activity and identity in the city.[65] In 1869, the English archaeologist John Turtle Wood (b.1821 d.1890), found the completely buried ruins of the temple at the foot of Ayasoluk Hill by excavating out along the line of the Sacred Way from the city's Magnesian Gate, which an inscription recorded as the starting point for a procession that carried statuettes to the temple.[66] The route of the Archaic Sacred Way was presumably quite flat as it ran along the edge of the sea covering the short distance across low-lying ground between the city and the temple. However, it must somehow have negotiated the river mouths and swampy ground that probably separated the two at this time.[67] Although the temple itself now sits in a hollow created by generations of excavators, it is thought to have originally stood on a low rise surrounded by marshy ground, and as such it would have been visible from certain parts of the city and for much of the length of the Sacred Way.

Samos

The Sacred Way to the Temple of Hera left the city of Samos and headed southwestwards for a distance of c.7 km over flat ground. Running close to the edge of the sea, it must have crossed the Imvrasos River near to which the temple complex originally stood. As at Ephesos, this swampy environment may originally have had cultic significance, but that detail of its setting is now lost due to landscape change. The remains of the temple are also covered by silt, but presumably it could originally be seen from some distance away. The temple would not have been the only thing to grace the horizon for approaching pilgrims, as a number[68] of colossal *kouros* statues were positioned beside the Sacred Way so as to make them visible from a distance.[69] Also lining the approaches to the temple were numerous other statues, including the famous Genelos Group – a family grouping of statues on a base.

Miletos

At c.16 km long, the Sacred Way from Miletos to Branchidai-Didyma is the longest in Ionia. It is also the best preserved and researched.[70] In common with the other three this Sacred Way adopts a relatively straight line between the city and the temple but, interestingly, in

---

[65]   Rogers 1991.
[66]   Wood 1877, 1890.
[67]   See Kerschner et al. 2008: pl. 50.
[68]   Fragments found during excavation indicate that there may have been as many as three monumental *kouroi* on the site originally (Guralnick 1996: 505).
[69]   R. Osborne 2007: 255.
[70]   Tuchelt et al. 1996; Herda 2006.

this case this is not the most ergonomic route. A simpler route would have been to follow the coast to Branchidai-Didyma, which is the line taken by the modern road. Instead the Sacred Way ascended the steep northern face of the Stephania escarpment, only to drop down the other side in a long descent toward Branchidai-Didyma. The effects of adopting this route will be examined below, but the reasons for this choice might have been that it was shorter than the coastal route, because it had cult significance, or because it did not expose the pilgrims to potential piratical raids from the coast.[71] Beyond the "Sacred Gate," where the road left the city, burials were sited, including the wealthy Lion Tomb, the entrance passage to which was flanked by lion sculptures.[72] The *Molpoi* inscription is a remarkable document that dates to c.450/49 BC. It appears to be a reinscription, with amendments, of an earlier Archaic period text.[73] This text describes an annual procession from the Temple of Apollo Delphinos in Miletos to his oracle at Branchidai-Didyma. The text notes a number of way-stations on the route, at which the procession should stop to make sacrifices, or sing *paeans* (hymns to Apollo). Some of these, such as the place of the Nymphs and the statue of Chares, have been firmly identified, but others, such as the altar of the Carian goddess Hekate at the city gates of Miletos, or the place of Dynamis, have not. The route of the Sacred Way has been successfully traced, or reasonably conjectured, on the ground for much of its length.[74] In its final few kilometers, the Sacred Way touches the coast at the harbor of Panormos (modern Mavi Şehir).[75] Panormos was probably the main access point to the temple at Branchidai-Didyma for many pilgrims, who arrived by sea.[76] From here, the final stretch of the Sacred Way rises up through a small gully toward the temple. Here the road surface is laid with stone slabs, from a later resurfacing, and was lined on either side with rows of lions and seated figures, both male and female.

Discussion: the Sacred Ways of Ionia

Sacred Ways always connect two places of cult significance – the sanctuary and the city, which was home to numerous sanctuaries of its own (see Table 5.1). Processions connected rural sanctuaries to the urban core, and vice versa, and the Sacred Ways discussed here can be seen as a manifestation of the processions.[77] As such they can be seen as the "physical embodiment" of the city–sanctuary relationship,[78] but they also represent the consolidation of a set of cult behaviors.

---

[71] Raiding was probably a common feature of life in Archaic Ionia, in which the oracle at Branchidai-Didyma may itself have played a role (see Chapter 7; Jackson 1995; Greaves 2000a: 51). In later history, Caesar was supposedly captured by pirates of the coast nearby, their intention possibly being to prey on pilgrims to Didyma (Plutarch *Caesar* 1–4).

[72] Forbeck and Heres 1997. See also Herda 2006 on the funerary elements of the *Molpoi* procession.

[73] *Milet* 1.3.133; Herda 2006. For an English translation and commentary see Gorman 2001: 176–86.

[74] See P. Schneider 1987.

[75] Greaves 2000a: 42–4.

[76] Herda 2006: 350.

[77] de Polignac 1995; R. Osborne 2007: 254–5.

[78] Greaves 2002: 117.

The Sacred Ways of Ionia share a number of common features: gateways where they enter and leave cities and sacred precincts,[79] high-status burials,[80] dedicatory statues (see Box 8.1), and minor cults.[81] The gateways are obviously a necessary feature of their progress out of the city and into the countryside which, as was noted in Chapter 5, marks an important transition. At the "Sacred Gate" of Miletos, where the road to Branchidai-Didyma emerged from the urban environment of the city into the rural world beyond, the *Molpoi* inscription records an altar to the Carian goddess Hekate, who was a "liminal" deity attributed with responsibility for crossroads and similar places of physical transition and change.[82] The presence of burials adjacent to the Sacred Ways is not just a reflection of their convenient physical location, but also a consequence of the behavior of processing along them, which would ensure that prominent funerary monuments positioned here would be seen by the whole community within the context of high-status ritual events.

With regard to the common features of their physical location, the Sacred Ways of Ionia are all adjacent to, or in some way connected with, the sea – as one would expect in this coastal region. Less obvious is the fact that, within the frame of modern aesthetic judgments, the locations of all four of the main temples are stunningly drab.[83] However, when considered from the perspective of an ancient viewer, and within the context of what we can now understand about changes that have taken place within the environment, their locations can be better understood. As mentioned above, it is now thought that the temples of Hera at Samos and Artemis at Ephesos originally stood in areas of marshland. In antiquity these would have been abundant with wild fauna and flora, and marshes appear to have had a religious significance from an early date.[84] As R.A. Tomlinson wrote when describing Ephesos: "The low-lying, marshy site is obviously similar to that of Hera on Samos and presumably reflects the particular needs of a local cult, established before the Greek settlement."[85] At Klaros and Branchidai-Didyma, the sanctuaries were sited over springs, which also have well-established cult associations. In the case of Branchidai-Didyma in particular, the spring here arose in an otherwise near-barren landscape, making it seem all the more miraculous.[86] Therefore although to the modern viewer these locations may appear uninspiring, they were imbued with religious meaning.

Phenomenology

Let us now consider, within our *Annaliste* framework, how such Sacred Ways might be experienced by individuals as they made their pilgrimages. The philosopher Martin Heidegger (b.1889 d.1976) believed that all life was essentially experiential, that is, to understand something we must understand it as it was experienced by the individual

---

[79] Kienast 2007, on Samos.

[80] e.g. Greaves 1999 and 2002: 87–9 on Miletos; Tsakos 2001 on Samos.

[81] e.g. those listed in the *Molpoi* inscription; see above and Table 5.1.

[82] Herda 2006: 282–5.

[83] On the location of Branchidai-Didyma, see Greaves 2002: 109.

[84] e.g. the Bronze Age fresco of ducks in a reed-bed from Akrotiri on Thera.

[85] Tomlinson 1976: 128.

[86] Greaves 2002: 10.

🐎🐎🐎 **Box 8.1** 🐎🐎🐎
The Chares Group

The so-called "Chares Group" of sculptures from the Sacred Way at Branchidai-Didyma is the largest and most important group of sculptures from Ionia.[a] Up until a century ago there were apparently as many as 60–70 statues to be seen, lining the approaches to the sanctuary.[b] The statues have been removed to museums across Europe and Turkey, including London, Paris, İstanbul, İzmir, and Balat (Miletos), but only 17 seated figures and two lions are now known to scholarship.[c]

Stylistically, the sculptures are dateable to the second quarter of the sixth century BC and the group includes both male and female figures. The fact that they are seated and the males are robed distinguishes them from the *kore* (female) and *kouros* (male) statue traditions of Greek sculpture, which are generally standing and the males nude. Although they were first found by archaeologists lining the Sacred Way, they may originally have been positioned in kin groups like the Genelos Group from the Sacred Way at Samos (see Figure 8.7).

The most famous statue in the group is a figure of a seated male that bears a *boustrophedon* inscription on the forward right leg of his chair that reads: "I am Chares, son of Kleisis, *archon* of Teichioussa. The statue is for Apollo."[d] Chares appears to have been an official appointed by Miletos to the small settlement of Teichioussa, which was on the eastern edge of its territory. This statue was possibly originally erected in a separate cult area dated to 570/50 BC, and similar to that found previously on the Sacred Way at "The Heights." The original location of this is unknown, but it may have been on the route from Teichioussa to Branchidai-Didyma or somewhere else in the vicinity. By the time of the *Molpoi* inscription, in the first century BC, the statue of Chares has become the penultimate stop on the *Molpoi* procession's progress from Miletos, where they evidently stopped to sing a paean to Apollo, before entering his sanctuary at Branchidai-Didyma.

Notes

[a]   J.M. Cook 1962.
[b]   Tomlinson 1976: 132.
[c]   Jenkins 1992: 188–9; Herda 2006: 327–50.
[d]   Didyma 2: 5–6 [trans. Boardman 1978: 96]; Herda 2006.

concerned. The archaeological theorist Chris Tilley developed this concept to create a phenomenology of landscape – a perspective by which we can start to appreciate landscapes as experience, not just as a physical space.[87] As an illustration of this, consider how an individual walking from Miletos to Branchidai-Didyma along the Sacred Way would experience the landscape. Walking through the intensively cultivated fields around Miletos he or she would ascend the north side of the Stephania escarpment via a steep path to arrive at the summit of the ridge. Here the pilgrim would be greeted by a vision of a completely new landscape – one that was sparsely populated and uncultivated in contrast to the fertile tilled fields behind him – in the middle of which rose up the Temple

[87]   Tilley 1997.

(a) Marble statue of Chares, ruler of Teichioussa, c.560 BC. © The Trustees of the British Museum.
(b) Marble statue of a woman seated in a chair from Didyma, c.530–510 BC. © The Trustees of the British Museum.

of Apollo that was his or her destination. This point is therefore a natural "epiphany point" in the individual's experience of the landscape. It is also a natural stopping point in the journey and it is perhaps no surprise that there was an intense concentration of cult activity here to mark this important point.[88]

Not only does the physical structure of the landscape affect the individual's experience of it, but so too do the human structures that become part of that landscape in medio-historical timeframes, such as the road itself. Consider how, when approaching the Temple of Hera at Samos, a pilgrim might first view the colossal *kouros* statues in the distance. Tilley would argue that the human eye is naturally drawn toward prominent

---

[88] Tuchelt et al. 1996.

human features in the landscape; they interrupt the natural landscape and socialize it. So our pilgrim on the road to the Temple of Hera, or standing on the summit of the Stephania, would see the prominent *kouroi* or temple buildings and experience the landscape not as a natural, unspoiled one, but a religious one. Unlike the physical structures of landscape that are essentially fixed in the *longue durée*, the meaning of archaeological structures and artifacts is negotiable. That is to say, societies attach their own meanings to artifacts, and those meanings can change as societies change.[89] Therefore, a statue that might "socialize" the landscape for a pre-Christian era individual might "paganize" it for someone viewing it from a Christian perspective.[90]

Finally, there are the microhistorical events that happened on the day of the pilgrimage itself that also affect how our pilgrim experienced the journey along a Sacred Way. The *Molpoi* inscription is, in effect, an itinerary of ceremonies and hymns to be performed and sung along the route between the city and the temple. These not only create another layer of social experience for the individual, but would also have created sensory experiences, such as the sound of music and the smell of burning sacrifices.

In this tripartite *Annaliste* perspective, the significance of the microhistorical events that are documented in the *Molpoi* inscription can be understood in a more nuanced context. This method also liberates us from the tyranny of close textual analysis. Consider our pilgrim's return journey, which is not covered in the inscription, which documents only a one-way itinerary. How would he or she have experienced the epiphanic moment when, having trudged up the long, slow ascent of the southern face of the Stephania escarpment, they first glimpsed the lush fields of Milesia laid out before them?

Cultural associations

Sacred Ways are not restricted to Ionian, or even Greek, culture. When looking for the cultural associations of the Ionian Sacred Ways it has been normal to look to Egypt, which was the inspiration for many of the artistic works displayed along their length and for the configuration of their arrangement. For example, the scale, technique, and styling of the monumental *kouroi* of Samos (e.g. see Figure 8.5) show Egyptian influence.[91] The arrangement of figures along the Sacred Way to Branchidai-Didyma would also, on first examination, appear to have an Egyptian influence. For example, the sanctuary on the summit of the Stephania features a semi-circle of seated figures reminiscent of the *dromos* (entrance passage) on the Serapeum Way at Saqqara in Egypt[92] and a row of sphinxes, similar to those at Saqqara and the lions of Delos, that are also thought to have been inspired by Egypt.[93] Perhaps the most obvious parallel is that between the rows of seated figures that flanked the final approaches to the *temenos* at Branchidai-Didyma and the colossi of Abu Simbel (Compare Box 8.1 and Figure 8.6). However, a recent re-evaluation

---

[89]   Shanks 1996: 120–3.

[90]   In this context it is interesting to remember that almost all of the statues that once lined the approaches to Didyma were decapitated, presumably by Christian iconoclasts. See Box 8.1 and Figure 8.7.

[91]   Guralnick 1996.

[92]   Discovered by Auguste Mariette in 1851 and never fully published. The site is described by Strabo (17.1.32). This arrangement of figures in a semi-circle may also be late in date.

[93]   Boardman 1999: 144–5.

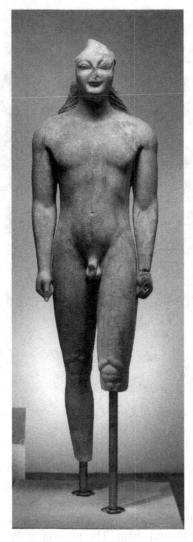

Figure 8.5   Colossal *kouros* from Samos (DAI Athens).

of the Chares Group by Alexander Herda has shown that these figures were probably repositioned in antiquity.[94] In their original alignment, they were probably arranged in a separate cult enclosure, like that found on the summit of the Stephania on the Sacred Way from Miletos to Branchidai-Didyma, or in a family group like the Genelos Group on the Sacred Way at Samos (Figure 8.7).[95] Herda's new interpretation would appear to suggest that their secondary arrangement was a later attempt to "Egyptianize" them by repositioning them not in their original groupings, but into a serried rank along the temple approaches. This element of Egyptian influence on the Sacred Ways of Ionia is,

[94]   Herda 2006.
[95]   Herda 2006: 327–50.

Figure 8.6   Abu Simbel. Courtesy of Chris Eyre.

in the case of the Chares Group at least, a later palimpsest overlaid on its earlier physical structures and sculptures. This again reminds us of the importance of not viewing these Sacred Ways as achronological fixed structures, but as axes of cult activity that were continuously developing and taking on new negotiated meanings as the values and aesthetics of society changed around them. The placing of Egyptian-influenced *kouroi* or other sculptures on these Sacred Ways does not mean that the Sacred Ways themselves were an Egyptian-inspired idea – especially if one discounts the arrangement of the very important Chares Group as being an Egyptian inspiration.

If the Sacred Ways of Ionia predate the superimposition onto them of a later Egyptophile cultural aesthetic, then are there also residual traces of pre-Greek cult activity that can be identified here? The processions that connected the settlements with their temples, if not the physical roads themselves, presumably date back as far as the earliest cult activity at those sites. Although it is hard to say precisely when *cult* activity started at these large extra-mural sites, there is certainly evidence for some form of activity from the Bronze Age at Samos, Ephesos,[96] and, to a lesser extent, at Branchidai-Didyma.[97] A feature of

[96]   Bammer 1990: 142.
[97]   Schattner 1992.

Figure 8.7 Reconstruction of the Genelos group from the Sacred Way at Samos (DAI Athens).

Bronze Age Anatolian and Aegean cult practice appears to have been the presence of extra-mural sanctuaries that related to phenomena in the landscape. Examples of this in an Anatolian context are sacred springs[98] and rock carvings,[99] and in an Aegean context, Minoan peak and cave sanctuaries. In post-Hittite Anatolia, these cult practices appear to have continued as neo-Hittite and Phrygian sacred rock carvings.[100]

At Ephesos, which can be equated with the Bronze Age Arzarwan capital of Apaša,[101] a number of interesting Bronze Age and early Iron Age cult installations have recently been identified at the site. First is a spring sanctuary on the north side of Ayasoluk,[102] which has been suggested as the site of the Bronze Age settlement,[103] just to the south of which lies the Temple of Artemis. Here a natural spring evidently fed a waterfall that emptied into a basin carved into the bedrock, surrounded by rock-cut niches. A bronze figurine of a Hittite priest has also been found on the north side of Panayır Dağı, which suggests further Hittite cultic activity here.[104] Also recently identified at Ephesos is a

---

[98]   e.g. Eflatun Pınar near Konya – Mellaart 1962.
[99]   e.g. Yazılıkaya at Boğazköy-Hattuša Collins 2007: 162.
[100] Roller 1999.
[101] Hawkins 1998; Büyükkolancı 2007.
[102] Bammer and Muss 2007.
[103] Büyükkolancı 2007.
[104] Hanfmann 1962.

neo-Hittite style rock relief found at the site of Balık Boğaz on Bülbül Dağı, just south of
the city, which features a human figure flanked by antithetical animals, one of which is
a deer.[105] It has also been argued that the statuettes found in the Temple of Artemis show
influences from neo-Hittite sculpture.[106] Finally, a rock-cut "shaft monument" of a type
known in Phrygia has been relocated and published close to the city, also on Bülbül
Dağı.[107]

If the convergence of these new pieces of evidence and interpretations points toward
there being a considerable amount of Hittite and post-Hittite Anatolian-style cult practice
at Ephesos, it could be suggested that the concept of sacred processions that linked settlements to such extra-mural cult sites might also have come from within Anatolia.[108] At
the Hittite capital of Hattuša, one of the city's most sacred places was Yazılıkaya, a narrow
cleft in the natural bedrock beyond the city walls, which was covered with over 100 m of
rock carvings depicting the Hittite pantheon and was where Hittite kings were buried.[109]
Although there is no secure evidence of a Sacred Way connecting Hattuša to Yazılıkaya,
the city was equipped with a number of highly elaborate ceremonial gateways. The Sacred
Ways of Ionia might therefore represent the physical consolidation of a set of cult practices that predate the period of Greek cultural predominance.

It is perhaps also significant to note that at least three out of the four major sanctuaries
with Sacred Ways attached were oracles – those at Klaros,[110] Branchidai-Didyma,[111] and
Ephesos.[112] Oracles were an important feature of Hittite cult practice.[113] The post-Hittite
Phrygian culture of Anatolia also practiced divination, and it appears that the group of
rock-cut cult installations known as "shaft monuments," similar to that found at Ephesos
(above), may have been where such oracles operated.[114]

The very gods worshipped in these temples may themselves also have found their
origins in Anatolia. Although studying the origins of these nebulous mythological constructs, which were subject to near-constant syncretism and negotiation, is fraught with
difficulties, it is worth noting that serious consideration has been given to the Anatolian
origins of Artemis at Ephesos[115] and Apollo,[116] although we may never precisely know
the character of the Anatolian gods that the Greeks conflated into their own deities to
create them.

---

[105]   İçten and Krinzinger 2004.
[106]   İşik 2003: 66–8.
[107]   Berndt-Ersöz 1998; Bammer and Muss 2006.
[108]   e.g. a procession, including musicians and acrobats, is depicted on the orthostats at the gate to the Hittite
site of Alaca Höyük (Collins 2007: 130).
[109]   Collins 2007. The theme of the Yazılıkaya rock carvings can also be interpreted as the meeting of two
"processions" of deities. Interestingly, Yazılıkaya was the scene of the Hittite New Year ceremony, as the *Molpoi*
procession marked the New Year in Miletos.
[110]   Parke 1985: 112–70, 219–24.
[111]   Parke 1985: 1–111; Fontenrose 1988.
[112]   Hogarth 1908: 191.
[113]   e.g. Ünal and Kammenhuber 1974; Collins 2007: 166–9.
[114]   Berndt-Ersöz 1998; Berndt-Ersöz 2003, esp. 191–3.
[115]   e.g. by Fleischer 1973.
[116]   Brown 2004 on Apollo.

The rituals practiced on these Sacred Ways may also have had pre-Greek origins. For example, according to the later reinscribed *Molpoi* inscription, two stone cubes (*gulloi*) were brought out toward the start of the procession and one was placed before the Carian Hekate at the gates of Miletos.[117] It was then adorned with wreaths and libations of undiluted wine were made. A second *gullos* was to be placed before the doors at Branchidai-Didyma. The origins of this obscure ritual act are unclear, but analogies made to later Greek cult practices have suggested that they might be aniconic images of Apollo, boundary stones, or associated with funerary cult.[118] However, no attempt has been made to understand this enigmatic ritual, which is evidently a crucial part of the *Molpoi* procession, in relation to Anatolian traditions, which were apparently often focused on stone.

In this rich blend of cults, there is little that one might consider canonically "Greek." Perhaps the way to best understand these Sacred Ways and their associated cults is to think of them as axes and foci of cult activity within the landscape, that had effectively become part of that landscape as it was experienced by the people who lived there. The origins of these Sacred Ways might have been the Anatolian (and Aegean) preference for extra-mural sanctuaries and the processions that presumably linked them to the (shifting) urban core. One might well imagine that into such a landscape the increasing predominance of the Greeks was at first accommodated, and then assimilated, during a medio-historical process of social change. Finally, texts such as the *Molpoi* inscription provide us with microhistorical snapshots of events seen through the language of Greek, that were probably ultimately of Anatolian origin.

This conclusion has been achieved by approaching the study of the Sacred Ways of Ionia by means of the *Annaliste* approach propounded by this book: starting with a detailed consideration of their landscape context and then considering their diachronic development as archaeological phenomena within that landscape, before finally considering the production of any historical texts within the context that emerges for this process of analysis. There are no ethnohistorical texts to test the hypothesis that the processions that may have been the origin of the Sacred Ways of Ionia were an Anatolia-inspired tradition that began in the Bronze Age or post-Bronze Age cult traditions of Anatolia, but if we restrict ourselves to standards of proof that accept only written texts as an acceptable basis of proof, then we fail to understand Ionia as it truly was – a dynamic culture that included non-Greeks and had developed within an Anatolian context.

"Foreign" Influences on Ionian Cult

As visible, high-status representations of the state and the collective identity of its people, religious sites have a particular importance for understanding ancient cultures. In particular the way in which cult centers can adopt and use the cult practices of "foreign" cultures can reveal the nature of the relationships between them. Elspeth Dusinberre, for example, has analyzed how Lydian and Persian cults were syncretized at Sardis as a means

---

[117] *Milet* 1.3: 133; Gorman 2001: 178–9, 184; Herda 2006: 249–59, 282–5.
[118] Herda 2006: 249–59.

to understanding the effects of Persian control of the Lydian kingdom.[119] In Ionia, the wealth, diversity, and localized nature of the evidence make a comprehensive analysis of cult practice here a complex undertaking. For the purposes of this book, a single theme will be highlighted that affects the way in which we understand the nature of the evidence base, namely the way in which cult needs to be understood in context and how the evidence for it has been identified by scholars. This discussion will be restricted to the contrast between Egyptian and "Anatolian" cult materials in the region.

Many sanctuaries in Ionia feature artifacts of Egyptian origin. In order to understand the role that this class of foreign artifact played in Ionian religion it is necessary to consider the precise nature of their deposition. The Ionian site that attracted the greatest concentration of Egyptian material was the Temple of Hera on Samos, which has considerably more of this type of material than comparable sites in mainland Greece or elsewhere in Ionia.[120] Other cult sites in Ionia also attracted votives of Egyptian, or Egyptianizing, material including the Sanctuary of Athena at Erythrai, the Sanctuary of Apollo at Kato Phana on Chios, the Sanctuary of Aphrodite at Miletos and the Oracle of Apollo at Branchidai-Didyma.[121] Although the presence of this high-prestige Egyptian material, which may have been brought back to the sanctuaries of Ionia by mercenaries or other travelers (see Chapter 7), may have influenced Ionian artists (see Chapter 9) it was only at a later date that Egyptian cults were adopted.[122]

In the Archaic period, Egyptian materials were very visible in the main sanctuaries, but they were deployed in a manner that was entirely consistent with the votive practices of the Archaic Ionians, who generally dedicated the most prestigious and valuable materials that they could afford to their gods.[123] In a few cases, it has been argued that the use of Egyptianalia in Ionian sanctuaries does go beyond their passive use as ornaments for dedication and appears to reflect an appreciation of their cult meanings in their original Egyptian contexts. For example, Günther Hölbl has argued that the types of Egyptian imports found in Ionian temples between the eighth and mid-sixth centuries BC include many scarabs and amuletic figurines that served to protect women and children in traditional Egyptian magic.[124] This would be entirely consistent with such artifacts being dedicated by mercenaries and travelers who left their families at home (see Chapter 7). Helga Bumke has also argued that a bronze statuette of the Egyptian god Bes found at the Oracle of Apollo at Branchidai-Didyma might have had some relation to the nature of cult at that site.[125] And the similarities between a new class of Klazomenian *sarcophagus* and Egyptian prototypes "cannot be accidental," according to Bilge Hürmüzlü.[126] In all these cases it can be seen that the decision to use Egyptian material as votives in Ionian

---

[119] Dusinberre 2003: 199.
[120] Boardman 2006: 524.
[121] Lamb 1935; Bumke 2002; Boardman 2006, Hölbl 2007.
[122] e.g. the temples of the Egyptian gods at New Priene and to Serapis at Miletos.
[123] Simon 1986 has shown that it was the socio-economic situation of the dedicator that determined the nature of votive offerings at Ionian cult sites.
[124] Hölbl 2007.
[125] Bumke 2002. See also Bumke 2007 on the dedication of Egyptian material at Samos.
[126] Hürmüzlü 2004: 197.

temples, even where an awareness of the cult meaning of those materials in their originating society can be demonstrated, or as inspiration for locally produced terracotta *sarcophagi*, is evidence of the Ionians' own agency at work – they actively chose what to deposit and which particular Egyptian cult meanings they were prepared to accommodate into their vision of their own gods.

Only later in the history of Ionia does the wholesale adoption of Egyptian cults occur, such as when a temple to the Egyptian god Serapis was built in Miletos in the third century AD. Also later in Ionian history, mythologizing traditions transpose motifs from Egyptian mythology onto Ionian deities, such as the story of Branchus' mother swallowing the sun – an Egyptian motif – appearing here in the foundation myth of the Branchidai-Didyma oracle.[127]

However, the same cannot be said of the Anatolian (i.e. "Phrygian"-style) cult sites, a number of which have recently been identified across Ionia. Firm evidence for Phrygian-style cult installations in Ionia includes four sanctuaries of Cybele at Phokaia,[128] the "Homer Stone" at Daskalopetra on Chios,[129] a shaft monument on Bülbül Dağı near Ephesos,[130] a sanctuary of Cybele at Galesion Hill near Ephesos,[131] rock-cut images of Cybele/Athena at Erythrai,[132] and rock-cut niches with terracotta images of a seated Cybele figure with lions from Priene.[133] Other possible Phrygian-style cult sites include a cult installation at Miletos[134] and a number of grave-like rock-cut niches with drainage channels situated in prominent rocky locations at Ephesos[135] and Myous.[136] These rock-cut features resemble Carian graves, which would originally have been capped by a stone slab,[137] but the provision of water channels, as at Ephesos, or steps, as at Myous, suggests post-funerary ritual usage, or even an entirely different form of non-funerary cult usage, despite their morphological similarity to graves.[138]

The fact that most of these sites have only been identified after extensive research into the Greek-style temple buildings at the same sites reflects the predilection of previous generations of Classical archaeologists for finding Greek-style sculpture and monumental buildings and the subsequent late adoption of survey methodologies to investigate areas beyond the urban core.[139] With the exceptions of the Sanctuary of Cybele by the harbor in Phokaia, the presumed cult installation on Kalabaktepe at Miletos, and the images of Cybele/Athena at Erythrai, all these sites are located beyond the confines of cities. Indeed,

---

[127] Burkert 1994: 51, citing Konon FGrH 26F 1.33; Varro in Schol. Stat. Theb. 8.198.
[128] O. Özyiğit 2003.
[129] Yalouris 1986: 179.
[130] Bammer and Muss 2006.
[131] Aydın 2007: 20, fig. 9. The only pottery found on the surface during survey here was Roman, although the monument itself would appear to be of an earlier date.
[132] See Chapter 5.
[133] See Chapter 5. The figures may be classical in date.
[134] Brinkmann 1990; Greaves 2002: 86.
[135] Bammer 2007: 105–8.
[136] See Chapter 5, esp. Figure 5.1.
[137] e.g. at Labraunda; see Hellström 2007: 148–9.
[138] Vassileva 2001: Bammer and Muss 2007.
[139] Greaves 2007a.

"remote settings" are the norm for cult sites of Cybele.[140] The recognition of so many "Phrygian"-style cult features in an area that would generally be considered to be beyond the geographical limits of the Phrygian kingdom will no doubt add to ongoing discussions about the extent and influence of this important culture[141] – a culture that existed on the edge of the Greek world and the cognizance of its writers.

Another difficulty has been that whatever cult practices took place here, they do not appear to have included the deposition of votives in the Greek manner. The resulting lack of surface finds by which to locate, identify, and date them is exacerbated by the preference for raised, rocky locations where there is little or no soil to retain any pottery that may have been deposited.[142] Their very nature as negative rock-cut features also means that there will be no architectural finds on the surface by which to locate and understand them. Whatever cult practices were performed at these sites, they appear to have left no archaeological trace. If one accepts that the rituals that took place before Hekate at the gates of Miletos during the *Molpoi* procession were of Anatolian origin, then libations and wreaths may have been involved.[143] The grave-like rock-cut basins found at Ephesos and Myous may have been associated with water cult[144] and the Phrygian-style shaft monument at Ephesos may have been used for divination.[145]

The nature of the relationship between the Greek and Anatolian cults of Ionia is a difficult one to prove, and each site must be treated individually. At Erythrai and Phokaia, for example, there appears to be a close physical proximity between the localities of the cults of Cybele and Athena and, at Erythrai, it can been argued that the iconography of the cult image was derived from, or at least compatible with, Phrygian images of Cybele (see Chapter 9). However, relating Anatolian-style cult installations such as these to their Greek counterparts is hard because of the lack of pottery, charcoal, or other dateable materials. Given this lack of dating evidence, it is possible to postulate a number of ways in which these cults may have interacted with one another during the Archaic period. First, the Greek cults could have swept the pre-Hellenic Anatolian cults aside with the arrival of the Ionian Migration. This would seem to fit with the overall historical metanarrative and general tone of the individual literary sources associated with the Ionian Migration, such as the foundation of Miletos (Hdt. 1.146 – see Epilogue). Secondly, they may have co-existed, each with its own separate social constituency within the city. The foundation myth of Ephesos suggests that the pre-existing cult of Artemis was allowed to continue after the Greeks founded their own temples and city (Pausanias 7.2.6) and some non-Greek cults evidently persisted in Ionia into the time of the fifth-century BC historians. Thirdly, there may have been syncretism between the two cult traditions in which they merged with one another. In this case it is interesting to note that although it can be seen that there are elements of Anatolian cult that have been accommodated into Greek cult practices (e.g. a seated cult image of Athena at Erythrai, similar to

---

[140]   Roller 1999: 109.

[141]   e.g. Vassileva 2001 on Bulgaria and G.D. Summers 2006 on central Anatolia.

[142]   Bammer 2007: 103.

[143]   *Milet* 1.133; Herda 2006.

[144]   Vassileva 2001; Bammer 2007; Bammer and Muss 2007.

[145]   Greaves forthcoming (3), citing Berndt-Ersöz 1998, 2003.

Phrygian-style images of Cybele), there is never any indication that there was any Hellenization of the Anatolian cults in the Archaic period.[146] This would be consistent with a pre-existing, and predominant, Anatolian culture being in place during the early years of Greek occupation in Ionia, with the Greek cults only rising to predominate at a later date. This hypothesis is purely speculative as more chronological and archaeological evidence would be needed to prove it, but it nevertheless presents a very different construct of Ionia to that based on the traditional narratives of Greek history (the first and second scenarios given above).

In conclusion, it can be seen that elements of Egyptian cult culture were accommodated into Ionian cult without effecting any major change upon it and in ways that demonstrate the agency and integrity of Ionian identity. Of the different historically attested groupings present in Archaic western Anatolia, those that would be indicated by the metanarrative of Greek history – the Carian/Lelegians and the Lydians – cannot be shown to have had any significant influence on any image of Ionian identity derived from literary or epigraphic sources. However, there is a persistent and increasing body of evidence to show that what might be described as "Phrygian"-style cults were present in largely unmodified form in Ionia. By way of contrast, Greek cults can be seen to have accommodated elements of "Phrygian"-style cult practice into them. Indeed a number of major *polis* cults appear to have developed out of Anatolian origins, becoming Hellenized only later.[147] The body of evidence for "Phrygian"-style cult is only likely to increase as archaeological surveys continue beyond the urban cores of the Ionian cities. If the primacy of the "Phrygian"-style cults in pre-Greek and early Archaic Ionia is accepted, then it would be ironic that Walter Burkert should have classified Cybele as a "foreign" deity[148] when, in Ionia, she is perhaps the only truly local deity for which we have evidence.

Burial Practices in Ionia[149]

Burials are not just a ritual activity; they are also very public events and for this reason they are useful indicators of community identity. For example, the fact that the famous painted terracotta *sarcophagi* of Klazomenai have enlarged, richly decorated rims that would be visible from the graveside when the coffin was laid in the grave suggests

---

[146] It is interesting to note that the function of the presumed Hittite water sanctuary on Ayasoluk at Ephesos was negotiated to take on a funerary function by the addition of a secondary grave (Bammer and Muss 2007), but evidence of such renegotiation of the function of the Phrygian-style monuments in Ionia is so far lacking. In fact, if the later pottery and figurines at Priene and Galesion Hill were dedications, then their primary cult function may have been maintained for centuries.

[147] e.g. Fleischer 1973 on the origins of Artemis at Ephesos as Anatolian mother-goddess; Greaves forthcoming (3) on Apollo at Branchidai-Didyma and above on the cult of Athena at Erythrai.

[148] Burkert 1985.

[149] The author is aware that a major study of burial traditions in Ionia is underway (by Olivier Mauriaud), and refers the reader to the forthcoming publication of that study for a more in-depth treatment than the brief overview offered here.

that some ceremony may have accompanied the act of burial.[150] When one considers burial practices in Ionia, one is immediately struck by the fact that there was a great variance in the burial practices between different sites, presumably reflecting the different character and identity of these communities.

A very brief survey, from north to south, will serve to illustrate the degree of variance that existed within Archaic Ionia. At Phokaia, burials in clay *sarcophagi* have been found at two locations within the city,[151] whilst to the west of the city three exceptional tombs have been found: a large *tumulus* (at Maltepe), a rock-cut Lydian tomb (the Şeytan Hamamı), and a monolithic "Persian"-style tomb carved out of the bedrock (Taş Kule).[152] Within Chios town, burials have been found in stone *sarcophagi*. At Klazomenai, in the seventh century BC cremation burials with grave goods were positioned in enclosed individual burial grounds, presumably for separate *genē* (descent) groups; by the sixth century BC unaccompanied burials were being made in painted *sarcophagi*. There were also a number of *tumuli* at the site.[153] The Archaic *necropoleis* of Erythrai, Teos, Lebedos, and Kolophon have all either yet to be found, or yet to be fully published. At Ephesos, burials in stone *sarcophagi* were found under the Roman *agora*; there are also *tumuli* on the nearby Kuyutepe Hill and rock-cut graves here and on Ayasoluk.[154] At Samos, 161 graves were identified in the West Cemetery, dating from the seventh and sixth centuries BC – the majority were marked by an amphora, 23 were unmarked, five were urn cremations under mounds, and one was a large built tomb.[155] A *necropolis* with *tumuli* was found outside of the settlement and other graves were marked by distinctive palmettes.[156] The *necropolis* and site of Old Priene have yet to be located. At Myous, a handful of undated rock-cut graves are visible at the site. At Miletos, seven stone *sarcophagi* with pitched marble slab lids and one earth-cut grave were found during rescue excavations under the modern village,[157] an undisturbed rock-cut chambered tomb with *dromos* and flanking lions was found,[158] and an isolated find of a palmette of a type used as grave markers in Athens indicates they may also have been used here.[159]

This plethora of different burial traditions can be accounted for in a number of ways. First, burial traditions were not conservative and they changed over time. For example, in Klazomenai not all of the six identified burial areas were in use at the same time, and new burial forms developed including the famous Klazomenian painted *sarcophagi*, which only came into use in the sixth century BC, prior to which cremation appears to have been the norm.[160] Secondly, there was social differentiation between the burials of the elite (e.g. the Lion Tomb at Miletos) and those lower down in society (presumably

---

[150] Cook and Dupont 1998: 121.
[151] Ö. Özyiğit 2003: 118–19, fig. 8.
[152] Cahill 1988.
[153] Hürmüzlü 2004; Ersoy 2007.
[154] Bammer 2007: 111; Bammer and Muss 2007.
[155] Morris 1987: 148; Tsakos 2001.
[156] Tsakos 2007.
[157] Müller-Wiener 1992, esp. 253.
[158] Forbeck and Heres 1997.
[159] von Graeve 1989.
[160] Ersoy 2007.

the stone *sarcophagi* and earth-cut graves that were found at the same site). Practices such as these could also change over time, and Ian Morris has argued that at some point in the sixth century BC Polykrates may have introduced a sumptuary law to limit expenditure of lavish burials.[161] Thirdly, there are distinctively local variations in burial practice – such as the painted *sarcophagi* of Klazomenai, which were a twist on the standard terracotta *sarcophagi* used elsewhere in Greece.[162] Finally, and perhaps most interestingly, there is the shifting allegiance of the social elite. For much of the Archaic period from c.700 BC onwards, the leaders of many cities in Ionia ruled by the permission or consent of the established powers within Anatolia – first Lydia and then Persia. At Phokaia, for example, we see the adoption of monumental styles of Lydian tombs – the Maltepe *tumulus* and the Şeytan Hamamı rock tomb.[163] Lydian-style *tumuli* are also evident at Klazomenai[164] and Ephesos.[165] The Lydian-style tombs of Phokaia are followed by a monumental "Persian"-style tomb – the Taş Kule[166] – although most Persians or Persianizers were evidently buried in local-style tombs.[167] Even Athens puts in an appearance in the south of Ionia, where there is Athenian influence apparent on the palmette found at Akyeniköy, near Miletos.[168]

These themes of lack of conservatism in burial practice, local diversity, social differentiation, and assimilation of the burial traditions of the dominant non-Greek elite can all be seen in the burials of Ionian colonies in the Black Sea.[169] For example, Damyanov has argued that cremation traditions at Berezan changed with the coming of Ionian colonists, but remained unchanged at Orgame and Histria.[170] We must, therefore, consider carefully what we mean when we talk about "Ionian" burial practices in colonial contexts, as Ionian traditions at home were obviously eclectic and adaptive.[171]

Conclusions

If religion is indeed an important medium for mediating the interaction of different cultures, then the nature of the relationships that are revealed by studying the cults of Ionia are perhaps unexpected. It has long been recognized that the very un-Greek cult images of Artemis at Ephesos must have had an Anatolian origin, but this would perhaps be expected as her cult was said to have pre-Greek origins even by ancient writers. However, what this new survey of the evidence shows is that there were also many other

[161]   Morris 1987: 148.
[162]   R.M. Cook 1981; Cook and Dupont 1998: 121–8.
[163]   Ö. Özyiğit 2003.
[164]   Ersoy 2007.
[165]   Bammer 2007.
[166]   Cahill 1988.
[167]   Ratté 1992: 160.
[168]   von Graeve 1989.
[169]   Avram 2007: 491 describes a diversity of burial practices in sites around the Milesian colony of Histria. See also Solovyov 2007 on Berezan; Vasilica Lungu speaking on Orgame in Cambridge, March 28, 2007.
[170]   Damyanov 2005.
[171]   Greaves forthcoming (2).

cult sites in Ionia that showed affinity with the traditions of Anatolia. Many of these can be seen to be "Phrygian" in style. The way in which these two cult traditions syncretized seems to be one in which the Greek cults adapted to the pre-existing "Phrygian" traditions of the region and there is not yet any indication that the "Phrygian" cults adapted themselves to Greek tastes. The Sacred Ways of Ionia, which constituted the most important concentration of cult activity in several key states, can be seen to be a "hybrid" of Anatolian and Greek traditions, possibly originating from processions which connected natural phenomena of the landscape with cult significance to the urban core. These cults did not originate in the Archaic period, rather it was a stage in a long process of syncretism that evidently began with the coming of Greeks to Ionia at the end of the Bronze Age (see Chapter 10), and which would continue after the end of the Archaic period. How that process of melding elements of Greek culture into the Anatolian can be seen to have been at work in the production of the craft items, or "art," will be the topic of our next and last chapter.

9

The Ornaments of Ionia

Introduction

The final thematic chapter of this book is the one where, for many people, their engagement with Ionia begins: the visual arts. The artworks of Archaic Ionia are plentiful and it would not be possible to provide a detailed survey of them here.[1] The purpose of this chapter is not to provide an overview of art in Ionia, but to understand the context within which art was produced, and to use that understanding of context as a means to consider what the Ionians' art can tell us about their cultural identity.

Anyone who has ever gazed at a urinal, a pile of bricks, or a soiled bed and wondered if it constitutes "art" or not has usually done so in the Pompidou Centre, the Tate Modern, or the Saatchi Gallery rather than a public convenience, a builders merchants' yard, or whilst sitting in their bedroom at home.[2] It is their context, both physical and social, that makes these things "art" in the modern world and, once removed from that context, their intended meaning is changed or lost (see Figure 9.1).

This reference to modern "art" might help us to realize the challenges we face in interpreting what we consider to be the "art" of Archaic Ionia, where we often understand neither the physical nor social context within which it was originally produced and intended to be viewed. However, such an analogy is also misleading because much of what we, as modern viewers, might consider to be ancient "art" were the products of craftsmen and the concept of "art for art's sake" did not exist in Archaic Ionia.[3] These craftsmen produced artifacts that, although beautifully elaborated, were ultimately always functional – even if that function was to be pleasing to the gods so that they would look

---

[1] Useful works for the reader wishing to find out more about Ionian art include: J.M. Cook 1962 on sculpture; Cook and Dupont 1998 on pottery; R.M. Cook 1981 on the painted *sarcophagi* of Klazomenai; von Graeve 2007 on figurines.

[2] These are, of course, references to Marcel Duchamp's *Fontaine* (1917), Carl Andre's *Equivalent VIII* (1966), and Tracey Emin's *My Bed* (1998).

[3] Such a concept was in fact a later invention – see Tanner 2003.

Figure 9.1 *My Bed* by Tracey Emin, 1998. © Tracey Emin, 2008. Courtesy of The Saatchi Gallery, London.

kindly on the individual who had commissioned that artifact. There is no sense in which the craftsman-like "artworks" of ancient Ionia, which we describe as "art," were in any way conceived of within a context analogous to modern dialectics about what constitutes "art." "Art" is therefore a term that must be used advisedly when discussing the ancient world and this should be borne in mind in reading this chapter, as well as the message about the importance of physical and social context to interpreting such artifacts.

Unlike the previous classes of material considered in this book, the influence of landscape on the production of artworks in Ionia is limited. The archaeological sources (i.e. the artifacts themselves) are, however, relatively plentiful, but to understand them in context it is necessary to consider not just those that survive, but also those that we know to have existed, but are now missing – Ionia's "lost" art treasures. In this way we can achieve a balanced understanding of the totality of Ionia's artistic output and influences within which we can then appropriately locate those most robust and discussed artforms – pottery and sculpture.

Having reviewed the available evidence in relation to the missing Ionian art, two themes will be developed in more depth: Ionian painted pottery in the Archaic period and how Ionian art can be "read" differently so as to distance it from the traditional approaches and narratives of Atheno-centric Classical archaeology and to try to identify "hybrid" Greek–Anatolian elements of the region's art that are uniquely Ionian.

"Art" and Landscape

One fundamental way in which landscape can affect the art of a region is through the availability of raw materials. Ionia had good supplies of local stone, including marble (see Chapter 3). There are also plentiful sources of clay in the region, from which to make pottery.[4] However, for the most prestigious artworks, Ionian craftsmen had to rely on imported copper, tin, gold, silver, and ivory.

The discussion of the Sacred Ways of Ionia in the previous chapter serves to highlight the importance of understanding artworks in their physical landscape setting. An interesting find from the Temple of Hera at Samos is the feet of a *kouros* statue in situ in the sanctuary,[5] but it is more common for statues to have been removed from their original context. This may have happened in antiquity for use as *spolia* (building materials), as happened to a lion from the Sacred Way at Branchidai-Didyma that became built into a field-wall,[6] or they can have been removed in recent history for display in museums (see Chapter 1). Sculptures could also be relocated, and their meanings renegotiated, in antiquity and this can have a considerable effect on their interpretation by ancient and modern viewers.[7] To better appreciate the phenomenology, visual impact, and meaning of such artworks in their original locations it is possible to develop 3D virtual reality environments in which artworks, buildings, and landscapes can all be recreated.[8]

Ionia's Lost "Art" Treasures

It is normal when writing about the history of a region to begin with its most celebrated and outstanding surviving artworks and to place lesser pieces into context alongside these. However, in doing so there is a danger that we project onto our understanding of the art of that region the aesthetic values of our own age because the very reason that such artworks were first excavated and transported to museums, where they became celebrated as great artworks, is that they were in concord with the tastes of contemporary society.[9] An alternative approach is to consider what artifacts we know to have existed in Archaic Ionia and then to place our consideration of those that have survived into a broader

---

[4]   Karin B. Gödecken identified 27 clay sources within the vicinity of Miletos alone (1988: 315).

[5]   Kyrieleis 1978: 387, fig. 3.

[6]   Weickert 1956.

[7]   e.g. the repositioning of the Chares Group in antiquity – Herda 2006: 327–50.

[8]   This has been done for Roman period Miletos by the Foundation of the Hellenic World, Athens (see Greaves 2002: 139, fig. 4.4).

[9]   See Chapter 1. See also Shanks 1996 on the "hype" that was created around the discovery of the Venus de Milo.

context with those that we might reasonably assume to have existed, but which have not survived.[10] Such an approach can give us new and interesting perspectives on art in the region.

The robust nature of terracotta and stone has resulted in the excellent survival of pottery and sculpture and the popular view today is that they represent the epitome of ancient artistic achievement. Yet in antiquity pottery and sculpture in stone can be seen to have been less esteemed than metalwork, which was much more highly valued. Certain forms of ancient Greek pottery, it has been argued, were created in imitation of more valuable metal vessels and certain features of their shape and decoration retain skeuomorphic characteristics that belie their original inspiration.[11] It has long been recognized that the artistic inspiration for so-called Greek "orientalizing" pottery, which includes the most important styles of Archaic Ionia, was the import of high-value bronzes and ivories from the Near East.[12] Other, more perishable, materials may also have been a source of inspiration to Ionian artists – including cloth and carved wood – which are largely absent from the archaeological record.

Let us briefly review three important classes of material that we know to be missing from Archaic Ionia and consider how they may have co-existed with, and influenced, the surviving artistic media of pottery and sculpture.

Metalwork

Metals are a rare find because they are subject to rust, robbery, and reuse.[13] Those examples that do survive, mostly from temple sites, indicate that Ionian artisans were working to a very high standard and with plentiful materials.[14] A significant number of the surviving finds appear to be special commissions for dedication in temples, such as the colossal knucklebone that is thought to come from Branchidai-Didyma, which bears an inscription that identifies it as being a dedication to Apollo (see Chapter 7 and Box 4.1). Although we might admire the artistry of many of these dedications, the primary reason that they were dedicated was not for their aesthetic merit, which would no doubt also be pleasing to the gods, but for their inherent value. Metal goods were probably treasured as much for their bullion value as for the quality of the workmanship that went into them.[15] On the East Staircase at Persepolis, for example, in a relief that apparently depicts a procession of peoples presenting tribute to the Persian king, the Ionians are shown carrying bowls, presumably made of metal, as part of their tribute payments.[16] However,

---

[10]   What Robin Osborne calls "the lost history of Greek art" (1998a: 9–11).
[11]   Vickers and Gill 1994.
[12]   Boardman 1996: 48–69.
[13]   Greaves' "three Rs" (2007b).
[14]   Key sites include the Temple of Hera at Samos, the Temple of Artemis at Ephesos, the Sanctuary of Aphrodite on Zeytintepe at Miletos, and the Lion Tomb at Miletos.
[15]   This is still the practice in the Indian subcontinent and much of Turkey today.
[16]   Schmidt 1953: 86, pl. 38, delegation 12. The two silver phiale bowls found in the Lion Tomb at Miletos may be the closest examples to the type of bowls depicted here (Forbeck and Heres 1997).

it would be unfair to think that metal votives did not also have symbolic value, as the dedication of arrowheads to Apollo or Artemis would have had a meaning that went beyond the monetary value of the metal they were composed of.[17]

Cloth

Cloth could be a highly valued commodity. In the Persepolis relief, mentioned above, the Ionians are also depicted bearing cloth. Cloth could be dedicated in temples, as when the Egyptian pharaoh Necho dedicated his cloak at Branchidai-Didyma (Hdt. 2.159), and cult images of the gods were sometimes presented with robes. None of these examples survive, but it has been suggested that the designs on local textiles may have been the inspiration for the designs and techniques of Ionian Wild Goat style pottery. As Robert Cook wrote:

> There is a striking difference between the animals of the Middle I Wild Goat style and those of the more or less contemporary Transitional style of Corinth. At Corinth the ideal was a precise outline and fine and exactly incised detail, with purple used freely to relieve the dark silhouette. In the Wild Goat style the drawing, though careful, is woolly and inner details are rendered by reserved areas and broadish stripes; nor do purple enhancements appear till the transition to Middle II. Corinthian suggests metalwork, the Wild Goat style textiles as its inspiration; but if so, the textiles may have been local.[18]

Wood

Another important artistic medium that does not get the consideration it deserves because of its poor survival rate is wood. The discovery in 1950 of an undisturbed burial chamber at Gordion in central Anatolia revealed that it was filled with elaborately decorated wooden furniture and artifacts.[19] Preserved in the anaerobic conditions inside the tomb these magnificent and intricate pieces of furniture provide a glimpse of a whole class of material that is missing from many ancient sites. On Samos, a fragment of wooden furniture with carved relief decoration has been preserved by the waterlogged conditions at the Temple of Hera.[20] One of the most remarkable objects to be found in central Anatolia in recent years – the Kerkenes ivory – is also thought to have been an inlay from furniture (see Figure 9.2).[21]

[17]   e.g. the arrowheads dedicated at the Sanctuary of Apollo at Kato Phana (see Chapter 7).
[18]   Cook and Dupont 1998: 38.
[19]   Simpson 1983; Simpson and Spirydowicz 1999. Inside the central wooden chamber of the so-called Midas Mound (MM) were also found bronzes, food, traces of cloth, an alphabetic inscription, and a single male corpse. The person interred here is not now thought to be Midas himself, but one of his predecessors.
[20]   Kyrieleis 1978: 395–6, fig. 13; Kyrieleis 1998.
[21]   Dusinberre 2002.

Figure 9.2 Ivory furniture inlay from Kerkenes Dağ. Excavated in 1996, this ivory furniture inlay is embellished with amber beads backed with reflective tin or silver and has traces of gold leaf. The doe, at left, was originally decorated with brightly colored enamel. It measures 29 cm. Conservation was carried out by Simone Korolnik in the Museum of Anatolian Civilisations, Ankara. The photographs were taken by Behiç Günel and Husein Sen. Image courtesy of Geoff and Françoise Summers.

Bone and ivory plaques from the Sanctuary of Aphrodite on Zeytintepe at Miletos suggest that in Ionia too furniture was inlaid with panels and dedicated in temples.[22] The statue of Chares from the Sacred Way at Branchidai-Didyma is seated on a chair that is carefully shaped, presumably in imitation of real furniture of the time (see Box 8.1). The use of high-value inlays, the placing of wooden furniture in royal tombs, and the dedicating of carved and inlaid furniture at temples shows that in Anatolia and Ionia wooden furniture was afforded a very high status. Wooden carvings were also created in imitation of sculptures in precious materials, such as ivory, gold, or bronze. At the Temple of Hera on Samos local artists can be seen to have produced carved wooden figurines in imitation of Egyptian prototypes.[23] We should not assume that such imitations were necessarily one-way and that they always sought to recreate or mimic artworks in more valuable materials. The *xoana* (cult statues) that had pride of place in many sanctuaries were an important class of high-prestige artistic woodwork and are known to have been adorned and imitated in other media. The cult statue in the Temple of Artemis at Ephesos was adorned with amber (see Box 10.1) and in the Temple of Athena at Emporio on Chios the wooden *xoanon* was surmounted by nine griffin *protomes* (decorative animal heads) made of lead, which were found in the collapsed remains of the *cella* (inner chamber) of the temple building.[24] Also at the Temple of Artemis at Ephesos, the *astragali* that were used for divination, and which were literally valueless in economic terms, were imitated in precious ivory inset with amber.[25] What gave these artifacts, the *xoanon* and the *astragali*, their importance was their cult significance and not their intrinsic value as judged by modern, or even ancient, economic standards. This is a useful perspective to bear in mind when we come to consider how we judge Ionian art in its local contexts.

[22]   Greaves 2002: 84.
[23]   R. Osborne 1998a: 47–8, fig. 21–22 compares an imported bronze figurine of the Egyptian goddess Mut, with a locally produced wooden carving.
[24]   Boardman 1967: 25–8.
[25]   Hogarth 1908: 190–2, pl. 36.

These examples of metalwork, cloth, and wood serve to illustrate how little we know about Ionian art because entire classes of important and influential materials are missing from the archaeological record. They also emphasize the continuing importance of context and the different values (monetary, artistic, and religious) placed on artifacts by different societies, including our own, and negotiated by those societies over time.

"Art" and Literature

The authors of ancient Greek and Roman literature admired and celebrated the artworks of Ionia. Pausanias, writing in the second century AD, described many artworks in ancient Greece that are now lost, including the cult statues of Branchidai-Didyma and Erythrai (2.10.4, 7.5.9). Unfortunately, such written descriptions are ambiguous and were produced as part of an ancient genre of writing about art that was a vehicle for philosophizing about nature and reality.[26] Such written sources can be valuable for telling us how temples were furnished and painted but the nature of historical writings is such that they do not describe the production processes of art or non-Greek perspectives on its meaning. Sometimes written sources can describe microhistorical events that affected lost artworks, such as when a temple is sacked, or draw attention to artworks that were in some way unusual, such as the cult image from Branchidai-Didyma which was apparently made of metal, not wood (Pliny NH 34.75; Pausanias 9.10.2). For Ionia the general lack of reliable historical sources is therefore compounded by the limitations of ancient writings about art.

"Connoisseurship" of Ionian Pottery

The study of Ionian pottery has lagged behind that of its mainland contemporaries, Corinth and Athens.[27] In mainland Greece the figural and narrative nature of the Corinthian style and Athenian Black Figure and Red Figure styles means that it is possible to relate scenes of human figures to the rich mythical traditions and historical texts from that region. For example, Robin Osborne has used images from mainland Greek art as illustrations to discuss key themes in Archaic and Classical history.[28] Such a method is possible and sustainable in Athens, but Ionia lacks sufficient ethnohistorical sources to provide a framework within which to discuss the narrative content of any figural scenes. Once again, the primacy afforded to historical texts over archaeological sources by methodologies such as Osborne's inevitably leads to Ionia becoming sidetracked from general surveys of Archaic and Classical art and new methodologies are required if the region is to be understood on its own terms, rather than those of its mainland Greek contemporaries.

[26] R. Osborne 1998a: 11.
[27] R.M. Cook 1992: 255.
[28] R. Osborne 1998a. Other examples of such approaches include Bérard et al. 1984 and Carpenter 1991.

Figure 9.3 Fikellura-style amphora with a running man, sixth century BC. © The Trustees of the British Museum.

That is not to say that all Ionian art is devoid of human figures. Later styles, such as the Fikellura style (see Figure 9.3), Chian Black Figure, and Klazomenian Black Figure and painted *sarcophagi*, do all feature human figures.[29] These styles all emerged in the later Archaic period and were inspired by Athenian vase-painting. In some cases, such as the Northampton Group, canonical scenes from Greek myth can be identified.[30] In others, there is a distinctly local twist to the depiction of mythical figures, such as the appearance of a war-like winged Athena who appears in battle scenes on Klazomenian *sarcophagi*.[31] Attempts to link figured scenes in Ionian pottery to instances of textual evidence from the region can appear strained because of the general paucity of the local historical framework within which to properly contextualize them.[32]

[29] Cook and Dupont 1998.
[30] Cook and Dupont 1998: 108.
[31] Cook and Dupont 1998: 121–8, esp. 17.3; Villing 1998: 162–3.
[32] e.g. Gödecken 1989, which tries to link a scene of a goat-rider from Miletos to the *Molpoi* inscription. There are many possible alternative interpretations for such an image and nothing in the *Molpoi* inscription directly indicates that riding goats was in any way connected with the procession.

The absence of human figures from early Ionian vase-painting can be viewed as an enduring inheritance of the so-called "orientalizing" period when, under the influence of the Near East, Greek vase-painting adopted many new images and motifs. Whereas the painters of mainland Greece are seen as "pioneering"[33] for the increasing sophistication of their use of human figures, Ionian vase-painting is, by implicit contrast, deemed to be merely decorative and not on a par with the representational "real art" of the mainland. Viewing Ionian vase-painting in this way tells us more about what contemporary commentators consider to be aesthetically acceptable than it does about the Ionians' attitudes to their own art. It is an approach that projects the values of contemporary Western thinking onto Ionian art, judges it, and finds it lacking. However, traditional Islamic art is consciously non-representational and the abrogation of creating images of Allah his prophet Mohammed (s.a.w.), or other figures has only served to inspire generations of Muslim artists to develop rich artistic traditions based on the use of geometric and natural patterns. Similarly, it is possible to interpret early Ionian art as being the product of a local tradition that favored non-figural art and remained close to its originating Near Eastern source materials. Only later in the Archaic period did local figural styles emerge in Ionia and these were evidently created in imitation of mainland Black Figure styles. Yet even these imitations were executed in the local reserve painting technique in South Ionia, or the application of lines of white paint in Klazomenai, and only in North Ionia was incision, the same technique as the mainland, used to execute figures.

The traditional study of Greek Archaic and Classical vase-painting owes much to the method of identifying the work of individual painters by means of "connoisseurship." "Connoisseurship" is the systematic study of the choices made by individual painters during the execution of a painting on a pot that allows them to be identified as all being produced by the same "hand" (i.e. an individual painter, a "school," or workshop). This might include the choice of pot form, elements of style or composition, or details of the execution, such as the attention paid to the hands or feet of human figures.[34] Although it is possible to identify the products of specific workshops or painters in this way, Ionian vase-painters did not sign their work as mainland artists sometimes did, with a *dipinti*, and we do not know the names of any Ionian vase-painters. Only in the later Ionian styles can the work of individuals such as the Altenburg Painter be securely identified.[35]

As such, the essence of the "connoisseurship" is the same as is applied to the creation of any other typological sequence in archaeology – the detailed and systematic study of the morphology of form (in this case of the decoration, and not just the pot). Although the very term "connoisseurship" carries with it an unhelpful connotation of elitism[36] and its practice was originally limited to a small number of scholars who had first-hand experience of seeing the pots, the advent of digital technology has the potential to democratize

---

[33] R. Osborne 1998a: 9.
[34] See R. Osborne 1998a: 88 for an example of how the work of different painters can be differentiated by their execution of ankles.
[35] Cook and Dupont 1998: 78–81. The Altenberg Painter was working in the Fikellura style.
[36] A. Villing pers. comm., May 14, 2009.

the practice of "connoisseurship" by making images of pots and their interpretations widely and freely available to all.[37]

However, "connoisseurship" is more than just the creation of a typology of vase-painting because the connoisseurs themselves, such as John Beazley (b.1885 d.1970), used their expert detailed knowledge to pursue the "Great Artist" and to identify creative individuals within the archaeological record.[38] A criticism of the "connoisseurship" approach to the study of Greek art is, therefore, that it often consolidates into defined "hands" not only the typological judgments of individual scholars, but also their aesthetic judgments. Having created their putative "artists," connoisseurs project onto them emotional and intellectual states that cannot be proven or tested. For example, Robert Cook describes the Albertinum Painter as being "bored" with his work.[39] Such a description might strike a chord with one who has seen a great many sloppily executed pots by the same hand, but it is not an objective criticism.

When writing about the Carian imitators of Wild Goat style Cook wrote: "Carian potters had managed well enough with simple linear patterns, but were bewildered by the more elaborate repertory of the Orientalising style."[40] In Cook's construction of western Anatolia in the Archaic period it is more likely that Carian artists were "bewildered" by these "new-fangled" lines of repetitive monochrome goat motifs, than that they and their clients had priorities other than the faithful reproduction of Greek pottery.[41] However, in his study of the orientalizing pottery of Caria and Ionia, İsmail Fazlıoğlu wrote: "The finds from Damlıboğaz suggest that local potters in Caria created an eclectic and local Early Orientalizing style by gradually adopting elements from South Ionia which they blended with provincial Geometric features."[42] That is to say, the local painters of Caria selected elements from the Ionian orientalizing style and actively combined it with features of the Geometric style that they chose to retain. This is evidence of the active creation of a "hybrid" pottery style, the significance of which will be discussed further below. Fazlıoğlu also notes that the Carian potters also preferred different forms to their Ionian neighbors,[43] especially "squat *oinochoe*" and *pyxides* (boxes), suggesting that they were intended for different purposes within the social context of their use in Caria.

What Cook dismissed as the "bewildered" imitators of Ionian pottery can therefore be constructed differently as active agents who catered for the different needs and tastes dictated by their local social milieu. Similarly, we do the Ionian potters no favors if we

[37]   A searchable online archive featuring some of John Beazley's photographs and notes, as well as updated material from other sources, is available at www.beazley.ox.ac.uk/index.htm. The author's own "pot-casting" project is just one of many projects aimed at opening up access to museum collections of Archaic and Classical Greek pottery.

[38]   For discussions of "connoisseurship" see Shanks 1996: 30–7; Boardman 2001: 128–38; and Snodgrass 2007: 19–23.

[39]   Cook and Dupont 1998: 126.

[40]   Cook and Dupont 1998: 64.

[41]   It is important to stress that sentiments such as this are more likely to be born of a great love and knowledge of the art of ancient Athens, than by any anti-Anatolian sentiments, as R.M. Cook did more than anyone else to further the study of the region's many local pottery styles.

[42]   Fazlıoğlu 2007: 255.

[43]   Fazlıoğlu 2007: 255–7.

judge them only against the aesthetic values of Western scholars or those of the Athenians, whose pottery is the benchmark for connoisseurs. We should therefore strive to construct understandings of Ionian art that try to avoid these traps that are inherent in traditional "connoisseurship" if we are to achieve an understanding of it as a product of its own, uniquely Ionian, cultural setting.

In effect, there are two dimensions to "connoisseurship" between which it is important to differentiate. The first is the typological categorization of decoration that is, and is likely to remain, the basis for the analysis of ancient painted pottery. The second is the subjective attribution of emotional states and value judgments by the connoisseurs to the individual "hands" that they have identified. In the opinion of this author, such writings blur the distinction between the consideration of artifacts as "objects" and as "art" and direct the reader toward the implicit historical narratives of the connoisseur. Although it could be argued that studying pottery not as "art" but only as typological artifacts reifies and de-personalizes the study of the ancient world, the systematization of the study of Ionian pottery uncouples it from the aesthetic judgments of individual connoisseurs, separates data from interpretation and, by making the criteria of allocation to typological categories explicit, opens it up to be engaged with and discussed by other researchers.

Case study: Two styles of Ionian pottery

One question that had long vexed pottery experts in Ionia was the nature of the relationship between two of South Ionia's major styles: Middle Wild Goat II and Fikellura.[44] Wild Goat style pottery dominated the region for about a century[45] and Fikellura appears to have been a later introduction. According to Udo Schlotzhauer the relationship between these two styles was "one of the most disputed questions in the scholarship of East Greek painted pottery."[46] The resolution of that question, by determining where and when they were produced, provides an interesting case study of the advances in scientific analysis and systematic excavation in Ionia between the start of the twentieth century (see Box 1.1) and the end.

The Wild Goat style was originally known as "Rhodian" or "Rhodian-Milesian" because of the large volumes of it that were first found on that island. The most accurate description to use would be the German term *Tierfries* ("animal frieze") because its distinctive decorative bands feature many different types of animals, not just goats.[47] The Wild Goat style shows evidence of its origins among the early orientalizing styles of Greece in its use of Near Eastern motifs such as sphinx-heads and lotus blossoms. It was traditionally divided into Early, Middle I, Middle II, and Late styles, with the latter two overlapping chronologically. The *krater* and round-mouthed *oinochoe* were common in the Early style, with the trefoil *oinochoe* and stemmed dish becoming common in the

[44] e.g. R.M. Cook 1992.
[45] Cook and Dupont 1998: 32.
[46] Schlotzhauer 2007: 289.
[47] This belongs to the SiA (Sudionish Archaisch) I and II phases defined by Kerschner and Schlotzhauer (2005, 2007).

Middle style (see Box 9.1). The distinctive decoration consists of cream or white slip being applied to the pot onto which are painted bold bands of decoration, outlines of animals and filling ornaments. The basic paint color was black or dark brown, but in the Middle and Late styles purple and then white colors were added. Goats are the most popular choice of animal but dogs, lions, sphinxes, griffins, hares, boars, rams, and foxes are also used, and were joined in the Middle I style by spotted deer and geese. These do not form narratives (e.g. a "chase" scene) because the figures rarely touch or appear to interact in any way. Between the animals are small filling devices, such as rosettes, triangles, and dots, and the bottoms of pots are decorated with rays or lotus flowers.

The Fikellura style takes its name from the site on Rhodes where it was first identified (see Figure 9.3). It was recently relabeled SiA II by Kerschner and Schlotzhauer.[48] It makes use of the same range of animal subjects as Wild Goat style, with the addition of partridges, but the scenes are more animated. A big difference is the abundant use of human figures in the Fikellura style, mostly *comasts* (male dancers, sometimes with padded buttocks) in revelry scenes. In contrast to the Wild Goat style, figures are not painted in outline, but in silhouette, with fine details in reserve.[49] Fewer figures were used and filling motifs were smaller, giving an effect of sparse decoration.

The nature of the relationship between these two styles has only been resolved in recent years by two innovations: scientific analysis of their fabric, and detailed stratigraphic excavations at Miletos.

The forms of clay analysis that were used to determine the place of manufacture of the different pottery styles in early Ionia are petrographic analysis and neutron activation analysis (NAA). Petrographic analysis involves taking thin-sections from pots so that their components can be studied under a microscope. Neutron activation analysis is a nuclear process for determining the composition of different elements that make up the analyzed material. For such analysis to be effective wasters from pottery kiln sites need to be analyzed in order to characterize the precise chemical composition of the products of those kilns and samples from individual pots can then be linked back to these known production centers by their chemical profiles.[50] Scientific analysis such as this has proved that both the Wild Goat and Fikellura styles were manufactured in Miletos, even though they were both first identified on Rhodes.[51] Not only can such analysis identify the place of production of identifiable pottery types, it can also be used to give insight into the pottery exchange patterns within a region and where a particular site received its pottery from. For example, at Ephesos NAA has identified imports from the Kalabaktepe artisans' quarter at Miletos, another source that is probably also yet to be located in Miletos, and two North Ionian sources.[52] Combined with typological analysis of the pottery it can now

---

[48]   Kerschner and Schlotzhauer 2005, 2007.

[49]   i.e. instead of incising the still-wet pot to cut away fine lines of the paint, as was the technique in Athenian Black Figure, the painter carefully left unpainted areas exposing the white slip beneath. In Figure 9.3 this can be noted on the line of the runner's torso and on his face.

[50]   The key work that established the profiles of a number of important production centers on the west coast of Anatolia from the Bronze Age to the Archaic period is M. Akurgal et al. 2002.

[51]   Cook and Dupont 1998.

[52]   Kerschner et al. 2002, 2007.

Box 9.1
The Garstang East Greek Bowl

The Liverpool Institute of Archaeology was founded in 1904 by Professor John Garstang, who researched and excavated extensively in Turkey throughout his career. This stemmed dish from the collections of the Garstang Museum of Archaeology at the University of Liverpool is an example of the standardized South Ionian Wild Goat style. This shape of bowl and pattern of decoration, including the use of the duck motif, is typical of the Middle Wild Goat II style.[a] In the new classification system for East Greek pottery it falls into the South Ionian Id (SiA Id) phase and can be dated to c.610–580 BC.[b] The style and fabric of the bowl appear to indicate that it was manufactured in Miletos.

Notes

[a] Cook and Dupont 1998.

[b] Kerschner and Schlotzhauer 2005: 42–4, fig. 41–42.

The Garstang East Greek bowl. © Garstang Museum of Archaeology at the University of Liverpool.

be shown that Archaic Ephesian pottery was receptive to influences from both North and South Ionia and also from Lydia. This analysis also helped prove the existence of local pottery production for the first time at Ephesos. The general pattern of pottery production and exchange that emerges for Archaic Ionia,[53] and the west coast of Anatolia in general,[54] is one of local production and consumption, with significant intra-regional exchange within Ionia and to other regional centers, and limited exchange with other regions, such as Lydia[55] and Athens.[56] This is the same as was observed by typological analysis of the coarseware amphorae from Miletos[57] and suggests that painted pottery largely mirrored the exchange of bulk goods, as was proposed in Chapter 4.

The systematic excavation of seven successive levels of settlement on Kalabaktepe Hill in Miletos, including kiln sites and wasters, not only conclusively proved that this was their production site, but also allowed for the chronological development of the Wild Goat and Fikellura styles to be traced through the seventh to fifth centuries BC.[58] Furthermore, the discovery at the Sanctuary of Aphrodite on the nearby Zeytintepe Hill of a number of "bilingual" vessels that bore both styles of decoration proved the co-existence of the two styles in the first third of the sixth century BC and showed that Fikellura had indeed developed out of Middle Wild Goat II.[59]

It can therefore be seen that the advances made in the stratigraphic excavation of pottery production centers and other sites in Ionia and beyond, combined with the systematic and wide-scale application of scientific analysis, enabled Kerschner and Schlotzhauer to develop a more refined pottery typology than was previously possible.[60] Their system is not rigid, and it can accommodate new regional styles and typologies as the results of ongoing excavations and analysis may require, and as it defines ceramic periods within Ionia, rather than just styles, it facilitates easier cross-referencing with the existing Attic and Corinthian typologies.[61]

"Reading" Ionian "Art"

The subjective element of much of the writing associated with traditional "connoisseurship" of ancient art judged it against the aesthetic values and vocabulary of contemporary society. Connoisseurs judge Ionian art against their own value-sets when they ascribed to it value-laden terms such as "satisfactory" or "slovenly," or describes it as displaying "carefully considered" use of paint.[62] Similarly, art historical approaches

---

[53] Klazomenai was an important pottery production center in North Ionia – Ersoy 2000, 2003.
[54] e.g. Berges 2006 on Knidos.
[55] Kerschner et al. 2002.
[56] Kerschner et al. 2008: 75–107.
[57] Naso 2005.
[58] Senff 2007; Kerschner and Schlotzhauer 2005, 2007.
[59] Schlotzhauer 2007.
[60] Kerschner and Schlotzhauer 2005, 2007.
[61] Kerschner and Schlotzhauer 2005, 2007.
[62] Cook and Dupont 1998: 39, 81, and 98, respectively.

that attempt to link Greek art to the *topoi* of ancient historical writings, such as that of Osborne,[63] are inherently Atheno-centric and although they may work for mainland Greece, it is an inappropriate methodology for Ionia, for which there are no ethnohistorical sources to balance those of the fifth-century BC Athenian historical genre. If we are to understand Ionia on its own terms, as a distinctive cultural region whose people had agency and autonomy, we need to find new ways of "reading" Ionian art, so that we can begin to view it by their own standards and not those of Athens or ourselves.

The discussion of Sacred Ways in Chapter 8 highlighted the importance of the physical setting of objects for understanding their meaning, for example the colossal *kouroi* of Samos and how they appropriated the landscape and negotiated its meaning for different generations of visitors. Understanding their social setting is much harder as we lack the detailed historical framework that exists for Athens but which is necessary for the proper interpretation of Ionian art. Just as "connoisseurship" of painted pottery values the Athenian Black Figure and Red Figure traditions over any that might have been produced in Ionia (or Caria), so too can the traditional interpretations based on historical reasoning favor mainland Greek material over less well-documented alternative local scenarios.

As an example of how Ionian art can possibly be misrepresented by traditional historical approaches, let us consider the Athena of Erythrai. Pausanias (7.5.9) described the cult statue in the Temple of Athena as being a large seated wooden image holding a distaff in each hand and wearing a *polos* (tall headdress). Although the age of the statue he is describing cannot be ascertained, it was probably Archaic in date; the temple itself dates back to the eighth century BC and he attributes this Athena to the sculptor Endoios, who was active in the second half of the sixth century BC. When attempting to "read" this image through Pausanias' description, we must be aware of two culturally specific contexts that influence our understanding of its meaning: his and our own. In her discussion of this lost statue, Alexandra Villing noted that it would be unusual for a weaver to hold a distaff (a stick on which wool is held during weaving) in each hand, and suggests that the statue is more likely to be holding a distaff in one hand and a spindle (a tool for spinning thread) in the other, as these two tools are quite similar in form and were used in conjunction during spinning.[64] She also notes that the precise meaning of the Greek word *ēlakatē* used by Pausanias is not clear and its ambiguity may be the source of this apparent misunderstanding.[65] Pausanias' reading of this image therefore reflects his own understandings (and possibly misunderstandings) of it and belies his own mental schemata, as delimited by the language of Greek.

While noting its Eastern influences, Villing goes on to conclude that this image "conformed best to the Greek ideal of the woman as comparatively passive"[66] and "such a borrowing of an iconographical motif could only have taken place if it conformed to

[63] R. Osborne 1998a.
[64] Villing 1998: 154–9.
[65] Villing 1998: 154–5, citing Bianchi 1953: 212.
[66] Villing 1998: 159, citing Jung 1982: 117–23.

Greek ideas."[67] She also demonstrates how this image of a seated, distaff-bearing Athena could be accommodated into the existing metanarrative of Greek history by relating the image to references of the spinning of the *Moirai* (the Fates) in canonical Greek literature, as well as East Greek authors such as Permenides and Homer. This interpretation and the process of argumentation by which it is achieved is typical of many traditional approaches to Ionian art that see the Greek element of Ionian society as predominant, in accordance with a historical scenario created by the literary sources of fifth-century BC Athenian literary and political writing (see Chapter 10 and Epilogue).

Villing's interpretation of a "comparatively passive" Athena would, however, only be true for a Greek viewer of the Classical period as her own work has shown that Ionian Athena was a warrior goddess. Anatolian iconography of this period typically depicted the great mother-goddess Cybele as being enthroned and framed in an architectural setting,[68] and therefore when viewed from an Anatolian perspective the seated pose of the Athena of Erythrai would evoke the divine authority of a female deity seated in her temple, not the domestic passivity of a Greek woman. In her construction of the social context in which the sculptors of Erythrai produced this statue, Villing appears to imply that conformity to Greek cultural ideals was essential. However, it is also possible to envision a specifically "Erythraian" social context in which the production of objects of such major significance might be deemed acceptable to both the "Greek" and the "Anatolian" elements within that society. This construct of a "hybrid" Ionian (or even just "Erythraian") cultural milieu that incorporated both Greek and Anatolian value-sets could also be taken to imply a degree of equality in the power relations between these two groups at the point of production of this statue.[69]

It has now been over a decade since Villing's interpretation of the Athena of Erythrai was first published,[70] and there have been many archaeological discoveries of Phrygian material in Ionia in the meantime, including the discovery of a number of rock-cut niches with images of Cybele/Athena below the temple at Erythrai itself and the discovery at Phokaia of a number of Cybele sanctuaries, one of which is situated immediately below the Temple of Athena there.[71] Nevertheless, a careful deconstruction of her analysis of this image serves to illustrate the way in which the mental schemata of scholars can often be subtly influenced by the existing metanarrative of Greek history. Within the *Wissenschaft* tradition of scholarship, being able to establish multiple points of contact between an image, artifact, or event and elements of canonical Greek culture remains the ultimate badge of "proof" (see Chapter 2). Such references and examples are often drawn from considerably later, or indeed earlier, sources and from across the Greek world – effectively creating a singular "Greek" culture that is both trans-regional and achronological. This

---

[67]   Villing 1998: 159. In choosing this example of Villing's reading of the Athena of Erythrai to illustrate how deeply ingrained Atheno-centric thinking is in standard approaches to art history, no criticism of her work is implied. Many other examples by other respected scholars could have been chosen to illustrate this point, including the author's own previous works.

[68]   Roller 1999.

[69]   Fitzjohn 2007. On hybridity, see Chapter 2.

[70]   First published 1998, reprinted 2002.

[71]   See Chapters 5 and 8.

is in contrast to modern understandings of Archaic Greece that recognize the disparate and localized nature of Greek ethnic identities at this time.[72]

In the opinion of the author, the Ionians were consciously combining Greek and local Anatolian traditions in their art – from the level of the minor art of vase-painting, up to the highest level of cult statues in their most important temples. Ionia was not just a geographical liminal zone, but also a cultural one situated between the Greek Aegean and Phrygian and Carian Anatolia. In actively combining elements of the traditions of these regions, Ionian artists were creating a hybrid culture that was uniquely "Ionian." This implies that artists were able to create and operate in a "third place," in which the two cultures could be combined.[73] This melding of the Greek and Anatolian cultures did not happen as a mathematical equation of the location of Ionia between the two regions, but through the agency of its people actively choosing to select and combine elements of each.

Scholars of the "Turkish School" are perhaps more inclined to be more mindful of the Anatolian influences on the art of Ionia than those who have been trained in other academic traditions (see Chapter 2).[74] For example, in discussing four figurines found in Lycia with parallels to Ephesos, Fahri Işık argued that they shared links to neo-Hittite sculpture.[75] He concluded: "Die Voraussetzung ist nicht schwer zu benennen: di Geburt der westanatolischen Kunst aus der ostanatolischen, d.i. die Geburt der Kunst des westlichen Zivilisation in Anatolien."[76] In Işık's reworking of the origins of Ionian art, it is Anatolia that "gives birth" to the art of Ionia, not vice versa, in contrast to some interpretations. This "Anatolio-centric" stance is not currently widely supported, but it presents an interesting counterpoint to the more common "Atheno-centric" stance implicit in literary positivist approaches. The fact is that, unless we accept as absolute truth the literary tradition that from the moment of their arrival in Ionia the Greeks dominated the whole region, then we will always have to consider each site, and each chronological phase, and even each artifact of Archaic Ionia on its individual merits if we are to find the often subtle evidence for the Anatolian dimension of Ionian art.

If we view artifacts primarily as aesthetic objects, then we inevitably judge them by the values of our own society. If we seek to find ways to accommodate them within contemporary, or near-contemporary, Greek historical writings then we can usually find ways to place them into the existing metanarrative with a reasonable degree of fit. If, however, we are to re-conceive of Ionia as a "third place" in which Greek culture was increasingly being overlaid onto a pre-existing Anatolian society in ways that were localized and chronologically progressive, then we must always seek to find evidence to balance the predominance of Greek historical sources. This may require us to admit different *types* of evidence because written Anatolian ethnohistorical sources do not exist to balance

---

[72]   e.g. J.M. Hall 1997.

[73]   Bhabha 2004.

[74]   e.g. E. Akurgal 1968.

[75]   Işık 2003.

[76]   "The premise is not difficult to see: the birth of west Anatolian art out of that of east Anatolia, that is, the birth of the art of Western civilisation in Anatolia." – Işık 2003: 68.

those of Athens. Evidence of the agency of Ionian local artists does exist, but it is subtle and we must always remember to look for it, and to look for it carefully.[77]

Conclusions

The production of "great artworks" is often considered to be one of the "higher functions" of any society – the closest that it is possible for archaeology to get to examining the core materials of its ethnic identity. Yet even from the lowly craft of vase-painting up to the creation of cult images we see that the "Greeks" of Ionia were actively combining local Anatolian traditions with those of the Greek Aegean. Specifically, it can be seen that mainland Greek innovations such as figural Black Figure vase-painting were accommodated within pre-existing local traditions and executed by local techniques. This can be seen to be happening at all levels of artistic production, including the most sacred and highly valued images of ancient Ionia – the *xoana* of its temples. If they were to be traced diachronically, the adoption of mainland Greek artistic templates could be seen to be a phenomenon of the later Archaic period – the latter half of the sixth century BC. Prior to this the Near East and Anatolia had been major sources of inspiration for Ionian craftsmen. In both these case studies the production of their art can be seen as the culmination of numerous conscious choices about material, form, and design that are the manifestation of the artists' agency – their ability to choose. How individual craftsmen made those choices was largely determined by the social institutions, settings, and traditions around them – the "habitus" of daily life – that was determined by the identity of the society around them.[78] What that identity may have been will be the subject of our final chapter.

---

[77] e.g. Wolfgang Schiering 2007 notes that it is not enough to understand Middle Wild Goat II pottery stylistically, but also to understand the local potting traditions that are evident in its manufacture.
[78] Knapp and van Dommelen 2008.

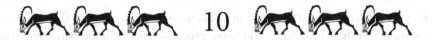 10

Who were the Ionians?

Introduction

The definition of "Ionia" taken in this book has been that of the 12 cities listed by Herodotos. This chapter seeks to examine the criteria by which he defined this area and whether or not Herodotos' "Ionia" has any currency as a transhistorical entity on the basis of its material culture alone – that is, whether there were core cultural traits and practices that existed across the region and across time which can be said to be truly "Ionian," and for which there are tangible remains. The preceding chapters have examined the archaeological evidence for different aspects of life in Ionia which could be said to have defined its culture. The role of these factors in defining Ionian ethnic identity will now be considered along with other less tangible, but in some ways more significant, factors in the definition of identity, such as language and historical traditions.[1]

In contrast to previous chapters, this chapter will begin by examining the literary and linguistic evidence for the existence of an Ionian regional identity, and explore why these have been central to previous studies of the region and its people. It is necessary to examine earlier attitudes to the mythic origins of the Ionians and their culture in Anatolia in order to appreciate how the new Archaeology-based approach (laid out in Chapter 2 and reiterated here) presents us with a different perspective on Ionian history.

Herodotos' Ionia

Using only historical sources, we can say very little for certain about the nature and function of the so-called Ionian League.[2] One way to define any such group is through actions

---

[1] For recent discussions of these issues see C. Morgan 2003 and Díaz-Andreu 2005.

[2] Roebuck 1955, 1979. Herodotos refers to them simply as "The Ionians," but the term "Ionian League" will be used here to avoid confusion with the Ionians as an ethnic or cultural grouping.

that they instigated and participated in collectively, although using this criterion the Ionians did very little that could be said to be "group actions." They apparently "possessed the Panionion" (Hdt. 1.142), which was a common sanctuary to Poseidon Hellenikos. It has been suggested that the recently discovered temple site at Çatallar Tepe, 800 m up in the Samsun Dağı range, should now be recognized as the site of the earliest Archaic Panionion,[3] and that Güzelçamlı, the site previously identified with the Panionion, is the later period of the site.[4]

As a political institution, it is presumed that the Panionion was also the place and the occasion when representatives of the different Ionian cities met to discuss issues of common interest and occasionally agreed to act in concert toward a common goal. However, prior to the Ionian Revolt, the Ionians appear to have done very little in unison. For example, their responses to the arrival of the Persians under Cyrus differed and whereas most Ionians resisted them, Miletos did not (Hdt. 1.69). The other cult that the Ionians apparently shared was the cult of Aphrodite Apatouria (Hdt. 1.147), although there is no suggestion that this has a unifying political dimension to it, as the cult of Poseidon Hellenikos evidently did.

During their revolt against Persia, the Ionians appear to have functioned as an ad hoc *symmachy*, which included non-Ionian participants such as Lesbos, under the leadership of Miletos. However, their unified front against the Persians apparently collapsed under pressure during the Battle of Lade, when the Samian ships fled the scene of the battle, leading to disaster for Miletos. This should not come as a surprise, as the Ionian League itself may have been born out of a war between the Ionian states that resulted in the annihilation of one of their number, Melie, and the redistribution of its territory.[5] There were also other recorded wars between Ionian states, as discussed in Chapter 7. This lack of evidence for any joint activities, and intermittent outbreaks of fighting between Ionian states, forces us to question just how deep-rooted the Ionian League was as a collective political force during the Archaic period.[6]

When the Ionians came under the control of Athens via the Delian League/Athenian Empire, the Athenian Tribute List inscriptions tell us that they were assigned to a single administrative district, called "Ionia." This district had been created for the purpose of gathering *phoros* for Athens and these inscriptions were an administrative tool whose function was to record contributions made by the different member states of the Delian League. These inscriptions were not an attempt to define the region and its people on ethnic grounds and they should not be used as such. One must also be careful to remember that Athens was an external power in the region. Although Athens was "Ionian" the Athenians were undoubtedly a very different kind of "Ionian" to their Anatolian cousins,

---

[3]   Lohmann 2007b. This identification is not yet proven. For example, there is nothing about the temple to connect it with Poseidon. An inscription connects it to Priene (*I Priene* 139) but the only evidence that Priene was responsible for the maintenance of the Panionion comes from later sources (Strabo 8.7.2, 14.1.20; Roebuck 1979: 56; C. Schneider 2004).

[4]   Kleiner et al. 1967.

[5]   Roebuck 1979: 60–1. See also Kleiner et al. 1967.

[6]   It is interesting to note that Thales of Miletos and Bias of Priene, two of the region's most famed thinkers, apparently both proposed greater centralization of the Ionian League (Hdt. 1.170).

who they were seeking to redefine into an administrative district. Finally, it is also important to remember that the Athenian Tribute Lists are post-Archaic in date and that the instigation and subsequent failure of the Ionian Revolt had been a massive event in the region, which can be expected to have had wide-ranging and permanent consequences that changed the character of the region considerably.[7] Later still, when Ionia had again fallen under Persian control, the Persians may have used the existing structures within Ionia through which to rule it, giving this administrative district an appearance of permanence.[8] The fact that these later trans-regional powers imposed onto Ionia a singular unitary identity and ruled it through pre-existing political structures which may only have appeared at the very end of the Archaic period further reinforced those structures, but does not imply that those structures were deep-rooted in the fabric of Ionian society or were of any great antiquity.

To sum up, all we can intuit from the historical records is that the Ionians may have used their common sanctuary and festivals at Panionion as a basis from which to engage in joint activities.[9] It may indeed be possible to infer quite a lot about the political organization of Ionia and the central role of the Panionion from Herodotos, and Ionia may indeed have been more organized than we have evidence for in extant literature,[10] but little of this can be arrived at or proven by archaeological means alone and we must put aside what we think we know of Ionia's political organization, which is mainly derived from later extra-regional sources, when we seek to define it and its non-political culture in the Archaic period.

For Herodotos, the defining characteristic of the Ionians' identity was their language and dialects – something for which there is epigraphic evidence, but which it is more difficult to link securely to archaeological cultures.[11] Language and the formation of oral and written traditions are vitally important elements in the creation and expression of ethnic identities.[12] There is tantalizing evidence that some form of Greek may have been used in Ionia in the late Bronze Age, based on possible Linear B evidence from Miletos.[13] Although we only have evidence of Linear B as a scribal language, and it is not known how widely it was spoken, if at all, the fact that Greek may have been spoken in late Bronze Age Ionia would have important implications for our understanding of the Greek "migration" (or "re-migration") to Ionia.

Whenever Greek first came to be spoken in Ionia, by the time he was writing in the fifth century BC Herodotos was able to distinguish four distinct groups within Ionia based on dialects (Hdt. 1.142):

---

[7]   e.g. mass colonization may have resulted from the failure of the revolt (Greaves 2007b).

[8]   Rubinstein and Greaves 2004: 1056.

[9]   Even responsibility for maintaining the Panionion was not a joint one as a later inscription suggests that this was Priene's duty (Roebuck 1979: 56). See note 3, above.

[10]   Rubinstein and Greaves 2004: 1056.

[11]   See Jeffery 1990 on epigraphic scripts of Ionia. Whereas formal inscriptions in stone could be argued to be the products of a small group of skilled craftsmen, the graffito of Archon son of Amoibichos at Abu Simbel (see p. 166, Figure 7.3) and the votives on pots from the Sanctuary of Aphrodite at Miletos are better evidence for the day-to-day use of those scripts and the language they represent.

[12]   J.M. Hall 1997.

[13]   Schiering 1979: 79, pl. 22.3; Niemeier 1998: 37; Greaves 2002: 63–6. Miletos was subject to more intensive Mycenaean influence than any other site on the Ionian coast (Niemeier 2005).

- *"Carian"* – Miletos, Myous, Priene
- *"Lydian"* – Ephesos, Kolophon, Lebedos, Teos, Klazomenai, Phokaia[14]
- *"The North Island Group"* – Chios and Erythrai
- *"Samian"* – Samos had its own dialect.

Herodotos was evidently able to differentiate between these groups and this has led to some discussion of what these groupings may have meant in terms of ethnicity and politics.[15] The distribution of these groupings clearly relates to the physical arrangement of the region. For example, the cut-off point between the "Carian" and "Lydian" groups is the physical wall created by the Mount Mykale horst ridge. South of this, the sites around the Gulf of Latmos could be argued to have formed a "Milesian *koine*"[16] but as we have negligible archaeological evidence from Myous and the site of Old Priene has yet to be found, it is not possible to connect this supposed subset of Ionian cities through their material culture. There is also such variance in local practices that even in the larger "Lydian" group it would be difficult to demonstrate that they had anything in common that differentiated them from the other Ionian dialectic groupings.

The Myth of the Ionian Migration

As outlined in Chapter 1, the Ionian Migration is a set of foundation stories from disparate sources that share a common strand about the movement of people from the Greek mainland to Ionia. The opinions of scholars vary on how much importance they attach to these stories – from total acceptance as historical fact, to total rejection.[17] In an extensive study of the pottery of the Protogeometric period, Irene Lemos has sought to selectively reintroduce the literary tradition into discussion of this period in those cases where it can be sustained by the archaeological evidence.[18] Her general conclusions are that there appears to have been a mass movement at about 1200 BC and that there were individual movements by groups of mixed population thereafter.

Some individual elements from the corpus of Ionian Migration stories can therefore apparently be confirmed by archaeology, when the literary evidence is applied retrospectively to the results of an archaeological analysis of a sufficiently large body of data. However, most of the Ionian foundation stories have been considerably "refashioned" in later history.[19] As an example of this, let us reconsider the template of a foundation myth that was current in fifth-century BC Athens[20] and which was applied to the foundation

---

[14]   See Kearns 1992.
[15]   Rubinstein and Greaves 2004: 1054.
[16]   Greaves' Milesian "mini-thalassocracy" (2000a).
[17]   e.g. Vanschoonwinkel 2006 and Cobet 2007, respectively.
[18]   Lemos 2002, 2007.
[19]   Nilsson 1986: 59–65.
[20]   This template may predate the fifth century BC. For example, it may have been an aid to storytelling in the oral tradition, similar to those used in the Homeric poems. Whatever its origins it is argued here that it is a literary trope, which may in some way reflect contemporary fifth-century BC practices when founding a colony, but which does not capture the historical realities of the events purportedly being described.

stories of Greek overseas settlements in the early Archaic period by later historians and poets (see Chapter 6):

- *Oikist* consults Delphi (usually about something unrelated)
- Oracle issues typically cryptic pronouncement
- *Oikist* ignores whole or part of the oracle's pronouncement
- His community (home or away) suffers
- *Oikist* realizes meaning of oracle and fulfills it
- New community flourishes.

This template matches very closely the foundation story of Ephesos in which the Ephesians struggled to found their city until an oracle had been correctly interpreted. This story was retold in the late second to early third centuries AD by Athenaios (8.62.361) from an original fifth-century BC story by Kreophylos.[21] In this story the Ephesian colonists had failed to successfully establish their colony for 20 years and were forced to live on an offshore island. Only when they had sought and successfully interpreted a cryptic oracular response regarding a fish and a boar were they able to move onto the mainland and build their city and temples.[22] This example shows us that despite their supposed antiquity, the series of foundation myths that constitute the core of the evidence for the Ionian Migration were reforged (or possibly even invented) in accordance with the conventions of fifth-century BC Athenian literary genres.

Not only were the structures of these stories recast into a fifth-century mold, the overall narrative of the ethnogenesis of the Ionian states was designed to suit the contemporary Athenian political agenda which was in the process of claiming Ionia as part of its empire. In this context the reinvented myths formed part of "a certain kind of oratory intended to excite patriotic sentiments."[23] These stories tell us a great deal about who the Athenians of the fifth century BC thought the Ionians of the Anatolian coast were, as reflected in their invention of the foundation traditions about them. However, what these stories do not tell us is anything about what the Ionians thought about their own identity or history. Lemos' detailed synthesis of the archaeology has shown that any physical evidence for the movement of peoples from the Greek mainland to the Anatolian coast shows that these took place at a date considerably before the start of the Archaic period, and the literary sources are all products of a post-Archaic literary genre. The discussion of the Ionian Migration therefore has no part in any serious consideration of the Archaic period, as it is a debate that seeks to meld pre-Archaic archaeological evidence from Ionia with the post-Archaic literature of Athens almost without reference to the intervening centuries.

Some commentators, including Lemos, might argue that the Ionian Migration myths preserve the essential historical "kernel" of a series of genuine historical events that

---

[21] Jacoby 1950: n. 417/1.

[22] For discussions of this myth and others connected with the foundation of Ephesos see Alzinger 1967, esp. 21–5, and Kerschner et al. 2008.

[23] Nilsson 1986: 85.

occurred in Ionia post-1200 BC. However, there is a danger that we might go beyond this to consider these literary tales of acts of foundation as archaeologically proven "events" that would lead to teleological arguments that Greek culture usurped that of Anatolia in Ionia at an early date.[24] In this book arguments and examples have been put forward that significant elements of Anatolian culture remained in Ionia throughout the Archaic period, a considerable period of time after the supposed dates of the Ionian Migration, and such examples should enable us to begin to question such teleological arguments that assume Greek cultural predominance in the region. By fetishizing texts we become blind to the subtleties of the archaeological record and by holding onto them too ardently we risk fossilizing the dynamic cultures of Ionia and Athens into the form they took in the writings of the fifth century BC. In fact, ancient societies revisited the core facts of their own collective memories and built them into new traditions, within the context of the contemporary social and political milieu, and this was central to their creation of their own dynamic ethnic identities that were often separate from their linguistic or material cultural identities.[25] An example of one such "core fact" of the collective memory of Ionia could be summarized as: "there was a time before the Greeks lived here." How this "core fact" (or indeed, this archaeologically proven "kernel" of historical truth) was woven into the stories and traditions of the different Ionian communities would vary between them and over time.

"Stories" and "tradition" were not the only elements that made up these identities, and other "raw material," such as monuments or customs, could also contribute to the formation of an ethnic group's traditions about itself.[26] This being so, visible monuments in the region could have played into the Ionians' perceptions of themselves. For example, Herodotos reports seeing two rock-carved images in Ionia: one on the road from Ephesos to Phokaia and one on the road from Smyrna to Sardis (Hdt. 2.106). He reports that these reliefs are in the form of seven-foot high armed male figures in Egyptian or Ethiopian garb. He also provides a false reading of the "Egyptian" hieroglyphic inscription on them and attributes them to the Egyptian king Sesostris. At least one of these images, that which is said to be "near Smyrna," can be securely identified with the Hittite relief and hieroglyphic inscription at Karabel (see Figure 10.1).[27] These reliefs presumably drew Herodotos' attention for a number of reasons: they were male, "foreign," and accompanied by a hieroglyphic inscription that he took to be Egyptian in origin. He weaves these visible monuments into a narrative about Ionia having once been conquered by the foreign male Egyptian historical character Sesostris. This demonstrates how Herodotos can formulate a narrative that incorporates obviously "foreign" elements of Ionian culture into an imagined history of the region of his creation. In this case, he invents the fact that Ionia had once been conquered by Egypt, a story that can be nicely accommodated within his narrative themes of Egypt as a great nation and of Ionia as being semi-"foreign," militarily weak and, therefore, open to invasion by outsiders. Another example of where

---

[24] On "events" see Chapter 1.
[25] Snodgrass 1991: 64; J.M. Hall 1997; Malkin 2003.
[26] Sourvinou-Inwood 2003, esp. 106 and 141, *contra* J.M. Hall 1997.
[27] Hawkins 1998.

Figure 10.1 The Karabel rock relief of "Sesostris" (actually a Hittite-style rock relief of Tarkasnawa, king of the Bronze Age kingdom of Mira). Photograph by Gertrude Bell 1907. © Gertrude Bell Photographic Archive at the University of Newcastle upon Tyne.

he does this is given in the Epilogue to this book. Interestingly though, Herodotos does not single out for such discussion the reliefs of Cybele in Ionia which we know to have existed at Phokaia and elsewhere; perhaps he simply did not consider these uninscribed reliefs of females to be "foreign" within the context of what he understood by "Ionian" identity.

Ionian Identity and Archaeology

In the total absence of ethnohistorical texts (see Chapter 1) we only have a construct of Archaic Ionian ethnicity that has been created by, or from, the texts produced within the context of fifth-century BC Athenian culture, such as Herodotos.[28] The reality of Archaic Ionian material culture is often at odds with the literary constructs of these later outsiders. For example, in fifth-century BC Athens the "East" was being epitomized as being weak and effeminate, yet the archaeological evidence for the "orientalized" Archaic

---

[28] Although Herodotos was himself a Carian by birth, at the time of his writing he was operating within the Athenian cultural milieu.

Ionians shows that they were constructing massive defenses and using their art to depict a war-like Athena.[29]

Not only did Athenian literary culture rewrite Ionian history so as to accommodate it within its own concepts of history and ethnicity, but so too has modern scholarship. An example of this is that the scholarly writing about the operation of the oracle at Branchidai-Didyma has often unquestioningly retrojected divination by means of the Classical Delphic practice of mantic trance onto the Archaic period at the site, for which the only firm archaeological evidence is for divination by cleromancy.[30]

If we are to avoid being influenced by the inherent Atheno-centricism of the ancient historical sources and the often one-sided nature of the traditional methods of art history and Classical archaeology, that call extensively upon references to the corpus of Athenian art and literature, then a new methodology is required. That methodology should seek to balance Aegean Greek and Anatolian influences within Ionia, even where the latter are less immediately perceptible, less well understood, and not as precisely dateable as those of Greece. It should also be an explicitly archaeological methodology, rather than a pseudo-archaeological justification of the metanarrative of ancient history. To do this it should apply some of the theories and practices of problem-based "prehistoric" archaeology (i.e. landscape archaeology and phenomenology, world-systems analysis, post-colonial third place theory, etc.) and progressively integrate historical sources into the framework established by these means (i.e. the *Annaliste* approach). As far as possible, this book has attempted to apply such a methodology and to provide a critique of the way in which traditional methodologies have sometimes unwittingly perpetuated Atheno-centricism in their study of Ionia.

Each of the thematic chapters of this book has sought to identify examples of cultural practices that were peculiarly Ionian. Chapter 3 emphasized the scale, diversity, and dynamism of the Ionian landscape and Chapter 4 examined the exploitation of that landscape for agriculture, of which trade was in large part a by-product. The cities of Ionia, discussed in Chapter 5, were shown to be positioned in relation to specific physical phenomena of their locality, to have had the outward appearance of defended contemporary Anatolian power centers, and to have influenced the *mentalité* of their inhabitants. In Chapter 6, Ionia's many colonies were shown to parallel the settlement preferences and processes of historical reinvention that can also be traced in the Ionian *metropoleis* themselves and were argued to be an extension of the world system of which Ionia was a part, but not the core. The survey of fortifications in Ionia presented in Chapter 7 shows that they were earlier than, and on a scale unprecedented in, those in much of mainland Greece and supports the interpretation that the Ionians were engaged, both politically and militarily, with Anatolia rather than with the *hoplite* states of the mainland. The recent recognition of a number of Phrygian cult sites across the region, discussed in Chapter 8, and the possible Hittite and neo-Hittite antecedents of some of the region's most important cult centers emphasize its strong Anatolian character. Finally, in Chapter 9, Ionian art was examined in a way that sought to construct new,

---

[29]   On defenses see Chapter 7; on Athena see Villing 1998.
[30]   Greaves forthcoming (3).

locally specific understandings of the region's art and its presumed relationship to Athenian culture.

Elements of Ionian cultural practice such as these differentiate it from those of contemporary Athens and mainland Greece, but they also differentiated the Ionian states from one another. Local pottery styles, funerary practices, and cult preferences are evident and are consistent with a general pattern of regionalism within the Archaic Greek world. Evidence of the adoption of Greek practices, such as the use of human figures in art, can be seen to be progressive, often coming late in the Archaic period, and always through the agency of the Ionian people.

Religion was an important mediator between ancient cultures.[31] In Ionia "hybrid" cultural forms combined elements of Greek and Anatolian cult iconography, showing the syncretism to the two cult traditions. The chronology of that process of syncretism will remain a difficult issue, but there is evidence to show that "Greek" cults accommodated into themselves elements of the pre-existing "Phrygian"-style practice, and it is not yet possible to show how (or if) the established "Phrygian"-style cults were modified by their encounter with Greek culture. When viewed only from the microhistorical perspective of the literary sources and the tradition of the Ionian Migration, it is hard to see how there could not have been a violent clash of cultures in this crucial meeting point between East and West. Yet, when viewed in mediohistorical timescales, and even in the *longue durée*, Ionian cults, such as the cult of Artemis at Ephesos (see Box 10.1), and burial rituals (see Chapter 8) can be seen to have been mutable in a way that would have facilitated syncretism and the accommodation of new populations, such as the Greeks, or new ruling elites, such as the Lydians or Persians. The landscape of Ionia was dynamic, and so were its cultures. Perhaps it is this message of the mutability of cultures when viewed from a slower historical tempo that has most relevance to the modern world, struggling to cope with its own clash of cultures and the divisions it has created between East and West.[32]

Conclusions

We waste too much time on seeking to "clarify" historical issues and to justify our interpretations of them by means of "objective" archaeological evidence.[33] In the opinion of the author, the means to understanding Ionian culture as a regional phenomenon is to apply to Ionia the methods of archaeological thinking that were developed for non-literary "prehistoric" cultures and then to reintroduce historical records in a measured and critical manner. Perhaps the most significant results of this critical review have been the realization that, once stripped of the weight of historical tradition, we actually know less about Archaic Ionia than we thought we did, that contrary to the impression given by that tradition there was no single "Ionian" identity but rather multiple local cultures existed, and that the evidence for "Phrygian"-style cult in Ionia has often been

---

[31] Dusinberre 2003: 199.

[32] See Greaves 2007a for further discussion of this theme.

[33] On archaeology's spurious claims to "objectivity" see Chapter 2.

🐏🐏🐏   Box 10.1   🐏🐏🐏
Artemis of Ephesos

The cult statue of Artemis of Ephesos is one of the most iconic images of Ionia. The origins of this image, like many aspects of Ionian culture, are complex and disputed – but they are unlikely to have been something that concerned her worshippers as much as they concern modern scholars.[a] The nature of the deity worshipped at the Artemision, and cults that were performed there, no doubt changed during the long history of the site, and the images that we are most familiar with come only from the very end of the temple's history of use.

Even ancient writers appreciated that the cult at Ephesos predated the arrival of the Greeks at the site and the foundation of their own city and temples (Pausanias 7.2.6), but finding archaeological evidence to prove continuity of cult activity at the site between the Bronze Age and the Archaic period has been difficult. Early attempts at excavating the site no doubt removed important archaeological contexts, unrecorded (see Box 1.1). Nevertheless, modern excavators have been able to locate areas of undisturbed stratigraphy and make systematic excavations of them.[b] However, even though these included finds of Bronze Age Mycenaean pottery, they have not conclusively proven the continuity of cult hypothesis.[c]

Much discussion has surrounded the cult image's egg- or breast-like appendages, which are commonly assumed to be a fertility symbol.[d] In the Roman period copy illustrated here, they have been accentuated to resemble breasts, but their true nature is unclear. A suggestion that they represent the scrotal sacs of sacrificed bulls that were used to adorn the original *xoanon* (wooden cult statue) has been widely publicized.[e] However, during excavation in the late 1980s a number of pendulous amber droplets, pierced for suspension as beads, were discovered, apparently where they had fallen when the temple was destroyed by a flood in the eighth century BC. The current interpretation is that it is these beads that adorned the original wooden cult image and are represented in the surviving Roman period statues from the site. The use of amber as a sacred material may have had its origins in Bronze Age Mycenaean cult practices, its natural iridescence being connected with solar cults, not fertility.[f]

Notes

[a]   LiDonnici 1992.
[b]   Bammer 1990; Kerschner 1997.
[c]   Bammer 1990: 142.
[d]   Bammer and Muss 1996: 73–5.
[e]   Seiterle 1979.
[f]   Muss 2008.

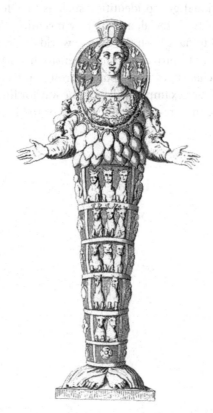

Artemis of Ephesos in an eighteenth-century engraving of a Roman marble copy of a Greek original, in the Vatican Museum.

overlooked. The construction of "traditions," such as the foundation myths of the Ionian Migration, and trans-regional group identities, such as the "Ionian League," were later products of conscious political, social, and literary invention that are inconsistent with what we now understand to have been the diverse world of the Archaic Greek culture.

This book did not set out to provide a comprehensive history of Ionia, but it is hoped that the methodological challenges it has posed through the critical review of available evidence and the discussion of examples will pave the way for the writing of such a history in a way that will balance the pre-Greek inheritance of the Ionians with later historical traditions about them.

Epilogue

Even those who started from the Government House in Athens and believe themselves to be of the purest Ionian blood, took no women with them but married Carian girls, whose parents they had killed. The fact that these women were forced into marriage after the murder of their fathers, husbands, and sons was the origin of the law, established by oath and passed down to their female descendants, forbidding them to sit at table with their husbands or to address them by name. It was at Miletos that this took place.[1]

By the time Herodotos came to write this passage, Miletos had been sacked by the Persians in retaliation for its revolt and Athens was the savior of Greece. Looking at Ionia, with its non-Greek origins and practices, he sought to construct a narrative of the origins of an Ionian society that had failed where Athens' had succeeded and which conformed to his overarching narrative structures and his opposing constructs of "Greek" and "barbarian." The Ionians he creates in this passage are Greek, but their "pure blood" has been diluted by intermarriage with a pre-Hellenic Carian population, whose achievements are reduced by his portrayal of them as a totally defeated and eradicated foe and whose culture is further debased (in his eyes) to becoming the preserve of women.

Alternatively, one could see this as an attempt to claim Greek ethnicity for the Ionians – a conscious reworking of the tradition of their origins that would make them acceptable to fifth-century Athenian concepts of "Greek" and "barbarian," and yet remained within the realms of the possible by incorporating key facts from the collective memory and experience of his audience. The "core fact" of this story is that Ionia had once been inhabited by a predominantly non-Greek Anatolian population, but by the time of his writing it was almost, but not entirely, Greek. After Lade, the political life of the Ionian cities was increasingly bound up with that of mainland Greece, but within their domestic space the Ionians were able to create a Third Place in which local dining customs, which appear no more alien to us than those practiced by many modern cultures, were

---

[1] Herodotos *Histories* 1.146 [trans. Sélincourt].

maintained and could be incorporated with the Greek into a "hybrid" identity that was uniquely Ionian.

This new interpretation, which is informed by the ideas laid out in this book, is neither definitive nor provable. Like all histories of the ancient world, it is a hypothesis based on the selection and interpretation of pieces of evidence, both archaeological and historical, that are used to construct a new narrative for Ionia. It is self-consciously aiming to invert a number of current received ideas and to re-envision Ionia as a part of the Anatolian world, in the hope of broadening out the possibilities for redefining, or reasserting, elements of the existing narrative and to allow for the creation of new interpretations of *Ionian* identity that are uniquely *Ionian*.

Glossary of ancient Greek [and modern Turkish] terms used in the text

Aeinautai   The "forever sailors," one of two political factions in a dispute in Miletos reported by Herodotos (5.28), the other group being the *cheiromachei*.

Agora   A market place.

Apoikia (pl. apoikiai)   Literally, an "away-settlement"; an overseas colony.

Archon   A ruler.

Astragalus (pl. astragali)   The foot bones of ungulates; knucklebones; Latin *tali*. In ancient times *astragali* were used as dice for casting lots and for oracles.

Asty   A city.

Beylik [Turkish]   An emirate or principality.

Bothros (pl. bothroi)   Pits in the ground; sometimes holding sacred offerings.

Boustrophedon   A system of writing in which text is presented alternately left-to-right and right-to-left; literally, "as the ox ploughs."

Cheiromachei   The "manual workers," one of two political factions in a dispute in Miletos reported by Herodotos (5.28), the other group being the *aeinautai*.

Chora (pl. chorai)   The territory of a *polis*.

Comast   A male dancer, sometimes depicted with padded buttocks, usually shown in art in a *comos* – a drunken dancing scene.

Diolkos   A dragway by means of which ships could cross the Corinthian isthmus.

Dipinti   Painted inscriptions, usually on pots.

Dodekapolis   A league of 12 cities.

Dromos   An entrance passage, usually to a tomb.

Emporion (pl. emporia)   A trading post.

Epoikoi   Settlers.

Hegemon   The leading or dominant power, often within the context of a group of states (a hegemony).

Heroon   A shrine dedicated to a hero.

Hoplite   A heavily armed infantry solider.

Klerouchy (pl. klerouchies)   A type of colony established by Athens in which the settlers retained Athenian status.

Koine   The common culture or language of a region.

Kore   A standing, robed female statue.

Kouros (pl. *kouroi*)   A standing male statue, usually nude.

Metropolis (pl. *metropoleis*)   Literally, a "mother-city"; the founding community of a colony.

Necropolis (pl. *necropoleis*)   Literally, a "city of the dead"; a burial ground.

Oikist   The founder of a settlement.

Panhellenic   Pertaining to the whole of Greece.

Pekmez [Turkish]   Condensed grape juice or must.

Pentekonter   A 50-oared warship.

Peraia   The extension of a territory to include an area of land on the opposing shore.

Phalanx   A formation of infantry soldiers in a line, or series of ranks.

Phoros   Tribute payments.

Phyle (pl. *phylae*)   A tribe.

Pithos (pl. *pithoi*)   A large open-mouthed storage jar.

Polis (pl. *poleis*)   A city-state.

Polos   A tall headdress, usually worn by female deities in art.

Proxenos   A guest-friend; relating to the Greek social institution of guest-friendship in which a citizen hosts a foreign ambassador in return for honorific titles.

Sarcophagos (pl. *sarcophagi*)   A stone or terracotta coffin in which a body is laid to decompose.

Stasis   A state of political stalemate.

Stele (pl. *stelae*)   A stone slab.

Symmachy   A military alliance.

Synoikise   The bringing together of settlements.

Tandır [Turkish]   A bread oven accessed from the top and usually sunk into the floor and set into a built structure.

Temenos   The sacred enclosure in which a temple is often located.

Trireme   A warship with three banks of oars.

Tumulus (pl. *tumuli*)   A burial mound.

Xoanon (pl. *xoana*)   The venerated cult statue in a Greek temple; usually carved from wood.

Bibliography

Adiego, I.J., 1997: Fragment d'une inscription lydienne. *Istanbuler Mitteilungen* 47: 156–7.

Akdeniz, E., 1996: 1995 Yılı Büyük Menderes Ovası ve Çevresi Yüzey Araştırmaları. *Araştırma Sonuçları Toplantası* 14: 233–54.

Akdeniz, E., 2002: Büyük Menderes Havzasında Prehistorik Yerleşim Dokusu. *Belletin* 66: 7–36.

Aksu, A.E., Piper, D.J.W., and Konuk, T., 1987: Quaternary growth patterns of Büyük Menderes and Küçük Menderes deltas, western Turkey. *Sedimentary Geology* 52: 227–50.

Akurgal, E., 1968: *The Birth of Greek Art: The Mediterranean and the Near East* [trans. W. Dynes]. London.

Akurgal, E., 1976: Phokaia (Foça). *The Princeton Encyclopedia of Classical Sites*: 708–9.

Akurgal, E., 1997: *Anadolu Kültür Tarihi*. Ankara.

Akurgal, E., 2002: *Ancient Civilizations and Ruins of Turkey*. New York.

Akurgal, E., 2007: Beiträge der Aiolier und Ionier zur Bereicherung und Gestaltung der griechischen Kunst und Kultur. In: J. Cobet, V. von Graeve, W.-D. Niemeier, and K. Zimmermann (eds.): *Frühes Ionien. Eine Bestandsaufnahme*. Mainz am Rhein: 639–44.

Akurgal, M., 2007: Hellenic architecture in Smyrna 650–546 BC. In: J. Cobet, V. von Graeve, W.-D. Niemeier, and K. Zimmermann (eds.): *Frühes Ionien. Eine Bestandsaufnahme*. Mainz am Rhein: 125–36.

Akurgal, M., Kerschner, M., Mommsen, H., and Niemeier, W.-D., 2002: *Töpferzentren der Ostägäis: Archäometrische und archäologische Untersuchungen zur mykenischen, geometrischen und archaischen Keramik aus Fundorten in Westkleinasien*. Wien.

Alcock, S., 1993: *Graecia Capta: The landscapes of Roman Greece*. Cambridge.

Alcock, S., 2007: The essential countryside: the Greek world. In: S.E. Alcock and R. Osborne (eds.): *Classical Archaeology*. Oxford: 118–38.

Alcock, S.E., and Osborne, R. (eds.), 2007: *Classical Archaeology*. Oxford.

Alty, J., 1982: Dorians and Ionians. *Journal of Hellenic Studies* 102: 1–14.

Alzinger, W., 1967: Alt-Ephesos: Topographie und Architektur. *Das Altertum* 13.1: 20–44.

Atakuman, Ç., 2008: Cradle or crucible: Anatolia and archaeology in the early years of the Turkish Republic (1923–1938). *Journal of Social Archaeology* 8.2: 214–35.

Ateşoğulları, S., 2002: *Arkeolojik söyleşiler I*. Ankara.

Austin, M.M., and Vidal-Naquet, P., 1977: *Economic and Social History of Ancient Greece*. London.

Avram, A., 2007: Das Territorium von Istros in archaischer Zeit. In: J. Cobet, V. von Graeve, W.-D. Niemeier, and K. Zimmermann (eds.): *Frühes Ionien. Eine Bestandsaufnahme*. Mainz am Rhein: 487–97.

Aybek, S., and Öz, A.K., 2004: Preliminary report of the archaeological survey at Apollonia ad Rhyndacum in Mysia. *Anadolu/Anatolia* 27: 1–25.

Aydın, B., 2006: A survey of Clazomenean close territory in Turkey – İzmir – Urla 1997. In: A. Erkanal-Öktü et al. (eds.): *Studies in Honor of Hayat Erkanal: Cultural reflections*. İstanbul: 95–105.

Aydın, B., 2007: Galesion Dağı ve Civarındaki Antik Yerleşimler. *Kubaba* 4.11: 16–29.

Bahn, P., 1996: *Archaeology: A very short introduction*. Oxford.

Balin de Bellu, E., 1965: *L'Histoire des Colonies, Grecques du Littoral Nord de la Mer Noire*. Leiden.

Bammer, A., 1968: Der Altar des jüngeren Artemisions von Ephesos: Vorläufiger Bericht. *Archäologischer Anzeiger* 1968: 400–23.

Bammer, A., 1990: A "periteros" of the Geometric period in the Artemision of Ephesus. *Anatolian Studies* 40: 137–60.

Bammer, A., 2007: Archäologische Überreste auf dem Bademliktepe bei Ayasoluk-Selçuk. *Anatolia Antiqua* 15: 103–11.

Bammer, A., and Muss, U., 1996: *Das Artemision von Ephesos*. Mainz.

Bammer, A., and Muss, U., 2006: Ein Felsdenkmal auf dem Bülbüldağ von Ephesos. *Anatolia Antiqua* 14: 65–9.

Bammer, A., and Muss, U., 2007: Ein frühes Quellheiligtum am Ayasolukhügel in Ephesos. *Anatolia Antiqua* 15: 95–101.

Baran, M., and Petzl, G., 1977/78: Beobachtungen aus dem nordöstlichen Hinterland von Teos. *Istanbuler Mitteilungen* 27/28: 301–8.

Barker, G., 1991: Two Italys, one valley: an *Annaliste* perspective. In: J. Bintliff (ed.): *The Annales School and Archaeology*. Leicester: 34–56.

Barker, G., 1995: *A Mediterranean Valley: Landscape archaeology and Annales history in the Biferno Valley*. London.

Bats, M., and Tréziny, H. (eds.), 1985: *Le territoire de Marseille: Actes de la table ronde d'Aix-en-Provence*. Aix-en-Provence.

Bay, B., 1999a: *Geoarchäologie, anthropogene Bodenerosion und Deltavorbau im Büyük Menderes Delta (SW-Türkei)*. [PhD thesis]. Bochum.

Bay, B., 1999b: Geoarchäologische Auswertung der Brunnengrabungen nördlich von Yeniköy. *Archäologischer Anzeiger* 1999.1: 77–88.

Bean, G.E., 1966: *Aegean Turkey: An archaeological guide*. London.

Beaumont, L., 2007: Chios: The Kato Phano archaeological project. In: J. Cobet, V. von Graeve, W.-D. Niemeier, and K. Zimmermann (eds.): *Frühes Ionien. Eine Bestandsaufnahme*. Mainz am Rhein: 137–48.

Beaumont, L.A., forthcoming: Chios in the "Dark Ages": New evidence from Kato Phana. In: A.M. Ainian (ed.): *The "Dark Ages" Revisited. An International Conference in Memory of William D.E. Coulson, June 2007*. Volos.

Beaumont, L., and Archontidou-Argyri, A., 1999: New work at Kata Phana, Chios: The Kata Phana Archaeological Project. Preliminary report for 1997 and 1998. *Annual of the British School at Athens* 94: 266–87.

Beaumont, L., and Archontidou-Argyri, A., 2004: Excavations at Kato Phano, Chios: 1999, 2000, and 2001. *Annual of the British School at Athens* 99: 201–55.

Becker, F., 1988: Ein Fund von 75 milesischen Obolen. *Schweizerische Numismatische Rundschau* 67: 5–41.

Béquignon, Y., and Laumonier, A., 1925: Fouilles de Téos. *Bulletin de Correspondance Hellénique* 47: 281–321.

Bérard, C., Bron, C., and Vernant, J-P., 1984: *A City of Images: Iconography and society in ancient Greece* [trans. D. Lyons 1989]. Princeton.

Berges, D., 2006: *Knidos: Beiträge zur Geschichte der archaischen Stadt*. Mainz.

Berndt-Ersöz, S., 1998: Phrygian rock-cut cult façades: a study of the function of the so-called shaft monuments. *Anatolian Studies* 48: 87–112.

Berndt-Ersöz, S., 2003: *Phrygian rock-cut shrines and other religious monuments: A study of structure, function and cult practice*. [Unpublished PhD thesis]. Stockholm.

Bhabha, H.K., 2004: *The Location of Culture*. London.

Bianchi, U., 1953: *Dios Asia. Destin, uomini e divinità nell'epos, nelle teogonie e nel culto dei Greci*. Rome.

Bintliff, J., 1986: Archaeology at the interface: an historical perspective. In: J.L. Bintliff and C.F. Gaffney (eds.): *Archaeology at the Interface: Studies in archaeology's relationships with history, geography, biology and physical science*. British Archaeological Reports International Series no. 300. Oxford: 4–31.

Bintliff, J., 1991: The contribution of an Annaliste/structural history approach to archaeology. In: J. Bintliff (ed.): *The Annales School and Archaeology*. Leicester: 1–33.

Blackman, D.J. (ed.), 1973: *Marine Archaeology*. London.

Blüm, I., 1999: Die Stadtmauern von Alt-Milet. Ergebnisse des Surveys 1996 und 1997. *Archäologischer Anzeiger* 1999: 53–76.

Blümel, W., 2007: Die Erforschung des Karischen. In: J. Cobet, V. von Graeve, W.-D. Niemeier, and K. Zimmermann (eds.): *Frühes Ionien. Eine Bestandsaufnahme*. Mainz am Rhein: 429–35.

Boardman, J., 1956: Delphinion in Chios. *Annual of the British School at Athens* 51: 41–54.

Boardman, J., 1967: *Excavations in Chios 1952–55: Greek emporio*. BSA Supplement vol. 6. Oxford.

Boardman, J., 1978: *Greek Sculpture: The archaic period*. London.

Boardman, J., 1986: Archaic Chian pottery at Naucratis. In: J. Boardman and C.E. Vaphopoulou-Richardson (eds.): *Chios: A conference at the Homereion in Chios 1984*. Oxford: 253–8.

Boardman, J., 1996: *Greek Art*. London.

Boardman, J., 1999: *The Greeks Overseas* (4th edn.). London.

Boardman, J., 2001: *The History of Greek Vases*. London.

Boardman, J., 2006: Greeks in the East Mediterranean (South Anatolia, Syria, Egypt). In: G.R. Tsetskhladze (ed.): *Greek Colonisation: An account of Greek colonies and other settlements overseas. Vol. 1*. Leiden: 507–34.

Boardman, J., and Vaphopoulou-Richardson, C.E. (eds.), 1986: *Chios: A conference at the Homereion in Chios 1984*. Oxford.

Bol, R., 2005: Der "Torso von Milet" und das Kultbild des Apollon Termintheus in Myus. *Istanbuler Mitteilungen* 55.

Bol, R., Höckmann, U., and Schollmeyer, P. (eds.), 2008: *Kult(ur)kontakte. Apollon in Myus, Milet/Didyma, Naukratis und auf Zypern, Akten Table Ronde Mainz 2004*. Mainz.

Bowden, H., 1996. Greek settlements and sanctuaries at Naucratis. In: M.H. Hansen and K. Raaflaub (eds.): *More Studies in the Ancient Greek Polis*. Stuttgart: 17–37.

Braudel, F., 1972: *The Mediterranean and the Mediterranean World in the Age of Philip II* [trans. Sian Reynolds]. New York.

Braun, T.F.R.G., 1982: The Greeks in Egypt. In: J. Boardman and N.G.L. Hammond (eds.): *The Cambridge Ancient History. Vol. III.3* (2nd edn.). Cambridge: 32–57.

Briant, P., 1994: À propos du boulet de Phocée. *Revue des Études Anciennes* 96: 111–14.

Bridges, R.A., 1974: The Mycenaean tholos tomb at Kolophon. *Hesperia* 43.2: 264–6.

Brinkmann, R., 1971: The geology of western Anatolia. In: A.S. Campbell (ed.): *Geology and History of Turkey*. Castelfranco Veneto: 171–90.

Brinkmann, V., 1990: Kalabaktepe – Der Westbau. *Istanbuler Mitteilungen* 40.

Brown, E.L., 2004: In search of Anatolian Apollo. In: A.P. Chapin (ed.): *XAPIΣ: Essays in honor of Sara A. Immerwahr*. Athens: Hesperia Supplements 33: 243–57.

Brückner, H., Müllenhoff, M., Gehrels, R., Herda, A., Knipping, M., and Vött, A., 2006: From archipelago to floodplain – geographical and ecological changes in Miletus and its environs during the past six millennia (Western Anatolia, Turkey). *Zeitschrift für Geomorphologie* N.F., Suppl.-Vol. 142: 63–83.

Brüggerhorr, S., Cheba, S., Leisen, H., and Warscheid, T., 1999: Untersuchungen zur Krustenbildung auf Marmoroberflächen in Milet. *Archäologischer Anzeiger* 1999.1: 99–108.

Bryce, T.R., 1986: *The Lycians. Vol. 1. Lycians in literary and epigraphic sources*. Copenhagen.

Bujskikh, A., 2007: The earliest East Greek pottery from Olbia Pontica. In: J. Cobet, V. von Graeve, W.-D. Niemeier, and K. Zimmermann (eds.): *Frühes Ionien. Eine Bestandsaufnahme*. Mainz am Rhein: 499–510.

Bumke, H., 2002: Eine Bes-Statuette aus dem Apollonheiligtum von Didyma. *Istanbuler Mitteilungen* 52: 209–19.

Bumke, H., 2006: Die Schwester des Orakelgottes: Zum Artemiskult in Didyma. In: J. Mylonopoulos and H. Roeder (eds.): *Archäologie und Ritual. Auf der Suche nach der Rituellen Handlung in den antiken Kulturen Ägyptens und Griechenlands*. Wien: 215–37.

Bumke, H., 2007: Fremde Weihungen für griechische Götter. Überlegungen zu den Bronzestatuetten ägyptischer Götter und Priester im Heraion von Samos. In: C. Frevel and H. von Hesberg (eds.): *Kult und Kommunikation. Medien in Heiligtümern der Antike*. Wiesbaden: 349–80.

Burkert, W., 1985: *Greek Religion: Archaic and classical*. Oxford.

Burkert, W., 1994: Olbia and Apollo of Didyma: A new oracle text. In: J. Solomon (ed.): *Apollo: Origins and influences*. Tucson: 49–60.

Büyükkolancı, M., 2007: Apaša, das alte Ephesos und Ayasoluk. In: J. Cobet, V. von Graeve, W.-D. Niemeier, and K. Zimmermann (eds.): *Frühes Ionien. Eine Bestandsaufnahme*. Mainz am Rhein: 21–6.

Cahill, N., 1988: Taş Kule: A Persian-period tomb near Phokaia. *American Journal of Archaeology* 92.4: 499–501.

Carpenter, T.H., 1991: *Art and Myth in Ancient Greece*. London.

Carter, J.C., 1994: Sanctuaries in the Chora of Metaponto. In: S. Alcock and R. Osborne (eds.): *Placing the Gods: Sanctuaries and sacred space in ancient Greece*. Oxford: 161–98.

Carter, J.C., 2006: *Discovering the Greek Countryside at Metaponto*. Ann Arbor.

Cartledge, P., 2006: *Thermopylae: The battle that changed the world*. London.

Caspari, M.O.B., 1916: The Ionian Confederacy – Addendum. *Journal of Hellenic Studies* 36: 102.

Casson, L., 1995: *Ships and Seamanship in the Ancient World*. Baltimore.

Cawkwell, G.L., 1992: Early colonisation. *Classical Quarterly* 42: 289–303.

Chadwick, J., 1973: The Berezan Lead Letter. *Proceedings of the Cambridge Philological Society* 199 (New series 19): 35–7.

Challis, D., 2008: *From the Harpy Tomb to the Wonders of Ephesus*. London.

Chase-Dunn, C., and Hall, T.D., 1997: *Rise and Demise: Comparing world-systems*. Boulder, CO.

Çiğ, M.İ., 1993: Mustafa Kemal Atatürk und die Archäologie in der Türkei. *Istanbuler Mitteilungen* 43: 517–22.

Çilingiroğlu, A., 2007: Properties of the Urartian Temple at Ayanis. In: A. Çilingiroğlu and A. Sagona (eds.): *Anatolian Iron Ages 6: The Proceedings of the Sixth Anatolian Iron Ages Colloquium held at Eskisehir, 16–20 August 2004*. Leuven: 41–6.

Çilingiroğlu, A., and Derin, Z., 2001: Armour and weapons. In: A. Çilingiroğlu and M. Salvini (eds.): *Ayanis I*. Rome: 156–87.

Clayton, P.A., 1994: *Chronicle of the Pharaohs: The reign-by-reign record of the rulers and dynasties of ancient Egypt*. London.

Cobet, J., 1997: Milet 1994–1995: Die Mauern sind die Stadt, Zur Stadtbefestigung des antiken Milet. *Archäologischer Anzeiger* 1997: 249–84.

Cobet, J., 2007: Das alte Ionien in der Geschichtsschreibung. In: J. Cobet, V. von Graeve, W.-D. Niemeier, and K. Zimmermann (eds.): *Frühes Ionien. Eine Bestandsaufnahme.* Mainz am Rhein: 729–43.

Cobet, J., von Graeve, V., Niemeier, W.-D., and Zimmermann, K. (eds.), 2007: *Frühes Ionien. Eine Bestandsaufnahme.* Mainz am Rhein.

Collins, B.J., 2007: *The Hittites and their World.* Atlanta.

Cook, J.M., 1962: *The Greeks in Ionia and the East.* London.

Cook, R.M., 1958: Speculations on the origins of coinage. *Historia* 7: 257–62.

Cook, R.M., 1961: Some sites of the Milesian territory. *Annual of the British School at Athens* 56: 90–101.

Cook, R.M., 1981: *Clazomenian Sarcophagi.* Mainz.

Cook, R.M., 1992: The Wild Goat and Fikellura styles: some speculations. *Oxford Journal of Archaeology* 11.3: 255–66.

Cook, R.M., 1993: A Carian Wild Goat workshop. *Oxford Journal of Archaeology* 12.1: 109–15.

Cook, R.M., and Dupont, P., 1998: *East Greek Pottery.* London.

Damyanov, M., 2005: Necropoleis and Ionian colonisation in the Black Sea. *Ancient West and East* 4.1: 77–97.

Dasen, V., 1997: Multiple births in Graeco-Roman antiquity. *Oxford Journal of Archaeology* 16: 49–63.

de Angelis, F., 2006: Going against the grain in Sicilian Greek economics. *Greece and Rome* 53: 29–47.

Debord, P., 1999: *L'Asie Mineure au IVe siècle (412–323 a.C.): pouvoirs et jeux politiques.* Bordeaux.

Demand, N.H., 1990: *Urban Relocation in Archaic and Classical Greece: Flight and consolidation.* Bristol.

de Polignac, F., 1995: *Cults, Territory, and the Origins of the Greek City-state.* Chicago.

de Souza, P., 1998: Towards thallasocracy? Archaic Greek naval developments. In: N. Fisher and H. van Wees (eds.): *Archaic Greece: New approaches and new evidence.* London: 271–94.

Díaz-Andreu, M. (ed.), 2005: *Archaeology of Identity: Approaches to gender, age, status, ethnicity and religion.* London.

Diehl, E., 1965: Fragmente aus Samos II. *Archäologischer Anzeiger* 1965: 823–50.

Dillon, M.P.J., 1997: A Homeric pun from Abu Simbel (Meiggs and Lewis 7A). *Zeitschrift für Papyrologie und Epigraphik* 118: 128–30.

Dobres, M.-A., and Robb, J., 1994: *Agency in Archaeology.* London.

Dougherty, C., 1993a: *The Poetics of Colonization: From city to text in Archaic Greece.* Oxford.

Dougherty, C., 1993b: It's murder to found a Greek colony. In: C. Dougherty and L. Kurke (eds.): *Cultural Poetics in Archaic Greece.* Cambridge: 178–98.

Dunham, A.G., 1915: *The History of Miletus: Down to the Anabasis of Alexander.* London.

Dupont, P., 1982: Amphores commerciales archaïques de la Grèce de l'Est. *La Parola del Passato: rivista di studi antichi* 37: 193–208.

Dupont, P., 1995/96: Amphores archaïques de Grèce propre en Mer Noire: État de la question. *Il Mar Nero* 2: 85–97.

Dupont, P., 2007: Diffusion des amphores commerciales de type Milesien dans le Pont archaïque. In: J. Cobet, V. von Graeve, W.-D. Niemeier, and K. Zimmermann (eds.): *Frühes Ionien. Eine Bestandsaufnahme.* Mainz am Rhein: 621–30.

Dusinberre, E.R.M., 2002: An excavated ivory from Kerkenes Dağ, Turkey: Transcultural fluidities, significance of collective identity, and the problem of Median art. *Ars Orientalis* 32: 17–54.

Dusinberre, E.R.M., 2003: *Aspects of Empire in Achaemenid Sardis.* Cambridge.

Ehrhardt, N., 1988: *Milet und seine Kolonien.* Frankfurt am Main.

Ehrhardt, N., 1998: Didyma und Milet in archaischer Zeit. *Chiron* 28: 11–20.

Ehrhardt, N., Lohmann, H., and Weber, B., 2007: Milet. Bibliographie vom Beginn der Forschungen im 19. Jahrhundert bis zum Jahre 2006. In: J. Cobet, V. von Graeve, W.-D. Niemeier, and K. Zimmermann (eds.): *Frühes Ionien. Eine Bestandsaufnahme*. Mainz am Rhein: 745–88.

Ergin, K., Guçlu, U., and Uz, Z., 1967: *A Catalogue of Earthquakes of Turkey and the Surrounding Area (11AD to 1964AD)*. İstanbul.

Erim, K., and Reynolds, J., 1970: The copy of Diocletian's edict on maximum prices from Aphrodisias in Caria. *Journal of Roman Studies* 60: 120–41.

Erkanal, H., 2008: Liman Tepe: New light on prehistoric Aegean cultures. In: H. Erkanal, H. Hauptmann, V. Şahoğlu, and R. Tuncel (eds.): *The Aegean in the Neolithic, Chalcolithic and the Early Bronze Age*. Ankara: 179–90.

Ersoy, Y., 1993: *Clazomenae: The archaic settlement*. [Unpublished PhD thesis]. Pennsylvania.

Ersoy, Y., 2000: East Greek pottery groups of the 7th and 6th centuries BC from Klazomenai. In: F. Krinzinger (ed.): *Die Agäis und das Westliches Mittelmeer*. Vienna: 399–406.

Ersoy, Y., 2003: Pottery production and mechanism of workshops in Archaic Clazomenae. In: B. Schmaltz and M. Söldner (eds.): *Griechische Keramik im kulturellen Kontext*. Münster: 254–57.

Ersoy, Y., 2007: Notes on the history and archaeology of early Clazomenae. In: J. Cobet, V. von Graeve, W.-D. Niemeier, and K. Zimmermann (eds.): *Frühes Ionien. Eine Bestandsaufnahme*. Mainz am Rhein: 148–78.

Ersoy, Y., and Koparal, E., 2008: Klazomenai Khorası ve Teos Sur İçi Yerleşim Yüzey Araştırması 2006 Yılı Çalışmaları. *Araştırma Sonuçlaı Toplantısı* 25.3: 47–70.

Ersoy, Y., Moustaka, A., and Skarlatidou, E. (eds.), 2004: *Klazomenai, Teos and Abdera: Mother City and Colonies. Proceedings of the Symposium, Abdera 20–21*. Thessaloniki.

Evans, C., 1998: Historicism, chronology and straw men: situating Hawkes' "Ladder of Inference". *Antiquity* 72: 398–404.

Fazlıoğlu, İ., 2007: Relations between Caria and Ionia on the basis of orientalising pottery. In: J. Cobet, V. von Graeve, W.-D. Niemeier, and K. Zimmermann (eds.): *Frühes Ionien. Eine Bestandsaufnahme*. Mainz am Rhein: 253–61.

Fitzjohn, M., 2007: Equality in the colonies: concepts of equality in Sicily during the eighth to sixth centuries BC. *World Archaeology* 39.2: 215–28.

Fleischer, R., 1973: *Artemis von Ephesos und der erwandte Kultstatue von Anatolien und Syrien*. Leiden.

Fletcher, A., and Greaves A.M. (eds.), 2007: *Transanatolia: Proceedings of the conference held at the British Museum*. Anatolian Studies Vol. 57. London.

Fontenrose, J., 1988: *Didyma, Apollo's Oracle, Cult and Companions*. Berkeley and Los Angeles.

Forbeck, E., and Heres, H., 1997: *Das Löwengrab von Milet (Winckelmannprogramm der Archaeologischen Gesellschaft zu Berlin)*. Berlin.

Forbes, H., 1996: The uses of the uncultivated landscape in modern Greece: a pointer to the value of the wilderness in antiquity? In: G. Shipley and J. Salmon (eds.): *Human Landscapes in Classical Antiquity*. London and New York: 68–97.

Foxhall, L., 1996: Feeling the earth move: Cultivation techniques on steep slopes in classical antiquity. In: G. Shipley and J. Salmon (eds.): *Human Landscapes in Classical Antiquity*. London and New York: 134–45.

Foxhall, L., 2007: *Olive Cultivation in Ancient Greece: Seeking the ancient economy*. Oxford.

Foxhall, L., Jones, M., and Forbes, H., 2007: Human ecology and the classical landscape: Greek and Roman worlds. In: S.E. Alcock and R. Osborne (eds.): *Classical Archaeology*. Oxford: 89–117.

Frei, P., and Marek, C., 1997: Die karisch-griechische Bilingue von Kaunos. Eine zweisprachige Staatsurkunde des 4. Jh.s v. Chr. *Kadmos* 36: 1–89.

Furtwängler, A., 2006a: Didyma. In: W. Radt (ed.): *Stadtgrabungen und Stadt forschung im westlichen Kleinasien.* Byzas 3. İstanbul: 73–80.

Furtwängler, A., 2006b: Didyma 2004. *Kazı Sonuçları Toplantısı* 27.2: 205–12.

Furtwängler, A., 2007: Didyma 2005. *Kazı Sonuçları Toplantısı* 28.2: 405–18.

Gallant, T.W., 1991: *Risk and Survival in Ancient Greece: Reconstructing the rural domestic economy.* Cambridge.

Gardner, P., 1911: The coinage of the Ionian Revolt. *Journal of Hellenic Studies* 31: 151–60.

Gates, M.H., 1995: Archaeology in Turkey. *American Journal of Archaeology* 100: 277–335.

Geertz, C., 1973: Religion as a cultural system. In: *The Interpretation of Cultures: Selected essays by C. Geertz.* London: 87–125.

Giannouli, V., 1996: Neue Befunde zur Wasserversorgung der archaischen Stadt Samos. *Archäologischer Anzeiger* 1996.2: 247–57.

Gibbins, D., 2000: Classical shipwreck excavation at Tektas Burnu, Turkey. *Antiquity* 74.283: 199–201.

Gill, D.W., 1994: Positivism, pots and long-distance trade. In: I. Morris (ed.): *Classical Greece: Ancient histories and modern archaeologies.* Cambridge: 99–107.

Gödecken, K.B., 1988: A contribution to the early history of Miletus. In: K.A. Wardle and E.B. French (eds.): *Problems in Greek Prehistory.* Bristol: 307–18.

Gödecken, K.B., 1989: Eine "Wilder Reiter"-Vase aus Milet. *Istanbuler Mitteilungen* 39: 129–42.

Goffman, E., 1959: *The Presentation of Self in Everyday Life.* London.

Gorman, V.B., 2001: *Miletos: The ornament of Ionia.* Ann Arbor.

Goudineau, C., 1983: Marseille, Rome and Gaul from the third to the first century BC. In: P. Garnsey, K. Hopkins, and C.R. Whittaker (eds.): *Trade in the Ancient Economy.* London: 76–87.

Grace, V.R., 1971: Samian amphoras. *Hesperia* 40.1: 52–95.

Graham, A.J., 1964: *Colony and Mother City in Ancient Greece.* Manchester.

Greaves, A.M., 1999: The shifting focus of settlement at Miletos. In: P. Flensted-Jensen (ed.): *Papers of the Copenhagen Polis Centre 5.* Copenhagen: 57–72.

Greaves, A.M., 2000a: Miletos and the sea: a stormy relationship. In: G. Oliver, T. Cornell, R. Brock, and S. Hodkinson (eds.): *The Sea in Antiquity.* Oxford: 39–61.

Greaves, A.M., 2000b: A note on the archaeology of Miletos. In: G. Oliver (ed.): *The Epigraphy of Death.* Liverpool: 111–16.

Greaves, A.M., 2002: *Miletos: A history.* London.

Greaves, A.M., 2004: The cult of Aphrodite in Miletos and its colonies. *Anatolian Studies* 54: 27–33.

Greaves, A.M., 2007a: Trans-Anatolia: Examining Turkey as a bridge between East and West. *Anatolian Studies* 57: 1–15.

Greaves, A.M., 2007b: Milesians in the Black Sea: trade, settlement and religion. In: V. Gabrielsen and J. Lund (eds.): *The Black Sea in Antiquity: Regional and interregional economic exchanges.* Århus: 9–21.

Greaves, A.M., 2008: Review of *Frühes Ionien. Eine Bestandsaufnahme* (eds. J. Cobet, V. von Graeve, W.-D. Niemeier, and K. Zimmermann, 2007). *American Journal of Archaeology* Fall: 10–11.

Greaves, A.M., 2009: Bronze Age Aphrodisias revisited. In: C. Gallou, M. Georgiadis, and G.M. Muskett (eds.): *DIOSKOUROI.* Oxford: 252–64.

Greaves, A.M., forthcoming (1): Herding, salt, and the "cognitive maps" of shepherds. In: T. Takaoğlu (ed.): *Ethnoarchaeological Investigations in Rural Anatolia 5.*

Greaves, A.M., forthcoming (2): "Greek" colonization: The view from Ionia. In: J. Lucas, S. Owen, and C. Roth-Murray (eds.): *Greek Colonization in Local Context*. Oxford.

Greaves, A.M., forthcoming (3): *Divination at Archaic Branchidai-Didyma*.

Greaves, A.M., and Wilson, A.T., forthcoming: *Aphrodite of Miletos*.

Greene, E., and Bass, G., 2004: 2002 Yılı Pabuç Burnu kazısı ön raporu. *Kazı Sonuçları Toplantısı* 25.2: 187–94.

Gresik, G., and Olbrich, H., 1992: Sicherungs- und Sanierungsarbeiten in Milet. *Istanbuler Mitteilungen* 42: 126–34.

Günel, S., 2003: Vorbericht über die Oberflächenbegenungen in den Provinzen Aydın und Muğla. *Anatolia Antiqua* 11: 75–100.

Günel, S., 2005: The cultural structure of Aydın-İkizdere region in the prehistoric age and its contribution to the archeology of Aegean region. *Anatolia Antiqua* 13: 29–40.

Günel, S., 2007: Çine-Tepecik Höyüğü 2005 Yılı Kazıları. *Kazı Sonuçları Toplantısı* 28.1: 231–46.

Guralnick, E., 1996: The monumental new kouros from Samos: measurements, proportions and profiles. *Archäologischer Anzeiger* 1996.4: 505–26.

Hackbeil, S., Massmann, W., and Stürmer, V., 1998: Ein wiedergewonnener klazomenischer Sarkophag. *Archäologischer Anzeiger* 1998.2: 271–80.

Hall, E., 1993: Asia unmanned: images of victory in classical Athens. In: J. Rich and G. Shipley (eds.): *War and Society in the Greek World*. London: 108–33.

Hall, J.M., 1997: *Ethnic Identity in Greek Antiquity*. Cambridge.

Hall, J.M., 2007: *A History of the Archaic Greek World ca. 1200–479 BCE*. Oxford.

Hall, T.D., 2006: [Re]periphalization, [re]incorporation, frontiers and non-state societies. In: B.K. Gills and W.R. Thompson (eds.): *Globalization and Global History*. London: 86–113.

Hall, T.D., and Chase-Dunn, C., 2006: Global social change in the long run. In: C. Chase-Dunn and S.J. Babones (eds.): *Global Social Change: Historical and comparative perspectives*. Baltimore: 33–58.

Hall, T.D., Kardulias, P.N., and Chase-Dunn, C., forthcoming: *Inter-regional Interactions, Archaeology, and World-Systems Analysis: A review*.

Hanfmann, G.M.A., 1962: A "Hittite" priest from Ephesus. *American Journal of Archaeology* 66.1: 1–4.

Hansen, M.H., 2006: *Emporion*: A study of the use and meaning of the term in the archaic and classical periods. In: G.R. Tsetskhladze (ed.): *Greek Colonisation: An account of Greek colonies and other settlements overseas. Vol. 1*. Leiden: 1–39.

Hansen, M.H., and Nielsen, T.H., 2004: *An Inventory of Archaic and Classical poleis*. Oxford.

Hansson, M.C., and Foley, B.P., 2008: Ancient DNA fragments inside Classical Greek amphoras reveal cargo of 2400-year-old shipwreck. *Journal of Archaeological Science* 35: 1169–76.

Harrison, T., 2002: The Persian invasions. In: E.J. Bakker, I.J.J. de Jong, and H. van Wees (eds.): *Brill's Companion to Herodotus*. Leiden: 551–78.

Hartog, F., 1988: *The Mirror of Herodotus: the representation of the Other in the writing of Herodotus* [trans. Janet Lloyd]. Berkeley.

Hawkes, C., 1954: Archaeological theory and method: some suggestions from the Old World. *American Anthropologist* 56: 155–68.

Hawkins, D., 1998: Tarkasnawa King of Mira: "Tarkondemos," Boğazköy, Sealings and Karabel. *Anatolian Studies* 48: 1–32.

Heilmeyer, W.-D., 1986: Die Einordung Milets in die Siedlungszonen der griechischen Frühzeit. In: W. Müller-Wiener (ed.): *Milet 1899–1980, Istanbuler Mitteilungen, Beiheft 31*. Tübingen: 105–12.

Heitsch, E., 2007: Ionien und die Anfänge der Griechischen Philosophie. In: J. Cobet, V. von Graeve, W.-D. Niemeier, and K. Zimmermann (eds.): *Frühes Ionien. Eine Bestandsaufnahme*. Mainz am Rhein: 701–12.

Held, W., 2000: *Das Heiligtum der Athena in Milet*. Mainz am Rhein.

Hellström, P., 2007: *Labraunda: A guide to the Karian sanctuary of Zeus Labraundos*. İstanbul.

Herda, A., 2006: *Der Apollon-Delphinios-Kult in Milet und die Neujahrsprozession nach Didyma: Ein neuer Kommentar der sog. Molpoi-Satzung*. Mainz.

Herrmann, P., 1995: Milet 1992–1993: Inschriften. *Archäologischer Anzeiger* 1995: 282–92.

Hind, J.G.F., 1984: Greek and Barbarian peoples on the shores of the Black Sea. *Archaeological Reports* 30: 71–97.

Hind, J.G.F., 1993: Archaeology around the Black Sea. *Archaeological Reports* 39: 82–112.

Hind, J.G.F., 1995/96: Traders and ports-of-trade (*emporoi* and *emporia*) in the Black Sea in antiquity. *Il Mar Nero* 2: 113–26.

Hodder, I., 1998: *The Archaeological Process: Towards a reflexive methodology*. Oxford.

Hodder, I. et al., 2000: *Towards Reflexive Method in Archaeology*. Cambridge.

Hogarth, D.G., 1908: *Excavations at Ephesos: The Archaic Artemisia*. London.

Hölbl, G., 1999: Funde aus Milet VIII. Die Aegyptiaca vom Aphroditetempel auf dem Zeytintepe. *Archäologischer Anzeiger* 1999.3: 345–71.

Hölbl, G., 2007: Ionien und Ägypten in archaischer Zeit. In: J. Cobet, V. von Graeve, W.-D. Niemeier, and K. Zimmermann (eds.): *Frühes Ionien. Eine Bestandsaufnahme*. Mainz am Rhein: 447–61.

Holland, L.B., 1944: Colophon. *Hesperia* 13: 91–171.

Holloway, R.R., 1984: The date of the first Greek coins: some arguments from style and hoards. *Revue Belge de Numismatique* 130: 5–18.

Horden, P., and Purcell, N., 2000: *The Corrupting Sea: A study of Mediterranean history*. Oxford.

Hueber, F., 1997: *Ephesos: Gebaute Geschichte*. Mainz.

Humphreys, S.C., 1972: Town and country in ancient Greece. In: P.J. Ucko, R. Tringham, and G.W. Dimbleby (eds.): *Man, Settlement and Urbanism*. London: 763–8.

Hürmüzlü, B., 2004: A new type of Clazomenian sarcophagus: The alteration of the burial customs in Clazomenae. In: R. Bol and D. Kreikenbom (eds.): *Sepulkral- und Votivdenkmaeler oestlicher Mittelmeergebiete (7. Jh. v. Chr. – 1. Jh. n. Chr.)*. Biblipholis 004: 195–8.

Hurst, H., and Owen, S. (eds.), 2005: *Ancient Colonizations: Analogy, similarity and difference*. London.

Huxley, G.L., 1966: *The Early Ionians*. London.

İçten, C., and Krinzinger, F., 2004: Ein wiederentdecktes Felsrelief aud Ephesos. *Jahreshefte des Österreichischen Archäologischen Instituts in Wien* 73: 159–63.

İşık, F., 2003: *Die Statuetten vom Tumulus D bei Elmalı: Ionisierung der neuhethitisch-phrygischen Bildformen in Anatolien*. Antalya.

Jackson, A.H., 1995: An oracle for raiders? *Zeitschrift für Papyrologie und Epigraphik* 108: 95–9.

Jacoby, F., 1930–94: *Die Fragmente der griechischen Historiker*. Leiden.

Jantzen, U., Felsch, R.C.S., Hoepfner, W., and Willers, D., 1973a: Samos 1971: Die Wasserleitung des Eupalinos. *Archäologischer Anzeiger* 1973: 72–89.

Jantzen, U., Felsch, R.C.S., Kienast, H., and Martini, W., 1973b: Samos 1972. *Archäologischer Anzeiger* 1973: 401–14.

Jantzen, U., Felsch, R.C.S., and Kienast, H., 1975: Samos 1973. *Archäologischer Anzeiger* 1975: 19–35.

Jeffery, L.H., 1990: *The Local Scripts of Archaic Greece: A study of the origins of the Greek alphabet and its development from the eighth to fifth century BC* (Revised edn. with a supplement by A.W. Johnston). Oxford.

Jenkins, I., 1992: *Archaeologists and Aesthetes: In the sculpture galleries of the British Museum 1800–1939*. London.

Johnson, M., 1999: *Archaeological Theory: An introduction*. Oxford.

Johnston, A., 1995/96: An epigraphic curiosity from Histria. *Il Mar Nero* 2: 99–101.

Jones, A., 2002: *Archaeological Theory and Scientific Practice*. Cambridge.

Jones, J.E., Sackett, L.H., and Graham, A.J., 1973: An Attic country house below the cave of Pan at Vari. *Annual of the British School at Athens* 68: 355–452.

Joukowsky, M.S., 1986: *Prehistoric Aphrodisias*. Providence, RI.

Jung, H., 1982: *Thronende und sitzende Götter. Zum griechischen Götterbild und Menschenideal in geometrischer und früarchaischer Zeit*. Bonn.

Kardulias, P.N., and Hall, T.D., 2008: Archaeology and world-systems analysis. *World Archaeology* 40.4: 572–83.

Karwiese, S. et al., 1996: Ephesos. *Jahreshefte des Österreichischen Archäologischen Instituts in Wien* 65: 5–74.

Karwiese, S. et al., 1998: Ephesos. *Jahreshefte des Österreichischen Archäologischen Instituts in Wien* 67: 6–78.

Kawerau, G., and Rehm, A., 1914: *Milet 1.3: Das Delphinion in Milet*. Berlin.

Kearns, J.M., 1992: *The languages of Lydian Ionia*. [Unpublished PhD thesis]. Los Angeles.

Kearsley, R.A., 1995: The Greek Geometric wares from Al Mina levels 10–8 and associated pottery. *Mediterranean Archaeology* 8: 7–81.

Keen, A.G., 2000: Grain for Athens: The importance of the Hellespontine route in Athenian foreign policy before the Peloponnesian War. In: G. Oliver, T. Cornell, R. Brock, and S. Hodkinson (eds.): *The Sea in Antiquity*. Oxford: 63–74.

Kerschner, M., 1997: Ein stratifizierter Opferkomplex des 7.Jh.s v. Chr. Aus dem Artemision von Ephesos. *Jahreshefte des Österreichischen Archäologischen Instituts in Wien* 66: 85–228.

Kerschner, M., 1999: Das Artemisheiligtum auf der Ostterrasse des Kalabaktepe in Milet. *Archäologischer Anzeiger* 1999.1: 7–51.

Kerschner, M., and Schlotzhauer, U., 2005: A new classification system for East Greek pottery. *Ancient West and East* 4.1: 1–56.

Kerschner, M., and Schlotzhauer, U., 2007: Ein neues Klassifikationssystem der Ostgriechischen Keramik. In: J. Cobet, V. von Graeve, W.-D. Niemeier, and K. Zimmermann (eds.): *Frühes Ionien. Eine Bestandsaufnahme*. Mainz am Rhein: 297–317.

Kerschner, M., and Senff, R., 1997: Die Ostterrasse des Kalabaktepe. *Istanbuler Mitteilungen* 47: 120–2.

Kerschner, M., Mommsen, H., Rocl, C., and Schwedt, A., 2002: Die Keramikproduktion von Ephesos in griechischer Zeit. Zum Stand der archäometrischen Forschungen. *Jahreshefte des Österreichischen Archäologischen Instituts in Wien* 71: 189–206.

Kerschner, M., Mommsen, H., and Schwedt, A., 2007: Das Keramikbild von Ephesos im 7. und 6. Jh v. Chr. In: J. Cobet, V. von Graeve, W.-D. Niemeier, and K. Zimmermann (eds.): *Frühes Ionien. Eine Bestandsaufnahme*. Mainz am Rhein: 221–45.

Kerschner, M., Kowalleck, I., and Steskal, M., 2008: *Archäologische Forschungen zur Siedlungsgeschichte von Ephesos in geometrischer, archaischer und klassischer Zeit: Grabungsbefunde und Keramikfunde aus dem Bereich von Koressos*. Vienna.

Khristchev, K., Georgiev, V., and Tchotchov, S., 1982: Salt production in ancient Anhialo: geological evidence. In: A. Fol (ed.): *Thracia Pontica I*. Sofia: 201–5.

Kienast, H.J., 1978: *Samos XV: Die Stadtmauer von Samos*. Bonn.

Kienast, H., 1992: Topographische Studien im Heraion von Samos. *Archäologischer Anzeiger* 1992.2: 171–213.

Kienast, H.J., 1995: *Samos XIX: Die Wasserleitung des Eupalinos auf Samos*. Bonn.

Kienast, H.J., 2007: Wege und Tore im Heraion von Samos. In: J. Cobet, V. von Graeve, W.-D. Niemeier, and K. Zimmermann (eds.): *Frühes Ionien. Eine Bestandsaufnahme*. Mainz am Rhein: 201–9.

Kim, H.S., 1994: *Greek Fractional Silver Coinage: A reassessment of the inception, development, prevalence and functions of small change during the late archaic and early classical period.* [Unpublished DPhil thesis]. Oxford.

Kim, H., 2001: Archaic coinage as evidence for the use of money. In: A. Meadows and K. Shipton (eds.): *Money and its Uses in the Ancient Greek World*. Oxford: 7–22.

Kimmig, W., 1975: Early Celts on the Upper Danube: the excavations at Heunenburg. In: R. Bruce-Mitford (ed.): *Recent Archaeological Excavations in Europe*. London: 32–64.

Kirk, K., and Greaves, A.M., 2009: Absorbing the shock of the early undergraduate experience. *Assessment, Learning and Teaching Journal* 4 (summer): 5–8.

Kleiner, G., 1966: *Alt-Milet*. Wiesbaden.

Kleiner, G., Hommel, P., and Müller-Wiener, W., 1967: *Panionion und Melie*. Berlin.

Knapp, A.B., 1992: Archaeology and *Annales*: time, space and change. In: A.B. Knapp (ed.): *Archaeology, Annales and Ethnohistory*. Cambridge: 1–21.

Knapp, A.B., and van Dommelen, P., 2008: Past practices: Rethinking individuals and agents in archaeology. *Cambridge Archaeological Journal* 18.1: 15–34.

Knipovic, T., 1971: Traces of Ionic and Attic influences in Olbian inscriptions of the 5th century BC. *Acta of the Fifth International Congress of Greek and Latin Epigraphy (Cambridge, 1967)*. Oxford.

Koenigs, W., 1996: "Rundaltäre" aus Milet. *Istanbuler Mitteilungen* 46: 141–6.

Koenigs, W., 2007: Archaische Bauglieder aus Stein in Ionien. In: J. Cobet, V. von Graeve, W.-D. Niemeier, and K. Zimmermann (eds.): *Frühes Ionien. Eine Bestandsaufnahme*. Mainz am Rhein: 669–80.

Kohl, P.L., 1987: The ancient economy, transferable technologies and the Bronze Age world-system: a view from the northeastern frontier of the ancient Near East. In: M. Rowlands, M. Larsen, and K. Kristiansen (eds.): *Centre and Periphery in the Ancient World*. Cambridge: 13–24.

Kopeïkina, V., 1972: The oldest fragment of painted pottery from the excavations on the island of Beresan. *Soviet Archaeology* 1973.2: 240–4.

Koray, K., 2005: The electrum coinage of Samos in the light of a recent hoard. In: E. Schwerheim and E. Winter (eds.): *Asia Minor Studien 54: Neue Forschungen zu Ionien*. Bonn: 43–55.

Kraay, C.M., 1976: *Archaic and Classical Greek Coins*. London.

Kraft, J.C., Brückner, H., Kayan, I., and Engelman, H., 2007: The geographies of ancient Ephesus and the Artemision in Anatolia. *Geoarchaeology* 22.1: 121–49.

Kurke, L., 1999: *Coins, Bodies, Games and Gold: The politics of meaning in archaic Greece*. Princeton.

Kyrieleis, H., 1978: Ausgrabungen im Heraion von Samos 1977. *Archäologischer Anzeiger* 1978: 385–96.

Kyrieleis, H., 1998: Cretan works of art in Samos. In: V. Karageorghis and N. Stampolidis (eds.): *Eastern Mediterranean: Cyprus-Dodecanese-Crete 16th to 6th cent. BC*. Athens: 277–86.

Lamb, W., 1935: Excavations at Kato Phana in Chios. *Annual of the British School at Athens* 35: 138–64.

Lambrianides, K., and Spencer, N. (eds.), 2007: *The Madra River Delta: Regional Studies on the Aegean Coast of Turkey 1. Environment, Society and Community Life from Prehistory to the Present*. London.

Lambrinoudakis, V., 1986: Ancient farmhouses on Mount Aipos. In: J. Boardman and C.E. Vaphopoulou-Richardson (eds.): *Chios: A conference at the Homereion in Chios 1984*. Oxford: 295–304.

Latacz, J., 2007: Frühgriechische Epik und Lyrik in Ionien. In: J. Cobet, V. von Graeve, W.-D. Niemeier, and K. Zimmermann (eds.): *Frühes Ionien. Eine Bestandsaufnahme*. Mainz am Rhein: 681–700.

Lazarov, M., 1982: Le commerce de Chios avec les cites Ouest-Pontiques (resumé). *Bulletin du Musée National de Varna* 18.33: 15.

Lemos, I.S., 2002: *The Protogeometric Aegean: The archaeology of the late eleventh and tenth centuries BC*. Oxford.

Lemos, I.S., 2007: The migrations to the west coast of Asia Minor: Tradition and archaeology. In: J. Cobet, V. von Graeve, W.-D. Niemeier, and K. Zimmermann (eds.): *Frühes Ionien. Eine Bestandsaufnahme*. Mainz am Rhein: 713–27.

Le Rider, G., 2001: *La naissance de la monnaie: Practiques monétaires de l'Orient ancien*. Paris.

LiDonnici, L.R., 1992: The images of Artemis Ephesia and Greco-Roman worship: A reconsideration. *The Harvard Theological Review* 85.4: 389–415.

Lloyd, S., and Mellaart, J., 1965: *Beycesultan 2: Middle Bronze Age architecture and pottery*. London.

Lohmann, H., 1995: Survey in der Chora von Milet. *Archäologischer Anzeiger* 1995: 293–328.

Lohmann, H., 1997: Survey in der Chora von Milet: Vorbericht über die Kampagnen der Jahre 1994 und 1995. *Archäologischer Anzeiger* 1997: 285–311.

Lohmann, H., 1999: Survey in der Chora von Milet: Vorbericht über die Kampagnen der Jahre 1996 und 1997. *Archäologischer Anzeiger* 1999: 439–73.

Lohmann, H., 2007a: Die Chora Milets in Archaischer Zeit. In: J. Cobet, V. von Graeve, W.-D. Niemeier, and K. Zimmermann (eds.): *Frühes Ionien. Eine Bestandsaufnahme*. Mainz am Rhein: 363–92.

Lohmann, H., 2007b: The discovery and excavation of the Archaic Panionion in the Mycale (Dilek Dağları). *Kazı Sonuçları Toplantısı* 28.2: 575–90.

London, G.A., 2000: Ethnoarchaeology and interpretations of the past. *Near Eastern Archaeology* 63: 2–8.

Lordkipanidse, O., 2007: Archaic Panticapaeum. In: J. Cobet, V. von Graeve, W.-D. Niemeier, and K. Zimmermann (eds.): *Frühes Ionien. Eine Bestandsaufnahme*. Mainz am Rhein: 591–605.

Luckenbill, D.D., 1927: *Ancient Records of Assyria and Babylonia, Part 1–2: Histories and mysteries of man*. London.

Magie, D., 1950: *Roman Rule in Asia Minor*. Princeton.

Makal, M., 1954: *A Village in Anatolia: Translated from the Turkish by Sir W. Deedes*. London.

Malkin, I., 2003: "Tradition" in Herodotus: the foundation of Cyrene. In: P. Derow and R. Parker (eds.): *Herodotus and his World: Essays from a conference in memory of George Forrest*. Oxford: 153–70.

Malkin, I., Constantakopoulou, C., and Panagopoulou, K., 2009: *Networks in the Ancient Mediterranean*. New York.

Marchese, R.T., 1986: *The Lower Maeander Flood Plain*. British Archaeological Reports International Series no. 292. Oxford.

Maslow, A H., 1943: A theory of human motivation. *Psychological Review* 50: 370–96.

Maslow, A.H., 1954: *Motivation and Personality*. New York.

Mattingly, D., 1996: First fruit? The olive in the Roman world. In: G. Shipley and J. Salmon (eds.): *Human Landscapes in Classical Antiquity*. London and New York: 213–53.

McNicoll, A.W., 1997: *Hellenistic Fortifications from the Aegean to the Euphrates*. Oxford.

Meier-Brügger, M., 1983: *Labraunda II.4: Die karischen Inschriften*. Stockholm.

Meiggs, R., and Lewis, D., 1969: *A Selection of Greek Historical Inscriptions to the End of the Fifth Century B.C.* Oxford.

Mellaart, J., 1962. The late bronze age monuments of Eflatun Pınar and Fasillar near Beyşehir. *Anatolian Studies* 12: 111–17.

Mellink, M., 1983: Archaeology in Asia Minor. *American Journal of Archaeology* 87.4: 427–42.

Mills, J.S., and White, R., 1989: The identity of the resins from the Late Bronze Age shipwreck at Ulu Burun (Kaş). *Archaeometry* 31.1: 37–44.

Mitchell, S., 1985: Archaeology in Asia Minor 1979–84. *Archaeological Reports for 1984–85* 31: 70–105.

Mitchell, S., 1999: Archaeology in Asia Minor 1990–98. *Archaeological Reports for 1998–99* 45: 124–91.

Möller, A., 2000: *Naukratis. Trade in Archaic Greece*. Oxford.

Morel, J.-P., 1983: La céramique comme indice du commerce antique (réalités et interpretations). In: P. Garnsey and C.R. Whittaker (eds.): *Trade and Famine in Classical Antiquity*. Cambridge: 66–74.

Morel, J.P., 2006: Phocaean colonisation. In: G.R. Tsetskhladze (ed.): *Greek Colonisation: An account of Greek colonies and other settlements overseas. Vol. 1*. Leiden: 358–428.

Morgan, C., 1989: Divination and society at Delphi and Didyma. *Hermathena* 147: 17–42.

Morgan, C., 2003: *Early Greek States beyond the Polis*. London.

Morgan, K., Evely, D., Hall, H., and Pitt, R.K., 2008: Archaeology in Greece 2007–2008. *Archaeological Reports for 2007–08* 54: 1–113.

Morris, I., 1987: *Burial and Ancient Society: The rise of the Greek city-state*. Cambridge.

Moucharte, G., 1984: À propos d'une découverte de monnaies de Milet. *Revue Belge de Numismatique* 130: 19–35.

Müller-Wiener, W., 1979: Arbeiten im Stadtgebiet. *Istanbuler Mitteilungen* 29: 162–73.

Müller-Wiener, W., 1986: Bemerkungen zur Topographie des archaischen Milet. In: W. Müller-Wiener (ed.): *Milet 1899–1980, Istanbuler Mitteilungen, Beiheft 31*. Tübingen: 105–12.

Müller-Wiener, W., 1992: Milet 1987. *Istanbuler Mitteilungen* 38: 251–90.

Muss, U., 2008: Amber from the Artemision from Ephesus and in the museums of İstanbul and Selçuk Ephesos. *Araştirma Sonuçları Toplantısı* 25.3: 13–26.

Myres, J., 1954: The Battle of Lade, 494 BC. *Greece and Rome* 23: 50–5.

Naso, A., 2005: Funde aus Milet XIX: Anfore commerciali arcaiche a Mileto: rapporto preliminare. *Archäologischer Anzeiger* 2005.2: 73–84.

Naumann, F., 1983: *Die Ikonographie der Kybele in der phrygischen und der griechischen Kunst*. Tübingen.

Nazarov, V.V., 2007: Archaic Berezan: results of recent archaeological investigations and its historical interpretation. In: J. Cobet, V. von Graeve, W.-D. Niemeier, and K. Zimmermann (eds.): *Frühes Ionien. Eine Bestandsaufnahme*. Mainz am Rhein: 541–9.

Newton, C.T., 1862: *A History of the Discoveries at Halicarnassus, Cnidus and Branchidae. Vol. 1*. London.

Newton, C.T., 1881: *Antiquities of Ionia*. London.

Nicholls, R.V., 1958/59: Old Smyrna: The Iron Age fortifications. *Annual of the British School at Athens* 53–54: 35–137.

Niemeier, W.-D., 1998: The Mycenaeans in western Anatolia and the problem of the origins of the Sea Peoples. In: S. Gitin, A. Mazar, and E. Stern (eds.): *Mediterranean Peoples in Transition*. Jerusalem: 17–65.

Niemeier, W.-D., 2005: Minoans, Mycenaeans, Hittites and Ionians in western Asia Minor: new excavations in Bronze Age Miletus-Millawanda. In: A. Villing (ed.): *The Greeks in the East*. London: 1–36.

Niemeier, W.-D., 2007a: Milet von den Anfängen menschlicher Besiedlung bis zur Ionischen Wanderung. In: J. Cobet, V. von Graeve, W.-D. Niemeier, and K. Zimmermann (eds.): *Frühes Ionien. Eine Bestandsaufnahme*. Mainz am Rhein: 3–20.

Niemeier, W.-D., 2007b: Westkleinasien und Ägäis von den Anfängen bis zur Ionischen Wanderung: Topographie, Geschichte und Beziehungen nach dem archäologischen Befund und den hethitischen Quellen. In: J. Cobet, V. von Graeve, W.-D. Niemeier, and K. Zimmermann (eds.): *Frühes Ionien. Eine Bestandsaufnahme.* Mainz am Rhein: 37–96.

Niemeier, B., and Niemeier, W.-D., 1997: Milet 1994–1995, Projekt "Minoisch-Mykenisches bis Protogeometrisches Milet": Zielsetzung und Grabungen auf dem Stadionhügel und am Athenatempel. *Archäologischer Anzeiger* 1997: 189–248.

Niemeier, W.-D., Greaves, A.M., and Selesnow, W., 1999: Die Zierde Ioniens: Ein archaischer Brunnen, der jüngere Athenatempel und Milet vor der Perserzerstörung. *Archäologischer Anzeiger* 1999: 373–413.

Nilsson, M.P., 1986: *Cults, Myths, Oracles and Politics in Ancient Greece.* Göteborg.

Osborne, C., 2004: *Presocratic Philosophy: A very short introduction.* Oxford.

Osborne, R., 1987: *A Classical Landscape with Figures: The ancient Greek city and its countryside.* London.

Osborne, R., 1998a: *Archaic and Classical Greek Art.* Oxford.

Osborne, R., 1998b: Early Greek colonization? The nature of Greek settlement in the West. In: N. Fisher and H. van Wees (eds.): *Archaic Greece: New approaches and new evidence.* London: 251–69.

Osborne, R., 2007: Cult and ritual: The Greek world. In: S.E. Alcock and R. Osborne (eds.): *Classical Archaeology.* Oxford: 246–62.

Owens, E.J., 1991: *The City in the Greek and Roman World.* London.

Özdoğan, M., 2001: *Türk Arkeolojisinin Sorunları ve Koruma Politikaları.* İstanbul.

Özgen, İ., and Öztürk, J., 1996: *Heritage Recovered: The Lydian treasure.* İstanbul.

Özyiğit, Ö., 1988: Spätarchaische Funde im Museum on Ephesos und die Lage von Alt-Ephesos. *Istanbuler Mitteilungen* 38: 83–96.

Özyiğit, Ö., 1994: The city walls of Phokaia. *Révue des Études Anciennes* 96: 77–109.

Özyiğit, Ö., 2003: Recent work at Phokaia in the light of Akurgal's excavations. *Anadolu/Anatolia* 25: 109–27.

Özyiğit, Ö., 2006: Phokaia. In: W. Radt (ed.): *Stadtgrabungen und Stadtforschung in westlichen Kleinasien.* BYZAS 3: 303–14.

Özyiğit, S., 1998: *Foça-Phokaia.* İzmir.

Parke, H.W., 1967: *Greek Oracles.* London.

Parke, H.W., 1985: *The Oracles of Apollo in Asia Minor.* London.

Parke, H.W., and Wormell, D.E.W., 1956: *The Delphic Oracle.* Oxford.

Parker, B.J., and Üzel, M.B., 2007: The tradition of tandır cooking in southeastern Anatolia: An ethnoarchaeological perspective. In: T. Takaoğlu (ed.): *Ethnoarchaeological Investigation in Rural Anatolia* 4. İstanbul: 1–43.

Peschlow-Bindokat, A., 1981: Die Steinbrüche von Milet und Herakleia am Latmos. *Jahrbuch des Deutschen Archäologischen Instituts* 94: 157–235.

Peschlow-Bindokat, A., 1996: *Der Latmos: Eine unbekannte Gebirgslandschaft an der türkishen Westküste.* Mainz.

Peschlow-Bindokat, A., 2001: Eine hethitische Grossprinzeninschrift aus dem Latmos. Vorläufiger Bericht. *Archäologischer Anzeiger* 2001.3: 363–78.

Peschlow-Bindokat, A., 2007: Zur Gründung der karischen Stadt Latmos. In: J. Cobet, V. von Graeve, W.-D. Niemeier, and K. Zimmermann (eds.): *Frühes Ionien. Eine Bestandsaufnahme.* Mainz am Rhein: 419–28.

Peters, J., and von den Driesch, A., 1992: Siedlungsabfall versus Opferreste: Essgewohnheiten im archaischen Milet. *Istanbuler Mitteilungen* 42: 117–25.

Pettegrew, D., 2001: Chasing the classical farmstead: Assessing the formation and signature of rural settlement in Greek landscape archaeology. *Journal of Mediterranean Archaeology* 14.2: 189–209.

Pfrommer, M., 1989: Zum Fries des Dionysostempels in Milet. *Istanbuler Mitteilungen* 39: 433–9.

Pironti, G., 2007: *Entre ciel et guerre: Figures d'Aphrodite en Grèce ancienne*. Naples.

Rackham, O., 1996: Ecology and pseudo-ecology: the example of ancient Greece. In: G. Shipley and J. Salmon (eds.): *Human Landscapes in Classical Antiquity*. London and New York: 16–43.

Raeck, W., 2003: Neue Forschungen an einem alten Grabungsort. *Istanbuler Mitteilungen* 53: 313–423.

Ratté, C., 1992: The "Pyramid Tomb" at Sardis. *Istanbuler Mitteilungen* 42: 135–61.

Real, W., 1977/78: Ausgewählte Funde aus dem Dionysos-Tempel. *Istanbuler Mitteilungen* 27/28: 105–16.

Rehm, A., and Harder, R., 1958: *Didyma 2: Die Inschriften*. Berlin.

Renfrew, C., 1980: The Great Tradition versus the Great Divide: Archaeology as anthropology? *American Journal of Archaeology* 84.3: 287–98.

Ridgeway, D., 1992: *The First Western Greeks*. Cambridge.

Robertson, C.M., 1940: Excavations at Al Mina, Suedia IV. The Early Greek Vases. *Journal of Hellenic Studies* 60: 2–21.

Roebuck, C., 1950: The Grain Trade between Greece and Egypt. *Classical Philology* 45: 236–47.

Roebuck, C., 1955: The early Ionian League. *Classical Philology* 50: 19–28.

Roebuck, C., 1959: *Ionian Trade and Colonization*. New York.

Roebuck, C., 1961: Tribal organization in Ionia. *Transactions and Proceedings of the American Philological Association* 92: 495–507.

Roebuck, C., 1979: *Economy and Society in the Early Greek World: The collected essays of Carl Roebuck*. Chicago.

Rogers, G.M., 1991: *The Sacred Identity of Ephesos: Foundation myths of a Roman city*. London.

Röhlig, J., 1933: *Der Handel von Milet*. Hamburg.

Roller, L.E., 1999: *In Search of God the Mother: The cult of Anatolian Cybele*. Berkeley.

Rowlands, M.J., 1972: Defence: a factor in the organization of settlements. In: P.J. Ucko, R. Tringham, and G.W. Dimbleby (eds.): *Man, Settlement and Urbanism*. London: 447–62.

Rubinstein, L., and Greaves, A.M., 2004: Ionia. In: M.H. Hansen and T.H. Nielsen (eds.): *An Inventory of Archaic and Classical Poleis*. Oxford: 1053–107.

Rumscheid, F., 1998: *Priene: A guide to the Pompeii of Asia Minor*. İstanbul.

Ryder, M.L., 1983: *Sheep and Man*. London.

Sabloff, J.A., 1986: Interaction among Classical Maya polities: a preliminary examination. In: C. Renfrew and J.F. Cherry (eds.): *Peer–Polity Interaction and Socio-political change*. Cambridge: 109–16.

Şahin, N., 1998: *Klaros: Apollon Klarios Bilicilik Merkezi*. İstanbul.

Şahin, N., Tanrıver, C., Akar, D.S., Taştemur, E., Ürkmez, Ö., and Önol, İ., 2007: Klaros 2005 (5. yıl). *Kazı Sonuçları Toplantısı* 28.1: 589–608.

Sakellariou, M.V., 1958: *La migration grecque en Ionie*. Athens.

Salviat, F., 1992: Sur la religion de Marseille grecque. In: M. Bats, G. Bertucchi, G. Congès, and H. Tréziny (eds.): *Marseille Grecque et la Gaule: actes du Colloque international d'Histoire et d'Archéologie et du Ve Congrès archéologique de Gaule méridionale (Marseille, 18–23 novembre 1990)*. Aix-en-Provence: 141–50.

Sarikakis, Th.Ch., 1986: Commercial relations between Chios and other Greek cities in antiquity. In: J. Boardman and C.E. Vaphopoulou-Richardson (eds.): *Chios: A conference at the Homereion in Chios 1984*. Oxford: 121–31.

Sartiaux, F., 1921: Nouvelles recherches sur le site de Phocée. *Comptes Rendus de l'Academie des Inscriptions et Belles-Lettres*: 119–29.

Schaps, D.M., 2004: *The Invention of Coinage and the Monetization of Ancient Greece*. Ann Arbor.

Schattner, T.G., 1992: Didyma, ein Minoisch-Mykenischer Fundplatz? *Archäologischer Anzeiger* 1992: 369–72.

Scheidel, W., Morris, I., and Saller, R., 2007: *The Cambridge Economic History of the Greco-Roman World*. Cambridge.

Schiering, W., 1979: Milet: Eine Erweiterung der Grabung östlich des Athenatempels. *Istanbuler Mitteilungen* 29: 77–108.

Schiering, W., 2007: Zur Klassifizierung der orientalisierenden ostgriechischen Tierfrieskeramik nach Zeitstufen und Landschaftsstilen. In: J. Cobet, V. von Graeve, W.-D. Niemeier, and K. Zimmermann (eds.): *Frühes Ionien: Eine Bestandsaufnahme*. Mainz am Rhein: 247–52.

Schlotzhauer, U., 1999: Beobachtungen zu Trinkgefäßen des Fikellurastils. *Archäologischer Anzeiger* 1999: 223–39.

Schlotzhauer, U., 2007: Zum Verhältnis zwischen sog. Tierfries- und Fikellurastil (SiA I und II) in Milet. In: J. Cobet, V. von Graeve, W.-D. Niemeier, and K. Zimmermann (eds.): *Frühes Ionien. Eine Bestandsaufnahme*. Mainz am Rhein: 263–93.

Schmidt, E.F., 1953: *Persepolis I*. Chicago.

Schneider, C., 1997: Grabung an der Stadtmauer 1995. *Archäologischer Anzeiger* 1997: 134–6.

Schneider, C., 2004: Poseidon und sein Volk. *Antike Welt* 35.3: 17–24.

Schneider, P., 1987: Zur Topographie der Heiligen Strasse von Milet nach Didyma. *Archäologischer Anzeiger* 1987: 102–29.

Schofield, L., and Parkinson, R.B., 1994: Of helmets and heretics: A possible Egyptian representation of Mycenaean warriors on a papyrus from El-Armarna. *Annual of the British School at Athens* 89: 157–70.

Schröder, B., Brückner, H., Stümpel, H., and Yalçin, U., 1995: Geowissenschaftliche Umfelderkundung. *Archäologischer Anzeiger* 1995: 238–44.

Seaford, R., 2004: *Money and the Early Greek Mind*. Cambridge.

Seiterle, G., 1979: Artemis: die Grosse Göttin von Ephesos. *Antike Welt* 10: 3–16.

Senff, R., 1995: Sondierungen am Südhang des Mengerevtepe. *Archäologischer Anzeiger* 1995: 224–8.

Senff, R., 2003: Das Aphroditeheiligtum von Milet. *Asia Minor Studien* 49: 11–25.

Senff, R., 2007: Die Ergebnisse der neuen Grabungen im archaischen Milet – Stratigraphie und Chronologie. In: J. Cobet, V. von Graeve, W.-D. Niemeier, and K. Zimmermann (eds.): *Frühes Ionien. Eine Bestandsaufnahme*. Mainz am Rhein: 319–26.

Shanks, M., 1996: *Classical Archaeology of Greece: Experiences of the discipline*. London and New York.

Shanks, M., and Tilley, C., 1992: *Re-constructing Archaeology: Theory and practice* (2nd edn.). London.

Sherratt, A., 1992: What can archaeologists learn from Annalistes? In: A.B. Knapp (ed.): *Archaeology, Annales and Ethnohistory*. Cambridge: 135–42.

Shipley, G., 1987: *History of Samos 800–188 B.C.* Oxford.

Shipley, G., 1996: Ancient history and landscape histories. In: G. Shipley and J. Salmon (eds.): *Human Landscapes in Classical Antiquity*. London and New York: 1–15.

Simon, C.G., 1986: *The archaic votive offerings and cults of Ionia*. [Unpublished PhD thesis]. Berkeley.

Simpson, E., 1983: Reconstructing an ancient table: The "Pagoda Table" from Tumulus MM at Gordion. *Expedition* 25.4: 11–26.

Simpson, E., and Spirydowicz, K., 1999: *Gordion Ahşap Eserler/Wooden Furniture*. Ankara.

Smith, M.E., 1992: Braudel's temporal rhythms and chronology theory in archaeology. In: A.B. Knapp (ed.): *Archaeology, Annales and Ethnohistory*. Cambridge: 23–34.

Snodgrass, A.M., 1980: *Archaic Greece*. London.

Snodgrass, A.M., 1985: The New Archaeology and the classical archaeologist. *American Journal of Archaeology* 89.1: 31–7.

Snodgrass, A.M., 1986: Interaction by design: The Greek city-state. In: C. Renfrew and J.F. Cherry (eds.): *Peer–Polity Interaction and Socio-political Change*. Cambridge: 47–58.

Snodgrass, A.M., 1987: *An Archaeology of Greece*. Berkeley and Los Angeles.

Snodgrass, A.M., 1991: Structural history and classical archaeology. In: J. Bintliff (ed.): *The Annales School and Archaeology*. Leicester: 57–73.

Snodgrass, A.M., 2002: The history of a false analogy. *Ancient West and East* 1.1: 19–23.

Snodgrass, A.M., 2006: *Archaeology and the Emergence of Greece: Collected papers on early Greece and related topics (1965–2002)*. Edinburgh.

Snodgrass, A.M., 2007: What is Classical Archaeology? Greek archaeology. In: S.E. Alcock and R. Osborne (eds.): *Classical Archaeology*. Oxford: 11–29.

Solovyov, S.L., 2007: Archaic Berezan: results of recent archaeological investigations and its historical interpretation. In: J. Cobet, V. von Graeve, W.-D. Niemeier, and K. Zimmermann (eds.): *Frühes Ionien. Eine Bestandsaufnahme*. Mainz am Rhein: 531–40.

Sourvinou-Inwood, C., 2003: Herodotos (and others) on Pelasgians: Some perceptions of ethnicity. In: P. Derow and R. Parker (eds.): *Herodotus and his World: Essays from a conference in memory of George Forrest*. Oxford: 103–44.

Stark, F., 1954: *Ionia: A quest*. London.

Stika, H.-P., 1997: Pflanzenreste aus dem archaischen Milet. Vorbericht zur Kampagne 1992. *Archäologischer Anzeiger* 1997: 157–63.

Stiros, S., and Jones, R.E. (eds.), 1996: *Archaeoseismology*. Athens.

Stümpel, H., Bruhn, C., Demirel, F., Gräber, M., Panitzki, M., and Rabbel, W., 1997: Stand der geophysikalischen Messungen im Umfeld von Milet. *Archäologischer Anzeiger* 1997: 124–34.

Summers, G.D., 2006: Aspects of material culture at the Iron Age capital on the Kerkenes Dağ in Central Anatolia. *Ancient Near Eastern Studies* 43: 164–202.

Summers, G.D., 2007: Public spaces and large halls at Kerkenes. In: A. Çilingiroğlu and A. Sagona (eds.): *Anatolian Iron Ages 6: The Proceedings of the Sixth Anatolian Iron Ages Colloquium held at Eskisehir, 16–20 August 2004*. Leuven: 245–63.

Summers, G.D., and Summers, F., 2006: Aspects of urban design at the Iron Age city on the Kerkenes Dağ as revealed by geophysical survey. *Anatolia Antiqua* 14: 71–88.

Summers, G.D., and Summers, F., 2008: A preliminary interpretation of remote sensing and selective excavation at the palatial complex, Kerkenes. *Anatolia Antiqua* 16: 71–88.

Tandy, D.W., 1997: *Warriors into Traders: The power of the market in early Greece*. Berkeley.

Tanner, J., 2003: *The Sociology of Art*. London.

Thirgood, J.V., 1981: *Man and the Mediterranean Forest: A history of resource depletion*. London.

Thomas, R., 2006: The intellectual milieu of Herodotus. In: C. Dewald and J. Marincola (eds.): *The Cambridge Companion to Herodotus*. Cambridge: 60–75.

Thompson, D., 2007: At the crossroads: prehistoric settlement in the Maeander Valley. *Anatolian Studies* 57: 87–99.

Thonemann, P., forthcoming: *The Maeander*. Cambridge.

Thureau-Dangin, F., 1912: *Une relation de la huitième campagne de Sargon*. Paris.

Tilley, C., 1997: *A Phenomenology of Landscape: Places, paths and monuments*. Oxford.

Tomlinson, R.A., 1976: *Greek Sanctuaries*. London.

Touchais, G., 1989: Chronique des fouilles et découvertes archéologiques en Grèce en 1988. *Bulletin de Correspondance Hellénique* 113.2: 581–700.

Treister, M.Y., 1996: *The Role of Metals in Ancient Greek History*. Leiden.

Treister, M.Y., 1998: Ionia and the North Pontic area. Archaic metalworking: Tradition and innovation. In: G.R. Tsetskhladze (ed.): *The Greek Colonisation of the Black Sea Area*. Stuttgart: 179–99.

Trigger, B.G., 1989: *A History of Archaeological Thought*. Cambridge.

Tritle, L., 2006: Warfare in Herodotus. In: C. Dewald and J. Marincola (eds.): *The Cambridge Companion to Herodotus*. Cambridge: 209–23.

Trundle, M., 2004: *Greek Mercenaries: From the Late Archaic period to Alexander*. London.

Tsakos, K., 2001: Die archaischen Gräber der Westnekropole von Samos und die Datierung der samischen Anthemienstelen. *Archäologischer Anzeiger* 2001.3: 451–66.

Tsakos, K., 2007: Die Stadt Samos in der geometrischen und archaischen Epoche. In: J. Cobet, V. von Graeve, W.-D. Niemeier, and K. Zimmermann (eds.): *Frühes Ionien. Eine Bestandsaufnahme*. Mainz am Rhein: 189–99.

Tsetskhladze, G.R., 1994: Greek penetration of the Black Sea. In: G. Tsetskhladze and F. de Angelis (eds.): *The Archaeology of Greek Colonisation*. Oxford Committee for Archaeology Monograph 40. Oxford: 111–35.

Tsetskhladze, G.R., 1998: Greek colonisation of the Black Sea area: Stages, models and native population. In: G.R. Tsetskhladze (ed.): *The Greek Colonisation of the Black Sea Area*. Stuttgart: 9–68.

Tsetskhladze, G.R., 2006: Revisiting ancient Greek colonisation. In: G.R. Tsetskhladze (ed.): *Greek Colonisation: An account of Greek colonies and other settlements overseas. Vol. 1*. Leiden: xxiii–lxxxiii.

Tuchelt, K., 1988: Die Perserzerstörung von Branchidai-Didyma und ihre Folgen archäologisch betrachtet. *Archäologischer Anzeiger* 1988: 427–38.

Tuchelt, K., 1991: *Branchidai-Didyma*. Zaberns Bildbände zur Archäologie 3. Mainz am Rhein.

Tuchelt, K. et al., 1996: *Didyma: Ein Kultbezirk an der Heiligen Straße von Milet nach Didyma*. Mainz.

Tuna, N., 1984: Ionia ve Datça yarımadası arkeolojik yüzey araştırmaları 1984. *Araştırma Sonuçları Toplantısı* 3: 209–22.

Tuna-Nörling, Y., 2002: Attische Keramik aus Phokaia (Eski Foça). *Archäologischer Anzeiger* 2002.1: 161–231.

Tuplin, C.J., 1987: Xenophon and the garrisons of the Achaemenid Empire. *Archäologische Mitteilungen aus Iran* 20: 167–245.

Ünal, A., and Kammenhuber, A., 1974: Das althethitische Losorakel Kbo XVIII 151. *Zeitschrift für vergleichende Sprachforschung* 88.2: 157–80.

van Andel, T.H., and Runnels, C., 1987: *Beyond the Acropolis: A rural Greek past*. Stanford.

van Wees, H., 2004: *Greek Warfare: Myths and realities*. London.

Vanschoonwinkel, J., 2006: Greek migrations to Aegean Anatolia in the Early Dark Age. In: G.R. Tsetskhladze (ed.) *Greek Colonisation: An account of Greek colonies and other settlements overseas. Vol. 1*. Leiden: 115–42.

Vassileva, M., 2001: Further considerations on the cult of Kybele. *Anatolian Studies* 51: 51–63.

Vestergaard, T., 2000: Milesian immigrants in Late Hellenistic and Roman Athens. In: G. Oliver (ed.): *The Epigraphy of Death*. Liverpool: 81–110.

Vickers, M., and Gill, D., 1994: *Artful Crafts: Ancient Greek silverware and pottery*. Oxford.

Villing, A., 1998: Athena as Ergane and Promachos. In: N. Fisher and H. van Wees (eds.): *Archaic Greece: New approaches and new evidence*. London: 147–68.

Villing, A., and Schlotzhauer, U. (eds.), 2006: *Naukratis: Greek diversity in Egypt: studies on East Greek pottery and exchange in the Eastern Mediterranean*. London.

Vinogradov, Y.G., 2007: Milet und Megara erschließen den Pontos Euxeinos In: J. Cobet, V. von Graeve, W.-D. Niemeier, and K. Zimmermann (eds.): *Frühes Ionien. Eine Bestandsaufnahme.* Mainz am Rhein: 465–73.

Vlassopoulos, K., 2007: Between east and west: Greek *poleis* as part of a world-system. *Ancient West and East* 6: 91–111.

Voigt, M.M., and Henrickson, R.C., 2000: Formation of the Phrygian state: the Early Iron Age at Gordion. *Anatolian Studies* 50: 37–54.

Voigtländer, W., 1986: Umrisse eines vor- und frühgeschichtlichen Zentrums an der karisch-ionischen Küste: Erster Vorbericht – Survey 1984. *Archäologischer Anzeiger* 1986: 613–67.

Voigtländer, W., 1988: Akbük-Teichiussa, Zweiter Vorbericht – Survey 1985/1986. *Archäologischer Anzeiger* 1988: 567–625.

Voigtländer, W., 2004: *Teichiussa: Näherung und Wirklichkeit.* Rahden.

von Gerkan, A., 1915: *Milet 1.4: Der Poseidonaltar bei Kap Monodendri.* Berlin.

von Gerkan, A., 1925: *Milet 1.8: Kalabaktepe, Athenatempel und Umgebung.* Berlin.

von Gerkan, A., 1935: *Milet 2.3: Die Stadtmauern.* Berlin.

von Graeve, V., 1989: Eine spätarchaische Anthemienstele aus Milet. *Istanbuler Mitteilungen* 36: 143–51.

von Graeve, V., 2005: Funde aus Milet XVII: Fragmente von Bauskulptur aus dem archaischen Aphrodite-Heiligtum. *Archäologischer Anzeiger* 2005.2: 41–8.

von Graeve, V., 2007: Zur Kunstgeschichte früher milesischer Terrakotten. In: J. Cobet, V. von Graeve, W.-D. Niemeier, and K. Zimmermann (eds.): *Frühes Ionien. Eine Bestandsaufnahme.* Mainz am Rhein: 645–68.

Voyatzis, M.E., 1990: *The Early Sanctuary of Athena-Alea at Tegea and the Other Archaic Sanctuaries in Arcadia.* Goteborg.

Wallace, R., 1987: The origin of electrum coinage. *American Journal of Archaeology* 91.3: 385–97.

Wallerstein, I., 1974: *The Modern World System I: Capitalist agriculture and the origins of the European world-economy in the sixteenth century.* San Diego.

Wallerstein, I., 2004: *World-Systems Analysis: An introduction.* Durham, NC.

Wallinga, H.T., 1987: The ancient Persian navy and its predecessors. In: H. Sancisi-Weerdenburg (ed.): *Achaemenid History I: Sources, structures and synthesis.* Leiden: 47–76.

Wasowicz, A., 1975: *Olbia pontique et son territoire: L'aménagement de l'espace.* Paris.

Weber, B.F., 1985: Die Grabung im Heroon III. *Istanbuler Mitteilungen* 35: 24–38.

Weber, B.F., 1995: Ein spätarchaischer Tempel auf dem Mengerevtepe bei Milet. *Archäologischer Anzeiger* 1995: 228–38.

Weber, B.F., 1999a: Die Restaurierungsmassnahmen in Theater von Milet: Arbeiten im September 1997. *Archäologischer Anzeiger* 1999.1: 115–24.

Weber, B.F., 1999b: Die Bauteile des Athenatempels in Milet. *Archäologischer Anzeiger* 1999.1: 415–38.

Weber, B., 2001: Die Restaurierungsmassnahmen im Theater von Milet: Arbeiten in den Kampagnen 1998–1999. *Archäologischer Anzeiger* 2001.3: 424–50.

Weber, B.F., 2002: Die Säulenordnung des archaischen Dionysostempels von Myous. *Istanbuler Mitteilungen* 52: 221–71.

Weber, B., 2007: Der Stadtplan von Milet: Einhundert Jahre Stadtforschung. In: J. Cobet, V. von Graeve, W.-D. Niemeier, and K. Zimmermann (eds.): *Frühes Ionien. Eine Bestandsaufnahme.* Mainz am Rhein: 327–62.

Weber, G., 1904: Zur Topographie der ionischen Küste. *Mitteilungen des Deutschen Archäologischen Instituts, Athenische Abteilung* 29: 222–36.

Weickert, C., 1940: Grabungen in Milet 1938. In: *Bericht über den 6. internationalen Kongress für Archäologie*. Berlin: 325–32.

Weickert, C., 1956: Zu Ionischen Löwen. *Mitteilungen des Deutschen Archäologischen Instituts (Athenische Abteilung)* 71: 146–8.

Wheeler, M., 1956 (reprint 2004): *Archaeology from the Earth*. New Delhi.

Whitley, J., 2001: *The Archaeology of Ancient Greece*. Cambridge.

Wiegand, T., 1911: *Siebenter vorläufiger Bericht über die von den Königlichen Museen in Milet und Didyma unternommenen Ausgrabungen*. Berlin.

Wild, J.P., 1977: Classical Greek textiles from Nymphaeum. *Textile Museum Journal* 4: 33–4.

Wille, M., 1995: Pollenanalysen aus dem Löwenhafen von Milet. *Archäologischer Anzeiger* 1995: 330–3.

Wood, J.T., 1877: *Discoveries at Ephesus: including the site and remains of the great temple of Diana*. London.

Wood, J.T., 1890: *Modern Discoveries on the Site of Ancient Ephesus*. London.

Woolley, L., 1953: *A Forgotten Kingdom: being a record of the results obtained from the excavation of two mounds, Atchana and al Mina in the Turkish Hatay*. London.

Wulzinger, K., Wittek, P., and Sarre, F., 1935: *Milet 3.4: Das islamische Milet*. Berlin and Leipzig.

Yakar, J., 2000: *Ethnoarchaeology of Anatolia: Rural socio-economy in the Bronze and Iron Ages*. Tel Aviv.

Yalçin, Ü., 1993: Archäometallurgie in Milet: Technologiestand der Eisenverarbeitung in archaischer Zeit. *Istanbuler Mitteilungen* 43: 731–70.

Yalouris, E., 1986: Notes on the topography of Chios. In: J. Boardman and C.E. Vaphopoulou-Richardson (eds.): *Chios: A conference at the Homereion in Chios 1984*. Oxford: 141–68.

Zimmermann, E., 1993: *Die Tierreste aus dem archaischen Milet / Westtürkei (7. bis 5. Jh. v. Chr.)*. [Magister]. München.

Zimmermann, K., 2007: Frühe Dachterrakotten aus Milet und dem Pontosgebiet. In: J. Cobet, V. von Graeve, W.-D. Niemeier, and K. Zimmermann (eds.): *Frühes Ionien. Eine Bestandsaufnahme*. Mainz am Rhein: 631–6.

Index

Note: an "n" after a page reference denotes a footnote on that page; page references in *italics* refer to illustrations.

Abu Simbel 15–18, 166, *166*, 188, *190*, 221n
Achaemenid 17, 167, 171
acropolis (-eis) 48, *48*, 78, 98, 100–1, 103, 106–7, 116, 147, 157–8, 172–3
Aegean 7–9, *8*, 11, 27, 38–9, 46–7, 51–2, 55–6, 59, 66, 68, 73, 79, 84, *85*, 91, 96, 99, 114, 118, 123–4, 129, 131, 150, 166, 168, 191, 193, 218, 226
aeinautai 92, 109, 169
Aeolis 19n, 56–7
Afghanistan 76
Africa, North 56
agency 28, 30, 38, 40, 42, 117, 130, 141–2, 146, 195, 197, 215, 217–18, 227
Agia Markella *125*
agora 4, 18, 98, 102–3, 198
agriculture 20, 40–1, *41*, 46, 56, 58, 66, 69–72, 74–5, 92, 93n, 94, 100, 102, 104, 109, 120, 180, 226
Ahmetbeyli valley 181, *182*
Ahmose 132, 167
Akron, to (the Heights) 112
Akrotiri 3, 185n
Akurgal, Ekrem 34, 96–8, 118, 157n
Akyeniköy 199
Albertinum Painter 210
Alcock, S. 44, 71n, 180
Ales, River 181

Alexander 170
Alexandria 80
Allah 209
Allalia 132
alliance(s) 13, 131, 154, 165
alluvium 4–5, *4*, 7, 46, 48n, 51–2, 56, 58–9, 61–3, 72, 101, 103, 105–6, 150, 157–8, 181
Allyates 155
Al Mina 81, 131–3, *133*, 167
Altenburg Painter 209
Altes Museum, Berlin 5
Amasis 132, 166
amber 4, 174, 206, *206*, 228
Amoibichos 166, 221n
amphora(e) 13, 72–5, 84–5, *85*, 90, 130, 139–40, 198, *208*, 214
amulets 194
Anatolia 8–9, 11–12, 17, 19–20, 27–8, 31, 35–6, 39, 46, 49, 52, 54, 56, 58, 61, 67–8, 76, 83, 102, 114, 116–19, 124–5, 142–3, 149, 154, 160–1, 163, 165, 169–70, 172, 180, 191–7, 199–200, 204–6, 210, 212n, 214, 216–20, 223–4, 226–7, 231–2
Anatolian Civilizations, Museum of *206*
animal(s) 1, 40, 43, 60, 75–6, 93, 152, 171, 177–8, 180, 192, 205–6, 211–12
Ankara 126n, *206*
Ankhilos 122

annaliste   28, 36–40, 38, 42, 44, 46, 58, 69,
    94, 115, 121, 142, 147, 185, 188, 193, 226
Antigonos I   50
Apaša   102, 191
Apatouria   220
Aphrodite   1, 6, 15–16, 18, 19n, 43, 57, 60,
    82, 107, 112, 113, 115, 127, 132, 134, 148,
    150–2, 171, 173, 175, 177, 178n, 194,
    204n, 206, 214, 220, 221n
apoikia(i)   120, 138–41, 138
Apollo   6, 14, 21, 78, 104, 113, *125*, 132, 152,
    154, 169, 173–7, 180–1, 181, 184, 186–7,
    192–4, 197n, 204, 206
Apollonia-on-the-Rhyndacus   15–16, 128, 143
Apollonia Pontica   122, 134
arable land   69, 74, 76, 91
arbitration   92, 110, 144, 154–5
Archaeological Society of Athens   103
archaeology   1–3, 5–15, 18–24, 26–46, 50, 52,
    56–8, 60–2, 64–8, 71, 73, 78, 83. 85, 89–92,
    90, 95–8, 100–3, 105, 108–12, 114, 118,
    121, 123–30, *133*, 136, 139, 140n, 141,
    143–4, 146, 148–9, 151–2, 154, 156–7, 160,
    163–4, 171–2, 174, 177–8, 180–1, 186, 188,
    193, 196–7, 202–4, 207, 209–10, 213, *213*,
    216, 218–19, 221–8, 232
Archaeology, Garstang Museum of   *133*, 213,
    213
architecture   6, 16, 19, 21, 36, 42, 97, 100,
    104–5, 107, 117–18, 135–6, 139, 146,
    149–50, 160, 168, 175–6, *176*, 196, 216
archon   14, 186
Archon   166, 221n
Argasa   108
Arinanda   49
Aristagoras of Miletos   13, 167
Aristodikus   154
Aristolochus   78
Aristophanes   83
Aristotle   79–80, 117, 136, 154n
armor   76, 146, 148–9, 152–3, 167
arrowheads   152, 205
art   6, 28n, 36, 41, 45, 70, 85n, 86–7, 91, 134,
    145, 148, 153, 188, 200, 201–18, 226–7
Artemis   4,6, 24, 102, 106, 113, 149, 155,
    172n, 173–8, 181, 183, 185, 191–2, 196,
    197n, 199, 204n, 205–6, 227–8, *229*
Artemision   15, 17, 24, 86, 95, 101, 114, 162,
    228

artifact(s)   2, 5–6, 10, 14, 16, 18, 20, 22, 26–7,
    29, 31–2, 65, 76, 78, 88, 90–1, 134, 137,
    145–6, 148, 151–3, 168, 178, 188, 194,
    201–3, 205–7, 211, 216–17
artworks   1, 90, 91n, 132, 146, 152, 201–3,
    206–7, 218
Arzarwa   191
ashlar   97, 100, 158
Assessos   14, 108, 112, 155–6, 180
Assyrian   167
astragalus(-i)   16, 21, 78, *78*
asty   95, 98, 101, 118
Atatürk, Mustafa Kemal   34
Athena   30, 48, *48*, 83, 97, 99, 106–7, 112,
    113, 117, 149, 151–3, 155–6, 164n, 169,
    173–5, 178, 180, 194–6, 197n, 206, 208,
    215–16, 226
Athenaios   70, 223
Athenian Empire   11, 19, 220
Athenian Tribute Lists   19, 220–1
Athens   5, 10–12, 15, 18–19, 61–2, 74, 87,
    91–2, 93n, 94, 103, 115–16, 135n, 141n,
    146, 153n, 158, 160, 170, 178, 180, *189*,
    191, 198–9, 203n, 207, 210n, 214–15, 218,
    220, 222–5, 227, 231
Attalids   16
Attic pottery   7, 12, 151, 178, 214
Attica   7, 93n, 152–3
Austria   33
autonomy   32, 146, 215
Avram, Alexandru   137, 199n
axe   152, 166
Ayanis   149
Ayasoluk Hill   *25*, 101–2, 174, 183, 191,
    197n, 198
Aydın   65

Bafa Gölü   77
Bahn, Paul   33
Bakkheion   97
Balat   106, 147n
Balat Museum, Miletos   5, 186
Balık Boğaz   192
barbarian(s)   130, 137, 143, 169, 232
Barca   56
Barker, Graham   39, 64
barley   74
basalt   19, 168
baths   197

battle(s) 12–13, 40, 72, 93, 110, 141–2, 146,
    150, 152–4, 164, *165*, 167, 169, 208, 220
battlefields 146, 148, 150
Battle of Lade 13, 72, 78, 93, 110, 142, 147,
    150, 154, 164, 165, *165*, 220, 231
Battle of Qadesh 169
Battos 129
Bay, Bilal 79–80
Bayraklı *see* İzmir-Bayraklı
Beazley, John 210
bees 75
Bell, Gertrude 24, *25*, *225*
Benndorf, Otto 24
Béquignon, Y. 99
Berezan 16n, 17, 92n, 123, 130, 135, 137,
    139, 199
Berlin 5, 153
Bes 194
beylik 118
Bias of Priene 13, 220n
Biferno Valley 39
Black Figure pottery 207–9, 212n, 215, 218
Black Sea 23, 56, 73–4, 76, 81, 84, 90n, 91,
    120, 123–4, 126–7, 131, 139–40, 199
boar 177, 223
Bodrum 85
Boeotia 39
bone(s) 1, 21, 56, 60, 75, 85, 177, 180, 206
border(s) 50, 54, 57, 68, 76, 100, 145
bosses 148
bothroi 178
Branchidai-Didyma 6–7, 14–18, 55, 78, 92,
    95, 106, 113, 114, 123, 130n, 132, 134,
    144, 149–50, 154, 167–8, 173–7, 180,
    181, 183–6, 188–90, 192–5, 197n, 203–7,
    226
Branchus 195
Braudel, Fernand 37–8, 38, 40, 42, 44, 46,
    57, 64, 67, 71, 180–1
breastplates 149
British Empire 91, 141
British Museum, London 5, 16n, 24, *82*, *88*,
    153n, *176*, *179*, *187*, *208*
bronze(s) 16, 18–19, 76–8, 92, 137, 148–9,
    152, 153n, 167, 177, 191, 194, 204, 205n,
    206
Bronze Age 6, 11, 38, 49, 99, 101–2, 114,
    124n, 149n, 157, 166, 174–5, 185n,
    190–1, 193, 200, 212n, 221, *225*, 228

Bug 122, 139
Bülbül Dağı 3, 102, 192, 195
Bulgaria 196
Bulgarian 23, 26
bullion 87–8, 167, 204
Bumke, Helga 194
burial(s) 15, 90, 97, 99, 103, 117, 130, 133–4,
    136, 138, 140, 146, 149–50, 157, 171,
    184–5, 197–9, 205, 227
Büyük Menderes 5, 45n, *47*, 50–1, *51*, *53*, 59,
    61–5, 70, 111
Byzantine 101, 105–6, 147n
Byzantium 123

cabotage 84–5, 93, 131, 135, 138–9
Caesar, Julius 55, 184
Cape Monodendri 173
Cape Poseidon 55
Cappadocia Gate *162*
Caria 8, 15, 19, 31, 64, 104, 166–7, 184–5,
    195, 197, 210, 215, 217, *225*, 231
Carian (language) 17, 222
Carian pottery 8, 81, 210
Çatallar Tepe 6, 19n, 148–9, 152–3, 175–6,
    220
cattle 75, 85
cella 206
Celsus, Library of 3, 95
cereal(s) 72, 74–5, 94
Çeşme 47
Chalcolithic period 114
charcoal 196
Chares 5, 14, 18, 153, 184, 186, *187*, 188,
    190, 203, 206
Chase-Dunn, Christopher 89
cheiromachei 92, 109
Cheramyes, Hera of 103
Chersonessos 140
Chios 7, 9, 21, 52–6, 64, 68, 72–5, 81, *82*,
    84–5, 93, 96–8, 108, 111, 116, 132–2,
    139n, 149, 152, 157, 164, *165*, 173, 194–5,
    198, 206, 222
chora(i) 14, 54, 56, 64, 66, 69, 71, 95, 100,
    103, 106–8, 115, 130–1, 138, 138, 140–1,
    145, 150, 156, 172
Christian *125*, 188
Church of St. John 101
Cimmerian(s) 9, 12, 117, 128n, 160
Çine-Tepecik 64

city(-ies)   3, 5–17, *9*, 19n, 21, 23, 39–40,
   42–3, 45, 48–9, 52, 55–7, 59, 61, 63,
   65–6, 68–71, 88, 89n, 91–120, 123–5,
   128, 130–2, 136, 138, 146–7, 150–2,
   154–63, 165, 169, 175–6, 180, 183–5,
   188, 192, 195–9, 222–3, 226, 228, 231
Classical Period   74, 99, 147n, 164–7, 216
clay   17, 80, 84, 198, 203, 212
cleromancy   226
climate   24, 57–8, 69, 72–4, 94, 129
cloth   76n, 79, 82–3, 92, 204–5, 207
Cobet, Justus   40, 117, 127n
coffin(s)   77, 152, 197
coin(s)   17, 22, 24, 76, 86–9, *88*, 91n, 111,
   139, 167, 178
coinage   74, 86–9, 91n, 167
Colchis   132, 139
Cold War   126
colonization   10, 57, 62–3, 70–1, 89, 120–44,
   138, 221n
colony(-ies)   16–17, 19, 23, 43, 63, 81, 82n,
   90–1, 117, 120–32, 134–44, 147, 199,
   222n, 223, 226
color(s)   86, 212
column(s)   48, 77, 176
comasts   212
commodity(-ies)   75, 79, 81, 84–5, 90–1, 121,
   139, 205
communication(s)   45, 49, 52, 55, 68, 96,
   101, 122
conjoncture(s), conjuncture(s)   37n, 38,
   39–41, 96
connoisseurship   207, 209–11, 214–15
conservation   20–1, *206*
context, archaeological   7–8, 15, 18–19, 22,
   83, 90, 148, 152–3, 156, 178, 203
Cook, J. M.   201n
Cook, Robert   205, 210
copper   76, 86, 122, 203
core   1, 53, 95, 97, 101–2, 106, 113, 116, 124,
   142, 147, 157, 184, 193, 195, 197, 200,
   226
Corinth   7, 152, 205, 207
Corinthian   7, 55, 133, 153, 205, 207, 214
cremation   140, 198–9
Crete   56
Crimea   140
Croesus   92, 155, 159, 162
cuirass   148, 152–3

cult(s)   15, 18, 20, 43, 60, 78, 86, 99, 102,
   104, *105*, 112, 113, 114–15, 118–19,
   127–8, 130, 132n, 133–5, 155, 157,
   171–200, 205–7, 215, 217–18, 220,
   226–8
customs   146, 224, 231
Cybele   97, 99, 104, 134, 164n, 169, 195–7,
   216, 225
Cyrene   128n, 129, 136, 139
Cyrus   97, 158, 220
Cyzicus   122

Damlıboğaz   8, 210
Damyanov   199
Danube   117n, 122, 167
Dardanelles   123
Darius   78
Daskalopetra   195
decorated pottery   79–81, 85, 91, 212
dedication(s)   15–19, 60, 78, 81, 83–4, 88, 92,
   103, 139, 148–9, 152–3, 155, 167–8, 174,
   177–8, 180n, 194, 197n, 204–6
deer   192, 212
defense(s)   41, 45, 101, 116–19, 141n, 147n,
   157n, 160–2, *162*, 170, 226
deforestation   58–9, 63, 65, 77, 164
Değirmentepe   97, 149n
deity(-ies)   17–18, 132n, 134–5, 149, 153,
   155, 172, 177–8, 185, 192, 195, 197, 216,
   228
Delian League   11, 19, 116, 155, 165, 220
Delos   188
Delphi   129, 173, 180n, 223
Delphinion   108
Delta, Büyük Menderes   62
Delta, Madra Çayı   39
Delta, Nile   131–2, 167
Demeter   106, 113, 173
demography   37, 38, 65, 70–1, 93–4, 107,
   137, 142–4, 147
dendrochronology   8, 160
de-population   151
destruction deposit(s)   12, 148, 150–1
dialect(s)   134, 221–2
Didyma   5, 16–17, 19, 21, 33, 108, 112–14,
   179, 184n, *187*, 188n
Dilek Dağları   47, 49n
diolkos   55
Dionysus   100, 104, 113, 130, 173

dipinti 16, 19n, 209
diplomacy 6, 24, 90, 90, 154–5, 161–2
distaff 215–16
divination 78, 192, 196, 206, 226
DNA analysis 73–4, 91
Dneiper 122
dodekapolis 4, 96
doe *206*
dogs 212
dress 145
dromos 188, 198
drought 75, 129–30
Dorians 11, 140–1
Doric 175
Dunham, Adelaide G. 91, 130
Dusinberre, Elspeth 172, 193
dyeing 171, 193
Dynamis 113, 184
dynamism, landscape 5, 7, 28, 57–8, 100, 106, 115, 226

Early Phrygian Destruction 9
earthquake 12, 106, 151
East Greek Pottery 124n, 133, *133*, 139, 149, 209, 211, 213, *213*, 216
East Staircase, Persepolis 204
economy 13, 20, 28, 38, 39–40, 41, 45, 54, 56, 66–72, 75–6, 79–80, 87, 89n, 90–4, 113–14, 119–20, 127, 142, 144, 161, 164–5, 177, 178n, 194n, 206
Egypt 75, 85, 89n, 91, 92n, 132, 141n, 166, 168, 188, 224
Egyptian 19, 90, 132, 155, 166, 168, 178, 188–90, 194–5, 197, 205–6, 224
Elea 124, 132
electrum 87, *88*
Elephantine 166
Eleusis 180
Emecik 81
Emin, Tracey *202*
Empire, British 91, 141
Empire, Roman 124
Emporio 54, 98, 108, 116, 149, 157n, 173, 178, 206
emporion 120, 131–3, 138–41, *138*, 143
enamel *206*
Endoios 215
enemy(-ies) 13, 74, 117n, 146–7, 150, 153–4, 162–3, 169–70

English (language) 23, 37, 52, 93, 118, 120, 126, 184
Enkelados 113
environmental archaeology 42, 60, 64–5
ephemeral streams 106
Ephesians 155, 223
Ephesos 1, 3–7, *3*, 10, 15, 17, 19n, 21–2, 24, *25*, 26, 33, 46, 49, 56, 58, 60n, 62n, 65, 71–3, 77, 81, 86–7, 95–7, 101–2, 104, 108, 110–11, 114, 116, 123, 149, 155, 157, 159, 162, 164, 168, 172n, 173–8, *176*, 181, 183, 185, 190–2, 195–6, 197n, 198–200, 204n, 206, 212, 214, 217, 222–4, 227–8, *229*
epigraphy 1–2, 14–20, 31, 41, 43, 70, 82, 101, 114n, 120, 127, 131, 134–6, 139, 172, 179, 197, 221
epiphany 113, 115, 187–8
epoikoi 137
erosion 41, 59, 62–4, 164
Ersoy, Yaşar 99, 117
Erythrai 10, 34, 47, 50, 53–5, 66, 83, 96, 98–9, 111, 123, 131, 147, *165*, 173, 175, 178n, 194–6, 197n, 198, 207, 215–16, 222
escarpment 106, 184, 186, 188
Eski Foça 7, 97, 125
ethics 23, 146
Ethiopia 224
ethnic identity 140, 144, 218–9
ethnoarchaeology 20–1, 26, 75
Euboea 93, 133
Eupalinos Tunnel 103
Europe 46, 89, 186
experimental archaeology 20–1, 26
extra-urban temples 7, 108, 114–15
Eyre, Chris *190*

Falkener, Edward 24
farming 20, 69, 72, 76, 91, 109, 120
farms 73, 110, 119
farmsteads 80, 108–10, 119
fauna 54, 174, 185
faunal evidence 1, 42, 79, 177
Fazlıoğlu, İsmail 8, 210
festival(s) 135, 174, 180, 221
Fikellura pottery 7, 81, 151n, 208, *208*, 209n, 211–12, 214
Final Neolithic Period 114
fish 52, 56–7, 60, 72, 77, 79, 149, 177n, 223
fish-hooks 149

Fitzjohn, Matthew   136, 216n
flood(s)   4, 51, 107, 124, 174, 228
flora   54, 174, 185
forest(s)   49–50, 66, 72, 77, 122
fortification(s)   40, 97, 100, 103, 108, 117,
       146, 156–9, 162–3, 226
foundation myth(s)   10–11, 121, 129–30,
       135, 137, 195–6, 222–3, 230
foxes   212
France   123
French (language)   23, 126
friendship(s)   17, 154
fruit   75
furniture   90, 205–6, 206

Galesion Hill   195, 197n
Garstang, John   133, 213, 213
Garstang Museum of Archaeology   133, 213,
       213
gate(s)   24, 113, 116, 156–7, 162, 163, 183–5,
       192n, 193, 196
gateway(s)   56, 185, 192
Gediz   50
geese   212
Genelos group   15, 92n, 183, 186, 189, 191
geoarchaeology   21, 62
geography   4, 10, 27, 37–9, 42–6, 48–9, 54,
       59, 65, 67–8, 70, 90, 106–7, 110, 112, 114,
       120–4, 126, 130–1, 139–42, 146–7, 164,
       166, 172, 180, 196, 217
Geometric period   64, 101, 147n, 181
geomorphology   60, 62–5, 68, 181
Georgian (language)   23, 126
German (language)   23, 126, 211
German Institute at Athens   103
Germany   32–5, 103
Geryon   153
Girard, Paul   103
GIS (geographical information system)   67,
       126, 173
glacis   116–17, 158, 161, 163
gneiss   77, 106, 116, 157–8
goat(s)   75–6, 208n, 210–12
god(s)   15, 19, 57, 88, 128–9, 132n, 149n,
       155, 169, 173n, 178, 192, 194–5, 201,
       204–5
goddess   43, 83, 112, 132, 134, 155, 177,
       184–5, 197n, 206n, 216
gold   76, 86, 168, 177, 203, 206, 206

Gordion   8–9, 12, 160, 205
gorgons   176
Gorman, Vanessa   169, 173n, 184n
grabens   47, 50–2, 55, 58
grave(s)   8, 15, 104, 105, 149, 195–9
Gravisca   140
grazing   50, 56, 66, 69, 72, 75, 83, 106
greaves   148
Great Artist   210
Greece   8, 12–13, 19, 27–8, 34, 50, 71–2, 80,
       91, 92n, 95, 116, 120, 123, 131, 133, 142,
       145, 153–4, 161–3, 168–9, 172, 175, 177n,
       194, 199, 207, 209, 211, 215, 217, 226–7,
       231
Greeks   11–12, 31, 36, 67, 72, 91, 93, 96,
       117n, 118, 130, 132–4, 137, 142–3, 148,
       150, 154, 167, 169, 172, 192–3, 196, 200,
       217–18, 224, 227–8
grid, orthogonal   21, 117
griffin(s)   206, 212
Gulf of Latmos   40, 49, 52, 59, 59, 61–3, 66,
       77, 103–5, 111, 173, 222
gullos (-oi)   193
Günel, Behiç   206
Güzelçamlı   23, 49, 111, 220
Gyges   101, 167
gymnasium   102

Hall, Thomas D.   89, 141
hares   212
harbor(s)   7, 21, 40, 43, 46, 53, 55–7, 61–2,
       65, 67, 75, 84, 90, 92, 95–9, 101–3,
       105–8, 110, 112, 113, 119, 122, 122, 124,
       147, 149, 151, 158, 164, 173, 181, 184,
       195
Harpagos   156, 158
Harrison, Thomas   169
Hattuša   191n, 192
Hawkes, Christopher   41
hegemon   170
Heidegger, Martin   185
Heights, The   112, 113, 186
Hekate   19n, 113, 184–5, 193, 196
Hekateus of Miletos   10
Hellenistic period   3n, 5, 10, 21, 48, 61, 65,
       80, 95, 97–8, 100, 103–4, 106, 151, 166,
       173, 175n, 181, 183
Hellenization   136, 197
Hellespont   56, 120, 123

helmet(s) 148, 153, 163
Hera 6–7, 13, 15, 103, 132, 173–5, 178, 181, 183, 185, 187–8, 194, 203, 204n, 205–6
Heraion 95, 103, 114, 168
Herakles 15, 113
herbs 75
Herculaneum 3
Herda, Alexander 14n, 16n, 184n, 189
herding 76, 108
Hermes 113
Hermos valley 50
Herodotos 1, 3n, 9–12, 14, 19, 31–2, 39, 44, 70, 96–7, 100–3, 116, 127–9, 131–2, 139, 143, 146, 149n, 150–2, 154, 156–8, 159, 160, 162–4, 167n, 168–9, 180, 219, 221–2, 224–5, 231
heroon 151
Hesiod 93
Hestia 113
Heunenburg 167
hierarchy of needs 41, 41, 44
hierarchy, settlement 108, 110
Hippodamos of Miletos 117, 136
Hissarlık 29
Histria 17, 81, 125, 130, 137n, 199
Hittite 50, 118, 191–2, 197, 217, 224, *225*, 226
hoard(s) 86–7, 89n, 178n
Hölbl, Günther 194
Hogarth, David 24
Homer 43–4, 146, 195, 216
hoplite 146, 152–4, 162–3, 167, 169, 226
Horned One 113
horst 47, 106, 222
Humei Tepe 106, 113
Hürmüzlü, Bilge 194
husbandry 75–6, 83, 93
Hydai 8
Hylaea forest 122n
hypothesis 30, 32, 114, 193, 197, 228, 232

iconography 134, 196, 216–17
identity(-ies) 6, 11–12, 26–8, 35, 65–7, 96, 114–18, 129, 134–5, 140, 144–7, 164, 171, 175, 178, 180, 183, 193, 197–8, 201, 217–19, 221, 223–7, 230, 232
Ikaros 49, 56, 111, 140
Imvrasos, River 174, 183
İncir Adası 97

inlay 205–6, *206*
inscription(s) 14, 22, 49–50, 61, 78, 111–12, 113, 114n, 134n, 135, 156, *166*, 179, 183–6, 188, 193, 204, 205n, 208n, 220, 221n, 224
insulae 117
intermarriage 137, 231
Ionianization 136
Ionian League 219–20, 230
Ionian Migration 10–12, 31, 196, 222–4, 227, 230
Ionian Revolt 10–14, 42, 78, 91n, 96, 110, 142, 155, 168–9, 220–1
Ionic 97, 175–6
Iran 78
iron 76–7, 122, 152, 155
Iron Age 64, 76, 83n, 116, 133, 191
island(s) 39, 46–7, 49, 52–8, 63, 65–6, 68–9, 72, 77, 79, 83, 85, 96–9, 102, 108, 111, 122–3, 130–1, 140, 145, 147, 150, 158, 211, 222–3
İstanbul 5, 186
isthmus 99, 122
Istria 122, 135, 137
Isık, Fahri 35n, 217
Italian (language) 23
Italy 117, 123
ivory(-ies)
İzmir 5, 24, 34, 97n, 186
İzmir-Bayraklı 34

jewelry 86
Johnson, Matthew 29n, 35
Julius Caesar 55, 184

Kadmos of Miletos 10
Kalabaktepe 5, 12, 18, 60, 72, 81, 84, 106–7, 113, 116, 125, 147n, 151, 157–8, 173, 177, 195, 212, 214
Kaletepe 113
Kampos 98
Karabel 224, *225*
Karantina 99
Kardia 131–2
Kardulias, P. Nick 89n, 141
Kastro, Mount 103
Kato Phana 21, 54, 98, *109*, *125*, 152, 171, 173–4, 194, 205n
Kaunos 17

Kayster   50, 101
Keil, Josef   26
Keraiites   113
Kerkenes Dağ   17, 117–8, 161
Kerkenes Ivory   205
Kerschner, M   113, 136, 211n, 212, 214
kiln(s)   81, 121, 214
Kirkis   166
Kithone, Artemis   106, 113
Kithone, Athena   173
Klarios, Apollo   181
Klaros   6, 101, 108, 114, 173, 181, 181, *182*,
   185, 192
Klazomenai   10, 26n, 58, 64, 71, 77, 80–1, 93,
   96, 99, 101, 108, 111, 123, 131–2, 134n,
   139n, 147, 152, 157–8, 197–9, 201n,
   214n, 222
Kleiner, Gerhard   31
Kleisis   186
klerouchies   123
Knidos   5, 81, 132n
knife   152
knucklebone(s)   16, 20, 78, 204
koine   123, 222
Kolaios of Samos   85
Kolophon   6, 26, 87, 96, 100–1, 108, 111,
   147, 178n, 181, 198, 222
kore   103, 113, 173, 186
Koressos   102
Korolnik, Simone   *206*
Kossinna, Gustaf   33
kouros (-oi)   153, 181, 183, 186–8, *189*, 190,
   203, 215
Kreophylos   223
Kroesus   15
Küçük Menderes   50, 60n, 101
Kümüradası   114
Kuşadası   65
Kuyutepe Hill   198
Kyme   154
Kyrene   56

Labraunda   17
ladder of inference   41
Lade, battle of   13, 72, 78, 93, 110, 142, 147,
   150, 154, 164, 165, *165*, 220, 231
Lambrianides, K.   39
landscape   3, 5, 7, 21, 28, 37–45, 41, 68–73,
   76, 91, 94–6, 100–1, 106–15, 119, 121–2,
   127, 130–1, 138, 142, 144, 161, 172–4,
   180–1, 183, 185–8, 191, 193, 200, 202–3,
   215, 226–7
landscape dynamism   5, 7, 28, 57–8, 100,
   106, 115, 226
landslide   3–4, 58, 102
language(s)
   – Carian   17, 222
   – English   23, 37, 52, 93, 118, 120, 126,
     184
   – French   23, 126
   – Georgian   23, 126
   – German   23, 126, 211
   – Italian   23
   – Lydian   17–18, 222
   – Modern Greek   23
   – Phrygian   17
   – Romanian   23
   – Russian   23, 126
   – Samian   222
   – Turkish   118, 126
   – Ukrainian   23
Latacz, Joachim   10
Latmos   64
Latmos, Gulf of   40, 49, 52, 59, *59*, 61–3, 66,
   77, 103–5, 111, 173, 222
Latmos, Mount   50, 76, 104
Laumonier, A.   99, 150
Laurion   87
lead   16–17, 76, 87, 92, 177, 206
leather   152
Lebedos   6, 9. 50, 66, 96, 100, 108, 111, 198,
   222
legumes   75
Lelegians   197
Lemos, Irene   222
Leros   140
Lesbos   1349n, *165*, 220
Leto   113
Library of Celsus   3, 95
Libya   85
Liman Tepe   99, 124n
liminal   57, 115, 185, 217
Linear B   221
linen   82
lingua franca   126
lion(s)   5, 56, 61, 149, 164n, 173, 184, 186,
   188, 195, 198, 203, 204n, 212
Lion Harbor, Miletos   56, 61, 164n, 173

literary sources   2, 10, 14, 32, 61–3, 68, 127,
   129, 136–7, 154, 172, 178, 196, 216, 223,
   227
literature   1, 2, 10–11, 14, 17, 20, 26, 29–32,
   36–7, 41, 43, 45, 61–3, 68, 82, 91, 95–6,
   116, 118, 124, 126–31, 133, 136–7,
   140n, 141–3, 146, 150, 152, 154, 160,
   172, 178–9, 196–7, 216–17, 219, 221–7,
   230
Liverpool, University of   133, 213, *213*
Livy   97
Lohmann, Hans   6, 50, 93n, 107, 220n
longue durée   37, 38, 39–40, 44, 58, 61, 70,
   94–5, 118, 169, 180, 188, 227
looms   82
loom-weights   16, 82–3
lotus   211–12
Louvre, the   5, *78*
Lycia   217
Lydia   12, 17, 81, 86, 92, 143, 159, 161–2,
   199, 214
Lydian(s)   12, 16–18, 63, 86, 97, 110, 117,
   142, 155–6, 158, 161, 163, 194, 197–9,
   222, 227
Lydian (language)   17–18, 222

Madra Çayı delta   39
Maeander   4, 21, 50, 52, 59, 61, 63, 65, 102,
   104, 110, 150
magic   194
Magna Graecia   123–4
Magnesia   4–5, 104
malaria   60, 65
Malkin, Irad   128, 138
Maltepe   97, 158, *159*, 198–9
mantic trance   17, 226
manure   76
maquis   66, 77, 113
marble   6, 17, 77, 94, *179*, *187*, 198, 203,
   229
marsh(es)   174, 183, 185
Maslow, Abraham   41
masonry, polygonal   99, 103, 158–9, 161
Massalia   122, *122*, 124–5, 134, 137n, 141n
mastic   73, 75, 98
Mavi Şehir   184
meat   75–6, 83
mediation   169
Medieval period   28, 36, 112, 116

mediohistorical   39–40, 58, 61–2, 69–70, 80,
   94, 107, 142, 147, 161, 165, 174, 180, 187,
   193, 227
Mediterranean   7, 37n, 46, 55, 64, 72, 74, *85*,
   95, 112, 115, 117n, 120, 123–4, 126, 140,
   164, 167, 174
Mediterranean polyculture   72
Mediterranée et le monde mediterranéen, la   37
Megara   123, 140n, 144
Megiddo   167
Melie   19n, 111–12, 220
Mende   85
Mengerevtepe   14, 108, 112, 156, 163n
mentalité   38, 115–16, 226
mercenary(-ies)   15, 87–9, 90, 92, 132, 141,
   146, 153, 166–8, *166*, 194
metal(s)   16, 76–7, 87–8, 90, 92, 94, 118, 139,
   148, 150, 204–5, 207
metalwork   118, 204–5, 207
Metaponto   117
methodology(-ies)   27–8, 30, 32, 35, 37,
   39–40, 42–3, 46, 60, 63–4, 121, 126, 172,
   180–1, 195, 207, 225, 226, 230
metropolis(-eis)   108–10, 120–21, 123, 125–7,
   129, 131–2, 134–6, 138, 140, 142, 144,
   226
microhistorical   37, 40, 80, 188, 193, 207, 227
Milesia   72, 108, 112, 113, 114, 188
Milesian Teichos   167
Miletos   1, 5–7, 10–18, 21–2, 30–1, 33, 34n,
   40, 43, 46, 49–50, *51*, 52, *53*, 55–7, 59–66,
   67, 70–7, 79–81, 83–4, *85*, 87, 90n, 91,
   92n, 93, 96–7, 99n, 101, 103–14, 113,
   116–17, 120, 123, 125–7, 131–2, 134–6,
   138, 139n, 142, 144n, 147–52, 154–8,
   160–1, 163–5, *165*, 167–71, 173–5, 177,
   178n, 181, 183–6, 189, 192n, 193–6,
   198–9, 203n, 204n, 206, 208n, 212–14,
   220–2, 231
milk   75–6
Millawanda   49
Mimas   47, 111
Minoan   151, 191
Mira   *225*
Modern Greek (language)   23
Mohammed *(s.a.w.)*   209
moirai   216
Molpoi inscription   14–15, 19, 112, 114n,
   179, 184–6, 188, 193, 196, 208n

Monodendri, Cape 173
mosque 107
mosquitoes 104
Mount Kastro 103
Mount Latmos 50, 76, 104
mudbrick 117, 157–8, 161, 167
murex 56, 79, 83
Mursili II 49
Museum of Anatolian Civilizations, Ankara
    206
museums 5–6, 8, 10, 18, 21, 24, 34, *82*, 86,
    88, 97n, 98, 107, 126, 133, 134n, 153n,
    176, *179*, 186, *187*, 203, *206*, *208*, 210n,
    213, *213*, *229*
Muslim 209
Muss, Ulrike 174, 197n
Mussair 149
Mycenaean 101, 221n, 228
Mykale 47, 49–50, 53–5, *53*, 57, 111, 122
Myous 5–6, 9, 21, 33, 46, 49, 52, 56, 59, 61,
    76–7, 96, 104–6, *105*, 108, 111, 147, 153,
    165, 173, 195–6, 198, 222
Mysia 15, 128n
myth(s) 10–11, 31, 121, 129–30, 135, 137,
    195–6, 208, 222–3, 230
mythology 13, 118, 153, 172, 192, 195

Naso, Alessandro 84, *85*
Naucratis 56, 75, 81, *82*, 131–2, 134, 167–8
navies 146, 164
Naxos 167
Near East 76, 87, 91, 118, 132–3, 151, 167–8,
    204, 209, 211, 218
Necho 155, 168, 205
necropolis (-eis) 97, 103, 198
negotiation 90, 115, 130, 141, 190, 192,
    197n, 207, 215
neighbor(s) 9, 49–50, 54, 57, 68–9, 72, 74–5,
    80, 111, 119, 130, 154, 157, 161, 165, 169,
    210
Nemirov 139
network(s) 71, 84–5, 89, 90–3, 90, 99, 110,
    122, 138–42, 138
neutron activation analysis (NAA) 212
New Archaeology 29–30, 32, 37, 219
New Priene 3n, 4, 103, 194n
Newton, Charles 5, 24
Niemeier, Wolf-Dietrich 147n, 149n, 174, 221n
Nile Delta 131–2, 167

North Africa 56
Northampton Group 208
North Island Group 222
Notion 101, 108, 181
nucleated settlements 102, 108, 119
numismatics 91, 127
Nymphs, the 113, 114, 184

oath(s) 155, 231
oikist 128–9, 137, 223
Oikus 15, 113
oinochoe 210–11
Oinoussai 54
Olbia-Borysthenes 122–5, 127, 130, 135, 137,
    139
Old Priene 3–4, 9, 49–50, 95, 103–4, 147,
    198, 222
Old Smyrna 34, 157, 163
Old Testament 133
olive(s) 72–5, 79–80, 98
olive oil 73, 75, 79–80, 92
olive presses 79–80
Olympia 148–9
Olympics 128
optical stimulated luminescence 61
oracle(s) 6, 14–17, 19–20, 55, 78, 90, 114,
    123, 129–30, 132, 134–5, 137, 139, 141,
    154–5, 168–9, 173, 180, 181, 184, 192,
    194–5, 223, 226
Orak Adası 97
oregano 73–4
ores 139
Orontes 132–3
orthogonal grid 21, 117
Osborne, Robin 129n, 172, 175, 178n, 180,
    204n, 207
Ottoman 24, 61–2
Oudamos 166
Özyiğit, Ömer 97, 134n, 156–7

Pabuç Burnu 85
Paestum 136
paleobotany 42, 60, 72–4, 91
palmette(s) 198–9
palynology 73, 77, 91
Panayır Dağı 3, 102, 159, 183, 191
panhellenic 148, 173
Panionion 34n, 111, 127n, 148, 154–5,
    175–6, 180, 220–1

Panormos 55, 184
Parians 110, 119, 144
Parion 131–2
Paris 5, 186
Paros 77, 92, 131, 155
Pasargadae 97
Patmos 140
Pausanias 63, 136, 141n, 177, 178n, 196, 207, 215, 228
Pedon 92n, 168
peer-polity interaction 175
Peisistratus 92
pekmez 72
Pelekos 166
Peloponnesian War 123
peninsula 5, 47, 53–7, 66, 72, 97–8, 100, 103–4, 106, 110–11, 122–3, 147n, 164n
pentekonter 164
peraia 54, 66
periphery 114, 139
peri-urban 112, 113
Permenides 216
Persepolis 92, 204–5
Persia 13, 90, 92, 123, 143, 158, 165, 170, 199
Persian War 12, 169
Peschlow-Bindokat, Annelise 64
Peters, Joris 177
petrographic analysis 212
Phalanthus 137
phalanx 153, 167
Pharaoh 132, 155, 166–8, 205
Pharmakoussa 55
phenomenology 181, 185–6, 203, 226
philosophy 13, 37, 41
Phokaia 7, 9–10, 13, 26, 34, 56–7, 87, 88, 96–8, 108, 116–17, 120, 123–5, 131–2, 134, 137n, 138, 140, 152, 155–8, 159, 160–5, 165, 173, 175, 195–6, 198–9, 216, 222, 224–5
phoros 19, 220
Phourni 56
Phrygia 8–9, 17–18, 104, 113, 114, 118, 191–2, 195–7, 200, 216–17, 226–7
Phrygian (language) 17
phyle 134
pig(s) 60, 75, 177
Pindar 127n, 128

pithoi 73
Pitton de Tournefort, Joseph 103
Pliny 120, 127, 207
Plutarch 55, 137n, 184n
de Polignac, François 96, 112
polis(-eis) 13, 49–50, 52–4, 56, 66–7, 69, 95–6, 107–8, 110–12, 114–16, 118–19, 131, 142, 144–6, 154–5, 157, 161, 163, 169, 172, 175, 197
polos 181n, 215
polyculture, Mediterranean 72
polygonal masonry 99, 103, 158–9, 161
Polykrates 56, 92, 103, 158, 161, 164n, 199
Pomorie 122
Pompeii 3
Pompidou Centre 201
population(s) 10, 17–18, 31, 46, 50, 55, 62–3, 65, 79, 93, 104, 107, 114, 116–17, 131–2, 135–44, 162–3, 174, 222, 227, 231
Poseidon 57, 113, 115, 173, 176, 220
Poseidon, Cape 55
Poseidonia 136
Potasimto 166
pottery
    Athenian 12, 133, 140, 207–8, 212n, 215
    Attic 7, 12, 151, 178, 214
    Black Figure 207–9, 212n, 215, 218
    Corinthian 7, 133, 207, 214
    East Greek 124n, 133, 133, 139, 211, 213, 213
    Euboean 133
    Fikellura 7, 81, 151n, 208, 208, 209n, 211–12, 214
    Mycenaean 228
    Red Figure 12, 151, 178, 207, 215
    Wild Goat 7, 81, 82, 84, 133, 152, 205, 210–14, 218n
prehistoric 20, 29, 36, 40, 147n, 151, 226–7
Priapus 122
Priene 3–4, 6, 9, 13, 15, 19, 33, 48, 49–50, 51, 52, 56, 59, 59, 77, 92n, 95–6, 103–6, 111, 147, 165, 168, 194n, 195, 197n, 198, 220n, 221–2
prisoners 146
processing 71, 77, 79–80, 83, 88n, 93, 99, 139
procession(s) 174, 183–5, 190, 192–3, 196, 200, 204, 208n
processualism 29–30, 32, 37
Proconnessos 77

proem 143
progradation 5, 51, 57–8, *59*, 61–3, 65–6
Prophitis Elias 98, 116
Propontis 56, 123, 131
propylon 181
Protogeometric Period 222
protomes 206
proxenos 142
Psammetichos 166–8
Pseudo-Skymnos 128
Pterians *206*
Pyrrha 108
Pythagorio 7, 103
pyxides 210

Qadesh, Battle of 169

radiocarbon 8, 61, 160
rams 212
Rassam cylinder 167
Red Figure Pottery 12, 151, 178, 207, 215
regionalism 11, 227
religion 15, 18, 40, 41, 46, 50, 56, 60, 81, 86,
    88n, 90, 106, 108, 114–15, 121, 129,
    134–5, 138, 145, 155, 171, 174, 179, 183,
    184, 188, 193–4, 199, 207, 227
reuse 148, 204
Rhodes 56, 132n, 168, 212
Rhône 122, 124
Rhône-Saône corridor 124
ritual(s) 152, 174, 180–1, 185, 193, 195–7, 227
robbery 148–9, 204
rock-cut 64, 99, 104, 113, 181, 191–2, 195–6,
    198, 216
Roebuck, Carl 19n, 91, 134n, 168n, 221n
Röhlig, J. 70n, 91
Roman(s) 2, 5, 10, 21, 58, 65, 95–6, 101–2,
    104, 106–7, 123–4, 134n, 151, 181, 183,
    195n, 198, 203, 207, 228, *229*
Roman Empire 124
Romanian (language) 23
rosettes 212
Russian 23, 126
rust 148, 204

Saatchi Gallery 201, *202*
Sacred Way(s) 18, 92n, 101, 106, 108, 112,
    113, 114–15, 174, 180–1, 181, 183–6,
    188–90, *191*, 192–3, 200, 203, 206, 215–6

sacrifice(s) 1, 43, 60, 135, 171, 177, 180, 184,
    188
Sahara 46
salt 122, 124n
Samian (language) 222
Samos 76–7, 9, 13, 15–16, 19n, 22, 33, 49n,
    52–7, 68, 72, 80–1, 84–5, 87, 92–3, 96–7,
    102–3, 105–6, 108, 111, 114, 116, 132,
    149, 153, 157–8, 160–1, 164, *165*, 168,
    173–5, 178, 181, 183, 185–91, *189*, 194,
    198, 203, 204n, 205–6, 215, 222
Samsun 131
Samsun Dağı 47, 49–50, *53*, 71n, 103, 148,
    220
sanctuary(-ies) 1, 6, 14–16, 18, 19n, 21, 43,
    50, 54, 60, 81, *82*, 88n, 92n, 97–8, 101,
    106, 108, 112–15, 132, 146, 148–52, 155,
    157, 164n, 171–4, 176–7, 178–80, 184–6,
    188, 191–5, 197n, 203, 204n, 205n, 206,
    214, 216, 220–1
Santorini 3
Saône 124
Saplıadası 108, 114
sappers 163
Saqqara 188
sarcophagos(-i) 77, 152–3, 178, 195, 197–9,
    201n, 208
Sardinia 123
Sardis 17, 117, 150, 161, 163, 169, 171, 193,
    224
Sartiaux, Felix 97, 158
sauroter 148, 153
scarab(s) 132, 194
Schliemann, Heinrich 24, 29, 43–4
Schlotzhauer, Udo 211–12, 214
sculpture(s) 1, 5–6, 13, 18, 21, 92, 153,
    178, 184, 186, 190, 192, 201n, 202–4, 206,
    217
Scythian 137, 139n, 141n
sea 1, 5, 7, 13, 17, 23, 37, 39, 43, 46–60,
    65–8, 72–4, 76, 77n, 79, 81, 83–4, 90n,
    91, 94, 96, 98, 100–2, 104, *109*, 112, 115,
    120, 123–4, 126–7, 131, 134, 139–40, 145,
    147, 150, 154–5, 173–4, 177n, 181, 183–5,
    199
sea-level 48, 58, 124
security 44, 130, 143, 147
Selçuk *25*, 65
Sen, Husein *206*

Serapeum Way   188
Serapis   194n, 195
Sesostris   224, *225*
settlement(s)   3n, 5–7, 9, 14, 21, 31, 40, 45–7,
    50–1, 53–4, 59–61, 64–6, 68, 81, 83,
    95–103, 105–112, 113, 114–16, 119–21,
    123–5, 127, 131–2, 136–41, 138, 147,
    156–7, 160, 162, 164n, 167–8, 183, 185–6,
    190–2, 198, 214, 223, 226
settlement hierarchy   108, 110
Seven Sages   80
Şeytan Hamamı   97n, 198–9
shaft monument(s)   192, 195–6
sheep   75–6, 83
sherds   109, *133*, 151n
shield(s)   148–9, 152–3, 178
ship(s)   55–6, 72–3, 75, 77, 84–5, 93, 110,
    164–5, *165*, 167, 170, 173n, 220
shipbuilding   77, 164
Shipley, Graham   96, 147n
shipwreck(s)   55, 73, 85, 99
Sicily   123, 136
siege(s)   75, 154–6, 158–9, 163, 165
Sikels   136
Silk Road   91
silver   76, 86–7, 139, 150, 203, 204n, *206*
Sinope   122, 128n, 132, 139, 143n
Sirince   73
Skylla capital   4
smelting   148
Smyrna   19, 34, 102, 157, 163, 224
Snodgrass, Anthony   11, 28n, 38, 58, 95, 107,
    112, 117, 149n, 175
socles   157–8
Socrates   13
soil(s)   3, 51, 59, 62–3, 69, 72–3, 76, 109, 148,
    151, 164, 173n, 196
soil analysis   109
Söke   65
Solon   146
Sostratos   *82*
Soter   113
source materials   1–2, 121, 143, 156, 171–2,
    180, 209
Spain   123
Sparta   115, 146, 158, 162, 170
spears   148, 178
spearheads   148n, 153
Spencer, Nigel   39

sphinx(es)   188, 211–12
spindle   215
spindle-whorls   82
spolia   160, 203
spring(s)   114, 173–4, 185, 191
stasis   109, 119. 155
stater(s)   87, *88*
statue(s)   5, 14–16, 18, 92n, 103, 153n, 168,
    174, 177, 178n, 183–6, *187*, 188, 203,
    206–7, 215–17, 228
statuette(s)   19, 183, 192, 194
stelae   15–16
Stephania   184, 186, 188–9
St. John, Church of   101
stone(s)   5–6, 15–16, 19, 48, 56–7, 77, 80, 90,
    97, 104–7, 116–17, 157–61, 163, 184, 193,
    195, 198–9, 203–4, 221n
story(-ies)   17, 41, 79–81, 121, 127–9, 136,
    139, 143, 154–6, 195, 222–4, 231
Strabo   128, 131, 132n, 141n, 188n, 220n
strategy   41, 101, 123, 150, 163
stratigraphy   8, 42, 81, 91, 93, 106, 151,
    156–7, 121, 214, 228
streams, ephemeral   106
subsistence   36, 41, 79, 94, 111, 142–3, 180
Summers, Geoff and Françoise   118, 162,
    196n, *206*
surplus   73, 79, 91, 93–4
Susa   16, 78, *78*
swamp(s)   5, 24, 52, 60, 66, 101, 103–4, 114,
    183
symmachy   165, 220
syncretism   192, 196, 200, 227
synoikise   50, 111

taboo   169
tactics   147n, 152–3, 163, 167
tandir   80
Taras   136–7, 141n
Tarkasnawa   *225*
Tartessos   85, 158, 162, 164n
Taş Burun   55, 57
Taş Kule   97, 198
Tate Modern   201
Tavşan Adası   114
technology(-ies)   7, 29, 38, 40, 50, 55, 67, 70,
    76, 82, 92, 126, 146–7, 152, 161, 163–4,
    170, 209
Teichioussa   14, 108, 114, 186, *187*

Tekağaç Burun   113, 115, 173
Tektaş   55, 85, 99
temenos   112, 113, 188
temple(s)   4, 6–7, 13–19, 22, 24, 30, *48*, 55,
     60, 76–8, 83–4, 88, 89n, 92, 95, 97,
     99–100, 102–4, 106–8, 110, 112–15, 117,
     125, 132, 135, 146, 148–53, 155–6, 161,
     164n, 168–9, 171–96, 181, 203–7, 215–18,
     220, 223, 228
Teos   13, 50, 55, 64, 85, 96, 99, 100, 132, 138,
     165, 198, 222
terracotta   6, 16, 82, 97, 135, 153, 195, 197,
     199, 204
territory(-ies)   19n, 49, 55, 58, 63–4, 66, 69,
     71–2, 83, 89, 95, 98, 101, 106, 107–8,
     111–12, 114–15, 119, 137–8, 140–4, 154,
     161, 186, 220
thalassocracy   222n
Thales of Miletos   13, 79–80, 220n
theater   5, 21, 100, 102, 105–7
Theater Harbor, Miletos   7, 84, 106–7, 113,
     151, 173
Theokles   166
Thera   128n, 129, 139, 185
Thermopylae, Battle of   12
Thrason   78
Thucydides   11, 123, 146, 157
Tierfries   211
Tilley, Chris   186–7
timber   50, 77, 90, 122, 163n, 165, 167
tin   76, 122, 203, *206*
to Akron (the Heights)   112
Tomlinson, R. A.   185
town planning   136
trade   7, 41, 48, 55–7, 61–2, 70–1, 73–7,
     79–81, 83–5, *85*, 87, 90–3, 102, 120–1,
     124n, 127, 130–1, 133, 135, 137–9, 138,
     164n, 168n, 226
tradition(s)   10, 19, 100, 109, 120, 128,
     134–8, 142, 144, 150, 152, 154, 164, 166,
     169, 174, 178–9, 186, 193–200, 207, 209,
     215, 217–19, 221–4, 226–7, 230–1
Tralles   65
Transitional   205
transport   49, 52, 54–5, 56n, 70, 73, 77, 84,
     130, 139
treaty(-ies)   154–5, 169
trireme   164
Trojan War   10

troops   78, 167
trophy   148
Troy   29, 43–4
Trundle, Matthew   166
Tsetskhladze, Gocha   90n, 126, 142
tumulus(-i)   97, 117, 158, 198–9
Tuna, Numan   99, 100n
Tuplin, Christopher   167
Turkey   5–6, 10, 20, 23, 32, 34–6, *47*, 54, 57,
     68, 73, 75, 80, 83n, 87, 116, 186, 204n,
     213
Turkish language   118, 126
Turkish School   35, 217
tyrant(s)   56, 92, 143, 158

Ukraine   139
Ukrainian (language)   23
University of Liverpool   133, 213, *213*
Urartu   149
Ürkmez   100
urn(s)   198

valley(s)   4–5, 7, 21, 28, 39, 46–7, *47*, 48–52,
     55, 59, 60–1, 63–5, 68, 70, 101–2, 110,
     181–2, *182*
vase-painting   152, 178, 208–9, 217–18
Vatican Museum   *229*
Vedius Gymnasium   102
vegetable(s)   75, 116
Vestergaard, Torben   61
view(s)   43, 101, 112, 115, 172–3, 187
viewshed analysis   173
Villing, Alexandra   215–16
vines   72, 74–5
Vlassopoulos, Konstantinos   142
von den Driesch, Angela   177
votive(s)   15–18, 86–7, 146, 148–9, 152, 168,
     171, 177–8, 194, 196, 205, 221
VR (Virtual Reality)   67, 203

Wallerstein, Immanuel   89, 141n
wall(s)   6, 40, 43, 48, 56, 73, 88, 97–8, 100,
     103, 106, 116–17, 118n, 146, 157–63, 165,
     167–8, 170, 175, 192, 203, 222
war(s)   10, 12–13, 24, 26, 49, 74, 111, 123, 126,
     144, 145–70, 178, 180n, 208, 220, 226
warfare   40–1, 41, 69, 76, 145–7, 153–5,
     163–4, 169–70
warrior(s)   146, 149, 152–3, 216

wasters   212, 214

water   7, 45, 50, 54, 57, 72, 92, 101, 103,
    107, 124, 172–4, 181, *182*, 195–6, 197n

water table   7, 107, 181, *182*

weapon(s)   146, 148–50, 152–3

Weber, Berthold   113, 117, 160n

well(s)   61, 107, 151

wheat   70, 74, 90, 91

Wheeler, Sir Mortimer   22

Wiegand, Theodore   103

Wild Goat pottery   7, 81, *82*, 84, 133, 152,
    205, 210–14, 218n

wine(s)   69, 72–3, 74, 84–5, 90, 98, 193

Wissenschaft   30, 34–5, 216

wood   18, 77, 161, 178, 204–7, 215, 228

Wood, John Turtle   24, 183

wool   75–6, 82n, 83, 91, 215

world-systems analysis   89, 90, 138, 140–2,
    226

xoanon (-a)   206, 218, 228

Yaşar Ersoy   99, 117

Yavan   133

Yazılıkaya   191n, 192

Yeşilova   63

Zeus   113

Zeytintepe   1, 6, 14, 18, 19n, 43, 60, 106, 113,
    115, 148, 150, 173, 177, 204n, 206, 214

Printed in the United States
By Bookmasters